# DEFINITELY BRITISH
# ABSOLUTELY AMERICAN!

Manuel de civilisation britannique et américaine destiné aux classes préparatoires HEC, aux Instituts d'Études Politiques, à l'ENA, aux ESJ...

Coordination générale : Fabien Fichaux
Docteur en Anglais
Professeur en classes préparatoires et maître de conférences à l'IEP de Paris

**Florence Binard**
Agrégée de l'Université et Doctorante à Charles V
Enseigne à l'IUT d'Évreux

**Monique Chéron-Vaudrey**
Agrégée de l'Université
Professeur en classes préparatoires au lycée Chaptal, Paris

**Odile Gouget-Escobar**
Professeur certifiée
Professeur au lycée Saint-Charles, Vienne

**Sarah Loom**
Titulaire du BA Hons et du MA Hons, University of Bristol (GB)
Agrégée de l'Université
Professeur en classes préparatoires au lycée Henri Martin, Saint Quentin
Expert près la cour d'appel d'Amiens

**Sophie Loussouarn**
Ancienne élève de l'École Normale Supérieure et Diplômée de l'IEP Paris
Agrégée de l'Université et Docteur en Anglais
Maître de conférences à l'IEP Paris et à l'université d'Amiens

**Guy Richard**
Agrégé de l'Université
Directeur des études et Professeur à l'IEP de Lille,
Coordinateur des enseignements d'Anglais

ISBN 2-7298-0722-5
©     Ellipses Édition Marketing S.A., 2001
       32, rue Bargue 75740 Paris cedex 15

Le Code de la propriété intellectuelle n'autorisant, aux termes de l'article L.122-5.2° et 3°a), d'une part, que les « copies ou reproductions strictement réservées à l'usage privé du copiste et non destinées à une utilisation collective », et d'autre part, que les analyses et les courtes citations dans un but d'exemple et d'illustration, « toute représentation ou reproduction intégrale ou partielle faite sans le consentement de l'auteur ou de ses ayants droit ou ayants cause est illicite » (Art. L.122-4).
Cette représentation ou reproduction, par quelque procédé que ce soit constituerait une contre-façon sanctionnée par les articles L. 335-2 et suivants du Code de la propriété intellectuelle.

www.editions-ellipses.com

# Avant-propos

L'idée de cet ouvrage est partie d'une constatation d'enseignant, de correcteur ou de membre de jury de concours : à l'issue du baccalauréat, les étudiants se trouvent cruellement démunis et dépourvus de connaissances sur les principaux sujets de civilisation, de culture, d'histoire ou même d'actualité des pays anglo-saxons.

Ces lacunes se traduisent non seulement à la lecture des copies (les « essais ») qui manquent souvent de fond, mais également lors des épreuves orales où nombre de candidats ne disposent que de connaissances par trop superficielles.

Bien que la priorité des épreuves d'anglais aux concours reste la qualité de l'expression et la correction de la langue, il est souvent bien délicat de dissocier le fond de la forme. Aussi cet ouvrage a-t-il pour vocation d'étoffer vos copies, de donner de la substance et de la matière à vos exposés oraux.

Sans prétendre à l'exhaustivité des sujets traités, il vise – à travers une cinquantaine de thèmes – à vous donner les bases de civilisation américaine et britannique.

Chaque dossier est construit selon le même schéma :
- trois pages de cours, où figurent les principaux éléments sur le thème traité ;
- une page de vocabulaire en contexte ;
- deux pages intitulées « Focus », où vous pourrez trouver toute une série d'informations ponctuelles sur le thème ;
- deux pages de corrigé-type d'épreuves de concours ou d'exercices variés (essai, commentaire de texte, de statistiques ou de *cartoon*, épreuves corrigées de concours, etc.), afin de vous montrer de façon très concrète comment utiliser vos connaissances à l'occasion des épreuves auxquelles vous êtes le plus souvent confrontés ;
- une fiche supplémentaire apporte des compléments d'information dans certains dossiers.

Bonne lecture et bonne préparation à tous.

Fabien Fichaux

# Table des matières

## CIVILISATION BRITANNIQUE

Introduction to Britain .................................................................. 8
1. Monarchy and the Establishment ............................................... 23
2. The Commonwealth .................................................................. 33
3. The United Kingdom and Europe ............................................... 43
4. Labour and Conservatives ......................................................... 51
5. Post Industrial Britain: A changing Britain ................................. 59
6. Blair's Third Way: Rebranding Britain ........................................ 67
7. Welfare to Work ........................................................................ 79
8. The National Health Service ..................................................... 87
9. Regions and Devolution ............................................................ 97
10. Ireland ..................................................................................... 105
11. Higher Education ..................................................................... 113
12. Sports in Britain ....................................................................... 123
13. The eccentric – an English beast? ............................................ 131
14. Home Sweet Home .................................................................. 137
15. Preservation of Nature ............................................................. 145
16. The British Media .................................................................... 153
17. British Cinema ......................................................................... 161
18. Religion in Britain .................................................................... 169
19. Ethnic Minorities ..................................................................... 177
20. Feminism in Great Britain ........................................................ 185
21. Gays and lesbians in England .................................................. 193

Introduction to the United States .................................................. 202
1. The Constitution ......................................................... 219
2. Lobbying................................................................... 229
3. The Land of the Free .................................................. 239
4. The Land of Opportunity ............................................ 249
5. The Land of the Big ................................................... 257
6. The changing face of entrepreneurship ..................... 267
7. A Nation of Immigrants ............................................. 275
8. The Case of the Black Community ............................ 283
9. Affirmative Action ..................................................... 293
10. Multiculturalism ......................................................... 303
11. Political Correctness .................................................. 311
12. Higher Education ....................................................... 319
13. Religion and Puritanism ............................................ 329
14. The Right to Bear Arms ............................................. 337
15. The Death Penalty ..................................................... 347
16. Scandals ..................................................................... 355
17. The Welfare State ...................................................... 363
18. The New Economy .................................................... 371
19. Globalisation ............................................................. 379
20. Hollywood ................................................................. 387
21. The Vietnam War and the American Psyche ............. 397
22. Sites of Memory ........................................................ 405
23. The US as Global Policeman ..................................... 415

Index ............................................................................... 423

# CIVILISATION BRITANNIQUE

# Introduction to Britain

The United Kingdom of Great Britain and Northern Ireland consists of four geographical and historical parts – England, Scotland, Wales, and Northern Ireland. Together, England, Wales, and Scotland constitute the larger of the two principal islands, while Northern Ireland and the Republic of Ireland constitute the second largest.

Apart from the land border with the Irish Republic, the United Kingdom is surrounded by the sea. The area of the United Kingdom is 94,251 square miles (244,110 square kilometres). At its widest the United Kingdom is 300 miles across. From the top of Scotland to the southern coast of England it is about 600 miles. The national capital city is London, situated on the River Thames in the southeastern corner of England.

Wales and England were unified politically, administratively and legally by the Acts of Union of 1536 and 1542. The 1707 Act of Union joined Scotland with England and Wales and there was a single parliament for Great Britain, although the three countries had previously shared a monarch.

Britain is a constitutional monarchy with the monarch as head of State. The monarchy and the House of Lords belong to "the dignified part of the Constitution", as Walter Bagehot wrote in *The English Constitution* (1867), whereas the Prime Minister, the Cabinet and the House of Commons belong to "the efficient part of the Constitution".

The monarchy is the oldest institution of government dating back to the 9th century and the monarch and the royal family are a source of unity and national spirit.

The United Kingdom is characterized by a long history and by political and cultural links with other areas of the world, the latter mostly a legacy of its large former empire. Even though the United Kingdom is a middle-sized and middle-ranking industrial country, it still has close ties with the 53 nations of the Commonwealth, of which the Monarch is the Head of State.

In postwar Britain, Margaret Thatcher became the defining figure in British politics as the "Iron Lady" and thus she has left her imprint on the country. Her election victories prove that she had a deep understanding of the mood of the British public in the late 1970s and 1980s. She understood that the British public were dissatisfied with an economy that failed to create prosperity and reward enterprise, and with public services (and public industries) dominated by producers of scandalously poor quality. The results of her reforms were spectacular and popular.

Tony Blair understood it and acknowledged the achievement of Margaret Thatcher. He has consistently used Thatcherite rhetoric to strengthen his "New" credentials.

Since 1997, Blair has launched ground-breaking reforms, ranging from Welfare to work, to devolution and he has committed himself to restoring the National Health Service. Nevertheless his government is constantly shattered by Northern Ireland's troubles which have led to terrorist actions, most notably by the Irish Republican Army (IRA).

The fight against hooliganism and the preservation of nature are also major priorities for Britain.

Over 29 million people in Britain over the age of 16 regularly take part in sport or exercise. Walking, swimming, yoga, football, and cycling are the most popular activities and the government is encouraging local authorities to ensure the provision of sporting facilities meets local needs and to preserve the right to ramble across the countryside.

Hence Britain is committed to environmental protection and has set the target of reducing emissions of greenhouse gases in Britain. Several government agencies and institutions such as the National Trust and the Royal Society for the Protection of Birds are involved in protecting Britain's natural heritage, supported by many local foundations.

As in every modern country, the media play an important part in Britain's everyday life, providing information and education, entertainment and communication.

Higher education has experienced a dramatic expansion since the Second World War. There are some 170 universities and higher education institutions, which enjoy academic freedom. About one in three pupils graduating from secondary school goes on to study at university.

Owing to its electoral system, Britain has a two-party system in which the Labour Party and the Conservative Party have been sharing power since the Second World War.

Britain is predominantly Christian, but most of the world's religions are represented in the country. Muslims are the second largest group and there are also Hindu, Jewish and Sikh communities.

## 1 – Population

There have been numerous changes in demographic patterns throughout the twentieth century, since Britain diversified ethnically and aged. In 1998 the population of the United Kingdom was estimated to be 59.2 million, the 18th largest in the world whereas in 1901 it amounted to 38.2 million.

Between the two world wars, Britain experienced a period of decreasing fertility characterised by delayed marriage, relatively high bachelordom and spinsterhood and virtually non-existent divorce and illegitimate births.

But since 1945, the family ties have weakened with the rising rates of divorce, separation, cohabitation and lone motherhood. The end of the century is characterised by an ageing population with low mortality and still lower fertility. The age structure of the population reflects the increasing longevity and changes arising from migration of persecuted people.

In 1998 one person in six was aged 65 and over compared with one in twenty in 1901. Besides, the annual number of deaths has remained stable this century with 661,000 deaths in the United Kingdom in 1998 compared with 632,000 in 1901. Infant and childhood mortality have fallen considerably and so have the death rates among older people. Consequently, the number of people living to the age of 100 or over increased during the second half of the twentieth century reaching 5,500 by 1996. Conversely, the population under the age of 16 fell from a third in 1901 to a fifth in 1998.

Apart from the increasing number of old people and the decreasing number of children, the pattern of immigration has changed and transformed major cities into racially mixed populations. Since 1945, new waves of immigration have arrived from the Carribean and South East Asia and there are 3 million people belonging to another ethnic group than the white group which makes up 94.5% of the population. In general, ethnic minority groups in Britain have a younger age structure than the white population, because of fertility rates.

There have also been changes in the occupational composition of the population. The number of men in the professional, managerial and supervisory grades has increased. So has the number of women in higher socio-economic occupations. There are now more women in the workforce but in 1999 men were three times more likely than women to be in the professional group and women tend to prevail in clerical and secretarial jobs.

The geographical distribution has also evolved. There was a great population increase in England between 1901 and 1998 amounting to 62%, whereas there was a small increase in Scotland amounting to 14%. The North West had the largest net loss of people due to internal migration while the South West had the largest net gain. England has the highest population density with 379 people per square kilometre in 1998 and Scotland the lowest with only 66 people per square kilometre. In

1998, 84% of the population of the United Kingdom lived in England. The population is highly urbanised with 90% of British people living in urban areas in 1991 and London has the greatest population density with 6.4 million people living in Greater London in 1991.

## 2 – National Income and Wealth

Men's incomes were higher than those of women regardless of age in 1996-97 and the top average income was that of men and women in their late forties. The gap between high incomes and low incomes grew rapidly in the United Kingdom in the 1980s but remained stable in the early 1990s.

During the 1990s, the growth in average earnings was more important than that of retail prices. Household income per head, adjusted for inflation almost doubled between 1971 and 1998. But the components of household income have changed since 1987. The proportion derived from wages and salaries fell from 60% to 56% in 1998 and there were rises in social benefits.

Yet, there is an uneven distribution of total income between households: 39% of people in single and couple households where all are in full-time work were in the top quintile in 1997-98. 29% of the self-employed were also in the top quintile in 1997-98. The average income of the top quintile group of households amounted to £33,590 in 1997-98.

The number of people living in households with low incomes rose from 13% in 1961 to 21% in 1992, but in 1997-98, there were 18% of households with low income, that is to say 60% of the median household disposable income. People from the ethnic minority communities are over-represented amongst low income households. Nearly 60% of Pakistani/Bangladeshi people were living in low income households in 1996-1998, compared with over 25% of Black and Indian people and 17% of white people. Workless households are over-represented in the bottom 20%. In February 1999, 2.6 million people in Great Britain had been granted income support for more than two years.

There is a geographical gap in the average gross earnings for full-time employees in the centre of England from Warwickshire in the south Midlands to Hampshire where the highest level is reached and in parts of Wales and Scotland where the lowest earnings are found.

In spite of the Equal Pay Act of 1970 and the Sex Discrimination Act which established the principle of equal pay for work, there is still a gender gap in the weekly earnings of men (£425.6 in April 1998) and women (£308.7 in April 1998). In 1999, women's weekly earnings were 74% of those of men, compared with only 54% in 1970.

The National Minimum Wage which came into effect on 1st April 1999 is £3.00 per hour for 18 to 21 year olds and £3.60 for those aged 22 or over.

Wealth is less evenly distributed than income. In 1996, the wealthiest 1% of individuals owned a fifth of the total marketable wealth. Half the population shared between them only 7% of total marketable wealth in 1996 and 30% of households had no savings at all in 1997-98.

There has been an increase in total household expenditure between 1951 and 1998. The patterns of expenditure have changed in the past forty years and households spent 48% in services in 1998, compared with 28% in 1963. Conversely, the amount of money spent on goods such as food, clothing and power fell from 63% in 1963 to 42% in 1998.

Household expenditure depends on the status of the household head. For example, the average expenditure of working age couples without children amounted to £441 per week in 1998-99, and those with children spent about £465 per week.

In 1997-1999, a white head of household spent 17% on motoring, 17% on leisure goods and services, 17% on food, 16% on housing, 14% on household goods, 6% on clothing, 6% on fuel, and 4% on alcohol and tobacco.

Furthermore, shopping on the Internet has become increasingly popular as more and more households acquire a personal computer.

## 3 – Figures on the Economy from 1979 to 1999

When Margaret Thatcher became Prime Minister in May 1979, her dominant aim was to master inflation, cut public expenditure and reduce taxation.

The main aim of government policy was to curb inflation, that is to say the rise in prices, which reached 21.9% in May 1981 and had fallen to 3.7% by May 1983, before rising again to 10% in 1990. The years after 1983 brought a continuing economic recovery, but the rate of unemployment did not fall until 1986.

The economic policy of the Thatcher government was two-fold: on the one hand, the market should expand and on the other hand, the role of the state should contract. It rested on cutting public expenditure, deregulation and privatization. Cutting public expenditure was intended to pave the way for cuts in taxation. Deregulation was meant to encourage competition. It involved the removal of exchange control and allowed the producer more freedom of action and the consumer more freedom of choice. From 1983 onwards, privatization developed and some 50 major public sector businesses have been privatized, including gas, electricity supply, railway services, coal and telecommunications. The privatization policy has involved denationalisation and deregulation. By 1987, the government had raised about £25 billion through privatization and 1 million jobs had been transferred from the public to the private sector.

Governmental policy towards the unions since 1979 meant to weaken collectivism and reduce union power.

On the other hand, the rate of expansion was due to high consumer spending. But there was a rise of unemployment in the 1980s as a consequence of policies designed to curb inflation.

After the recession of 1990-92, the British economy experienced continuous growth and low inflation. Domestic demand slowed with Gross Domestic Product at 3.5% in 1997 and at 2.2% in 1998.

There has been a substantial decline in inflation since 1990 and in 1998 the rate of inflation amounted to 2.6%.

The nature of the labour market has changed radically in the past two decades. Britain has shifted away from an old regulated market with high unionisation and secure jobs to a deregulated one. This new labour market is characterised by low unionisation, flexible employment and job insecurity.

Since 1988, there has been a rise in levels of employment. In spring 1989, there were 26.7 million people in employment and 1.8 million were unemployed and in spring 1999, 27.3 million people were in employment and 1.7 million people were unemployed. The percentage of workforce unemployed fell from 8.8% in 1988 to 6% in 1999. There has been a significant growth of employment among women. Between spring 1971 and spring 1999, the number of women in employment in Britain increased from 56% to 72%.

The next big expansion was in imports and exports and by the 1980s imports were growing twice as fast as exports and a large balance of payments deficit emerged. By 1990, the proportion of British trade with Commonwealth countries had decreased to 10% while trade with the European Community had grown to over 50%.

There was also an improvement in the standard of living and an increase in spending.

## 4 – Politics

The House of Commons and the House of Lords are the two chambers of Parliament, but the House of Commons is the dominant chamber and a fundamental institution of British government. It is now the efficient part of the Constitution together with the Prime Minister and the Cabinet. It consists of 659 MPs elected as representatives of parties (the Labour Party, the Conservative Party, the Liberal Democrats and other smaller parties). It remains important as a legislative and scrutinising body, as a representative body and as a forum for national debate. It has political legitimacy and is the major theatre of politics, but as the power of the executive has increased the golden age of the Commons is over.

First of all, the House of Commons has a legislative function as most legislation originates from government and emerges from its passage through Parliament. The House of Commons provides the legitimacy of law and the machinery for the making of law derived from its legislative sovereignty. The House of Commons scrutinizes the legislation and the proceedings of government through several organs: the official opposition, the Standing Committees, and the Select committees. Standing Committees consider legislation in detail, clause by clause and can make amendments. Select Committees deal with the departments of Agriculture, Defence, Education, Employment, Environment, Foreign Affairs, Health, Home Affairs, National Heritage, Science and Technology, Scottish Affairs, Trade and Industry, Transport, Treasury and Civil Service, and Welsh Affairs. Currently each committee comprises 11 MPs formally appointed by the House of Commons itself. They have an absolute right to demand any information they require for the purposes of their enquiry and have some influence on policy both in the short term and in the long term. They constitute a great advance on Commons machinery to scrutinise the executive.

Secondly, the House of Commons has a representative function. It expresses the mind of the English people on all matters. The Member of Parliament (MP) is a representative of a party, of common interests and of his constituency expressing the grievances of the public.

Thirdly, the House of Commons has a teaching function and is the focus of national debate on Prime Minister's Question Time and at the beginning and end of major debates.

The official opposition and its Leader have formal standing and the official opposition has some rights and privileges illustrated in the presence of a Shadow Cabinet.

It can ask questions to the government during Question Time and Prime Minister's Question Time. Question Time helps to maintain an investigatory control over the executive. The occasion provides a chance to judge ministerial dexterity. On average, it takes between two and three minutes to deal with each question. Any question must relate to a matter for which the Minister is directly responsible to Parliament. Every Wednesday, questions are put to the Prime Minister, in Prime Minister's

Question Time, the focal point of which is the contest between the two main party leaders.

The key to understanding the powers of the Commons lies in the relationship between government and the House of Commons as the representative body. Yet, the House of Commons has yielded powers to the executive embodied by the Prime Minister Tony Blair.

The House of Commons has little effective capacity to challenge the actions of government. It has largely lost the function of initiating legislation. It no longer uses its powers to control financial and administrative matters.

Furthermore, the House of Commons is poorly representative, being forced by the electoral system into a false two-party pattern. It is dominated by the Labour Party and the Conservative Party, restricting individual opinion and dissent. The majority party chooses a government and hands the parliamentary power of its majority to the government, which thus acquires the command of the House of Commons. The composition of the House of Commons should reflect the political views of the electorate better and Select Committees should reflect the political views in the Commons. But, the private Member of Parliament has yielded independence to party and to interest groups.

Finally, the House of Commons has surrendered most of its powers to the executive. The growing powers of the PM and the functions of the Cabinet have overruled the powers of the House of Commons and ministers dominate the House of Commons.

Thus the House of Commons has become the passive forum in which the struggle is fought between great political machines. This is an unusual arrangement in legislatures which are mostly based on the principle of the separation of powers.

## 5 – Electoral system

The body of rules governing the British electoral process has often been seen as one of the keys to understanding the causes of the country's political stability. Recently the electoral system has been the subject of criticism. Particular controversy has surrounded the British method of translating votes into seats, the so-called first-past-the-post system.

There was a slow extension of the electorate in the 19th century thanks to the Reform Act of 1832 and 1867 which added voters from the working classes of the towns and cities.

The Representation of the People Act of 1918 gave the vote to all men of 21 and to women over 30. In 1969, there was a lowering of the voting age to 18.

All British citizens are allowed to vote, except peers who may not vote in elections to the House of Commons because they have the right to sit in the House of Lords.

For national elections, Britain uses a Single Member Simple Plurality system (SMSP) (often known as "first-past-the-post"). Britain's first-past-the-post electoral system is not neutral in converting the share of seats won. It causes a distortion between the share of votes and the share of seats and can be thought of as a system of disproportional representation. Britain's electoral system overrewards the single most popular party and favours the Labour and Conservative parties which can concentrate political support in certain areas whereas it tends to discriminate against parties with widely distributed electoral support. The first-past-the-post system is a key factor in the maintenance of the British party system because it militates against the breakthrough of a third party, not only in terms of electoral geography but also in terms of tactical voting.

The greatest change could come from a reform of the voting system. The introduction of a more proportional system in European elections may lead to a greater representation of minor parties such as the Green Party. But the most far-reaching impact would come through any change to the voting system for the House of Commons.

When Tony Blair was elected in 1997, he was committed to reforming the electoral system for general elections and he appointed Lord Jenkins to chair a Committee on electoral reform. The Committee suggested adopting the alternative vote which is not proportional, but is often defined as a form of proportional representation. It is preferential voting in single-member constituencies. The Alternative vote ensures that no Member of Parliament (MP) can be elected on a minority vote. It would thus be fairer than first-past-the-post, under which many MPs can be elected even though more votes have been cast against them than for them. But the Prime Minister has not implemented such electoral reform yet, because it would have four implications: it would increase the number of parties, smaller parties would be represented, there would be a fragmentation of existing parties, and it would end one party domination in the legislature.

It would also affect the accountability of the executive, since responsibility for policies would no longer be located in a single party, but would be split between two or more parties. Coalition government which has been the exception in UK politics could become the norm, with less legislation and more policy stagnation requiring a new culture of co-operation in order to be effective.

There is at present a widespread movement across the political spectrum which supports a modernisation of Britain's constitution, with electoral reform taking a central role in helping to improve the quality of British democratic and political life. The Alternative vote is surely the most reasonable system of electoral reform for the House of Commons.

If approved by referendum, it will not be implemented before 2005.

## 6 – Local government and London

There are 39 counties in England incorporating 296 districts. In addition there are 32 London boroughs together with the City of London and 36 metropolitan districts.

Local government is government for local people by local people and British citizens aged 18 and over and registered to vote in current electoral areas are entitled to elect local councillors.

Local authorities provide a wide range of services for their local communities and exercise powers given to them by Parliament. They have an impact on economic development and provide housing, education, social services, police and fire services.

The spending of local governments is financed by central government grants and the redistribution of revenue from the national non-domestic rate.

One of the major priorities of Blair's government was good local government and decentralisation. Blair wants local councils to promote the economic, social and environmental well-being of their area. Blair's government is increasing the role of local councils in economic development and restoring some of their influence over grant-maintained schools.

Blair's government is in favour of directly elected mayors which would make it easier for the public to identify with their local authority.

The Lord Mayor of London was responsible financially for the centre of London, but London was so far the only Western capital without a directly elected mayor and an elected city government. A consultation paper on a *New Leadership for London* in 1997 underlined the need to restore democratic city-wide Government to London and an assembly both directly elected. Its aim was to bring decision-making closer to the people.

Consequently, the creation of the Greater London Authority was held as a means to improve London's competitiveness. Londoners voted in a referendum on whether the capital should have an elected mayor in May 1998. On May 4th, 2000, Ken Livingstone was elected Mayor of London with 41% of the votes. His victory was seen as a sign of Blair's decreasing influence, since the new Mayor stood as an independent who rallied Labour supporters, Tories and Lib Dems against Blair's candidate Frank Dobson.

The role of the Mayor includes proposing the budget, devising strategies and promoting actions to implement London-wide strategies, but he does not have the power or the money to do a lot of things. He has no responsibility for London's schools and hospitals and he does not have the power to levy taxes. The mayor has to work with a 25-seat Greater London Assembly in which no party has control.

The role of the Assembly involves approving the budget and strategies, approving appointments, and scrutinizing the Mayor. The Greater London Authority will deal with transport policy, ranging from the integration of roads, rail, bus, tube to the steady improvement in the quality of the underground. It will be in charge of economic development and regeneration and environment protection, improving the capital's environment, air quality and waste management.

## 7 – What future?

Throughout history, Britain has shown a great power of resilience, constantly following the trend of history, avoiding upheavals: evolution seems to be the line rather than revolution. Ever since the Glorious Revolution praised by Edmund Burke in contrast with the French Revolution a century later, the English have been aware of changes, taking U-turns whenever necessary. More recently, the Queen cut her Civil List facing public criticism and a bill on privacy was passed when the media became threatening for the Royal Family. Even if in popular imagination the UK remains the kingdom of "Pomp and Circumstance", however questioned it is, it enters the 21st century equal to itself, retaining its traditions. The Opening of Parliament remains the yearly ceremony which attracts many tourists together with British subjects. The flimsy aspect of the Crown seems everlasting though fragile. It could easily be tipped over by a family crisis. And yet great family events such as the 100th birthday of the Queen Mother proved out to be a cement for the nation. Indeed, the Queen Mother was closely associated with the misery of London during World War II, together with her two daughters Queen Elizabeth and Princess Margaret.

The aristocracy has also followed the trend, either out of obligation, for lack of money, or because of heavier taxes when they did not sell and tried to maintain their estates. They were the first to find solutions, transforming their stately homes into natural parks as the Duke of Bedford did just after the war at Woburn Abbey, or even into luxury hotels for tourists in quest of tradition. Aristocrats also turn to the City and business.

The Duke of Westminster still owns one tenth of London in the city of Westminster.

Public schools which have adapted to the need of progress remain among the best schools in the United Kingdom. They shape a character, impart a style of living, a tone of voice and a way to speak, not to mention dress codes, thus abiding by the legacy of the tradition which still consists in excellence and courage. The upper classes are opening up more and more to deserving people who do not really belong, but who succeed in buying aristocratic estates or vie with aristocrats for fame and fortune: Elton John, Richard Branson have thus become great favourites of the Royals.

Yet another serious crisis is shattering Britain presently: bovine spongiform encephalopathy or "mad cow" disease originated in Britain and is now worsened by another epidemic: foot and mouth disease. Death seems to bring British farming to the brink of collapse, viewed by Europeans and an Irish government minister as "the leper of Europe". The British economy has been too long out of control and the whole system is now questionable: from the agricultural policy which will boil down to destroying livelihoods and bringing to a standstill much of the world's trade in beef, pork and lamb to transport with the recurrent derailments which caused heavy damage and casualties.

## 8 – Key dates and events in British history

*Roman Britain (55 BC-AD 440)*

| | |
|---|---|
| 55-54 BC | Caesar lands in Britain. |
| c.50 | London founded. |

*The Anglo-Saxon Age (440-1066)*

| | |
|---|---|
| 751 | Adam Bede publishes *The Ecclesiastical History of the English People*. |

*The Middle Ages (1066-1485)*

| | |
|---|---|
| 1066 | The Battle of Hastings: the Normans conquer England. |
| 1215 | The Magna Carta is imposed upon King John by the barons. The beginning of the Black Death and the plague epidemic. |
| 1381 | The Peasants' Revolt. |
| 1485 | The War of the Roses ends with the death of Richard III at the Battle of Bosworth. |

*Tudor Britain (1485-1603)*

| | |
|---|---|
| 1509 | Henry VIII ascends the throne and strengthens the powers of the monarch. |

| | |
|---|---|
| 1534 | Henry VIII breaks apart with Rome and becomes the Supreme Governor of the Church of England. |
| 1536 | Henry VIII dissolves the monasteries and church estates are sold by the Crown. |
| 1547 | Henry VIII dies. |
| 1549 | The first Book of Common Prayer is published. |
| 1558 | Elizabeth I ascends the throne. |
| 1588 | The Spanish Armada is defeated by the fleet of Elizabeth I. |

*Stuart England (1603-1688)*

| | |
|---|---|
| 1603 | James I becomes King of Britain. |
| 1604 | The Gunpowder plot is the last major Catholic conspiracy. |
| 1642 | The Civil War begins. |
| 1649 | Charles I is executed and the line of succession is interrupted. |
| 1653 | Cromwell becomes Lord Protector. |
| 1658 | Cromwell dies and is succeeded by his son as Lord Protector. |
| 1660 | The monarchy is restored and Charles II ascends the throne. |
| 1665 | The Great Plague. |
| 1666 | The Great Fire of London. |
| 1685 | Charles II dies and James II ascends the throne. |
| 1688 | The Glorious Revolution begins and Mary and William of Orange ascend the throne. |

*Britain In the Eighteenth Century (1688-1815)*

| | |
|---|---|
| 1689 | The Bill of Rights protects the liberties of the subject and the powers of Parliament. |
| | The Glorious Revolution and the Bill of Rights. |
| 1707 | By the Act of Union, England and Scotland merge with Wales. |
| 1714 | Queen Anne dies and George I ascends the throne. |
| 1776 | Adam Smith publishes *Wealth of Nations*. |
| 1790 | Edmund Burke publishes *Reflections on the Revolution in France*. |
| 1800 | Ireland merges with Britain and the United Kingdom of Great Britain and Ireland is created. |
| 1815 | The Battle of Waterloo ends the Napoleonic Wars. |
| 1832 | The First Reform Bill extends the franchise and puts an end to the rotten boroughs. |

*The Victorian Age (1837-1901)*

| | |
|---|---|
| 1851 | The Great Exhibition opens in London. |
| 1867 | The Second Reform Act further extends the Reform Bill of 1832. |
| 1884 | The Fabian Society is founded. |
| 1901 | Queen Victoria dies and Edward VIII ascends the throne. |

*The Twentieth Century*

| | |
|---|---|
| 1911 | The Parliament Act cuts the financial powers of the House of Lords. |
| 1918 | The Representation of the People Act extends the franchise to all men over 21 and to women over 30. |
| 1942 | The Beveridge Report calls for a social security system. |
| 1944 | Butler Act on Education. |
| 1945 | For the first time the Labour Party wins a landslide victory in the general elections. Clement Attlee becomes Prime Minister. |
| 1946 | National Health Service Act. |
| 1947 | India becomes independent. |
| 1952 | George VI dies and Elizabeth II ascends the throne. |
| 1963 | Britain refused entry to the EEC. |
| 1964 | Harold Wilson becomes Prime Minister. |
| 1973 | The United Kingdom joins the European Community. |
| 1977 | Jubilee of Queen Elizabeth II. |
| 1979 | Margaret Thatcher becomes Prime Minister; she would win two further elections. |
| 1981 | The Prince of Wales marries Lady Diana Spencer. |
| 1990 | Margaret Thatcher resigns and John Major becomes Prime Minister. |
| 1997 | The Labour Party dubbed New Labour by Tony Blair wins the general elections on May 1st and Tony Blair, the Leader of the Party, becomes Prime Minister. |
| 1999 | Elections to the Scottish Parliament and to the Welsh Assembly. |
| 2001 | The Labour Party wins the general elections again on June 7th and Tony Blair remains Prime Minister. |

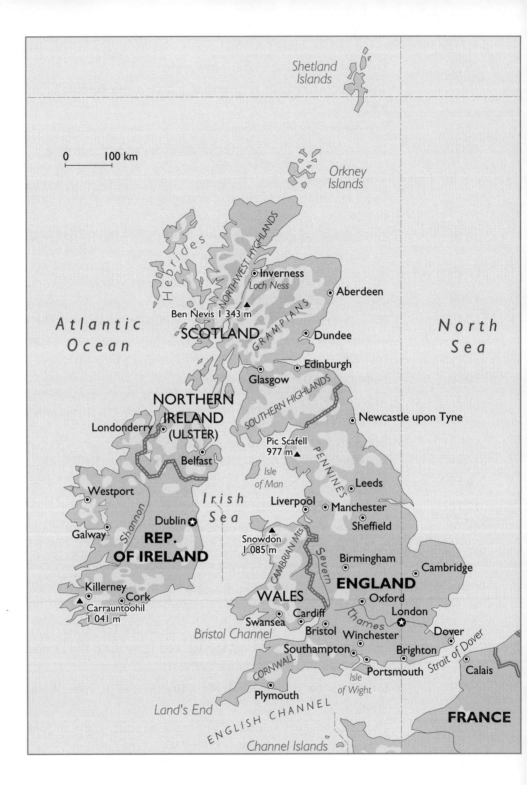

# Monarchy and the Establishment

*Sophie Loussouarn*

The British monarchy is the only one on the grand imperial scale left in a world full of republics. Only a few "bicycle monarchies" remain elsewhere. It is the *apex of a privileged and outdated pyramid. The Monarchy is embedded in the traditional core of the *Establishment: the Church of England, the Lords, the landowners, the top military men and the very wealthy.

The monarchy belongs to the dignified part of the British Constitution together with the House of Lords, as opposed to the efficient parts, that is the Cabinet, the Prime Minister and the House of Commons. Queen Elizabeth II is the Head of State and the Head of the Commonwealth. She has performed official duties since 1952.

In 1994, Blair put forward a reform of the British monarchy to turn it into a Scandinavian style of court. Since then, Blair has become Prime Minister and a longer-term modernization programme is under consideration for the succession of Prince Charles or his son Prince William. Some royal advisers want the monarchy to become less *aloof, more open and more in touch with the people.

What will the plan to modernize the British monarchy consist in? Will it hasten the process towards a more Scandinavian monarchy, a monarchy symbolizing a much more classless society?

## The historical background

The *Crown is an element of stability and an element of social unity and the monarch is an element of continuity; it is a way of linking the past, the present and the future. The monarchy dates back to the 9th century and the continuity was broken only once during the period of rule by the council of state and Oliver Cromwell (1649-1660). The line of succession was broken with the execution of Charles I in 1649 but it was restored with Charles II.

The monarchy and its associated activities provide a symbol for nation and state. The monarch is a *figurehead at the apex of society. The monarch is a unifier above the *party fray. All British citizens are subjects of the queen. The symbolic power of *royalty is enormous. It sells magic, history, state, nation, but also some attractive notions, like class, privilege and social unreality. Ritual is a way of consolidating the institution and ceremonies such as the Coronation, the State Opening of Parliament, royal marriages and jubilees are means of increasing the popularity of the monarch.

## The remaining constitutional powers of the monarch

The monarchy has lost some of its powers but it still provides an essential constitutional mechanism in the formation and dissolution of governments. So far, the functions of the monarch are legally the following. The Monarch *summons, *prorogues and dissolves Parliament. The Queen opens Parliament with a Speech which is written by the Prime Minister and outlines the Government's programme. In theory, Parliament draws its existence from the Monarch. The Monarch has the right to be consulted, to encourage and to warn. No bills passed by Parliament can become law without the Royal Assent. But the Monarch has not refused a bill that passed through the House since 1707 and the role of the Sovereign in the *enactment of legislation is today purely formal.

The Monarch is the Fountain of Justice. In the United Kingdom, all jurisdiction derives from the Crown, but the Monarch acts on the advice of the Ministers. On the one hand, the Queen can pardon or show *mercy to those *convicted of crimes. On the other hand, the Queen can do no wrong and cannot be *sued in courts of law.

The Queen appoints the Prime Minister and makes appointments to many important state offices, on the advice of the Prime Minister. She appoints and *dismisses government ministers, judges, members of the diplomatic corps. As the Head of the Army, the Monarch alone can declare war and peace on the advice of responsible Ministers and appoint officers and as the Head of the established Church of England, she is the Defender of the Faith and appoints bishops on the advice of the Prime Minister. Besides, the Monarch is the Fountain of Honour and confers life *peerages, *knighthoods and other honours, such as the *Order of the Garter, the *Order of the Thistle, the Order of Merit and the Royal Victorian Order.

### Reforms of the Monarchy

Most of the powers of the Monarch have already been transferred to the Prime Minister and Parliament, but other proposals to modernize the Monarchy include transfers of powers to the Speaker of the House of Commons. Yet the monarch would remain Head of the Army and Head of the judicial system.

Among the constitutional reforms of the Monarchy, the question of succession has been raised. The sons of the sovereign and their descendants have precedence over daughters in succeeding to the throne. The sovereign succeeds to the throne on the death of his or her predecessor. The automatic succession is summed up in the phrase "the King is dead; long live the King!" So the Coronation follows the accession. But the Monarch could be elected from the members of the established Hanover-Windsor dynasty. This would widen the field of choice.

Moreover, the Monarch has been governor of the Church of England since 1543. It is worth noting that it is true only of England. The Queen is linked to the Church of England and promises to maintain it in the *Coronation Oath. There could also be a disestablishment of the Church of England as the state's official religion and a removal of the monarch's position as the head of that church.

The modernization of the Monarchy includes bringing it closer to the people. The Windsors have often been said to be *manacled by protocol and tradition. Reformers want the Monarchy to be closer to the people instead of being out of touch. They want the Crown to come down from the apex of the establishment pinnacle. The education of the Royal Family should be in touch with the age and the royal children should go to state schools instead of Eton and Gordonstoun. Reformers are in favour of a bicycle Monarchy. They want the royal family to be more approachable like the Monarchy in the Netherlands. But this raises the question of the mystique of the monarchy. The Monarchy is magic because it displays great wealth and aristocratic connections, because it is set apart from its subjects.

## Monarchy has to adapt if the institution wants to survive

Even though the Monarchy is still popular, profound changes are going on.

It is certainly the most revered of the British institutions, though its image and that of individual members of the Royal Family has been seriously damaged in recent years. Despite numerous problems for the Royal Family over the past two decades, the proportion in favour of a monarchy rather than some form of a presidential system has remained stable at four in five of the public. The Queen has often been in the list of the most admired people. The people are not interested in the labour of administration, they are fascinated by the magic and the *pageantry.

But, there is talk of cutting down the expenses of the monarchy. It started with the reform of the Civil List. Since 1993, the Queen has accepted to pay *income tax. The Queen *funded the restoration of Windsor Castle and opened up the royal finances to public scrutiny. Furthermore, the future of *grace and favour apartments at Kensington Palace is the subject of intense internal debate.

The institution might be reformed, as it has been throughout history, according to changed circumstances. It might also be abolished, in which case there is a need to consider what might replace it in the constitution. The obvious alternative to hereditary monarchy which would satisfy the requirement for a democratic head of state is an elective presidency. The main objection is that an elected president would inevitably be a politician. There is no good reason to believe that an elective presidency would have serious disadvantages, either of efficiency or of dignity over an hereditary monarchy. But the Monarch is independent and holds a reserve power to control politicians' behaviour. Unlike politicians who are chosen at random, the monarch is above politics and can be admired as an abstraction.

# Vocabulary

| | |
|---|---|
| aloof | hautain |
| apex | sommet |
| befit (to) | convenir |
| convicted | accusé |
| coronation oath | serment du couronnement |
| Court of Appeals | cour d'appel |
| crown, Crown | couronne, Couronne, Reine |
| decay | décadence, déclin |
| dismiss (to) | renvoyer |
| enactment | application |
| Establishment | pouvoirs établis |
| figurehead | figure de proue |
| franchise | droit de vote |
| fund (to) | subventionner |
| grace and favour apartments | appartements attribués à une personne pour la durée de sa vie, par la Reine |
| honour system | décorations |
| income tax | impôt sur le revenu |
| judiciary | pouvoir judiciaire |
| knighthood | chevalerie |
| legislature | corps législatif |
| manacled | emprisonné |
| mercy | miséricorde, grâce |
| mores | mœurs |
| Order of the Garter | Ordre de la Jarretière |
| Order of the Thistle | Ordre du Chardon |
| pageantry | apparat, pompe |
| party fray | mêlée des partis politiques |
| peerage | pairie |
| peer (life/heriditary) | pair à vie ; pair héréditaire |
| press (to) ahead | faire avancer |
| prevail over (to) | surpasser, l'emporter sur |
| prorogue (to) | proroger |
| ranking | classement |
| rebalanced | rééquilibré |
| royalty | la famille royale |
| scrutiny | contrôle |
| shorn of | dépouillé de |
| be sued (to) | être poursuivi |
| summon (to) | convoquer |
| tramlines of policy | les voies de la politique |

# Focus...

◆ **Quotations**

***Walter Bagehot on the Monarchy***
"To state the matter shortly, the sovereign has, under a constitutional monarchy such as ours, three rights – the right to be consulted, the right to encourage, the right to warn. [...] The characteristic advantage of a constitutional king is the permanence of his place. This gives him the opportunity of acquiring a consecutive knowledge of complex transactions, but it gives only an opportunity. The king must use it." (*The English Constitution*, Hammersmith: Fontana Press, 1867)

***Kingsley Martin on the Establishment***
"Probably the best definition of the Establishment is that it is that part of our government that has not been subjected to democratic control. It is the combined influence of persons who play a part in public life, though they have not been appointed on any public test of merit or election. More important still, they are not subject to dismissal by democratic process. They uphold a tradition and form a core of continuity in our institutions. They are privileged persons and their positions are not as a rule affected by changes of government."
(*The Crown and the Establishment*, London: Hutchinson, 1962)

◆ **The class structure**

Three elements make up class:
- Class is shaped by history.
- Class has a very strong subjective element.
- There are areas of inequality in power, authority, wealth, income, job situation, material conditions and lifestyles. There are wide differences between "them" and "us" in lifestyles, attitudes and customs.

The class of origin remains an important factor in recruitment to higher status occupations.

In 1990, more than half of the people said they were working-class, 1% upper class, and 17% said they belonged to no class at all. The middle classes were left with a miserable 28%.

From 1942 to 1990, the elites still composed a unitary dominant class and had a continuing hold on political power, even though the homogeneity of the Establishment was being questioned. At the top, to belong to the upper classes still offered disproportionate access to positions of power. More than one third of the Labour Cabinet of 1964 were traditional upper-class figures and six members were the products of the most exclusive public schools.

The sons of executives, senior civil servants and higher grade professionals were the most likely to remain at the same social level as their fathers. The higher civil service continued to be dominated by the upper classes.

The maintenance of family connections was a facet of the upper-class ethos and upper-class people had greater freedom of choice. The specificity of the upper-class family was the putting-down at birth of the son's name for the father's public school and the son's succession to the appropriate Oxford or Cambridge college.

# Commentary of a Text

## Concours de sortie de classement de l'ENA, mars 1999

"What is Power?" by Will Hutton (*The Observer*, 1 November 1998)

> The British have an almost unshakeable belief in the existence of that mystical governing élite, the Establishment. A network of exclusive London clubs supposedly plays host to a cluster of civil servants, businessmen and financiers who are united by family, education and conservative views, and who allegedly run the country. The Establishment may have been breaking down ever since the war, but most British believe it remains in place, laying down the *tramlines of policy and ensuring that the interests of the powerful and wealthy are safeguarded. It does not intervene directly of course, and its influence is based as much on access to power as formal authority; famously it is not what you know but who you know that counts.
>
> However, it only takes one glance at our list of the 300 most powerful people in Britain to realise that such a notion is in advanced *decay. There are certainly leadership groups and networks in Britain – and education at the better public schools and Oxbridge remains the best passport to the upper echelons of power, even in the new industries – but there is no longer a cohesive power élite, with shared *mores and political assumptions, that could be called the Establishment. Power has become diffused, and lies as much with scientific prowess or writing one of the leading TV soaps as holding a position in the political hierarchy. Nor can conservatism govern whoever is in power.
>
> Yes, there remain quietly influential meals in London clubs, and anybody who underestimates the cache of class, received pronunciation and dress codes in uniting the powerful underestimates the role of class in Britain. But birth no longer confers automatic access to power. If business and finance are even more powerful, that is because corporate power and the capital markets are objectively more powerful; not because those who run them use the right clubs and are members of the right families. The steady march of foreigners up the power list is testimony to the new emerging order, as is the high placing of those in the media and popular culture. Power is a sophisticated concept; it has always meant more than just the capacity of any one individual to make something significant happen in economy or society that would not otherwise have taken place. What has happened today is that these alternative power sources and influences have mushroomed, putting the old formal power networks in the shade. Our ordinary lives are shaped not principally by what is happening in the apparatus of the state, from the military to the courts, but by what is happening beyond, in the wellsprings of economy and society. Cultural and social change is now so fast and so palpably driven from below rather than from the top that those who have invented new means of seeing art are plainly at least as influential – if not more – than the Master of the Rolls or any chief constable.

Signs of the new times are all around. Six of the top names on the list are from overseas, as *befits an age in which financial markets and the media are increasingly globalised. This is a media age. Another feature of the list is the high *ranking accorded to finance.

There are very few women on the list. There are only seven in the top 100, and Cherie Booth and the Queen are special cases. Despite talk of girl power and the rise of women, what is striking is that the powerful still tend to be white, Anglo-Saxon men in their mid-fifties; women have still to break through to the real power and leadership groups, especially in business and finance.

*In this article published in* The Observer, *Will Hutton highlights the changing nature of power in Britain over the past twenty-five years. The article challenges the traditional notion of the Establishment and focuses on the perceptible widening in the social origins of many élite groups. The Establishment is made up of a very small minority of top people (drawn from politics, business, the City, the learned professions and the arts) who play the key role in decision-making.*

*The conservative networks of power are determined by birth, education, values and club membership. In spite of the social and cultural changes brought about by globalization, the journalist underlines the importance of the class system in the entrance to positions of power and social esteem in Britain. The élite is overwhelmingly public-school and Oxbridge educated. The Establishment is held together less by shared economic interest than by a common culture which separates it sharply from the rest of society. The Establishment has certain dress codes for gentlemen and ladies who dress up for parties and for formal events.*

*Even though the Establishment has a similar privileged educational background and lifestyle, élite positions are changing and the ruling class in Britain is no longer as homogeneous as it used to be. Britain is no longer ruled by a single monolithic Establishment and certain élite groups are becoming more open to newcomers. Some upstarts buy the castles of the ruined aristocracy but dress in jeans. Change, however slow it may be, has taken place in the world of finance and in the world of the media, which shape culture and society. Pop music and football have *prevailed over culture. Businessmen, TV stars and supermodels have overtaken politicians, civil servants and trade union leaders in the list of most famous people.*

*Yet, power remains in the hands of white Anglo-Saxon men in their fifties and women tend to be excluded from power and top positions in business and finance.*

# MORE ABOUT...
## ...THE REFORM OF THE LORDS

Tony Blair was committed to reforming the upper chamber which is awaiting a second stage of previous rounds of reforms: those of 1911 and 1949. Change in the composition of the House of Lords was on the government's agenda in 1997. What will the political and social impact of the reform be?

### THE POWERS OF THE HOUSE OF LORDS

The House of Lords is unlike any other European institution. It is the upper chamber and is part of the British Parliament together with the House of Commons. The Lords meet in the Palace of Westminster and this is where the Queen opens Parliament and delivers the Queen's Speech each year in October or November.

The powers of the House of Lords have been considerably reduced in the twentieth century.

Along with the monarchy, the peers have now joined the dignified part of the Constitution.

Constitutionally, the Upper House remains an essential part of the legislative process.

But the formal powers of the House of Lords are limited by the financial privilege of the House of Commons and by the Parliament Acts of 1911 and 1949. With the Parliament Act of 1911, the Lords completely lost their power to delay or reject money bills at all and now by convention do not even debate the annual Finance Bill. The 1949 Act cut short the period for which the Lords could delay legislation by reducing the period between first and second reading from two years to one.

In spite of the limitations imposed by the Parliament Acts of 1911 and 1949, the House of Lords today retains some important functions. First of all, the House of Lords is a forum of debate on matters of current interest. Secondly the House of Lords has the power to revise House of Commons bills and to introduce bills of a legal character. Thirdly the House of Lords has powers of *scrutiny and subjects government policy and administration through questions and through the work of its select committees. Finally, the House of Lords is the ultimate Court of Appeal in the UK.

### THE MEMBERSHIP OF THE HOUSE OF LORDS

Before the 1999 reform, it was determined by birth, creation and position.

Nearly two thirds (751) of its approximately 1,200 members were hereditary peers.

Under one third (400) are life *peers. All *peerages are conferred by the Sovereign who acts on the advice of the Prime Minister. A life peerage is both the highest honour awarded in the UK and the necessary qualification for membership of the upper chamber.

There are 26 spiritual Lords: the archbishops of Canterbury and York, the Bishops of London, Durham and Winchester, and the 21 senior bishops of the Church of England.

There are law Lords who assist the House in its judicial duties. They concentrate their contributions of bills which involve the judicial system, the administration of justice or law reform.

The reform of the Lords is nothing new. It had been on the Labour agenda since 1968, when Harold Wilson was Prime Minister.

Tony Blair went into the election of 1997 committed to abolishing the voting rights of hereditary peers. With a huge majority in the Commons, the Blair government wanted to force the hereditary peers out of the House of Lords by the year 2000. They decided that only 92 hereditary peers would remain in the transition period before the hereditary peers are totally removed.

The first 17 hereditary peers remain because they are office holders in the House of Lords. In November 2000, the reform was achieved since 751 unelected aristocrats chose 75 hereditary peers who will remain in the House of Lords. Among the remaining peers are the active peers, the life peers, the law Lords and the spiritual Lords.

The Lords reform has less to do with a concern for democracy and meritocracy and more to do with determination to neutralize one of the few checks on the power of the Commons. *Shorn of the hereditary peers and *rebalanced by additional Labour peers, the House of Lords will rarely be able to vote down the government.

The reform of the House of Lords is characteristic of New Labour which will end 800 years of history.

Tony Blair wants to *press ahead with the second stage of his modernization programme. The minimalist scenario would see the removal of the hereditary peers, but with reform stopping at this point. The House of Lords would then consist simply of life peers, all appointed by the current and the previous governments; and the bishops and law Lords. This might provoke a further bout of questioning about the legitimacy of the second chamber, and a further debate about its functions: is it simply a revising chamber? Is it a House of experts or of corporate and professional interests? Reforms that boost the democratic legitimacy of peers may reduce their inhibition in using existing powers to revise primary legislation and veto secondary legislation. Similar questions about functions arise on a maximalist scenario. If the House of Lords became an elected chamber, what would be the basis of the *franchise? To preserve its role of complementarity it would need to be elected on a different franchise from the House of Commons. But it need not be directly elected. Full reform of the House of Lords will need to consider the case for a supreme or constitutional court for the whole of the UK separate from the Appellate Committee of the Lords.

# 2. The Commonwealth

*Sophie Loussouarn*

The Commonwealth is a voluntary association of 54 sovereign states. It is one of the world's most vigorous international groupings *embracing countries which are widely different in size, wealth, levels of development, race, culture and religion. The total population of the Commonwealth *makes up over a quarter of the world's population.

The Commonwealth emerged from the process of decolonisation and the transformation of the British Empire. For Britain, it was a means of retaining its links with the former colonies and the Commonwealth now *fosters international co-operation and trade links.

The contemporary Commonwealth is a considerably different body from that which existed in 1931, 1949 or even in 1960. It has no formal constitutional structure, its members preferring to rely on unwritten conventions and accepted procedures. The Commonwealth has no formal charter but prospective members are expected to accept and commit themselves to the Commonwealth's *core values and principles as set out in the Harare Declaration of 1991. It benefits from shared practices and beliefs and from the shared language of English.

The Queen, symbol of the free association of independent member nations, is Head of the Commonwealth.

## The historical background

The Commonwealth traces its origins to the development of British colonial policy. In 1884, the British politician Lord Rosebery called the Empire "a Commonwealth of nations". In 1917, the Imperial War Conference recognised that "the constitutional relations of the component parts of the Empire... should be based upon a full recognition of the Dominions as autonomous nations of an Imperial Commonwealth".

Dominions were described as "autonomous Communities within the British Empire, equal in status, in no way subordinate one to another in any aspect of their domestic or external affairs, though united by a common *allegiance to the Crown and freely associated as Members of the British Commonwealth of Nations". Formal recognition of this fully independent status came with the passing by the British Parliament of the Statute of Westminster in 1931.

The modern Commonwealth emerged from the movement of decolonisation of British colonies after the Second World War. Two Commonwealth members were created, India and Pakistan followed by Ceylan in 1948. These developments gave direction to the new multiracial Commonwealth of equals which began to emerge as an essential part of postwar British foreign relations. Since 1949, the great majority of former British, Australian and New Zealand dependencies have *achieved independence and the majority have chosen to join the Commonwealth.

A new period in Commonwealth membership began in 1957 when Ghana achieved independence and joined the association. Commonwealth membership expanded rapidly as British rule over many countries ended in Africa, Asia, the Caribbean, the Mediterranean and the Pacific and almost all these nations chose to join the association on independence. The Commonwealth symbolises "the transformation of the Crown from an emblem of dominion into a symbol of free and voluntary association" as Queen Elizabeth II declared in a speech for the Silver Jubilee in 1977.

### The British monarch as Head of the Commonwealth

There are no constitutional functions attached to the title of Head of the Commonwealth, but it remains crucial as the symbolic link uniting all member states. Furthermore, the Monarch is the outward and visible mark of the special relationship which exists between the member states. Whether they are republics, indigenous monarchies, sultanates, elected chieftaincies or realms where the Queen remains *Head of State, members of the Commonwealth recognise the Queen as Head of the Commonwealth.

In those countries where the Queen remains as Head of State it has become established that the Queen acts as the Head of each individual state rather than as monarch of Britain. This change in practice has also affected Australia, Canada and New Zealand where the Queen is formally designated Queen of each individual country.

Her Majesty Queen Elizabeth II has been head of the Commonwealth for over 40 years and has visited every Commonwealth country except the two new members, Cameroon and Mozambique. In a Christmas broadcast from New Zealand in 1953, the Queen underlined the uniqueness of the association when she said: "The Commonwealth bears no resemblance to the empires of the past. It is an entirely new conception built on the highest qualities of the spirit of man: friendship, loyalty and the desire for freedom and peace."

The Queen maintains close links with the Commonwealth in many ways, especially with Commonwealth Day on the second Monday in March each year; the Queen delivers an annual Commonwealth Day Message and attends a multi-faith *observance at London's Westminster Abbey. The service includes a procession of the flags of member countries borne by their *nationals. Besides, the Queen attends the Commonwealth Games which still reflect the spirit of friendliness in which they were conceived in 1891 and which are organized every four years and are open to amateur competitors from throughout the Commonwealth.

The official aspect of the Commonwealth is its *machinery in London run by the Commonwealth Secretariat, established at the 1965 Prime Minister's Meeting to foster understanding between the constituent governments. Intergovernmental consultation is its main mode of operation, including Commonwealth Prime Ministers' Meetings.

### Reinventing the Commonwealth

In spite of its racial and religious diversity, the Commonwealth today is a community based on a shared heritage, since most countries have a common language and similar legal and educational systems. Since the Harare Declaration, the Commonwealth has laid the stress on values and goals such as good *governance and respect for human rights, sustainable development, protecting the environment, improving the life of women, and fighting crime, drug abuse and the spread of AIDS. Education and training rank among the Commonwealth priorities to enable economic and social development. The Commonwealth aims at shared prosperity through financial and technical assistance, thanks to the Commonwealth Fund for Technical Co-operation and to the Commonwealth Development Corporation. Besides, 53% of the aid budget of Britain's Department for International Development goes to Commonwealth countries, to help improve the quality of life.

The Commonwealth seems to be going well especially after a majority of Australians voted in favour of retaining the British monarchy on November 6th, 1999. However members of Blair's government *advocate various reforms which would diminish the role of the monarch and of Britain within the Commonwealth. In November 1999, a *think-tank called the Foreign Policy Centre *patronised by Tony Blair and presided over by Robin Cook published a *pamphlet entitled "Reinventing the Commonwealth".

Among the changes put forward, a Commonwealth President could *chair Commonwealth meetings, a debate could be organized over the Head of the Commonwealth. Besides the pamphlet suggested moving the Commonwealth's headquarters from London to Delhi or Lagos, and making the rules of membership more transparent.

The authors *question the role of the Queen and suggest turning the Commonwealth into a democratic club, focusing on trade and human rights.

Such reforms would certainly not attract interest in Commonwealth business in Britain, if the headquarters move from London to Delhi or Lagos. Furthermore the monarch is still very popular as a symbolic head of the Commonwealth.

# Vocabulary

| | |
|---|---|
| achieve (to) independence | obtenir l'indépendance |
| advocate (to) | préconiser, conseiller |
| allegiance | fidélité, obéissance |
| asset | atout |
| chair (to) | présider |
| constituent government | gouvernement mandant |
| core values and principles | principes de base |
| domestic affairs | affaires intérieures |
| embrace | regrouper, comprendre |
| encompass (to) | embrasser, englober |
| equities | actions ordinaires |
| exact (to) | exiger |
| external affairs | affaires extérieures |
| foster (to) | engendrer |
| governance | administration |
| Head of State | chef de l'État |
| insurance | assurance |
| intertwined | entrelacé |
| loosen (to) | se défaire, se relâcher |
| machinery | rouages administratifs |
| make up (to) | constituer, comprendre |
| national | ressortissant |
| observance | service religieux |
| pamphlet | brochure, opuscule |
| patronised | encouragé |
| question (to) | mettre en question |
| reluctant | réticent |
| shattered | brisé |
| self-governing | autonome |
| swaps trading | échange sur titre et sur devise, marché entre banques, échange de transactions à court terme |
| think-tank | groupe d'experts |
| trade in equities | marché des actions ordinaires |
| be undermined (to) | être amoindri |

# Focus...

The Commonwealth includes 13 of the world's fastest growing economies and 14 of the world's poorest.

Britain's Department for International Development devotes over 50% of its aid budget to the developing countries within the Commonwealth.

◆ **Chronology**

| | |
|---|---|
| 1777 | The first four provinces of Australia were granted responsible government; Queensland followed in 1859, Western Australia in 1893. |
| 1873 | Queen Victoria was made Empress of India. |
| 1907 | Australia achieved dominion status. |
| 1908 | New Zealand became a dominion. |
| 1909 | South Africa became a dominion. |
| 1926 | The Inter-Imperial Relations Committee defined their position in what became known as the Balfour Declaration. The dominions became described as "autonomous communities within the British Empire, equal in status, in no way subordinate one to another in any aspect of their domestic and external affairs, though united by a common allegiance to the Crown and freely associated as Members of the British Commonwealth of Nations". |
| 1931 | The Statute of Westminster recognized the independence of the *self-governing colonies under a common allegiance to the Crown. |
| 1947 | India and Pakistan became independent and chose the Commonwealth. |
| 1948 | The Commonwealth Development Corporation was set up by Britain to support the private sector in developing Commonwealth countries. |
| 1949 | A great majority of British dependencies achieved independence and chose the Commonwealth. |
| 1961 | South Africa withdrew from the Commonwealth. |
| 1965 | The Maldives achieved independence in 1965, but did not join the Commonwealth until 1982. |

| | |
|---|---|
| 1972 | Pakistan withdrew from the Commonwealth but rejoined in 1989. |
| 1994 | Return of South Africa to the Commonwealth. |
| 1995 | Mozambique became the first country to join which had not previously had such links with Britain. |
| 1999 | Referendum on the future of monarchy in Australia. |

◆ **The Commonwealth Principles
defined in the Singapore Declaration (1971)**

"The Commonwealth does not have a formal constitutional structure, its members preferring to rely on largely unwritten conventions and accepted procedures. However, its members have subscribed to several statements of shared principles which they believe should govern the conduct of the world's nations and peoples, in order to create a peaceful, equal, just and prosperous global community.

The Commonwealth of Nations is a voluntary association of independent sovereign states, each responsible for its own policies, consulting and co-operating in the common interests of their peoples and in the promotion of international understanding and world peace.

Members of the Commonwealth come from territories in the five continents and five oceans, include peoples of different races, languages and religions, and display every stage of economic development from poor developing nations to wealthy industrialised nations. They *encompass a rich variety of cultures, traditions and institutions."

# Essay

## The United Kingdom: From A Major World Power To A Middle-Sized Regional Power?

*Britain has moved from being a major world power to being a middle-sized regional power. In 1900, Britain was an imperial power. But the economic pattern has changed in the past few years and Britain is no longer a leading power in the world. Today Britain is struggling to retain its unity and independence. The twentieth century has been a century of national decline. What factors led to this decline? How did Britain react to these changing circumstances?*

*Decline is bound up with war. A country of Britain's size cannot hope to win two world wars and still remain a superpower. World War I shattered old Europe while \*exacting a terrible price from the UK in both gold and blood. World War II gave vast tracts of Eastern Europe to the Soviet Union.*

*Britain's importance in international affairs began to decrease after 1945, but was not fully acknowledged until the 1960s. Until the 1960s, the UK was one of the leading world powers.*

- *Britain was an independent nuclear power.*
- *Britain held a permanent seat on the Security Council of the United Nations.*
- *Britain was responsible for policing much of the world. In 1945, Winston Churchill described Britain's role in terms of being at the intersection of three majestic circles.*
- *The first was the Commonwealth circle which was a legacy of Britain's imperial power and embraced much of Africa and Asia as well as the dominions of Canada, New Zealand and Australia.*
- *The second was Britain's special relationship with the United States.*
- *The third was Britain's close relationship with Western Europe.*

*Taking a close look at the map, we can still assert that the Commonwealth spreads from East to West and the main \*assets of Britain are Australia, New Zealand, Canada, India and South Africa, Britain's population only amounting to a thirtieth of the whole Commonwealth population.*

*The loss of Britain's Empire and her transformation from a world power to a middle-sized regional power took place within a space of* twenty-five years. Britain was *reluctant to accept that her former place in the world had vanished forever and was very much in favour of an association with the Commonwealth and a special relationship with the United States. The history and culture of Britain and the United States were *intertwined and out of the close cooperation during the Second World War developed the special relationship. But the special relationship was strained during the Suez crisis in 1956 and weakened considerably during the 1960s and the 1970s. The Suez crisis showed that Britain could no longer sustain its old imperial world role. By the end of the 1960s, the British could no longer claim to exercise a dominant part in world affairs. Britain has had to adapt and make far-reaching changes in its foreign policy.

Since then, British policy-makers moved from an Atlanticist to a European outlook. As the links with the Commonwealth *loosened and the special relationship with the United States was redefined, Europe played a more prominent part in Britain's foreign policy. Britain became a member of the European Union in 1973 and is now one of the fifteen member states of the European Union.

In spite of its being a middle-sized regional power, Britain is a world leader in the provision of financial and business services and tourism is another major growth area. In spite of having 1% of the world's population, Britain is the fifth largest trading nation in the world, accounting for about 5.7% of world trade in goods and services. Britain is responsible for 10% of world exportation services and the nation's exports are in the region of US $266 billion. Furthermore London has one of the largest international insurance markets and Stock Exchanges. London is the world's largest centre for international bank lending (19% of the global market), international bonds – primary markets (60%) and secondary markets (75%) -, international *trade in equities (60%), *swaps trading (30%), marine insurance (28%) and aviation insurance (38%).

Britain's comparative wealth has declined and its part in world affairs has also contracted. Britain has become a trading partner with a great culture and a democratic tradition instead of being a world power of the first order. In spite of all the symptoms of declining prestige in the world, the Commonwealth survives, moreover Britain has the prospect of the European Union while maintaining a close relationship with the United States.

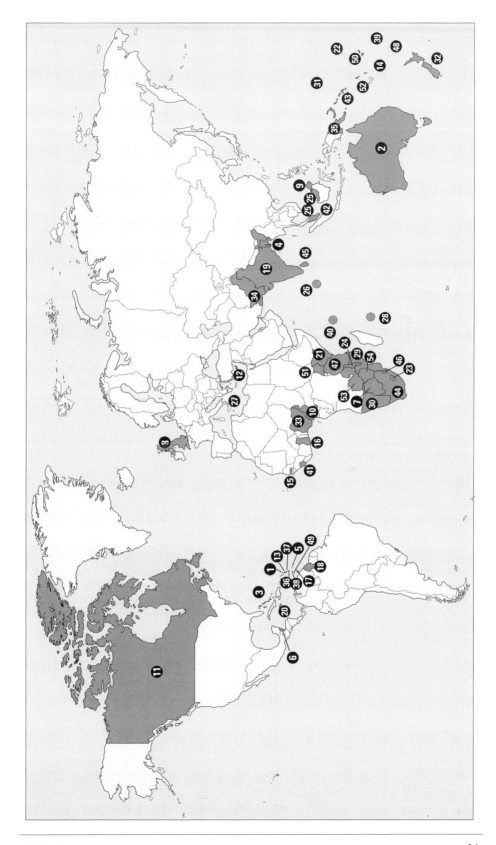

Civilisation britannique

1. Antigua & Barbuda
Cap.: St John's
2. Australia
Cap.: Canberra
3. The Bahamas
Cap.: Nassau
4. Bangladesh
Cap.: Dhaka
5. Barbados
Cap.: Bridgetown
6. Belize
Cap.: Belmopan
7. Botswana
Cap.: Gaborone
8. Britain
Cap.: London
9. Brunei Darussalam
Cap.: Bandar Seri Begawan
10. Cameroon
Cap.: Yaoundé
11. Canada
Cap.: Ottawa
12. Cyprus
Cap.: Nicosia
13. Dominica
Cap.: Roseau
14. Fiji
Cap.: Suva
15. The Gambia
Cap.: Banjul
16. Ghana
Cap.: Accra
17. Grenada
Cap.: St George's
18. Guyana
Cap.: Georgetown
19. India
Cap.: New Dehli
20. Jamaica
Cap.: Kingston
21. Kenya
Cap.: Nairobi
22. Kiribati
Cap.: Tarawwa
23. Lesotho
Cap.: Maseru
24. Malawi
Cap.: Lilongwe
25. Malaysia
Cap.: Kuala Lumpur
26. Maldives
Cap.: Malé
27. Malta
Cap.: Valetta
28. Mauritius
Cap.: Port Louis
29. Mozambique
Cap.: Maputo
30. Namibia
Cap.: Windhoeck
31. Nauru
Cap.: Nauru
32. New Zealand
Cap.: Wellington
33. Nigeria (suspended)
Cap.: Abuja
34. Pakistan
Cap.: Islamabad
35. Papua New Guinea
Cap.: Port Moresby
36. St Kitts & Nevis
Cap.: Basseterre
37. St Lucia
Cap.: Castries
38. St Vincent & The Grenadines
Cap.: Kingstown
39. Samoa
Cap.: Apia
40. Seychelles
Cap.: Victoria
41. Sierra Leone
Cap.: Freetown
42. Singapore
Cap.: Singapore
43. Solomon Islands
Cap.: Honiara
44. South Africa
Cap.: Pretoria
45. Sri Lanka
Cap.: Colombo
46. Swaziland
Cap.: Mbabane
47. Tanzania
Cap.: Dar es Salaam
48. Tonga
Cap.: Nuku'alofa
49. Trinidad et Tobago
Cap.: Port of Spain
50. Tuvalu
Cap.: Funafuti
51. Uganda
Cap.: Kampala
52. Vanuatu
Cap.: Port Vila
53. Zambia
Cap.: Lusaka
54. Zimbabwe
Cap.: Harare

**COMMONWEALTH COUNTRIES**

| COUNTRY | ADJECTIVE | COUNTRY | ADJECTIVE |
| --- | --- | --- | --- |
| Australia | Australian | Malta | Maltese |
| The Bahamas | Bahamian | Mauritius | Mauritanian |
| Bangladesh | Bangladeshi | Mozambique | Mozambican |
| Barbados | Barbadian | Namibia | Namibian |
| Botswana | Tswana | Nauru | Nauruan |
| Brunei | Bruneian | New Zealand | New Zealander |
| Burma | Burmese | Nigeria | Nigerian |
| Cameroon | Cameroonian | Pakistan | Pakistani |
| Canada | Canadian | Papua New Guinea | Papuan |
| Cyprus | Cyprian; Cypriot | Seychelles | Seychellois |
| Dominica | Dominican | Sierra Leone | Sierra Leonean |
| Fiji | Fijian | Singapore | Singaporean |
| The Gambia | Gambian | South Africa | South African |
| Ghana | Ghanaian | Sri Lanka | Sri Lankan |
| Grenada | Grenadian | Swaziland | Swazi |
| Guyana | Guyanese | Tanzania | Tanzanian |
| India | Indian | Tonga | Tongan |
| Jamaica | Jamaican | Trinidad | Trinidadian |
| Kenya | Kenyan | Uganda | Ugandan |
| Lesotho | Sotho | Zambia | Zambian |
| Malawi | Malawian | Zimbabwe | Zimbabwean |
| Malaysia | Malaysian | | |

# The United Kingdom and Europe

*Sophie Loussouarn*

As the Commonwealth circle declined and the special relationship with the US was redefined, Britain adapted by giving greater prominence to the European circle. Britain was reluctant to accept that its future lay in Europe. Britain's unique historical experience and its geographical situation different from European neighbours account for Britain's view of European unity and cooperation.

Britain's relationship with the European Union has been one of the dominant issues in British politics in the last fifty years. It has also been one of the most divisive. The debate has moved through a number of phases:

- The British government initially refused to participate in the negotiations which led to the setting up of the EC in the 1950s. Until the 1960s, most British political leaders did not see the British relationship with the continent as fundamental.
- The UK then applied to join in the 1960s and was twice *rebuffed.
- Britain was a late entrant to the European Community and became a full member in 1973.
- Since 1973, however, the relationship between the British government and other European governments has been marked by distrust and conflict. Many leading members of the British business community and some of the political elite had come to accept that a unified European market would be an inevitable response to the challenge of the American economy.

What is at stake in the European controversy in British politics is a major choice about Britain's role in the global political economy which involves questions of interest, ideology and identity.

## *The historical background*

Britain remained rather *aloof from developments in Europe during the early postwar years.

In 1945, Attlee welcomed the Schuman Plan but felt unable to join in. It was the most crucial of the opportunities which the Labour government missed between 1945 and 1951.

In 1946, Churchill called for the creation of a United States of Europe with Franco-German reconciliation providing the first crucial step. Even though Churchill did not believe Britain should play a major role in such a Europe, he can be held as one of the Founding Fathers of the European Community.

In the long *run, it was Britain's economic decline which, more than any other factor, led Britain to move into the European circle. But Britain was opposed to a common market. British politicians were concerned about the way in which European unity was being achieved. They were concerned by the concept of supra-nationalism. The idea that national governments should sacrifice sovereignty to European institutions was not attractive in Britain. Furthermore, Britain preferred international *free trade to the idea of a customs union.

Britain announced that they would not join the Six. Nevertheless, the European Free Trade Agreement was signed in November 1959 and it included Britain, Norway, Sweden, Denmark, Austria, Portugal and Switzerland.

By the early sixties, Macmillan announced the British intention to apply for membership of the EEC in July 1961, but the Prime Minister faced considerable opposition within the British Conservative Party and the French President, General de Gaulle, declared Britain unfit for membership in January 1963, vetoeing its entry into the EEC.

Then, Wilson's Labour Government applied for EEC entry in May 1967, but the second British attempt to join the EEC was again vetoed by De Gaulle in November of the same year.

After the *withdrawal of General de Gaulle in April 1969, the new Conservative government elected in 1970 began the negotiations leading to the successful entry of Britain into the EEC on 1st January, 1973. Two-thirds of the British people voted in favour of membership in the 1975 referendum.

### Blair's Britain in Europe: a new opportunity

For fifty years Britain has had a choice: to build a new world role for itself based on full and active membership of Europe or to face a future of increasing isolation and impotence. 1998 was the 25th anniversary of the UK's entry to the EU.

The advantages of membership of the European Union are described in terms of the economic benefits of being part of the *Single Market and the political gains in joining together with other member states in common actions in foreign policy and in international trade talks.

Tony Blair wants Britain to be a reliable ally in the institutions of which he is a member and a leader in Europe. His vision of Europe is of an alliance of independent nations choosing to cooperate to achieve the goals Britain cannot achieve alone. He is against a European federal superstate.

According to him, there are only three options for Britain in Europe: the first one is to come out, the second is to stay in but on the *sidelines, the third is to stay in, but in a leading role.

An increasing number of conservatives favour the first option that is to come out of Europe. But withdrawal would be disastrous for Britain. It would put millions of jobs at risk, it would dry up inward investment and it would destroy Britain's *clout in international trade negotiations. The third option is the path the New Labour government wants to take as the Blair government wants to make a fresh start in Europe, with the credibility to achieve reform.

Britain's six month presidency of the European Union in 1998 was an opportunity to bring Britain's vision closer by engaging people's interest in economic reform and the fight against unemployment, in a tougher approach to crime, in the search for a healthier environment and in EU enlargement. Britain sought to build a Europe which brought practical benefits and genuinely responded to people's concerns: more open, more transparent and free from the burden of unnecessary regulation.

But there was a low turnout of voters in the 1999 European elections. Fewer than one elector in four made it to the *polls in Britain and voters in Labour seats were particularly reluctant to vote. Not only did many of those who voted Labour in 1997 stay at home, but many who didn't stay at home voted for someone else. Just 58% of those who had voted Labour in 1997 and cast a vote on June 10th remained loyal.

### The euro debate

The UK has to address the question of its own membership and to join when appropriate conditions are *met.

According to Blair, ruling out membership in the first wave was absolutely right, because of the different state of the UK cycle and the high level of the pound. There were formidable obstacles in the way of Britain being in the first wave of membership.

The arguments for joining is that it would have given Britain more influence over the project's design.

But New Labour thinks that to exclude British membership of EMU for ever would be to destroy any influence Britain has over a process which will affect Britain whether it is in or out. Blair is aware that *standing aside in the longer term could well impose high costs, as European industry restructures in response to the euro.

In any event, there are three preconditions which would have to be satisfied before Britain could join during the next Parliament: first, the Cabinet would have to agree, then Parliament and finally the people would have to say yes in a referendum.

Those who want Britain to join the euro have powerful arguments: lower European interest rates, the end of the *currency exchange costs and fluctuations within Britain's biggest market and lower prices once easy comparisons are possible across the Continent.

But opponents point to the booming UK economy where foreign investment is *soaring and unemployment and taxes are lower than in Germany and France and argue Britain would be crazy to lose control of monetary policy to a central bank Germany and France dominate, when the euro is so weak.

In October 1999, Blair was joined by Michael Heseltine, the former Conservative deputy Prime Minister, his colleague Kenneth Clarke and Charles Kennedy, the new Liberal Democrat leader for the launch of a new lobby group, "Britain in Europe". After months of hesitation, Blair was finally ready to start the counter-offensive against growing Conservative xenophobia. He concentrated on the merits of European Union membership because it is vital to jobs, trade, industry and investment. Blair is now leading "the patriotic cause" against the prejudices of "some Eurosceptic parody of a federal superstate" and he is in favour of joining a successful single currency if economic tests can be met and if people *back the move in a referendum.

# Vocabulary

| | |
|---:|:---|
| affluent | riche |
| aloof | hautain, arrogant |
| apex | apogée, sommet |
| apply (to) for membership | poser sa candidature |
| back (to) | soutenir |
| bogus | faux |
| clout | influence, pouvoir |
| commissionner | commissaire |
| the corporate world | le monde des affaires |
| currency | monnaie, devise |
| single currency | monnaie unique |
| hard currency | devise forte |
| soft currency | devise faible |
| customs union | union douanière |
| deadline | échéance, délai |
| delay | retard |
| entrepreneurial spirit | esprit d'entreprise |
| free trade | libre-échange |
| give (to) an impetus to | donner l'impulsion à |
| implement (to) | mettre en œuvre |
| influential | influent |
| ingenuity | ingéniosité |
| jingoistic | nationaliste |
| Single Market | Marché unique |
| meet (to) the conditions | remplir les critères |
| outlet | débouché |
| perceptive | perspicace |
| polls | urnes |
| rebuff (to) | repousser, rejeter |
| resilience | ressort, résistance |
| in the long run | à long terme |
| be (to) on the sidelines | rester sur la touche, ne pas se mêler à une affaire |
| soar (to) | prendre son essor, faire un bond, monter |
| stand (to) aside | se tenir à l'écart |
| unfettered | sans entraves |
| vie (to) with | rivaliser |
| withdraw (to) | se retirer |
| withdrawal | retrait |

# Focus...

Over 50 per cent of British trade in goods and services is within the EU. Eight of Britain's top 10 trading partners are in Europe.

3.5 million British jobs, and one seventh of all UK income and production, depend on sales to European countries.

All EU citizens have the right to live and work in any member state. 100,000 Britons work in other EU countries; another 350,000 live there. In 1997 there were 34 million visits made by UK citizens to other EU countries.

◆ **Message from the Prime Minister, Tony Blair**

"Our membership of the European Union delivers real benefits to every region of the UK. EU funds make a vital contribution to local development through investment in environmental, education and research projects. Businesses throughout the country rely heavily on the trade and investment that the single market brings. EU membership provides jobs for millions of British workers and helps to guarantee the future prosperity of all areas of the UK."

◆ **The institutions of the European Union**

*Council of the European Union*
The Council of the European Union is in charge of policy-making. Member states are represented by the ministers dealing with the subjects debated. Britain presided over the Council from January 1st to June 30th 1998. The Council makes decision by unanimity, by a qualified majority or by a simple majority.

*European Commission*
The European Commission is the executive organ of the community. It is the biggest of the European Union's institutions. At the *apex of the Commission, there are 20 commissioners who are appointed by member governments for a four-year term of office, which is renewable. The Commission is the civil service of the European Union. It initiates policy proposals to the council, implements the decisions taken by the Council of the European Union and ensures that EU treaties are respected by all the member states.

*European Parliament*
The European Parliament has 626 directly elected members and Britain has 87 seats. The Parliament is consulted on a wide range of

issues before the Council takes final decisions. The Parliament votes the Community's annual budget in agreement with the Council. The Community budget amounts to some 86 billion euros which is very small compared to national budgets.

### *Court of Justice*
The Court of Justice is composed of 15 judges who interpret the meaning of the Treaties and the decisions taken by the Council of the European Union and the Commission. It has the final word on all aspects of community law.

# Essay

Comment upon the following lines written by Hugo Young in the *Guardian Weekly*, on 10th January, 1999:

"The euro presents massive political challenges, but there seems no point in being outside it, since Britain's future is entirely bound up with its success or failure.(...) But the threat to national identity now strikes me as *bogus. We are all invaded by America. If cultural defences are needed, it's against transatlantic domination."

*Britain is still divided between Europhiles and Eurosceptics. Britain has long given priority to the Empire and America over Europe and the EU is not much loved in Britain. In fact, the relationship of Britain to European integration must be set against a background of changing economic interests. Hugo Young's view is that of a European who is aware of the implications of the euro for Britain and who holds American hegemony as a threat to British culture. According to him, Britain cannot be a good European if it rejects the euro and it is ridiculous to be afraid lest the European Union might endanger national identity.*

*There is no doubt that the introduction of the Single European Currency is a political challenge for Britain and that Britain will eventually have to join if it is to be an \*influential member of the European club. In Hugo Young's opinion, it is impossible to support the EU without supporting the euro and every country that wants to be called European ought to belong to the euro. Europeans welcomed the euro as a success, even though it meant giving up sovereignty. Most European citizens and politicians responded positively to the introduction of the euro which is popular in most European countries. It is held as an opportunity of growth and influence. But European governments had to give up sovereignty and simply kept the right to appoint the European Central Bank's senior officials.*

*The only drawback is the lack of openness and democracy in the ECB, which was meant to be more independent than the US Federal Reserve or Germany's Bundesbank.*

*On the one hand, the euro represents an opportunity for the City of London, since it is aimed at giving an \*impetus to European industry, at making it more efficient and competitive against American industry.*

*On the other hand, it implies closer political integration for Britain and a repudiation of nationhood as traditionally understood, since* the euro is likely to promote closer cooperation between the countries of "Euroland".

In spite of the contrasting views on the single currency, there is no denying that it will have a prominent impact on the world economy. If Britain had joined right from the start, this would have had more influence over the project's design. Moreover, a fixed exchange rate would have increased competition in the British market.

The euro being so weak at present, the British are very sceptical of the single currency and only 24% of people are in favour of joining whereas 63% are against according to a recent opinion poll. While most Britons are reluctant to embrace the euro, some think that opposing the single currency amounts to the same thing as opposing the EU itself.

In his *perceptive analysis of the relationship with Europe, Hugo Young underlines the danger of American domination over culture. To his mind, European integration is no threat to the British identity. The English language and literature are preserved as part of the world's inheritance, since European cultures have mingled and grown together throughout the centuries. There is no reason why they should be afraid since their language is the language of the EU, a language of culture which has become the language of business, the language of the global economy and of new technology. Moreover, no EU member has lost its national identity because of EU membership, so why would Britain have anything to fear? Europhobia thus appears as a criticism of the continent by some *jingoistic Britons proud of their insular state.

Nevertheless the danger of American hegemony should not be overlooked with the risk of a standardized culture setting the artistic and linguistic criteria for other less powerful countries. Britain within the EU will have to prove its capacity to *vie with the *resilience, the *ingenuity and the creativity of a new country *unfettered by the traditions of the Old World. There are far more harmful consequences for Britain and western countries with the Hollywood film industry, American video games and e-business than with European cultures which cannot be held as rivals.

The Euroscepticism of some British Conservatives endangers Britain's role in Europe and in the world and weakens the UK, whose destiny is linked to the EU and not to the United States. Withdrawing from Europe would relegate Britain from the premier divisions of nations and it would be the "real end of one thousand years of history", as Tony Blair said at the 1999 Labour Party Conference.

# 4 Labour and Conservatives

*Sophie Loussouarn*

The Labour Party and the Conservative Party are the two major political parties in Britain today. The general election of June 7th, 2001 brought a *landslide victory to Tony Blair and New Labour, though there was a 12% drop in turnout to 59% of eligible voters compared to the figures of May 1997. The Conservative Party is much older than the Labour Party which celebrated its centenary at the 1999 Labour Party Conference. The two major political parties share different values and their core support remains different in spite of recent changes in the British electorate. Whereas the traditional Labour Party is committed to collectivist values, to the defence of the poor and to a strong executive, conservatism justifies existing orders within society, rejects abstract principles in politics and seeks to avoid any role for the state in economic life. In spite of the decline in class-based voting since 1951, two-thirds of the working classes voted Labour in the postwar years, while four-fifths of the middle classes voted Conservative. The Conservative party has been the dominant party throughout the twentieth century, even though conservatism is currently in decline. Between 1918 and 1997, the Conservatives were in government for 58 years (75% of the time), ruling either alone or as a dominant partner and enjoying several uninterrupted *spells in power (1931-1945, 1951-1964 and 1979-1997).

## *The Labour Party*

The Labour Party is identified with the ideology of socialism. However British socialism has been gradualist, parliamentary and reformist. It has been influenced by the ethical socialism of the Independent Labour Party, the collectivism of the Fabian Society and by the trade unions which were the major link with the working classes.

The Party was formed in 1900 but its socialist constitution dates back to 1918. After the Second World War, Labour won an *overwhelming victory in the 1945 general election under the leadership of Clement Attlee. The Labour government carried out nationalisations and set up the Welfare State. During the Wilson years (1964-1970) and the Callaghan government, the Labour Party pursued revisionist policies based on high public spending, industrial interventionism and the introduction of comprehensive schools. In the May 1997 general election, Labour won a landslide victory which was repeated in 2001. Tony Blair's socialism is a reflection of the ethical tradition of the party, yet it rejects the idea that the welfare provision can always be funded through sustained economic growth.

Constitutionally, the Labour Party is less hierarchical and more democratic than the Conservative Party. At the national level, there are five elements of organization:

the Labour leader who has the power to appoint the Cabinet and allocate *Shadow Cabinet *portfolios in opposition, the Parliamentary Labour Party, the National Executive Committee which is the central administrative authority in the party, the annual conference held annually and the Labour Party headquarters at Walworth Road. Owing to the authority inherent in the position, the Labour Party leader wields great power and balances the claims of parliamentarians, trade unionists and constituency activists. The functions of the National Executive Committee (NEC) range from supervising all the work of the Labour Party outside Parliament to formulating policy proposals and making annual reports for the party conference. The annual conference in the autumn decides the policies which make up the party programme and elects the NEC to manage the party on a day-to-day basis. At a local level, the Constituency Labour Parties select parliamentary candidates and coordinate union sponsorships.

The Labour Party has been heavily reliant upon trade unions for income since they have contributed three quarters of income since 1945. But the Labour Party has managed to diversify fund-raising lately and 40% of its income now comes from membership and small donations, while trade unions account for 30% of the funds, the rest coming from donations greater than £1,000 (20%) and from commercial activities (10%).

## The Conservative Party

There is a Conservative tradition in Britain which dates back to the seventeenth century. Conservatism has Tory foundations. While the Whigs wished to limit royal authority, the Tories supported the monarchy. The Whigs upheld religious dissent, whereas the Tories were the party of the Church of England. Modern conservatism originated as a reaction against the French Revolution and was based on the opposition between Edmund Burke (1727-1797), the founder of modern British conservatism and Thomas Paine (1737-1809), the herald of political radicalism. Modern conservatism continued in the nineteenth century in opposition to political and economic radicalism and became a synonym of gradualism, paternalism and patriotism. After 1945, the paternalist tradition of the Conservative Party enabled conservatism to adapt to the interventionist Welfare State and managed economy. Nowadays conservatism is on the defensive and is characterized by tensions and disagreement over Europe. Yet Tories won the European Parliament elections in 1999 and 593 local council seats in May 2000.

The Conservative Party is a hierarchical party and all efforts are targeted towards the assistance of the parliamentary party. At the national level, the Conservative Party consists of four main elements: the leader, the Parliamentary party, the National Union and Conservative Central Office. Authority is concentrated in the hands of the leader who appoints the party chairman. The Conservative Party emerged from Parliament and it meets weekly in the 1922 committee when Parliament is sitting. Created at the Carlton Club in 1922, the committee provides the collective focus of *backbenchers when the party is in government and it includes all MPs except the leader when it is in opposition. The National Union is the third fold of the Conservative Party, representing and supervising party membership. It is a large body with around 3,600 members which originated in 1867 in order to create a nationwide conservative organization coordinating the work of Conservative Associations, encouraging the creation of new ones and disseminating Conservative ideas to the new working-class electors after the Second Reform Act. It is a channel of communication between party members and the leadership. It holds its annual meeting during the four-day Conservative Party Conference which takes place in the autumn, in order to demonstrate solidarity with the leadership and to inspire party activists. As for Conservative Central Office, it was founded by Disraeli in 1870 and it is the organizational centre of the party. Staffed by officials, this professional element of the party is a means of stimulating constituency activity. Its main tasks are money-raising, the organization of election campaigns, assistance with the selection of candidates, research and political education. At a local level, conservative constituency associations perform three major tasks: campaigning for the party in local and national elections, fund-raising, and selecting parliamentary candidates.

Now the Conservative Party faces a leadership crisis as William Hague, the Tory leader who was elected in 1997, has constantly accused Tony Blair of using Tory rhetoric and of borrowing Conservative themes. Hague resigned in June 2001. As we go to press, Kenneth Clarke looks the most likely successor, although the party is divided. A new vision will be needed to the new leader as Labour has successfully attracted the centre ground and is opening up to Europe with the likelihood of a referendum on the euro.

Apart from the two major parties, which have won the general elections since 1945, the Liberal Democrats emerged as a third party. The Liberal Democratic Party is very strong at the political *grass-roots as illustrated by its successes in *by-elections and local elections. Yet, in parliamentary terms they are a minor party and have not held power alone since 1915.

As long as the electoral system remains the same, the two party system which, many claim, has rewarded the Labour Party and the Conservative Party since 1945 will endure and no third party will break through.

# VOCABULARY

| | |
|---|---|
| alleviate (to) | adoucir |
| backbencher | député sans portefeuille |
| biased | partial |
| blatant | flagrant |
| bridge (to) the gap | combler l'écart |
| by-election | élection partielle |
| clear-cut | bien défini, tranché |
| constituency | circonscription |
| deter (to) | dissuader |
| disparage (to) | déprécier, décrier |
| down-trodden | opprimés |
| fat cats | riches |
| fringe party | parti marginal |
| frontbencher | membre du Cabinet fantôme |
| party grandees | caciques du parti |
| grassroots | base |
| grassroots movement | parti populaire |
| herald | précurseur |
| highlight (to) | mettre au premier plan |
| incumbent | candidat sortant |
| landslide victory | raz-de-marée |
| likely | vraisemblable, probable |
| pay (to) lip-service to | rendre hommage |
| loathe (to) | détester |
| mainstream party | parti principal |
| official / civil servant | fonctionnaire, administratif |
| overwhelming victory | victoire écrasante |
| Parliament is sitting | le Parlement siège |
| pollster | sondeur, enquêteur |
| portfolio | un portefeuille ministériel |
| be (to) reliant upon | dépendre de |
| reluctant | réticent |
| reshuffle | remaniement |
| ruling party | un parti au pouvoir |
| Shadow Cabinet | gouvernement de l'opposition |
| sheer | pur |
| spells | périodes |
| spin-doctor | conseiller en communication |
| tenet | principe |
| pay (to) tribute to | rendre hommage à |
| whip | chef de file |
| wipe (to) out | effacer |

# Focus...

In the 2001 general election, the Labour Party won 413 of the 659 seats. They lost 6 seats. The Conservative Party won 166 seats and the Liberal Democrats won 52 seats.

◆ **The two-party system**

Britain has been traditionally regarded as a two-party system. Political parties in the form of Whigs and Tories can be traced back to the seventeenth century, the Tories being more reluctant to embrace change and the Whigs being a little less fearful of innovation. In the 1830s the division between the parties became more clear-cut and the two-party system began to function, with Whigs on the one side and Tories on the other.

Since 1945, voters in half of all seats at general elections had a choice of candidates from the two main parties only. First, elections produced majority rule, without the need for coalition partnerships, except in the February 1974 general election where there was a minority Labour government and a surge in the Liberal Party support. Secondly, there was a degree of alternation in government. Since 1945, the Conservatives won 7 elections and Labour won 6 elections. Conservative/Labour have a hold on the party system.

Forecasting the likely future shape of the UK's party system is extremely difficult since one of its vital elements, the electoral system for Westminster, remains uncertain. Should the government decide to move to a proportional system, this would have the potential to increase the number of parties from which voters could choose and to create new forms of government, based on coalitions between parties.

◆ **The electoral system**

For national elections, Britain currently uses the first-past-the-post system, which is cohesive and restrictive. It creates high entry barriers and thus deters the creation of new parties. Moreover, the first-past-the-post system is biased in favour of mainstream parties. It tends to discriminate against fringe parties. The first-past-the-post system is a key factor in the maintenance of the British party system because it militates against the breakthrough of a third party, not only in terms of electoral geography but also in terms of tactical voting.

The greatest change could come from the reform of the voting system. The introduction of a more proportional system in the

European elections may lead to a greater representation of minor parties such as the Green Party. But the most far-reaching impact would come through any change to the voting system for the House of Commons.

Electoral reform surfaced in the mid-nineteenth century and was taken up again in the 1970s and 1980s, when the two party system began to be challenged by the Liberal Party. In 1997, the Labour Party manifesto put forward a referendum on the voting system. The Labour Government is now studying the Jenkins Report which advised a mixed system of alternative vote with Top-up seats. The system recommended by the Jenkins Commission is a variant of the Additional Member System used in Germany and adopted in New Zealand, following a referendum in 1993.

# Commentary of a Text

*Concours de classement de sortie, ENA, mars 1999*

## "Labour's Royal Telegram" by Robert TAYLOR (*The Spectator*, 2nd January, 1999)

New Labour's amnesia about its history before Mr Blair may be due to *sheer ignorance. More likely, it derives from a deliberate strategy to remove Labour history from the public eye.

The current silence over a centenary Mr Blair and the modernisers would most like to forget reflects uncannily the similar neglect by the media of the party's original birth. It was in the pious surroundings of the Memorial Hall in London's Farringdon Street that the Labour representation Committee was formed on 27-28 February 1900 at a meeting of trade union delegates, Fabians, members of the Independent Labour Party and the Marxist Social Democratic Federation.

The mood of today's Labour leadership suggests it would rather overlook the whole occasion.

But the dislike of the party's past has deeper significance than a mere obsession with modernity and the appeasement of big business.

New Labour's superficial attempts to rewrite the party's history first began with a lecture Mr Blair delivered to the Fabian Society in July three years ago to commemorate the 50th anniversary of Labour's 1945 election triumph.

True, Mr Blair on that occasion paid appropriate *lip-service to the successes of the Attlee government. "Its achievements make me proud to call myself a democratic socialist," he assured the Fabians. But his main concern was to criticise the party's ethos and structure. It is clear from rereading the text of his address that Mr Blair sought to identify himself and his party with the New Liberalism of pre-1914 Britain.

But it is in his over-identification of Labour with the organised working class that Mr Blair has proved to be the most mistaken. His dislike of the activities of the trade unions in the party seems to be atavistic and unyielding, based on prejudice not knowledge. It stems in part from an understandable personal horror of the disorder some unions inflicted on the country during the 1978-79 winter of discontent but also from his own Conservative party and public school background, far from the manual workers.

However, there is a more fundamental explanation for Mr Blair's inclination to *wipe out 100 years of Labour History. He wants to deny or marginalise the wider achievements of the Labour movement by suggesting that the trade union connection both hampered and ultimately sabotaged Labour's destiny as a natural party of government. In order to do this, he and his colleagues have to resort to caricature, exaggeration or plain untruths to justify a simplistic picture of the party's history. It is true the trade unions were crucial to the creation of the Labour Party in 1900, although they were always keen to underplay their own importance in its structure and policy-making. However, it was the Fabians and above all the Independent Labour party who provided most of its political thought by helping to develop an ideology of Labourism.

The most *blatant attempt to rewrite the party's history has come not from Mr Blair, but from the cynical, opportunistic Philip Gould, the arch-consultant who still claims he is a senior adviser to the Prime Minister. In his chilling book, *The Unfinished Revolution*, Mr Gould describes the Labour party of Attlee, Gaitskell, Wilson and Callaghan as "dogmatic and statist, ignoring and marginalising the core liberal concepts of individual responsibility, self-reliance and civic rather than state action."

Here is the party's history being manipulated and distorted. For New Labour, the party's past is there to be erased from the common memory or used selectively to browbeat Old Labour. It reflects the triumph of the world of the consultants, the *spin-doctors and the *pollsters over the dying manual working class and those whom New Labour describes patronisingly as the "socially excluded".

*Robert Taylor deals with New Labour's way of celebrating Labour's 100th birthday and of looking at its past. The journalist recalls the circumstances in which the Labour Party was formed in 1900. Trade Unions, Fabians and members of the Independent Labour Party took part in its setting up. But the New Labour leadership wants to do away with its roots and to give up some of its \*tenets. New Labour seeks to be modern and compromise with the super-rich and big business.*

*Even though Tony Blair paid \*tribute to the achievements of the Attlee government at the 50th anniversary of Labour's 1945 landslide victory, he is critical of the party's ethos and structure and defines himself as a social democrat who is closer to the Liberals than to Old Labour. Blair \*disparages the role of trade unions within the party and \*loathes the social unrest they brought about during the winter of discontent in 1979.*

*Far from denying the prominent part of the unions in the creation of the Labour Party, the journalist acknowledges that they mostly behaved sensibly and moderately. In his book* The Unfinished Revolution, *Mr Gould, a senior adviser of Tony Blair, urged to bridge the gap between Liberals and Labour. New Labour means to forget about Labour's history at a time when consultants and spin-doctors have overpowered the vanishing working classes. The Labour Party is changing and tends to favour the new middle-class people of the suburbs rather than the professional middle classes keener on social citizenship and public service.*

# 5     Post Industrial Britain: A changing Britain

*Guy Richard*

Since the end of World War II, Britain's major parties had been committed to economic recovery and social reform (in the form of the "welfare state"), but the consensus was to be put to the test in the seventies.

Indeed, Britain then had to wage war on two different fronts: rising prices and growing unemployment. The 1974-1979 worldwide recession only made matters worse, bringing into sharp focus the irrelevance of the British economy which relied too heavily on old-time types of activities like steel-mills, coal-mines and shipyards. The British had to face it: their economy was rapidly slipping, productivity dropped and Britannia no longer ruled the waves. Moreover, trade unions wanted to make themselves heard and strikes became a familiar way to voice workers' grievances. Miners brought down a Conservative government in 1974 and clashed with a Labour government during the "winter of discontent" of 1979, a move with calamitous consequences, both economically and politically.

Many analysts thought some drastic policy would have to be carried out to break the deadlock, Britain may have been ripe for Mrs Thatcher's strong-arm approach.

## *Thatcherism: ten years that shook Britain*

Margaret Thatcher will go down in history as Britain's longest-serving Prime Minister (with one exception: Lord Liverpool: 1812-1827). Together with W. Churchill, she will rank as Britain's greatest Prime Minister in the twentieth century. She is one of the few politicians who gave her name to the policy she initiated.

### *The formative years*

Was she a born leader or did she have to fight for it? Originally, the odds were against her since she was born in 1925 into a lower middle-class family (her father was a grocer) in Grantham, a small town in the Midlands. Mr Roberts, her father, was involved in local politics, he was a councillor and he must have set an example for her: "like father, like... daughter". She was admitted to Oxford in the 1940s and had to clear two *hurdles: Oxford was still a male preserve for the elite. As she was a woman from the lower middle classes, she had to fight against prejudice and to work her way up. She was dogged and eventually graduated in chemistry and law: she was a high-achiever indeed!

But politics was something in which she was interested and she ran for Parliament. She became an MP in 1957 after two failures. Once again she might have given up, but she showed determination. In 1970, the then Prime Minister, E. Heath, appointed her Secretary of Education and her tough love approach earned her the first nickname of "the milk *snatcher" (cf. p.63). In 1975, she managed to win the Conservative Party leadership, a "first" in a traditionally male-dominated party. In 1979, the Conservative Party won the general election and she was appointed Prime Minister by the Queen, a real achievement for a grocer's daughter from a small provincial town.

## A mixed record

She had always been a staunch believer in the virtues of a free market and was determined to put her ideas to the test. In order to do so, there were a few obstacles she had to overcome:
- the British people's apathy as she considered Britons' resolve had been weakened by decades of Labour government meddling;
- the power of the unions, which she regarded as a state within the state and which she wanted to curb. She seized on the miners' strike to bring the unions to heel (cf. Focus, p. 63). She spoke of her vision of a "free, classless and open Britain" which she could achieve through private ownership. She vowed she would create a nation of home-owners and shareholders thanks to a bold privatisation programme and she delivered on her promise. When she left office 70% of Britons owned the house they lived in and 20% held shares.

In foreign affairs, she wanted Britannia to rule the waves again, fought the Falklands war, was America's best ally in tense East-West relations, but was shrewd enough to size up Gorbachev as a leader who could be trusted. Unfortunately, however determined she may have been to put Britain back on the international scene, she failed to play the card of European integration and gradually *fell out over that major issue, both with the British and her own party faithful. This was to cause her downfall.

John Major's nomination to the Conservative Party leadership and subsequently, as Prime Minister, was a compromise within his own party. He was radically different from his predecessor, both in manner and in character. Hers was a confrontational style whereas he was congenial and consensus-minded. Under the circumstances, being Prime Minister was not an easy task since he knew Margaret Thatcher still enjoyed the support of many Conservative MPs and was all too happy to criticise him from the wings, thus undermining his credibility.

The odds were against him indeed. He found it hard to assert his authority and be his own man, as he was under constant pressure from his own *party's rank-and-file and from the Murdoch press which criticised him for his pro-European leanings. Nevertheless, he managed to score a few points in some specific fields:
- he established Britain's role as a reliable ally during the Gulf War (January/February 1991) and did not capitalize on victory to *call a snap election,

unlike Mrs. Thatcher in 1983, after the 1982 Falklands War;
- he scrapped the controversial poll tax, which had caused Mrs Thatcher's *ouster.

But he had to withdraw Britain from the Exchange Rate Mechanism (ERM), which meant a de facto devaluation of the pound, a decision Britons felt as a humiliation.

Although a breakthrough was made in some pressing problems like education, NHS (National Health Service) reform, Northern Ireland and Europe, little could be accomplished with so much opposition and so little *leeway.

What John Major was best at was surviving. His caretaker government will have to be reassessed, not so much as a failure as a *stepping-stone between Mrs Thatcher's iron rule and Tony Blair's "cool Britannia" approach.

The Thatcher legacy is undoubtedly *here to stay and will have to be reckoned with, positively and negatively. One must bear in mind her advocacy of a "get-rich" approach through hard-work and self-reliance contributed to a widening gap between the haves and the have-nots in Britain, a growing divide between North and South. Besides, the welfare state, a safety net that had been painstakingly woven by years of (mostly Labour) policies, started unravelling. Infrastructures showed signs of neglect, homelessness became visible. This is a heavy burden her successors have had to deal with.

## VOCABULARY

| | |
|---:|:---|
| adamant | inflexible, intransigeant |
| browbeat sb. (to) | impressionner qqn |
| clear a hurdle (to) | franchir une haie |
| cripple (to) (adj.: crippling /crippled) | paralyser ; paralysant ; paralysé |
| determination/doggedness | détermination ; ténacité |
| determined/dogged (to be) | être déterminé, tenace |
| fall out with sb. over sth. (to) | se brouiller avec qqn à propos de qch. |
| greed (adj.: greedy) | avidité, cupidité |
| hat trick | le fait de remporter 3 élections consécutives |
| hector sb. (to) | rudoyer qqn |
| here to stay (this is) | cela n'est pas près de disparaître |
| hurdle (to clear a) | surmonter un obstacle |
| landslide (victory) | victoire écrasante |
| launch a campaign (to) | lancer une campagne |
| leeway | liberté d'action, marge de manœuvre |
| marketer/marketeer | partisan de l'économie de marché |
| meddle in sb.'s business (to) (adj.: meddlesome) | se mêler des affaires d'autrui |
| office (to be/to leave/to take) | être en fonction ; prendre ; quitter ses fonctions |
| ouster/oust (to) | éviction ; évincer |
| overnight | du jour au lendemain |
| overwhelming victory | victoire écrasante |
| party's rank-and-file (+ accord au plur.) | militants de base, la base |
| plummeting | qui s'effondre |
| poll tax (the) | taxe d'habitation (calculée selon le nombre de personnes) |
| resign/step down (to) | démissionner |
| sap sb.'s energy (to) | saper l'énergie de qqn |
| scrap a project (to) | abandonner un projet |
| selfishness (adj: selfish) | égoïsme ; égoïste |
| skyrocketing/soaring | qui monte en flèche |
| slip (to) (for sb.'s popularity) | décliner |
| sluggish economy | économie qui tourne au ralenti |
| snap election (to call a) | décider une élection anticipée |
| snatch (to) | saisir brusquement |
| square/settle accounts with sb. (to) | régler des comptes avec qqn |
| stepping-stone | tremplin (fig.) |
| tenet | doctrine ; un dogme |
| voted out (to be) | être mis en minorité (et devoir se retirer) |

# Focus...

◆ **Thatcher's two nicknames**

"**The milk snatcher**": When she was Secretary of Education, she decided to cut the free milk programme in primary schools. Since the '50s, British children had been given a free bottle of milk every day, which she regarded as an uneconomical measure. She came to be known as "the milk snatcher" (i.e. the one who takes milk away from babies) but, however unpopular such a move was, she stuck to it since it saved money.

NB. Reintroducing such a programme is one of New Labour's pledges. Besides, it would also contribute to getting rid of Britain's milk surplus…

"**The Iron Lady**": a nickname Russian diplomats gave her during a summit in the mid-eighties. She would *hector her partners, be it in the Cabinet, in European summits or in tense East-West talks. Toughness was a virtue she would go by.

◆ **Her decade as Prime Minister**

**1979** She was appointed Prime Minister after a Conservative victory in the general election.

**1990** She was voted out by her own party and had to step down.

◆ **The landmarks of her premiership**

**1981** The IRA activists' hunger strike.

**1982** Victory in the Falklands war.

**1984** The miners' strike/the IRA bomb attack in Brighton.

**1990** Controversy over the *poll tax.

◆ **"A lady who would never bow"**

In **1981**, she ignored IRA activists who had gone on a hunger strike to be granted political prisoner status. Their leader, Bobby Sands, and nine of his comrades-in-arms, were to starve to death. Nor was she *browbeaten to the negotiating table when an IRA bomb exploded in her hotel in Brighton in 1984, during a Conservative Party Conference.

In **1982**, the Argentines reclaimed the Falkland Islands (which they call "the Malvinas") as theirs and she did not hesitate to dispatch British troops 8,000 miles from home to retake them. It was a short, but bloody war and the Union Jack flew over Port Stanley again.

The Thatcher government decided to close unprofitable coal pits in **1984**. Miners went on a strike which was to last nearly a year but

Civilisation britannique

when they eventually had to resume work, their demands had not been met (cf. the films *Brassed Off* by Mark Herman – in French "Les Virtuoses" – 1997 and *Billy Elliot* by Stephen Daldry – 2000). Mrs Thatcher capitalized on their defeat to pass union-bashing legislation in Parliament, thus curbing the unions' influence in labour disputes.

In **1990**, she wanted to introduce a new flat poll tax, based on the number of people in a household, not on the family's income, which people viewed as an unfair measure. They took to the streets, sometimes violently, and the bill had to be *scrapped.

**Her downfall:** She had always insisted on a team of players but after ten years in office, all her Cabinet ministers had left her one by one. Her confrontational style and *adamant opposition to Europe had come to antagonize even her staunchest supporters. She eventually had to walk into the sunset…

◆ **Maggie's sound bites**

**On her childhood:** "My father left school at the age of 13 and he had to make his own way in the world."

"It's nice to be brought up in a community spirit, in a community atmosphere."

**On her character:** "What has the women's movement ever done for me?"

"My policies are not based on some theory, but on things I and millions were brought up with: an honest day's work for an honest day's pay, live within your means, put a nest egg by for a rainy day, pay your bills on time, support the police."

"When a woman is strong, [people say] she is strident, if a man is strong, [people say] gosh, he is a good guy."

"I am a naturally hard worker. I was brought up that way. It is a sin to be idle."

**When she took office,** she quoted St Francis of Assisi:

"Where there is discord, may we bring harmony, where there is error, may we bring truth, where there is doubt, may we bring faith, where there is despair, may we bring hope."

**On Gorbachev:** "I like Mr Gorbachev, I know we can do business with him." (1987).

"I would implicitly accept his word."

**On Europe:** "I want my money back." (during several summits on a Common Agricultural Policy).

When invited to give an address on Europe's future, she retorted: "It's rather like inviting Genghis Khan to speak on the virtues of peaceful coexistence."

# Essay

Just before the May 1997 general election in Britain, *Newsweek* ran the following headline:

*Whatever the outcome, Thatcher's legacy is secure.*

**Did such a prophecy hold true?**

*After eighteen years of Thatcherism, Britain allegedly needed a break with an era characterized by its leader's overbearing personality. It was to be a landslide victory for Labour which had been out of office during the "long Tory night". The* Newsweek *headline thus looks a bit paradoxical: why did the American weekly claim Mrs Thatcher would be the winner, whatever the results of the election? Did such a prophecy eventually come true?*

*When she took office in 1979, Mrs. Thatcher had vowed she would "give the country a good shake" and she was true to her word indeed. Opening the floodgates of the market, she did contribute to boosting whole sectors of Britain's economy. The bold privatisation she embarked on enabled more Britons to become home-owners and share-holders. She ruled the country with an iron fist and her European counterparts, British miners and Argentine generals experienced her single-mindedness the hard way. She was so determined that she did not even realise she was no longer backed by her own constituents.*

*One would have expected Tony Blair's New Labour to put an end to, or even wipe the slate clean of the Thatcher legacy, but it hardly seems to be the case. Witness the unions' declining influence within Labour and in the country at large: what Mrs Thatcher had started may have been completed by T. Blair... Likewise, a Labour Prime Minister came to the Royal Family's rescue on several key occasions and always seems eager to give the Royals a helping hand. Britain is definitely not going to become a republic in the near future, although a Lords reform is now under way, with the number of hereditary peers reduced to 92 since November 1999...*

*The Welfare State was badly battered by the Tories and New Labour tends to prefer back-to-work schemes to welfare benefits. "People should help themselves": Mrs Thatcher's, or T. Blair's words?*

*The US could rely on Britain as a staunch ally during the Kosovo crisis just as Mrs Thatcher sided with R. Reagan during the euromissile crisis. The transatlantic tie is far from being severed. Besides, joining the euro is still an open question for Britain...*

*Therefore, the Thatcher legacy is here to stay. T. Blair is most unlikely to dump it, as he is well aware British society has changed since the late seventies and he seems bent on adopting a middle-of-the-road approach. Politicians have to be pragmatic, and T. Blair is a quick learner.*

# Blair's Third Way: *Rebranding Britain

*Sophie Loussouarn*

The recent paper signed by Prime Minister Tony Blair and German Chancellor Gerhard Schröder, entitled Europe: *The Third Way – Die Neue Mitte*, begins boldly:

"Social democrats are in government in almost all the countries of the Union. Social democracy has found new acceptance – but only because, while retaining its traditional values, it has begun in a credible way to renew its ideas and modernize its programs. It has also found new acceptance because it *stands not only for social justice but also for economic dynamism and the *unleashing of creativity and innovation."

The term "The Third Way" shows a need to have a unified ideology. But the German model of the Third Way remains quite different from the Anglo-Saxon one and the best definition of the Third Way is whatever Blair actually does. It is neither Old Left nor the New Right, but it is a name for democratic socialism peculiar to the British or it is a middle way between social democracy and neo-liberalism. Blair's Third Way means to promote equality, social cohesion and a dynamic economic market.

### The 1997 election

In 1997, Labour's election campaign was smooth and efficiently run and Labour's agenda centred on five *pledges: education, crime, health, jobs and economic stability. The triumph of the Labour Party on May 1st, 1997 was reminiscent of the 1945 victory with Clement Attlee. The Labour Party emerged with a 179-seat majority and a total of 418 Labour MPs, including a record 101 Labour women. It was a revolution after the four consecutive election defeats Labour had suffered.

There are several reasons which account for such a landslide, among which the exhaustion of the Conservative Party after eighteen years in office, the changing vote of the electorate with the support of a new type of middle class, the commitments of the Labour manifesto and the new leadership of the party. Tony Blair made the Labour Party electable. He projected the image of a leader and he rebuilt the Labour party in his own image. Blair was elected to modernize what was outdated and to make fair what was unjust, and to do both by the best means available, irrespective of dogma or doctrine. Blair's task was to build a modern country and to achieve a long-term change in England.

On the morning of 2nd May, Prime Minister Tony Blair, addressed the nation:

"I know well what this country has voted for today, it is a mandate for New Labour and I say to the people of this country we ran for office as New Labour, we will govern as New Labour. This was not a mandate for dogma, or for doctrine or a return to the past, but it was a mandate to get those things done in our country that desperately need doing for the future of Britain. And this new Labour government will govern in the interests of all our people, the whole of this nation, that I can promise you."

On 15th, May 1997, Blair unveiled the first effective Labour programme for nearly 20 years. Tradition was maintained in the ceremonial accompanying the Queen's processional ride from Buckingham Palace to Westminster to deliver the Queen's Speech in the House of Lords. The tone of change was apparent in the new government's programme. At its heart were measures to improve education and health, tackle crime and a big constitutional package, including bills to provide for early referenda on a Scottish Parliament and Welsh assembly to devolve powers to the Scots and Welsh and a new London authority was to be created with an elected mayor.

There was commitment to high and stable levels of employment and a fundamental attack on youth unemployment.

## Blair's reforms

Rebranding Britain implied a range of constitutional and social reforms.

Constitutional reform was at the heart of the Labour manifesto and involved the end of the hereditary principle in the House of Lords, the reform of party funding to end *sleaze, and more independent local government.

The reform of social policy included on the one hand the reform of the welfare state and the policy of "Welfare to Work" and on the other hand measures to save the NHS with quality targets for hospitals and more spending on patients in real terms every year. It also meant to help parents balance work and family, to tackle homelessness and to help retired people.

Blair's Third Way also involved a reform of the education system with more spending on education, improving teaching and cutting down class sizes. The new economic policy meant to promote investment, with no increase in income-tax rates and budget to get people off welfare and into work. Furthermore there were new measures to help small businesses and to boost local economic growth.

Anthony Giddens, Great Britain's chief Third Way theorist, emphasized the need of combining wealth creation and social cohesion in several contexts, including the great changes wrought by globalization, the new dialogue with science and technology and the transformation of values and lifestyles.

There are six policy areas of the Third Way:
- a new style of politics or "second wave of democratization";
- a new relationship that joins state, civil society and market;
- *supply-side policies incorporating social investment notably in education and infrastructure projects;
- fundamental reform of the welfare state by creating a new balance of risk and security. Third Way reforms of the Welfare State not only involve

compulsory savings but, above all, the strict insistence on everyone working, including the disabled. Benefits are withdrawn unless people accept training or new jobs;
- a new relationship to the environment evolving out of ecological modernization;
- a strong commitment to transnational initiatives in a world of *fuzzy sovereignty.

### New Labour and the Third Way: beyond Left and Right?

The Third Way has been described as a combination of neoliberal economics and social democratic policy. The first word is optimism. It accepts the needs of global markets but adds key elements of social well-being. Another buzz is flexibility.

Perhaps this is where the Third Way actually divides Labour. Old Labour is threatened by risk and sees flexibility as insecurity, so it tries to hold on to old certainties.

New Labour, on the other hand, emphasizes new opportunities of individual initiative and the way people can enhance their well-being by coping with new challenges. The positive, future-oriented sense of opportunity makes the Third Way attractive to those who do not feel threatened, including the new global class of people who hope to benefit from changed forces of production.

There is something almost elitist about the Third Way, but the principles put forward by Blair find widespread support and epitomize the *mainstream of British opinion. The Labour Party reshaped its image with New Labour. New Labour is pragmatic and harmonizes social justice and economic efficiency. There is therefore an opposition between New Labour's populism and Old Labour's *blinkered dogmatism. New Labour is aware that Britain needs a market economy with competitive strength, but it also needs a society that includes all citizens rather than *disfranchising an underclass.

Blair's Third Way is an attack on tradition and ancient institutions. Blair's reforming zeal expresses his wish to transform and modernize the country. The reforms launched in Britain are likely to foster a different turn of mind in thinking about politics, with more devolved structures, more consensual politics, a greater role for constitutional law and electoral reform. The nature of democracy in Britain underwent fundamental changes with the granting of devolution to Scotland and Wales in 1999, with the end of voting powers for hereditary peers in the House of Lords and with the election of the London Mayor in May 2000. But the reform of the National Health Service is costing more and taking longer than voters expected. Violent crime is up by 4% since 1997. Besides, class sizes for older primary children have begun to fall, but those in secondary schools have risen slightly. Finally, with Tony Blair the powers of the Prime Minister have increased and he is exercising supreme and centralised power. As James Lewis wrote in his article "New Century, Same Politics", "there has been much talk of rebranding Britain for the new millennium, but little success despite the Prime Minister's efforts." (*The Guardian Weekly*, 5th January, 2000)

# VOCABULARY

| | |
|---:|---|
| appoint (to) | nommer |
| bailiff | huissier |
| read (to) for the Bar | préparer le barreau |
| barrister, Queen's Council | avocat à la Cour |
| blinkered dogmatism | dogmatisme à œillères |
| cope (to) with | faire face à |
| counterpart | homologue |
| devote (to) | consacrer |
| disfranchise (to) | priver qqn de ses droits civiques |
| foster (to) | encourager |
| fuzzy | flou, confus |
| governance | gouvernement |
| the judicature, judiciary | la magistrature |
| knock-on effect | répercussion |
| law school | Faculté de Droit |
| life expectancy | espérance de vie |
| lionize (to) | faire une célébrité de |
| loosen (to) | se relâcher |
| maiden speech | premier discours d'un député |
| the mainstream | courant dominant |
| platform | programme d'un parti |
| pledge | promesse |
| premiership | fonction de Premier Ministre |
| purchasing power | pouvoir d'achat |
| rebrand (to) | rénover |
| revamp (to) | modifier, améliorer |
| Home Secretary | ministre de l'Intérieur |
| Secretary of State | ministre |
| the Shadow Cabinet | le gouvernement de l'opposition, gouvernement fantôme |
| sleaze | corruption |
| spokesman | porte-parole |
| stand (to) for | symboliser, représenter |
| state-ownership | étatisation |
| supply-side policies | politique de l'offre |
| 10 Downing Street | résidence du Premier Ministre |
| unleash (to) | déclencher |
| upbringing | éducation |
| wedlock (out of) | illégitime |

# Focus...

◆ **Robin Cook on New Labour**

"What New Labour does offer is a distinct and consistent approach, an approach which is entirely within a long tradition of progressive thinking but which reflects the needs and nature of modern society."

(*The Economist*, May 2nd, 1998)

◆ **Blair's Cabinet after the 2001 General Election**[*]

- The Deputy Prime Minister and First Secretary of State is the Rt Hon John Prescott MP.
- The Chancellor of the Exchequer is the Rt Hon Gordon Brown MP. He was Tony Blair's shadow chancellor before 1997. He is the scholarship boy made good, with a first-class degree from Edinburgh. In the City, Brown is respected for giving the Bank of England the power to set interest rates. The euro appeals to his technical, revolutionary mind.
- The President of the Council and Leader of the House of Commons is the Rt Hon Robin Cook MP.
- The Lord Chancellor is Lord Irvine of Lairg, who is in charge of the administration of the law and courts and has a staff of 12,000 people. Lord Irvine is the collosus of domestic policy, legislation and constitutional reform. He is very close to the Prime Minister. The two men talked daily before the 1997 election. His Department has played a very important part in the devolution process in Scotland and in Wales. Lord Irvine presides over a full-scale Ministry of Justice. His influence is all-pervasive at the heart of the Government.
- The Foreign Secretary is the Rt Hon Jack Straw MP.
- The Home Secretary is the Rt Hon David Blunkett MP, who is in charge of the administration of justice, police, prisons, immigration, public safety and public morals which has a staff of 50,000 people.
- The Secretary of State for Environment, Food and Rural Affairs is the Rt Hon Margaret Beckett MP. She is in charge of housing, local government and inner cities and the environment and has a staff of 8,000 people.
- The Secretary of State for International Development is the Rt Hon Clare Short MP.

---

[*] This information is accurate at the time of going to press. However, Cabinet reshuffles are not uncommon.

- The Secretary of State for Work and Pensions is the Rt Hon Alistair Darling MP.
- The Secretary of State for Transport, Local Government and the Regions is the Rt Hon Stephen Byers MP.
- The Secretary of State for Health is the Rt Hon Alan Milburn MP.
- The Secretary of State for Northern Ireland is the Rt Hon Dr John Reid MP. The Northern Ireland Office is in charge of economic and social policies, law and order, and security policy relating to Northern Ireland. It has a small staff of 200 people. He had to resign from the office of Secretary of Trade in December 1998 on account of a financial scandal.
- The Secretary of State for Wales is the Rt Hon Paul Murphy MP.
- The Secretary of State for Defence is the Rt Hon Geoff Hoon MP.
- The Chief Secretary to the Treasury is the Rt Hon Andrew Smith MP.
- The Secretary of State for Scotland is the Rt Hon Helen Liddell MP.
- The Leader of the House of Lords is the Rt Hon The Lord Williams of Mostyn QC.
- The Secretary of State for Trade and Industry is Patricia Hewitt MP.
- The Secretary of State for Education and Skills is the Rt Hon Estelle Morris MP.
- The Secretary of State for Culture, Media and Sport is the Rt Hon Jessa Jowell MP.
- The Parliamentary Secretary, Treasury and Chief Whip is the Rt Hon Hilary Armstrong MP.

# Comment upon the following statistics

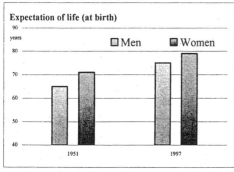
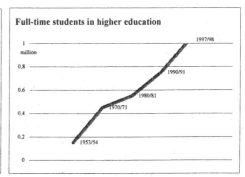
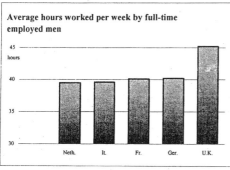
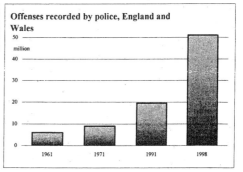
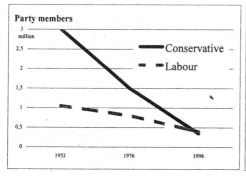
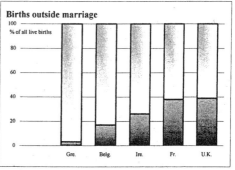
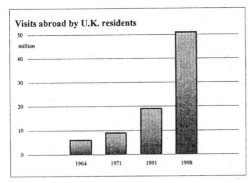
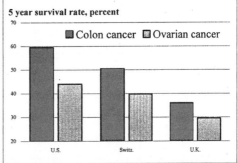

Civilisation britannique

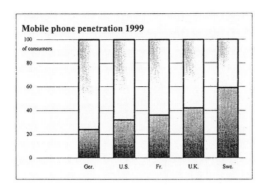

## " Baby Blair's Britain is... "(*Time*, 5th June, 2000)

The American weekly magazine, *Time*, *devoted its cover story to Blair's Britain in the issue of 5th June 2000, when Leo Blair was born. In these statistics, journalist J.F.O. McAllister looks at the changing face of Britain between 1951 and 1999, compared to other western countries. The nine charts focus on *life expectancy (Chart 1), higher education (Chart 2), working hours (Chart 3), crime (Chart 4), political party membership (Chart 5), family life (Chart 6), travelling abroad (Chart 7), health (Chart 8) and mobile phone ownership in 1999 (Chart 9).

Chart 1 draws a parallel between the state of Britain at the end of Attlee's government in 1951 and at the beginning of Blair's *premiership in 1997. The first chart highlights the improvement in the health of British men and women since the setting up of the National Health Service (NHS) in 1948. Within 46 years, men's life *expectancy has risen from 65 to 75 and women's life expectancy has risen from 75 to 85. Nevertheless, in 2000, fifty years after the creation of the NHS, cancer remains a major killer. Compared to the United States, where 60% of patients suffering from colon cancer and 45% of patients suffering from ovarian cancer survive, in the UK the five-year survival rate averages 35% for colon cancer and 30% for ovarian cancer. There is no denying that if the NHS was a success when it was created by Bevan, it needs reforming, taking into account the increasing population and the new waves of immigrants.

Chart 2 stresses the democratization of higher education in Britain. When Churchill was Prime Minister in 1953, there were 200,000 full-time students at university, whereas after Wilson's premiership in 1970, the number of students had doubled. It doubled again between 1970 and 1990, reaching 800,000, and when Blair took office in 1997 Britain could pride itself on 1 million full-time students. Indeed, in 1992, the polytechnics became universities, which accounts for the growing number of full-time students.

Chart 3 shows that the British work an average of 45 hours per week, whereas Germans and French people work slightly over 40 hours and the Dutch and Italians fewer than 40 hours per week. Indeed, France has gradually cut down the number of working hours from 40 to 39 hours and finally to 35 hours, just being implemented. In Great Britain, the level of unemployment has fallen and the employment policy gives incentives to the creation of new jobs, especially for young people.

Chart 4 underlines that in spite of the low level of unemployment in Britain, the crime rate in 1998 was five times higher than in 1964 with 50 million offences, hence the commitment of the Blair government to tackle crime. The demise of the car and wool industry and the closing of manufacturing industries accounts for a rise of violence and crime mostly in the North of Britain.

Chart 5 sets off the decreasing interest in politics from 1952 to 1998. Indeed, after the war, the British Conservative party was very powerful and party membership was at its peak at the time of Churchill's premiership. The lack of trust in politicians and the growing number of scandals (sleaze, party financing and sex scandals) account for the gradual fall in party membership.

Besides, Chart 6 highlights the *loosening family ties in Britain, which seems to be a very permissive society with a rate of 40% of births out of *wedlock, compared to fewer than 30% in Ireland and 1% in Greece. The loss of family values and the fall in religious belief could be held responsible. As a matter of fact, there is a striking difference between Greece where religious practice is still very strong and the UK and France.

Chart 7 together with Chart 9 show the increasing number of visits abroad by UK residents between 1964 and 1998 and the penetration of mobile phones in the UK in 1999 compared to other western countries. This reflects the improving living standards and purchasing power of the British people. Whereas less than 20% of the population travelled abroad in 1964, by 1998 almost all UK residents visited countries outside the UK. Britain has benefited from the economic boom and over 40% of consumers in Britain own a mobile phone which is more than France (below 40%) or the United States (30%) or Germany where ownership is slightly over 20%, but less than Sweden which reaches 60%. Since the 1990s, the strength of the pound *and the competitiveness of Britain has enabled many British to buy secondary homes abroad especially in Spain, Portugal and France.*

*The nine charts reflect the changing face of Britain. The improvement in the NHS has had a \*knock-on effect on life expectancy, and the health of the British nation could be compared to that of other European nations such as France or Germany until recently. The growing number of students at university reflects the democratization of Britain, yet the number of students in France is higher with 2 million students in 1997. The labour market has adjusted to globalization and deregulation and the British work longer hours than their European counterparts. As a consequence, the purchasing power of the average Englishman is higher which accounts for the ownership of mobile phones and the number of visits abroad. Blair's Britain is thus wealthier and healthier than Attlee's Britain, the only shadow is the high crime rate.*

# MORE ABOUT...
## ...TONY BLAIR

### BIOGRAPHY

Tony Blair was born on May 6th, 1953 in Edinburgh, Scotland. His conservative *upbringing was privileged. His father was a law lecturer and a *barrister and Tony Blair was educated at the elite boarding school Fettes College in Edinburgh from 1964 to 1971 before going up to Oxford in 1972. He graduated from St John's College in 1975, and was called to the bar the following year. Like his father, he became a lawyer and specialized in employment and commercial law. In 1976, while working as a lawyer, Blair met his wife Cherie Booth, a Catholic whom he married in March 1980. Tony Blair is a very strongly religious person who was deeply influenced by his father's conservatism.

### Blair's entry into politics

He joined the Labour Party in 1975 and in 1983 he was elected to the House of Commons as Member of Parliament for Sedgefield, a northern coal-mining region near his hometown of Durham. He was promoted to Opposition *Spokesman on Trade and Industry from 1987 to 1988. He entered Labour's *Shadow Cabinet in 1988. From 1988 to 1989, he was Shadow Secretary of State for Energy, then from 1989 to 1992 he became Shadow Secretary of State for Employment and from 1992 to 1994 he was Shadow Home Secretary and member of the National Executive Committee of the Labour Party.

He entered politics at a time when the Conservative Party was ruling and when the Labour Party lost four consecutive general elections from 1979 to 1992. After John Smith's sudden death in May 1994, Tony Blair was elected leader of the Labour Party on 21st July 1994, at the age of 41. He was the youngest leader ever. What accounts for his success was that the Labour party was weak and its formerly powerful politicians had lost political weight. As a moderniser, Blair began to transform the Labour Party, setting aside militant leftism and shifting towards the centre of British politics. Blair remodelled and redefined Labour, embracing new ideas and policies. By mid-1995 he had *revamped the Labour Party's *platform, promoting free enterprise, anti-inflationary policies, crime prevention and a commitment to European integration. He rewrote Clause IV of the Labour Constitution advocating "common ownership of the means of production, distribution and exchange" and had it replaced with a more modern statement of objectives, putting a commitment to enterprise alongside the commitment to justice. He created New Labour to meet the challenges of a different world and to give Britain a different political choice. Blair accepted the Thatcher legacy but he also reacted to Thatcherism. Even though Tony Blair has followed market economics, he attacked Conservative neo-liberal economic individualism. Under his leadership, the Labour Party defeated the Conservatives in municipal elections in May 1995. Furthermore, Blair transformed the Labour Party from a defensive, ideologically hung-up vote-loser to a party of government with a 179-seat majority. Blair set out 177 commitments in the Labour manifesto and in May 1997, the Labour Party won a landslide victory at the general election.

### Blair's premiership

Tony Blair was *appointed Prime Minister and was the youngest Prime Minister since Pitt the Younger in 1783. He moved to 10 Downing Street and disclosed his distinctive approach of new centre and centre-left politics in the Queen's Speech. He wanted to renew faith in politics through a government that will govern in the interests of the many.

Blair holds views traditionally deemed Liberal and Conservative. He is liberal on matters of education, welfare and technological change, but conservative on law and order issues and family values. Blair's vision is one of national renewal, with a modern welfare state and a country playing a pivotal role in the world. Blair made the historic decision to grant the Bank of England the right to determine interest rates independently from the government. He launched the constitutional reforms of Scottish and Welsh devolution in 1997. In April 1998, Blair signed the peace agreement that led to self-rule in Northern Ireland in 1999. Then followed the reform of the Lords and the social reforms.

He improved the quality of government services and dealt with long-term unemployment. Tony Blair explained that trade unions could not expect special deals from Labour when it was in office. He urged Britain's unions to modernize and he meant to weaken further the links between the unions and the party. Blair has broken the traditional government cycle .

But the British do not pay the same attention to Blair's theory of the "Third Way" as do Bill Clinton, Gerhard Schroder, Lionel Jospin and Massimo D'Alema. Whereas Tony Blair is *lionized by his *counterparts for his special contribution to "progressive *governance", the British remain rather indifferent. Moreover, few Britons hold their Prime Minister as "a leader in ideas and influence", and many view him as a control freak.

Tony Blair is a pragmatist who has a more enterprising and more compassionate vision of a modern Britain. But he is becoming less popular; one poll highlighted that 34% of people were satisfied with the job he's doing while 33% were not.

As a politician, Blair cultivates a persona in which Margaret Thatcher's resolute approach is the model.

# 7   Welfare to Work

*Sophie Loussouarn*

Welfare to Work is a continuation of the social policy which was launched after World War II, when the Welfare State was set up in Britain. The government was very committed to the prevention of a rise in unemployment and introduced the National Insurance Bill at the end of 1945.

When Tony Blair won the May 1997 election, one of the Government's top priorities was to *tackle unemployment and social inequalities, to modernize the structure of social security and to make the welfare state active in supporting work. The Government published a green paper on Welfare Reform entitled *New Ambitions for Our Country – A New Contract for Welfare.* The objectives of the Government were to cut down the number of unemployed people, to increase the percentage of disabled people in work, to reward work and to discourage reliance on benefits. At the 1999 Party Conference, Tony Blair reasserted his wish to "help people into work" and "give extra help to those who can't work". Creating jobs is at the centre of New Labour's strategy to support economic growth. Work, *training for work, and education for work are the surest ways to end exclusion. The aim is to include the excluded through work, intervention, deals and to discourage welfare dependency.

## The historical background

Wartime changes paved the way for the development of the welfare state in Britain. The architects of these new policies were W.H. Beveridge (1879-1963) and J.M. Keynes (1883-1946) both Liberals, both academics (Beveridge was a former Director of the London School of Economics and Keynes a Cambridge don) and both temporary civil servants during the war. The **Beveridge Report (1942)** called for a new social-security system based on compulsory social *insurance and fixed subsistence-level *benefits in return for flat-rate *contributions. Sir William Beveridge conceived an inexhaustible unemployment benefit scheme, with provisions for compulsory training to apply to the long-term unemployed. Beveridge's objective was to banish the "giant evils" of *Want, *Disease, *Squalor, Ignorance and *Idleness from Britain. The White Paper on **Employment Policy (1944)** accepted the maintenance of "a high and stable level of employment" as one of the "primary aims and responsibilities" of government after the war. Keynes allocated post-war government a central role in maintaining consumer demand for goods and services at a level sufficient to preserve full employment.

The main welfare state measures introduced by the wartime coalition and the Labour government (1945-51) were broadly continued by Conservative governments in the 1950s. During the period 1945-1970, there was a consensus in terms of welfare and social policy. The Wilson government (1964-1970) introduced a *redundancy pay scheme and the benefits were most apparent for workers experiencing short-term problems of loss of work through sickness and unemployment. With the rise in unemployment from 1970 to 1979, the Heath government introduced new policies in the field of employment, restructuring the public employment service. The reform of employment policy was meant to help create and fill jobs and meet the demands of employers and workers. From 1979 to 1990, the Thatcher government *curbed social security costs by cutting insurance benefits, tightening the qualifying rules for unemployment benefit, preventing youngsters and full-time students from getting *entitlements and preventing *claims from unemployed people not actively seeking work. Half a century after the Beveridge Report and despite the creation of a welfare state, Britain remains a society plagued by social and economic problems.

### *Helping people into work*

The New Labour government wants to tackle unemployment by getting people into work and by creating a more personalised and flexible benefit system which will reduce *disincentives to work. The Blair government intends to help the unemployed and other disadvantaged people into work, through its Welfare to Work programme. More than £5 billion will be invested in Welfare to Work:
- £3.15 billion for young people
- £350 million for the long-term unemployed
- £200 million for lone parents
- £1,300 million for schools
- £200 million for people with disabilities.

The aim is to find a balance between the needs of employers and employees and to give incentives to enterprise. The government's goal is to help improve careers guidance and training and to promote lifetime learning so that people can compete in a changing labour market.

The government means to increase the educational standards and skills of the workforce. Employers are encouraged to invest in the training and development of their employees and individuals are encouraged to take responsibility for their own training and development. The government funds training, enterprise and vocational education programmes.

As a measure to tackle unemployment, the Blair government has launched the New Deal which is co-ordinated by the Department for Education and Employment. The word echoes Roosevelt's policy in the United States during the 1930s.

The categories of people targeted by the New Deal are young people aged 18 to 24, long-term unemployed aged over 25, single parents and people with disabilities.

**The New Deal for young people** started in April 1998. Young people aged 18 to 24 who have been unemployed for six months or more are invited into their local Jobcentre where they meet their New Deal Personal Adviser. The first step is known as the

"Gateway to New Deal" and consists in an intensive period of counselling, advice and guidance on finding work. If the young person does not manage to find work at the end of the Gateway, which lasts four months, the deal includes various options: a job with an employer who is given a £60 subsidy a week for six months; a job with a voluntary sector organisation for six months; a job with the Environment Task Force for up to six months; or the option to carry on in full-time education or training for up to twelve months, towards a recognised qualification. By 2002 New Deal will help 250,000 young unemployed people.

**The New Deal for people aged 25 or over** who have been unemployed and claiming benefits for two years or more was launched in June 1998. Employers receive subsidies of £75 per week for six months to take on long-term unemployed aged 25 or over. In order to help these people back into work, the New Deal is backed by the following measures: Training for Work which focuses on getting people into work, Work Trials which encourages employers to take on people who have been unemployed for six months or more on trial, Jobfinder grants which are available to people unemployed for more than two years to help fund their costs on returning to work, and finally, Workwise which is targeted towards people who have been unemployed for more than a year.

**The New Deal for lone parents** devotes £200 million to helping 500,000 single parents find work. When their youngest child reaches school age, single parents not in work are asked into their local Jobcentre where they meet their New Deal Personal Adviser. The first stage of New Deal for Lone Parents was launched in eight areas in July 1997 and extended to all single parents on Income Support by October 1998. It offers single parents a chance to refresh or learn new skills and increase their employment prospects.

Finally there is an **Employment Rehabilitation *Allowance for people with disabilities** in order to increase their employment prospects by improving their work readiness, jobfinding skills and techniques. The Employment Rehabilitation Allowance amounts to £38 per week.

The New Deal involves a different way of looking at the jobless. Its aim is to provide the various categories of unemployed people with better *skills, self-confidence and work prospects. Among the incentives to move into work is the Back to Work Bonus which aims to encourage people to keep in touch with the labour market and allows claimants in receipt of Income Support and the Jobseeker Allowance to receive a tax-free sum of up to £1,000 when they move off benefit into work. Finally the Blair Government set up Employment Zones for a two-year period starting in April 2000. The 15 Zones are meant to deliver innovative solutions to the problems faced by areas where long-term unemployment is particularly high or persistent. In the year 2000, Britain had the lowest level of unemployment of any European economy.

# VOCABULARY

| | |
|---|---|
| allowance | allocation |
| application | candidature |
| (subsistence-level) benefit/income support | revenu minimum |
| (unemployment) benefit | allocation de chômage |
| bonus | prime |
| claims | revendications |
| (flat-rate) contribution | contribution à taux fixe |
| curb (to) costs | maîtriser les coûts |
| disease | maladie |
| disincentive | facteur dissuasif |
| dismiss (to) | congédier |
| dwindle (to) | diminuer, s'amenuiser |
| entitlement | allocation à laquelle on a droit |
| fairness | équité |
| idleness | oisiveté |
| insurance | assurance |
| irrelevant | hors de propos |
| layoffs/redundancies | mises au chômage technique |
| probation | essai |
| resign (to) | démissionner |
| retailer | détaillant |
| retire (to) | prendre sa retraite |
| skill | compétence, aptitude |
| squalor | misère, conditions sordides |
| staff reductions | réductions de personnel |
| tackle (to) a problem | s'attaquer à |
| target (to) | cibler |
| threshold | seuil |
| thriving | prospère |
| trade union | syndicat |
| training | formation |
| turnover | chiffre d'affaires |
| unionization | syndicalisation |
| wages | salaire |
| want | besoin |
| wholesaler | grossiste |
| workforce | main d'œuvre |
| work trial | période de travail à l'essai |

# Focus...

In June 1999, Britain's workforce in employment amounted to 27.4 million while 1.68 million people were unemployed.

Women make up nearly half of the workforce.

In 1999, 6% of the workforce was unemployed, compared to 10.5% in 1993. Unemployment stands at 1.68 million. The British level of unemployment is below the EU average.

During Autumn 1998, the number of unemployed young people aged 16 to 24, as a percentage of those economically active, was under 14%.

◆ **Social Security**

The key objectives of the social security system are to promote incentives to work, to reduce poverty and welfare dependency, and to strengthen community and family life. The Social Security system is financed by the National Insurance Fund and by general taxation. The benefits which cover unemployment, maternity, widowhood, retirement and sickness are dependent upon the payment of contributions. But child benefit, working families' tax credit, income support for some people not required to be available for work and benefits for the disabled are non-contributory and are financed from general taxation.

In 1998-1999, there was a growth of 0.6% a year of social security spending from £93.2 billion to £95.8 billion.

◆ **Industrial Relations**

Trade Unions are recognised by 88% of the top companies in Britain. However trade union membership has declined. Union membership, union values and union behaviour plus the end of closed shops account for the dwindling strength of trade unionism. Union membership now stands at 31% of all employees. In 1979 it was 55%. At the end of 1994 there were 260 unions in Britain with a total of 8.2 million members. In 1998, out of 27 million employed people there were only 6.75 million members of trade unions affiliated to the Trade Union Congress.

The unions' core values are different from those of the market economy which holds enterprise and profit as the key elements. Trade unions seek to humanise the workplace and are still against a global economy, against some forms of work flexibility embraced by certain companies and against competitiveness. They have to reconstruct themselves with the grain of the modern economy.

Trade unions are weaker and weaker owing to the changes in industrial relations since the 1970s as well as to the influence of New Labour tenets. Tony Blair explained that trade unions cannot expect special deals from Labour when it is in office. He urged Britain's unions to modernize and he means to weaken further the links between the unions and the party.

But the Government published a White Paper on Fairness at Work in 1998 so as to encourage partnership between employers and employees in the workplace and guarantee the right of employees to join a trade union on a voluntary basis.

## Comment upon the following statistics

Table 1
Composition of the population by the economic status of the family

|  | 1994/5 (%) | 1998/9 (%) |
|---|---|---|
| Self-employed head/spouse | 11 | 9 |
| One or more full-time employees | 48 | 51 |
| Part-time employees | 6 | 8 |
| Aged 60 or over | 18 | 17 |
| Unemployed head/spouse | 7 | 4 |
| Other not in work | 10 | 11 |
| **Total population (millions)** | 55.8 | 56.6 |

Source: Analytical Services Division, Department of Social Security

Table 2
Proportion of employment and *turnover in small, medium and large businesses (1996)

|  | **Number** | **Employment** | **Turnover** |
|---|---|---|---|
| Small businesses | 99.1% | 45.9% | 42.3% |
| Medium businesses | 0.7% | 12.4% | 14% |
| Large businesses | 0.2% | 41.7% | 43.7% |

Table 3
Employment by industry sector in Great Britain (Winter 1997/8)

|  | Millions | % |
|---|---|---|
| All employees | 23 |  |
| All service industries | 17 | 72 |
| Manufacturing industries | 4.7 | 20 |
| Construction | 1.2 | 5.1 |
| Electricity, gas, other energy and water supply | 0.3 | 1.2 |
| Agriculture and fishing | 0.2 | 0.8 |
| Private sector | 17 | 74 |
| Public sector | 6 | 26 |

Source: Office for National Statistics

Civilisation britannique

**Analyse the three tables of statistics, comment upon the collected figures and put them into perspective.**

The three tables underscore recent trends in employment in Britain. Table 1 focuses on the evolution of employment in British families from 1994/5 to 1998/9. Table 2 points out the differences in employment and turnover according to the size of the firm while table 3 stresses the imbalance between the private sector and the public sector and the number of employees by industry.

Table 1 testifies to the rising level of employment and the falling rate of unemployment in Britain over the past five years. The growth in the number of part-time employees is largely due to the increasing number of women in employment.

As can be seen in Table 2, even though large companies have the highest turnover in Britain, small firms with fewer than 50 staff provide 45.9% of the private sector *workforce. Governmental support to small and medium-sized companies has helped maintain the level of employment in firms, which do not have the resources of large companies.

Table 3 shows the importance of the service sector which accounts for almost three quarters of all employees. There has been a huge rise in employment in the service sector in the past few years, owing to the increasing number of banks, to the growing size of *retailers, and to the thriving state of British tourism.

Britain excels in high-technology industries such as chemicals, plastics, pharmaceuticals, electronics, aerospace, offshore equipment and printing which account for 20% of employment.

In 1997/8, the construction industry came third in the number of people employed, thanks to substantial projects such as the Channel Tunnel, the London Docklands and the Millennium Dome. Energy and natural resources employ 282,000 people, since Britain has a more varied energy supply than many other countries. However agriculture and fishing employ the lowest number of people in Britain, owing to mechanization and despite the agri-environment programmes which provide incentives to farmers to respect the environment.

Finally, the private sector accounts for three quarters of employment, since Britain's economy is based mainly on private enterprise with the increasing number of small firms (which amount to 99.1% compared to 0.2% of large companies) and since some 50 major public sector businesses have been privatised since 1979. The public sector has thus been dwindling ever since and represents one quarter of British employment.

# 8   The National Health Service

*Sophie Loussouarn*

The National Health Service (NHS) is one of the pillars of the *Welfare State. The NHS was founded in order to provide effective and appropriate treatment and care when necessary, while making the best use of the *available resources. It was an innovation of the 1945-1951 Labour government and it was driven by a belief in fairness, quality and public service. The NHS came into existence in 1948 as the only universal National Health Service where treatment was free at the point of access for everyone who lived in Britain. It was established under the National Health Service Act, 1947, the National Health Service (Scotland) Act, 1947, and the NHS Act (Northern Ireland), 1948. It consolidated and extended the existing health services and meant to improve the health of the nation. The NHS was an immediate success with the public and has remained popular ever since. Over the period from the late 1940s to the 1990s, the health of the UK population has improved for every age group and demand for treatment has grown faster and faster.

More than fifty years after its creation, the NHS provides a *comprehensive range of care and employs one million people. It has a yearly budget of £41 billion and Britain spends 5.9% of GDP on public health care. But the NHS *falls short of the standards patients expect and staff want to provide. The NHS sets national standards to improve performance and it is over-centralised. The New Labour government which has been in office since 1997 is therefore *committed to restoring the NHS: it means to reform the structure of the NHS, to end the delays and develop new forms of public/private partnerships. The new NHS will be built on the same values, revitalised for the next fifty years.

## The basic principles of the NHS

The NHS offers all forms of medical treatment to all members of the community, without *regard to their means or to any insurance qualification. The great majority use the service, and almost all the hospitals and the members of the medical and allied professions *take part in it.

Its objectives are to promote health, to prevent ill health, to diagnose and treat injury and to care for those with *long-term illness and *disability.

It is mainly funded by taxes which cover 82% of health costs and by the contribution of employers and employees which cover 12.2% of the costs. In addition, health authorities are free to raise funds from voluntary sources and some NHS hospitals take private patients who pay the full cost of their treatment.

Two-thirds of all expenditure is devoted to *staff costs and one tenth of the yearly budget is spent on medicines. Hospitals and community services for people aged 64 and over account for two-fifths of the overall health costs even though they represent 16% of the population.

## The organisation of the NHS

The NHS is a massive and complex organisation.

The Secretary of State for Health is *accountable to Parliament for the *provision of health care services and he discharges his responsibility through health authorities and boards.

The Department of Health is responsible for protecting the health of the nation, and providing financial help and social care.

Within the Department of Health, the NHS is managed by the NHS Management Executive which launches policies and has eight regional offices working in partnership with the health authorities in their region.

Health services are administered by 100 health authorities in England, five in Wales, 15 health boards in Scotland and four health and social service boards in Northern Ireland. The task of these health authorities is to analyse the health care needs of the people in their area and to manage the services provided by doctors, dentists, *pharmacists and opticians.

There are three levels of free care available to users of the NHS:

- Primary care is provided by family doctors, dentists, opticians and pharmacists working within the NHS. The 28,937 English *General Practitioners are the gatekeepers to other services and *refer patients to specialists when necessary.

The 1997 NHS Primary Care Act introduced greater flexibility in the delivery of primary health care.
- Secondary care deals with further treatment in the 300 district general hospitals which provide care for the elderly, maternity and *emergency services. It is managed by NHS Trusts.
- Tertiary care deals with specialist services for rare cancers and craniofacial services.

The NHS in Scotland, Wales and Northern Ireland is separate from that in England. The Scottish Executive is in charge of the NHS in Scotland, the National Assembly for Wales is in charge of the NHS in Wales and the Secretary of State for Northern Ireland is responsible for the NHS in Northern Ireland.

## New Labour and the reform of the NHS

Modernizing the NHS is one of the top priorities of Blair's government.

New Labour wants to achieve five goals: improving the health of everyone, ensuring patients get prompt care and treatment, delivering excellence everywhere, guiding people through the health and social care systems and investing public money wisely to get the best results.

New Labour means to improve hospitals and GP services, meet high-quality standards in hospitals, reduce waiting lists, contain health spending by influencing the decisions of medical staff and by introducing a partnership of all health bodies with GPs and nurses, reduce the death rate from heart disease and improve the effectiveness and speed of access to cancer services.

In February 1998, the Government launched a new strategy, "Our Healthier Nation", which aims to end the inequalities in health, to encourage healthy eating and exercise, to encourage prevention and to discourage drug and alcohol misuse and smoking.

In July 1998, the Government announced it would provide an extra £20 billion over the next three years.

The new Health Act 1999 promotes partnership within the NHS and between the health service and local authorities. The Primary Care Groups and Trusts, teams of GPs, community nurses and social services staff took control of most of the NHS budget from April 1999. New legal duties of quality of care and of partnership were introduced to improve standards of care. The National Institute for Clinical Excellence and the Commission for Health Improvement were created to make the delivery of health care more uniform, to appraise treatments, recommend standard protocols and launch therapies proven both beneficial and cost-effective. Health Action Zones were launched in the poorest areas of the country covering 13 million people. Finally a *telephone hotline was introduced to provide health advice and to reduce pressure on hospitals.

Furthermore the Blair Government published a Plan for Investment and Reform (PIR) in the NHS which aims at giving the British people a health service fit for the 21st century. The March 2000 Budget settlement has devoted more money to provide *NHS facilities (7,000 extra beds in hospitals, over 100 new hospitals by 2010, over 3,000 GP *premises modernized and 250 new scanners) and to increase NHS staff in order to cut the waiting times for treatment. So as to take the needs of the patient into account, power will be devolved from the Government to the local health service. A Modernisation Agency will be set up to spread best practice. The contracts of GPs and hospital doctors will be modernised. Nurses will have greater opportunity to extend their role and will be able to supply medicines by 2004. Finally, patients will have more influence over the way the NHS works.

Since 1997, New Labour has launched the most *far-reaching reforms since 1948 and aims to improve the standards of the NHS and adapt it to change, including patients, carers and NHS staff to develop local charters.

## Vocabulary

| | |
|---:|:---|
| be (to) accountable to | être responsable devant |
| asset | atout |
| available | disponible |
| backlog | arriéré |
| blurring | brouillage |
| buttress (to) | étayer |
| be (to) committed to | s'engager à |
| comprehensive | complet, détaillé |
| dedication | dévouement |
| disability | handicap |
| downsides | aspects négatifs, défauts |
| the emergency services | les urgences |
| fall (to) short of | ne pas atteindre le but, être en-dessous de l'attente |
| far-reaching | d'une portée considérable |
| forthcoming | à venir |
| General Practitioner (GP) | généraliste |
| litmus test | test décisif |
| long-term illness | maladie de longue durée |
| midwife | sage-femme |
| NHS facilities | installations du système de santé |
| nurse | infirmier, infirmière |
| outpatient | malade en consultation externe |
| overshoot (to) | outre-passer |
| take (to) part in | participer à |
| pharmacist | pharmacien |
| physician | médecin (non chirurgien) |
| (GP) premises/surgery | un cabinet de généralistes |
| provision | la fourniture |
| refer (to) to a specialist | envoyer en consultation chez un spécialiste |
| without regard to | indépendemment de |
| rough-and-ready | rudimentaire |
| scarce | rare |
| shabby | minable |
| squalid | misérable, sordide |
| staff | personnel |
| surgeon | chirurgien |
| surgery | consultations, soins |
| telephone hotline | numéro vert |
| Welfare State | État-Providence |
| work (to) flat out | travailler d'arrache-pied |

# Focus...

Britain spends 5.9% of GDP on public health care, whereas Germany spends 8.2%.

At birth and during the first month of life, the risk of death in families of unskilled workers is double that in professional families.

The total number of patients waiting for inpatient treatment at NHS hospitals in England rose by 10,800 (1%) between 1st April and 30th June, 2000; the number of patients in England's adult population waiting over 12 months rose by 2,600 (5.3 %) to 50,700; 1 patient had been on the waiting list for longer than 18 months. By the end of June 2000, 444,000 people had been waiting more than 13 weeks from the date of their referral to an outpatient appointment (an increase of 11 per cent since the end of March 2000).

◆ **William Beveridge on the National Health Service**

"Restoration of a sick person to health is a duty of the state prior to any other. A comprehensive national health service will ensure that for every citizen there is available whatever medical treatment he requires, in whatever form he requires it, domiciliary or institutional, general, specialist or consultant, and will ensure also the provision of dental, ophthalmic and surgical appliances, nursing and midwifery and rehabilitation after accidents."

(Beveridge Report, 1942.)

◆ **R.M.Titmuss on inequality in health**

"We have learnt from 15 years' experience of the Health Service that the higher income groups know how to make better use of the Service; they tend to receive more specialist attention; occupy more of the beds in better equipped and staffed hospitals; receive more elective surgery; have better maternity care; and are more likely to get psychiatric help and psychotherapy than low income groups–particularly the unskilled."

(*Commitment to Welfare*, 1963.)

◆ **Community Health Councils**

There are more than 200 Community Health Councils in England and Wales. They were created in 1974 to find out what people wanted and recommended.

They provide information about NHS services.

They give advice to patients on how to get special help.

They also help with complaints and advise the local health authority how to improve services.

◆ **Frank Dobson's plan for the Patient's Charter**

"Patients will be expected to be courteous to staff, just as they would expect staff to be courteous to them [...] It measures what is easily measurable. It has nothing to do with outcomes. If we are going to have a Patient's Charter that works, it has got to relate to outcomes. The merit of measuring time spent on waiting lists, or waiting in *outpatients is that time is easy to measure."

Frank Dobson was Blair's Health Secretary from 1997 to 1999.

# Commentary of a Cartoon

*IEP Paris, épreuve écrite de passage en deuxième année, 2000*

Britain's Health Service On Critical List (*Guardian Weekly*, January 20-26, 2000). Comment upon the following cartoon.

> This cartoon is a close up of an empty grave inviting the next victim of the National Health Service to jump right in. The signpost on the right-hand side reads "Fast efficient NHS direct, No Beds, No Staff, No Fuss, Cut Out the Middlemen, Jump Right In!" In the background, on the left another signpost displays a skeleton and the logo NHS praising its effective work and *dedication to "your" cause: "*working flat out for you". The viewer can't help feeling concerned since it is addressed to him, unaware that he will soon be flat out. To comfort him, a headstone beckons in the centre background "spare beds" with a bitter implication, R.I.P. ("Rest in Peace"). Nevertheless "you" should not be blind to the blatant truth that if the NHS is fast and efficient, it is not the result expected by the patient who cannot find a bed or

*nurse in hospital which seems to be a shortcut between life and death via sickness.*

*The cartoon is a bitter, scathing denunciation of the health service in the year 2000, fifty odd years after the NHS was launched by Bevan in 1948. The NHS is indeed a \*litmus test for New Labour which promised an improvement of the system after eighteen years of Conservative rule. Tony Blair even went as far as pledging that the government would bring British spending up to the European level. Nevertheless, he could not even prescribe one remedy that would cure the crumbling health system. In the winter of 1999-2000, patients could not find beds in hospitals during the influenza epidemics. Moreover, people have to wait overtime and die because of cancelled operations.*

*As a matter of fact, New Labour is showing the same attitudes to taxes and public spending as the Conservatives. Blair's government is rationing health care so that staff are overworked and insufficient. Whereas Germany has 9.6 doctors for 1,000 people, Britain has 1.6. While France has 8.7 beds, Britain has 1.6 per 1,000 people. Those figures \*buttress the cry of revolt. The cartoonist uses macabre puns and grave humour to voice his indignation together with the poor British people, the middleman, the intermediary, who cannot afford to pay for better health care.*

# MORE ABOUT...
# ...THE NHS

### *Jury de classement de sortie de l'ENA, mars 1999*

"THE HEALTH SERVICE AT 50"(*THE ECONOMIST*, JULY 4TH 1998)

Depending on how you examine it, the National Health Service appears to be either in fine form for its age – lean, fit and adaptable – or chronically malnourished, in poor physical shape and verging on senility.

On the one hand, the NHS seems remarkably cost-effective compared with America's obese health-care system: by the *rough-and-ready measures of average life expectancy and infant mortality, the health of the two countries' populations is much the same, even though America spends twice as much of its national income on health than Britain does. Dollar for dollar, America spends three times as much on each person as Britain.

On the other hand, the NHS does have some worrying symptoms: a queue of almost 1.5m patients waiting for hospital treatment; old and often *shabby buildings; and lack of assessment and accountability among doctors that can lead to spectacular failures.

Those who are concerned for the future health of the middle-aged NHS fear that, as a service almost entirely funded from taxes, it will be especially difficult for it to cope with the ever-rising expectations of the public at a time when the population is ageing and when expensive new treatments are appearing by the day. Despite all this, the NHS's 50th birthday should be a cause for celebration, not gloom. No longer does one child in 15 die before the age of 11, as was the case before the health service was invented. A boy born today in an NHS hospital is expected, on average, to live for 75 years, compared with just 66 years in 1948.

It was a reckless promise to make, especially at a time when Britain was ravaged by war and virtually broke: to meet every health need of every person in the country, for free. But, in early 1948, each home in Britain was sent a leaflet announcing that from July 5th a new National Health Service would "provide you with all medical, dental, and nursing care. Everyone – rich or poor, man or woman or child – can use it or any part of it. There are no charges, except for a few special items."

Since the turn of the century there had been much talk about the need for such a universal health-care system but little to show for it. In most of Britain, the hospitals were *squalid, overcrowded, inefficient – and the rich were treated at home by expensive private consultants.

But towards the end of the second world war, with victory in sight, the British people's attitudes and expectations changed, and despair gave way to optimism. Amid a growing mood of national solidarity, it was assumed that the country's ancient class divisions were dissolving. Rationing meant that everyone got his fair share, and it also planted in the public's minds the idea that fair shares meant equal shares. These cultural changes meant that a high-quality, egalitarian health service, funded through a progressive tax system, was no longer a pipedream but a serious prospect.

Following Labour's election victory a few months after the war's end, the job of making the NHS fell to Aneurin Bevan, the new health minister.

In its early years, the NHS greatly *overshot its budget. Bevan assumed that it was simply due to a *backlog of untreated cases and that the cost of the NHS would fall as the nation became more healthy. How very wrong he was.

The idea, that demand for health care is finite, and that some given sum of money would therefore clear the NHS's backlog, is one of the central myths on which the service was built.

Another is that its creation separated medicine from money, allowing doctors to offer treatments based entirely on their judgment of the patient's need, not their cost.

A third myth is that the NHS can offer equal service to all, regardless of who or where they happen to be.

*Fifty years after the introduction of the NHS,* The Economist *looks at one of the essential parts of the British Welfare State and lays the stress on the basic principles of the system and on the medical myths.*

*The journalist draws a comparison between the British NHS and the American health system, the former being more cost-effective than the latter. In spite of its \*assets, there are numerous \*downsides in the day-to-day working of the NHS, ranging from waiting lists, to the bad condition of the buildings, not to mention medical errors.*

*In the \*forthcoming years, the NHS will face numerous challenges, such as the rising number of elderly people and the increasing costs of new treatments. However the decrease in child mortality and the improvement in the health of the poor are achievements the NHS can pride itself on.*

*The setting up of the NHS was a turning-point in Britain where medical care for workers was \*scarce before 1948, where hospitals were sordid and where there was a two-tier health system, one for the poor and one for the rich.*

*The Second World War, together with the \*blurring of class cleavages and the new sense of equality and solidarity account for the creation of a high quality, universal, egalitarian health service providing medical, dental and nursing care.*

*The founder of the NHS believed that health care demand would be limited, that doctors could decide on treatments regardless of health costs and that all patients would be equally cared for, whoever they were and wherever they were.*

# 9 Regions and Devolution

*Sophie Loussouarn*

The New Labour government put *devolution at the top of its political agenda. Devolution is a form of subsidiarity passing power back to the people. It is "the transfer to a subordinate elected body, on a geographical basis, of functions at present being exercised by Ministers and Parliament" as Vernon Bogdanor wrote in *Devolution in the United Kingdom* (Oxford University Press, 1999). It originated from the Labour Party with the launching of the 1979 referendum, but the struggle for devolution lasted two decades.

In September 1997 two referenda were organized in Wales and Scotland. Both Scotland and Wales decided in favour of devolution. It was an unprecedented event since the union of Wales with the United Kingdom in 1536 and since the Act of Union of 1707. Wales has not had the same degree of autonomy as Scotland within the British government framework, since the Act of Union of 1707 left the Scottish legal, educational and church systems untouched. The devolution programme launched in September 1997 aimed at making the government of the United Kingdom more efficient and bringing *decision-making closer to the people.

## The referenda on devolution in Scotland, Wales and Northern Ireland

In the September 1997 referendum, the large majority of over 70% in favour of the Scottish devolution contrasted with the small majority of 50.3% in Wales. It was *ground-breaking legislation. It meant that there would be a Scottish Parliament and a Scottish Executive as well as a Welsh Assembly which would remain part of the British structure, with power originating from Westminster. The Scottish Parliament will be more powerful than the Welsh Parliament. However, the Welsh Parliament will give a political expression to the Welsh identity, granting the Scots and the Welsh more power over their own affairs.

A referendum was held in Northern Ireland in May 1998 and over 71% of voters were in favour of devolution. It will progressively remove the unitary veil from Britain's union structure to make explicit the quasi-federal relationships between Westminster and the new governments in Edinburgh, Cardiff and Belfast.

The 1997 and 1998 results were an historic event: they heralded a *watershed in British constitutional history.

## The Scottish Parliament, the Welsh Assembly and the Northern Ireland Assembly

*1 – The Scottish Parliament*

The Scottish Parliament is a new and powerful symbol of nationhood. It gives representation to the 5.1 million people of Scotland. Instead of the *first-past-the-post

Civilisation britannique

system used in British elections, the Additional Member System is now used. In Scotland, there are 73 Members of the Scottish Parliament (MSPs) representing constituencies and 56 members selected from eight regions. The Scottish Parliament thus has 129 members altogether.

In the elections on 6th May, 1999, there was a *turnout of 58%. The Labour Party came first with 56 seats, rivalled by the Scottish National Party with 35 seats. The Conservatives were relegated to third place (with 18 seats) and the Liberal Democrats came fourth (with 17 seats). It meant that there would be a Labour-Lib Dem coalition to help form an administration that would get a programme through the Parliament's four year term.

It met for the first time on May 12th, 1999. All 129 members were required to make an oath to "be faithful and bear true allegiance to Her Majesty Queen Elizabeth, her heirs and successors, according to law". Lord Steel, a former Lib Dem leader was elected presiding officer, or speaker. He was co-chairman of the Scottish Constitutional Convention which drew up the plans for the Scottish Parliament.

The Scottish Parliament was inaugurated on July 1st, 1999 by the Queen, M. Dewar, the Prime Minister and Lord Steel. The Scottish Parliament will have four-year terms and it will be temporarily housed in the assembly hall of the Church of Scotland. The Scottish Parliament adds an extra *tier of government.

The Scottish Parliament will have law-making powers over health services, education, local government, transport, social services, housing, criminal and civil justice, economic development, the environment, agriculture, sports and the arts. The Scottish Parliament will have limited tax-making powers and Westminster will control the Constitution, defence, foreign affairs, macroeconomic policy, financial services, financial markets, immigration and nationality, employment law and social security.

### 2 – The Welsh Assembly

The Government of Wales Act 1998 created a National Assembly for Wales with 60 members: 40 *constituency members, elected from existing Westminster constituencies and 20 additional members selected from five regions. In the elections on 6th May, 1999, Labour won 28 seats in the 60-member assembly, Plaid Cymru took 17, the Conservatives 9, and the Liberal Democrats 6. The Queen opened the assembly on 26th May.

The assembly will have executive power and powers of secondary legislation only and will be dependent upon Westminster for its annual block grant. The Welsh assembly will *wield more limited powers than the Scottish Parliament, but it takes over most of the Secretary of State's functions, regarding the Welsh language, water, arts and heritage, industry, education, economic development, social services, environment, housing, health, highways, local government and tourism. The British government will still be in charge of economic policy, defence, foreign policy, the justice system, broadcasting and sport. Schemes for future legislation will be prepared in Whitehall by officials who are no longer responsible for their administration in Wales. Welsh legislation will have to take its chance each year in the long queue of measures put forward by Whitehall departments. There will be no capacity to amend existing statutes except through Westminster. With just 60 members, the Welsh assembly in Cardiff will feel like a poor relation in its powers and status.

Dafydd Wigley, head of the Welsh nationalist Party, Plaid Cymru, says the nationalists simply want more control over things that are close to them, such as health and education. It is less likely that devolution will give a *boost to regional parties in Wales.

*3 – The Northern Ireland Assembly*

The Good Friday Agreement of 1998 provided for the setting up of an elected Assembly in Northern Ireland. Elections to a new Northern Ireland Assembly were held on 25th June, 1998. The Ulster Unionist Party came first with 28 seats, the Social Democratic and Labour Party came second with 24 seats, the Democratic Unionist Party came third with 20 seats, and Sinn Fein won 18 seats.

The Assembly wields *devolved power over agriculture, the environment, education, employment, enterprise and investment, health, culture and the arts. Besides, the Northern Ireland Executive was established on 2nd December, 1999.

## The implications of the new devolved powers for British politics

The devolution legislation provides a constitution for Scotland and Northern Ireland and for the first time questions the British constitution. The creation of a new Scottish Parliament and a Welsh assembly is part of a commitment to modernizing the constitution of the United Kingdom.

It raises the question of sovereignty. The British Parliament has passed some of its day-to-day power to a directly elected Scottish Parliament representing the people of Scotland and to a directly-elected Welsh assembly. There is a risk of competition between Westminster, the Scottish Parliament and the Welsh assembly. Political power will be shared between different levels of government, with Parliament being *squeezed between the European Union and the devolved assemblies. There will be formal division of powers between two levels of government. The devolution legislation allocates legislative and executive power to Westminster and Whitehall on the one hand, and the devolved governments and assemblies on the other. There will be greater and more public intergovernmental bargaining between Edinburgh, Cardiff, Belfast and London.

Tensions between different parts of the country may be exacerbated. What devolution will decisively test is whether the shared identity of being British will survive the passing of historic interests which brought the Union into being. The new political institutions will sharpen people's sense of dual identity, with people seeing themselves as Scottish, Welsh, Irish or English as well as British.

# Vocabulary

| | |
|---:|:---|
| Additional Member System | forme de représentation proportionnelle |
| array of | étalage de |
| ban (to) | interdire |
| bias | préjugé |
| bigotry | fanatisme |
| give (to) a boost to | relancer |
| (political) bribery | corruption électorale |
| canvass | démarche électorale |
| congenial | agréable |
| constituency | circonscription |
| culprit | accusé, coupable |
| debunk (to) | tourner en dérision |
| decision-making | processus de décision |
| devolution | décentralisation |
| devolve power (to) | décentraliser le pouvoir |
| devolved powers | pouvoirs décentralisés |
| discrepancy | écart |
| downturn | baisse |
| estrange (to) sb from | séparer qqn de |
| first-past-the-post system | scrutin majoritaire uninominal à un tour |
| ground-breaking | révolutionnaire |
| herald (to) | annoncer |
| hindrance | obstacle, entrave |
| mastermind (to) | organiser, diriger |
| merger (economic) | fusion |
| from the outset | au commencement, au début |
| proceedings | débats d'une assemblée |
| raft of legislation | masse de législation |
| root (to) out | extirper |
| scathing | acerbe, mordant, cinglant |
| squeeze (to) | exercer une pression sur qqn |
| at stake | en jeu |
| staple industries | industries de matières premières |
| thriving towns | villes prospères |
| tier of government | niveau de gouvernement |
| (electoral) turnout | participation électorale |
| upshot | le résultat |
| watershed | un tournant |
| wield (to) power | exercer du pouvoir |

# Focus...

### ◆ Chronology

55 and 54 B.C. Julius Caesar *masterminded the first Roman landings in Britain.

122     The Romans began building Hadrian's Wall to mark the northern frontier of Britain.

1066     At the Battle of Hastings, William the Conqueror defeated King Harold of England and under the Norman dynasty the centralization of the realm was achieved.

1536-43 England and Wales were formally integrated by the Acts of Union and English became the official language for Wales.

1649-50 Ireland was conquered again by Cromwell.

1707     The Scottish Parliament voted itself out of existence. The Act of Union between Scotland and England and Wales was voted by the English and Scottish parliaments and the country of Great Britain was formed.

1801     The Union between Great Britain and Ireland became effective.

1966     The Welsh nationalist Party, Plaid Cymru, won their first seat at Westminster.

1969     Prince Charles was made Prince of Wales at Caernarvon Castle.

1974     The Scottish Nationalist Party won 11 seats at Westminster.

1979     Devolution was rejected in a referendum.

1996     The Stone of Scone, Scotland's coronation stone of ancient kings, was returned from London to Edinburgh Castle, 700 years after having been removed by Edward I.

1997     Referendum on Scottish and Welsh devolution.

1999     Elections to the Scottish Parliament and to the Welsh Assembly.

### ◆ The Scottish National Party (SNP)

The SNP was founded in 1934 and is very powerful in Scotland. They are nicknamed "Tartan Tories" but yet identify themselves as moderate left-of-centre on economic and social questions. With the discovery of North Sea oil off the coast of Scotland, the SNP could claim that Scotland would be economically better off with independence. The basic aim of the SNP is Scottish independence within the European Union and the Commonwealth. With the election of the Scottish Parliament in May 1999, the SNP has achieved its aim and they have 35 seats in the 129-member Scottish Parliament.

◆ **Plaid Cymru**

The Welsh Party was founded in 1925 and it is associated with the left and socialism. It seeks full self-government for Wales based on socialist principles, the promotion of the Welsh language, and the restoration of Welsh culture.

It has contested all elections to the Westminster Parliament since 1945, but it remained unrepresented until July 1966. The party won two other seats in the February 1974 elections and the 1992 election yielded the party's best result with 4 MPs.

◆ **Regional government in England**

The Blair government launched eight English Regional Development Agencies (RDA) which started work on April 1st, 1999. It is in keeping with the European Union's concept of a Europe of regions. The total budget of the RDAs will rise from £1.24 billion in 2000-01 to £1.7 billion in 2003-04.

# Commentary of a Text

*Concours de classement de sortie de l'ENA, mars 2000*

"The Scottish Parliament's Plan for a Reign of Terror" by Alan Cochrane (*The Spectator*, 14th August, 1999).

> We now have in Scotland a generation of politicians who know nothing, have done nothing and plan to do nothing – other than to be politically correct. At official level we are seeing something like a reign of terror, which is new, and which also emanates from something ancient in the Scottish psyche.
>
> This week the composer James MacMillan caused a sensation at the Edinburgh Festival with his perceptive analysis of what he considers to be pervasive Scottish anti-Catholic *bigotry: "It is a very Scottish trait," said Mr MacMillan, "a desire to narrow and restrict the definition of what it means to be Scottish. This tendency to restrict, to control and to enforce conformity and homogeneity is an obsessive and paranoid flaw in the Scottish character."
>
> Look at the parliament itself. It has been determined, from the *outset, that it should be as different as possible from that dreadful place at Westminster. For one thing, it should be family-friendly – i.e., it shouldn't expect its 129 members to turn up very often. Rather, they should spend as much time as possible with their families and the rest of us should be content to pay them the princely sum of £40,000 a year to do so. The *upshot is that the Edinburgh parliament intends to sit for one-and-a-half days a week, a total of nine hours.
>
> When they can be bothered to turn up, our new legislators have interesting priorities. Step number one is to banish racism. Scotland must be an anti-racist land – that is, as the Americans say, a "given". Scotland's Deputy First Minister in the Labour/Liberal Democrat coalition government is Mr Jim Wallace, leader of the Scottish Lib Dems. He also holds the justice portfolio and his very first initiative was to set up not one but two "task forces" to investigate and *root out "institutionalised racism".
>
> Sexism is also a heinous sin. When the earnest young nationalist, Duncan Hamilton, complained about the appalling standard of debating in the parliament's chamber, he was denounced as a sexist pig. The fact that the *culprits were predominantly women and that their public-speaking skills were dreadful was lost in the cacophony of feminist fury.
>
> Then take the matter of religion. Should the parliament open its *proceedings with prayers? This is a matter taxing its finest brains. They have set up a committee to ponder whether the Assembly should have a wholly Christian aspect or whether it should reflect what is called Scotland's multiracial society – it isn't, by the way – and have the wee bits of prayers for everyone: you know, a minute for the Presbyterians, a minute for the Catholics, 30 seconds for the Muslims and Jews, and even a period of silence for the atheists.

The Episcopal Bishop of Edinburgh, Richard Holloway, is not the most popular man in the Anglican communion. But he has been talking no less than sense when he says that if this is to be the way of it, then better no prayers at all.

Their multicultural devotions complete, our tribunes will embark on spreading PC throughout the land. The biggest *raft of legislation that is likely to come before the parliament when it resumes its labours next month will concern the real battle of Scotland – that between town and country.

Donald Dewar, the First Minister plans to allow "communities" to buy the estates on which they live when they come up for sale, through the use of Lottery cash.

Then last week, Lord Watson of Invergowrie provided details of his bill that will *ban fox-hunting in Scotland.

Taken together, these measures will confirm what many believe to be the decidedly anti-rural *bias among Scotland's new legislators.

Scotland's acquisition of its own parliament was supposed to enable us better to decide our domestic priorities, without let or *hindrance from those nasty English. The early signs are that our legislators are trying to create a country in which a great many Scots will feel like foreigners.

*Alan Cochrane ridicules the Scottish Parliament in a *scathing article from the Conservative weekly,* The Spectator.

*Scottish devolution brought to the fore a new aspect in Scottish society even though it could be viewed as a revival of the Scottish spirit. The Scottish character is often laughed at as being narrow-minded and conservative. Among the new Scottish politicians, there are plenty of novices who behave with Scottish straightforwardness and sternness.*

*From the beginning, the Scottish Parliament was meant to be utterly different from the British Parliament in terms of size and attendance. A Parliament for 5 million people is inevitably different from a Parliament for 59 million people. The new Parliament is informal and criticised as amateurish.*

*The Scottish legislators rank among their top priorities the banishment of racism, sexism and the religious question not to mention land reform. The question of prayers before parliamentary debates is at *stake. Furthermore, communities should be able to buy the estates currently owned by English millionaires. Scotland's bill to ban fox-hunting is part of the extremely controversial rural debate. The Scottish Parliament appears keener to tackle moral issues than Westminster.*

*Paradoxically, the Scottish Parliament which should have brought decision-making closer to the Scots is *estranging them from Scottish politics.*

# 10 Ireland

*Sophie Loussouarn*

The fundamental cause of the partition of Ireland is the relationship between England and Ireland. The impact of England was very limited at first. In 1155 the Pope, Adrian IV, made Henry II of England Lord of Ireland. Settlements took place under Elizabeth I. After 1649, the English government aimed at solving the Irish problem by means of further plantations. In 1782, an independent Irish Parliament was formed, but after Wolf Tone's rebellion was defeated in 1798, England and Ireland were united and the Irish were given seats in the House of Commons at Westminster. In the twentieth century, the Irish problem still endures and has damaged Britain's international reputation. Nevertheless, throughout the 1990s, the Irish economy constantly improved and unemployment has been declining since 1993. New investments in growth industries such as computer software and network services contributed to the 2,500 new jobs created in 1999.

## The Union and the national question

Ireland was part of the United Kingdom from 1800 to 1922. The Act of Union of 1800 provided that Ireland would be represented by 100 members in the House of Commons. Unionism emphasized the link with Britain as a guarantee of religious and civil liberties and of economic prosperity. In 1829, Catholic emancipation was *conceded. But the Union faced opposition before the Great Famine of the 1840s. The Irish Land Question became a permanent crisis because absentee English landlords continued to exploit the poor Irish peasants. The Union raised the question of change in political status, change in land law, institutional structures including the Catholic majority and cultural authenticity. Charles Stewart Parnell had a personal ascendency over the national movement from 1879 to 1889. Protestantism had been the mobilizing force of resistance to Home Rule since the 1880s. Home Rule was revived at the beginning of the 20th century and the revolutionary element gathered strength. In 1916, the nationalists staged an insurrection known as the *Easter Rising in Dublin and declared the establishment of a republic. During 1917, Sinn Fein, which was created in 1905, was transformed into a coherent political movement. Meanwhile the most extremist volunteers formed a unit called the Irish Republican Army (IRA), advocating violent methods such as shooting policemen. Ireland was in a state of virtual civil war and there were attacks on Catholic shipyard workers beginning in Belfast. The Government of Ireland Act was passed in 1920. However violence continued for two years. Eventually, the Anglo-Irish Treaty was signed on December 6th, 1921, leading to the construction of the Irish Free State. The *partition of

Ireland was the consequence of Irish national revival and Northern Ireland was born in a crisis. Partition was meant to preserve protestantism and to remove British rule from all Irish domestic affairs in accordance with the principle of self-determination. The 1920s were thus a turning point in Irish history. The two Irish states had liberal pluralistic constitutions and intended to cater for Nationalists in the North and Unionists in the South. A provisional government was established in Ireland, creating a democratic political system and a constitution was published in June 1922. But even after the direct threat of republican military action had disappeared in the summer of 1922, a more general insecurity persisted.

A new constitution was adopted in 1937 and Ireland was given a new name: Eire. Irish was then declared the national language and the Catholic and Roman Catholic Church was recognized as the guardian of the faith.

## The second republic and the thirty years' crisis

In 1949, Eire officially became a republic and left the Commonwealth. Britain recognized the status of Ireland. Ireland was modernizing and there was a gradual erosion of insularity. The 1960s were a turning-point in the social evolution of Ireland.

The Catholics in the North felt that they had been for too long treated like second-class citizens. That's why in 1968 the Northern Ireland Civil Rights Association organized marches and *demonstrations. The civil rights crisis broke out in 1969. Riots followed in Londonderry and Belfast in 1969 and British troops were deployed to control them. Rioters threw *petrol bombs and stones and the army and the Royal Ulster Constabulary *retaliated with tear gas. In 1972, *paratroopers opened fire on an illegal civil rights march in Derry, where 13 civilians were killed and 29 injured. That day has since been remembered as "Bloody Sunday". The bombings continued throughout most of the seventies, eighties and nineties. In 1979, the IRA killed a public figure, Lord Mountbatten, a cousin of the Queen and former viceroy of India. It represented a direct assault on the Crown.

For twenty years after the *collapse of the Sunningdale settlement the republican movement continued its war against Britain and Ulster loyalism. The troubles have inspired several film directors with films such as Pat O'Connor's *Cal* (1984), Neil Jordan's *The Crying Game* (1992), Jim Sheridan's *In the Name of the Father* (1993) and Roger Michell's *Titanic Town* (1998).

A far-reaching political step was taken with the Anglo-Irish Agreement signed at Hillborough Castle in 1985.

In 1994, the IRA called for a historic ceasefire and London accepted to start negotiating. The Irish-American community helped the peace process. Gerry Adams, leader of Sinn Fein, was granted a visa in order to be allowed to enter the USA. Gerry Adams had been regarded as a terrorist, his voice was *dubbed whenever he spoke on British television. Thanks to the joint efforts of former US President Bill Clinton, Democratic senators and the American ambassador in Dublin, Gerry Adams was finally welcomed in New York and treated by the media almost like a head of state. A few months later, it became possible for Irish and British leaders to meet and begin the peace process. An agreement was finally reached on Good Friday in 1998, after 22 months of intensive negotiations that involved eight of the ten Northern Irish political parties. The talks were *chaired by former US Senator George Mitchell and included British prime minister Tony Blair, Irish prime minister Bertie Ahern, and President Bill Clinton. The accord gave the Republic of Ireland a voice in Northern Irish affairs. The loyalist paramilitary groups supported the agreement. However the dream of a peaceful Ireland was shattered in August when a bomb attack in Omagh (Ulster) killed 28 people. It was *regarded by many as the worst atrocity in thirty years. Nevertheless Parliament reopened in Stormont in September with David Trimble as Prime Minister. John Hume (Catholic) and David Hume (Protestant) received the Nobel Peace Prize for their joint effort to reach a peaceful solution to the Troubles. On May 30th, 2000, Britain returned *home rule powers to the Northern Ireland Assembly.

Since then there have been several *outbursts of violence, especially every summer in July when Protestant Loyalists (Orangemen) celebrate the Protestant victory at the Battle of the Boyne: they organize parades and march through Catholic areas, which the Catholics regard as a provocation.

## *Irish identity*

There is a distinct Irish nationality with its own language and culture. The cultural community flourished in Ireland from the eighteenth-century onwards and has developed in recent years. The early twentieth-century experiences of independent Ireland reveal the human search for freedom of expression. In the first years of the twentieth century, W.B.Yeats (1856-1939), James Joyce (1882-1941) and John Millington Synge (1871-1909) reflected the Irish identity. Some of Yeats's poems dealt with Irish nationalism and the revolution. James Joyce, who was born in Dublin, devoted all his writing to Dublin. His book of realistic short stories *Dubliners* (1914) described the *dreariness of a ruined city inhabited by helpless characters and *Ulysses* (1922) depicts a day in the life of Leopold Bloom in Dublin. Nowadays, the Nobel Prize winner Seamus Heaney who is an Ulster Catholic and has been influenced by Joyce is the guardian of Irish poetry and writes about the hard life of Irish farmers and craftsmen and the violence going on in Northern Ireland. He is placed, as he said later "between the marks of English influence and the *lure of the *native experience".

# VOCABULARY

| | |
|---:|:---|
| car bomb | voiture piégée |
| chair (to) | présider |
| collapse | effondrement |
| concede (to) | concéder |
| covetous | avide, cupide |
| demonstration | manifestation |
| dreariness | monotonie |
| dub (to) | doubler |
| Easter Rising | soulèvement de Pâques |
| Home Rule | autonomie |
| intent on | déterminé |
| IRA (Irish Republican Army) | forces armées irlandaises |
| lure | attrait |
| MBE (Member of the British Empire) | distinction, décoration |
| native | nationale |
| outburst | éclat, déchaînement, explosion |
| outpost | bastion |
| oversee (to) | être témoin de |
| paratrooper | parachutiste |
| partition | séparation |
| petrol bomb | cocktail Molotov |
| pounding | frénétique, qui martèle |
| prejudice | préjugé |
| prevail (to) over | l'emporter sur |
| protracted | prolongé, qui traîne |
| Provisional IRA | IRA, IRA provisoire |
| rail (to) against | s'en prendre à |
| ransom | rançon |
| regard (to) | estimer |
| resentment | amertume, rancune |
| resent (to) | en vouloir à |
| retaliate (to) | répliquer, riposter |
| retaliation | représailles |
| scathing | acerbe, cinglant |
| settlement | colonie |
| spatter (to) | éclabousser |
| stand (to) for | représenter, signifier |
| starvation | famine |
| take (to) after | ressembler à |
| on the verge of | à la limite de, au bord de |
| be wrecked (to) | faire naufrage, échouer |

# Focus...

- **Chronology**
  - 432   Saint Patrick introduced Christianity to Ireland and the country developed into a centre of Gaelic and Latin learning. Irish monasteries acted as universities attracting intellectuals from all over Europe.
  - 1171   Henry II became Lord of Ireland but local rule endured for centuries.
  - 1690   King James II and his French supporters were defeated by the Protestant King James II at the Battle of Boyne.
  - 1801   Act of Union between England and Ireland which became the United Kingdom of Great Britain and Ireland.
  - 1846   The Great Potato Famine was the peak of the steady decline of the Irish economy. Roughly a million people died of *starvation and fever, even more left for North America.
  - 1869   Disestablishment of the Church of Ireland.
  - 1907   Foundation of Sinn Fein.
  - 1922   Ratification of the Anglo-Irish Treaty.
  - 1937   The Constitution changed the name of the nation to Eire.
  - 1949   Ireland Act (cession of the six counties with the consent of the Parliament of Northern Ireland).
  - 1955   The Republic of Ireland was admitted to the United Nations.
  - 1973   Like Britain, Ireland joined the European Economic Community.
  - 1990   Mary Robinson was elected the republic's first woman president in the presidential election.
  - 1992   Irish voters approved the Maastricht treaty by a large majority in a referendum.
  - 1993   The Irish and British governments signed a joint peace initiative.
  - 1997   Mary McAleese became the President.
  - 2001   Treaty of Nice rejected.

- **Political parties in the Republic of Ireland**
  - Fianna Fail (FF) was founded in 1926. It is the party of government for Ireland since it is the youngest party. Its main figure was Eamon de Valera. The party and the leader assumed power in 1932 and were to hold it for most of the next four decades. Sean Lemass was the second leader of Fianna Fail.

- Fine Gael (FG) was founded in Dublin in April 1923. The party emphasized liberalism and pluralism.
- The Irish Labour Party is the oldest party in Ireland. No national election was fought by Labour until 1922. It was four years in government in the 1980s.
- The Democratic Left was made up of the official IRA and the *Provisional IRA. The former was socialist/revolutionary, the latter had nothing of that communist expression. In 1970, Sinn Fein, the political wing of the IRA emerged.
- The Irish Greens: the Green Party has existed in Ireland since 1981 and scored its first victory in the 1989 election.

◆ **Northern Ireland Representation in the House of Commons (June 2001)**

| Party | Seats |
|---|---|
| Ulster Unionist | 6 |
| Social Democratic & Labour | 3 |
| Democratic Unionist | 5 |
| Sinn Fein (the members have not taken their seats) | 4 |

Northern Ireland elects 18 Members of Parliament (MPs) to the House of Commons and, by proportional representation, 3 of the 87 UK representatives to the European Parliament (MPEs).

# Essay

A SONG by John LENNON

**Commentary of "Sunday Bloody Sunday"**

> "You anglo pigs and scotties
> Sent to colonize the North
> You wave your bloody Union Jack
> And you know what it's worth !
> How dare you hold to *ransom
> A people proud and free
> Keep Ireland for the Irish
> Put the English back to sea."

*This is the third stanza of a protest song John Lennon wrote a few days after the event which took place on Sunday January 30th, 1972. Catholic Bogside turned into a battlefield, with the "confrontation in mass between the Catholic populace and the Army" as read* The Times. *The \*prejudice of the Catholics against the regime, their \*resentment of the ban on processions and parades for a year by the Orange organizations inflamed their hatred of the British Army. Hooligan elements took over and soldiers found it hard to keep control. Bloody Sunday represented a massive propaganda victory for the Provisional IRA.*

*John Lennon, who had Irish origins, was absolutely outraged. He had previously been involved in Peace movements, and in 1969 he returned his \*MBE in protest at British involvement in the Nigerian War. Then he left Great Britain to settle in New York City where his anti-establishment attitude provoked a four-year wrangle for his "green card".*

*Lennon carries on with an insulting tone in the third stanza with the words "pigs" and "scotties" which refer to the settlers who came from England and Scotland at the time when the Plantation of Ulster started in the 17th century. Ireland's history over the last 300 years is one of a \*protracted struggle for land. The song comments upon Irish nationalism and the violent opposition to British hegemony. Ireland has always fought for land and power.*

*The plantation of Ulster opened a period in which the Protestant English gentry confiscated land and \*oversaw a massive influx of*

*Scottish settlers. There was a lot of violence between the Anglo-Scottish settlers and the native Irish inhabitants.*

*Then he directly attacks the symbol of Britain: its flag, the Union Jack. The adjective "bloody" refers to the blood stains it is \*spattered with and the blood people shed for its sake, but it is also a \*scathing insult applied to the values it \*stands for. Lennon is really revolted and resents the lack of liberty of the Irish people, \*railing against the British with the shout "How dare you...!" which stands on the \*verge of a threat. He advocates a very primitive reaction to solve the problem: "Put the English back to sea", just as if they were invaders, reminding us of the Spanish who were \*wrecked on the coast after the defeat of the Armada by the troops of Elizabeth I...*

*The whole song underlines that the nationalists were \*intent on independence from Britain. Indeed, the Republic of Ireland which came into existence with the 1948 Republic of Ireland Act has never proved a satisfactory creation. In the last stanza of the song John Lennon goes as far as comparing Belfast to "concentration camps" emphasizing the lack of communication between the two communities who are aliens to each other. Consequently the English are held responsible for the division and the war, they are viewed as enemies and unlawful invaders. There is no room in Ireland for whoever is not Irish. Lennon clearly asserts that the war in Northern Ireland is a colonial war and Ireland the last \*outpost of the British Empire. In view of the present situation, thirty years of continuous fight have proved there is no solution and terrorism is gradually \*prevailing over the peace negotiations. As a matter of fact, in early March 2001 a car bomb exploded in front of the BBC television centre in West London.*

*When John Lennon wrote this song, he was \*taking after Bob Dylan and other American singers who protested against the Vietnam war and a dehumanized and \*covetous society. This new trend of protest song became quite popular and was meant to arouse people's awareness and indignation all over the western world. He voiced his anger using provocative words, a \*pounding music beat and an aggressive tone in order to reach out to the heads of state.*

# 11     Higher Education

*Sophie Loussouarn*

The higher education sector is now, thanks to the 1988 Education Act, much easier to define. It is made up mainly of the universities and colleges of higher education which lead to degree level and beyond this to Ph.D and D.Phil. level. Higher education has been brought more firmly under the authority of central government. On the one hand, Britain's 80 universities still enjoy a great deal of academic freedom in selecting their own students, defining their courses, awarding their degrees and recruiting their staff, but they depend on the government for funding. On the other hand, colleges of higher education offer a truly public sector alternative and have become free-standing statutory corporations. As for higher education students, they receive some financial support from their local education authority.

In the past, access to higher education was too restricted, but there are six times as many young people going on to higher education now as in the early 1960s. In 2000, Britain sent 35% of young people to university compared to 14% in 1987. In 1998, almost 190,000 students graduated from universities in England, over 100% more than in 1985. Besides, men have been outnumbered for some years in British higher education, and in 2001, 54% of the applications for university were from women.

## *British universities*

British universities have a tradition of elitism and excellence, in spite of the considerable differences which exist between them owing to the historical circumstances of their birth.

The universities of Oxford and Cambridge date back to the thirteenth and fourteenth centuries and are among the best universities in the world. They are and have always been the institutions at the top of the educational hierarchy. They attract many of the brightest students of their generation and award the most prestigious certificates. The two universities share the same ideology and have the authority to make authoritative statements about values. They are the main universities of the elite and shape a homogeneous group with a common cultural identity rooted in the idea of a liberal education centred on the arts and humanities. Scientific and technical studies are disparaged. Indeed, the Establishment is mostly interested in finance and administration.

The teaching at Oxford and Cambridge is based on the *tutorial system (the *don teaches one or two students, sometimes more) and the *academic year is divided into three terms. Oxford has 38 colleges and Cambridge has 31 colleges and the colleges have separate legal identities.

The Congregation in Oxford and the Regent House in Cambridge wield control and are the guardians of the constitutions of their universities. The two universities remain in control of their own government machinery and are governed by their scholars through a range of committees. Since 1945, the two universities have expanded, but there has been a feeling that Oxbridge colleges should not grow too much for fear of destroying the idea of a college as a small and intimate community. Moreover, the balance between teaching and research has *shifted in favour of research so that by 1960 it had become one of the leading centres of research and the number of postgraduates had increased. Oxford and Cambridge compete with each other in the academic field and are institutions where the future leading politicians and civil servants used to go to learn the proper sociocultural values and form the right social ties. Eight of the last ten prime ministers went to Oxford. Three out of four senior judges went to Oxford or Cambridge. Two out of three of the most senior civil servants are Oxbridge graduates.

Unlike the English universities, Scottish ones have blended high learning and class-consciousness. Among the Scottish top 10 are Edinburgh founded in 1583, St Andrews founded in 1410, Glasgow founded in 1451 and Aberdeen founded in 1495.

Apart from Durham, founded in 1832, the nineteenth-century universities are very different from Oxbridge and are known as "redbrick" universities.

London University was founded in 1836 to provide university education for young people who could not attend Oxford or Cambridge because they did not belong to the Anglican higher classes.

At the end of the 1950s, new universities appeared to *accommodate the increasing number of students. And in the following decade, the Wilson government created other universities and launched the Open Universities which were meant for mature students who followed correspondence courses. Open Universities widened access to higher education for adults between twenty-five and forty-five and provided an opportunity for life-long education.

## Polytechnics and Colleges of Higher Education

According to the 1988 Reform, the 30 *polytechnics and 65 Colleges of Higher Education became statutory corporations funded by the Polytechnics and Colleges Funding Council.

Polytechnics date back to the 1960s and were created by the Labour government to meet the increasing demand for vocational, professional and industrially based courses in higher education. They were funded with generosity and developed with an enthusiasm which higher education would never see again. They filled the gap between university and further education work and placed an equal emphasis on academic and practical work, bearing in mind the needs of industry. Thus the expansion of higher education in the 1960s took place in the framework of the newly created binary system with universities remaining as autonomous bodies established by royal charter and the polytechnics developing as the highest level institutions within the public sector controlled and financed by the local authorities. Polytechnics were entitled to grant degrees and to take postgraduates for Ph.Ds, but they were often seen as the second best in higher education. They offered a wide range of courses in keeping with their vocational role, among which business and administration were the most popular, followed by engineering and technology, arts, science and social studies, *let alone agriculture for a minority of students. But the polytechnics were reworked by the Conservative government by the 1992 Act. This allowed polytechnics to change their titles to universities.

Unlike polytechnics which prepared for business, industry, engineering and technology, Colleges of Higher Education lead to socially-oriented professions, ranging from teacher training to the caring professions, art and design, the media and public administration. Most of the students of the Colleges of Higher Education were young women studying on a small campus of two to five thousand students in a rural setting.

This considerable expansion in higher education was intended to ensure that opportunities for higher education would be spread more representatively among the population, especially the working classes.

## The future development of higher education in a learning society

Higher education has a major contribution to make to lifelong learning and the Dearing Report stressed the need to widen access to include those who have traditionally been under-represented in universities.

On July 23rd, 1997, the National Committee of Inquiry released a report entitled Higher Education in the Learning Society which underlined the prominent role of higher education in the development of people, society and the economy. Blair's government *endorses the need to extend opportunities for lifelong learning to ensure that people are equipped with the skills and knowledge required to respond to the technological changes of our age. According to the report, higher education is meant to enable individuals to develop their capabilities to the highest levels throughout life, to increase knowledge and understanding, to serve the needs of the economy and to play a major role in shaping a democratic, civilised and inclusive society.

Blair's government wants all who can benefit from it to have the opportunity to carry on to higher education. The Government now has a goal of enabling 50% of the population to enter higher education and does not want higher education to depend upon ability to pay. £8 billion of public funds will be devoted to supporting higher education. In particular, many students should benefit from part-time degree courses. Solving this requires hard choices, but a more efficient system of funding, a fairer system for repaying *loans, together with *fees for better-off parents, has meant more students than ever before are now going into higher education.

# Vocabulary

| | |
|---|---|
| academic (adj./n) | universitaire |
| accommodate (to) | loger, recevoir |
| allegedly | prétendument |
| apply for (to) | poser sa candidature |
| BA degree | licence ès lettres |
| BSc degree | licence ès science |
| bursary | bourse d'études |
| decry (to) | dénigrer, décrier |
| don | professeur |
| drop out (to) | abandonner |
| dropout | étudiant qui abandonne ses études |
| endorse sth (to) | appuyer, souscrire à |
| fall headlong (to) | tomber la tête la première |
| fees | frais de scolarité |
| fellow | chargé de cours |
| first | diplôme avec mention très bien |
| graduate school (US) | troisième cycle |
| grant | allocation d'études |
| lecture | conférence |
| lecturer | maître de conférences |
| let alone | sans compter |
| liberal arts | lettres et sciences humaines |
| loan (student –) | prêt, emprunt |
| major in (to) | se spécialiser en |
| MA degree | maîtrise ès lettres |
| MSc degree | maîtrise ès sciences |
| pass (to) an exam | être reçu à un examen |
| Ph.D./D Phil | thèse |
| polytechnics | institut professionnel d'enseignement technique |
| postgraduate | étudiant en thèse |
| research | recherche |
| self-educated | autodidacte |
| seminar | séminaire |
| shift (to) | changer |
| sit (to) an exam | passer, subir un examen |
| spark (to) off | déclencher |
| tuition | instruction, enseignement |
| tutorial | travaux dirigés |
| undergraduate | étudiant qui prépare sa licence |
| vocational training | formation professionnelle |
| wield (to) control | exercer le contrôle |

# Focus...

The average *tuition cost at Oxford amounts to £6,000 a year compared with the £14,000 fees of top American universities.

Britain now sends 35% of young people to university, which is more than the American rate of 30%.

50% of the students at Oxbridge come from private schools.

54% of the applications for university places in 2001 were from women.

In 2000, David Blunkett, the Education and Employment Secretary announced a £68 million package which included £17 million for non-repayable bursaries for mature students.

◆ **The public school system**

> Boarding schools pave the way to Oxford and Cambridge. They are great British traditions which flourished as institutions designed to instil virtues of independence, self-reliance and physical vigour. The most famous public schools for boys are Eton, Harrow, Westminster, Winchester, Rugby and St Paul's. But since the 1960s, the boarding school has been the target of ridicule.
>
> In 1999, there were only 73,000 children going to boarding school owing to the high tuition fees and to changes in lifestyles. Indeed, some schools charge over £15,000 a year and more and more parents want to see more of their children.

◆ **A criticism of the Oxbridge system**

> "Teachers have argued for centuries about whether the primary function of education is incarceration or self-development. Oxbridge's unique achievement has been to combine the worst aspects of both models.
>
> The do-it-yourself degree may have been the perfect system for the intellectual development of Newton, Wordsworth and Asquith, but the complete absence of regulation, training and external supervision of lecturing, tutoring or student welfare today seems like self-development gone mad. For the lucky few who are very bright, self-assured and provided with a decent tutor, the system continues to work miracles."
>
> (*New Statesman*, 16th October, 1998)

Civilisation britannique

### ◆ Open Universities

Open Universities were launched in 1966, using distance-learning methods to offer higher education to those who had missed out earlier in life. It meant to serve the needs of adults for part-time study to degree level by the new and adventurous means of using television and radio as principal teaching media. Some mocked the Open University as a glorified correspondence college. It was also a brilliantly original institution which took the ideals of social equality and equality of opportunity more seriously than any other part of the British education system. It provided a means for anti-university governments to meet the demands of graduates on the cheap.

# Essay

**Is British Higher Education elitist or meritocratic?**

*British higher education has changed a lot since the 1960s and the number of students who register for university has increased. But competition for university places in 2001 looks like being slightly less intense than in recent years, although popular courses in the leading institutions are still certain to be oversubscribed. Britain offers a wide range of universities and colleges which has improved access to learning opportunities. Oxford and Cambridge, arguably, offer the best education and they dominate the controlling positions in the civil service, the law, banking and the media. Hence the assault on Oxbridge elitism. Apart from the exclusive education of Oxbridge, does British higher education aim at a meritocracy with equal opportunities?*

*Oxford and Cambridge are \*allegedly elitist and the system is often criticized as undemocratic, since many of the most cherished positions in British society are occupied by Oxbridge graduates. The two finest British universities have a magic of their own which has fascinated students and writers throughout the centuries. But how fair is the recruiting system? Does the competitive atmosphere of the Oxbridge system enable self-development? Do the students really benefit from the three years of elite undergraduate education? Can the students who graduate from those exclusive universities remain in touch with the rest of the population?*

*The admission procedures have often been criticized because admissions are controlled by colleges rather than the universities. Applications are made to individual colleges, some of which favour state school applicants while others are more traditional. The fairness of the college entrance examination has been questioned and there has been criticism of the Oxbridge admissions lottery. In June 2000, Laura Spence, a brilliant student from an ordinary comprehensive school in the north-east of England failed to secure a place at Magdalen College, Oxford, to study medicine. This \*sparked off a national controversy, and Laura Spence was, subsequently, accepted by Harvard, one of America's elite universities. Gordon Brown, the Chancellor of the Exchequer, decried the selection process, which tends to favour privately-educated students. Even though Oxford and Cambridge have tried to widen access in abolishing their entrance exams and in selecting their students by interview, this process has been viewed as more class-biased.*

*The social composition of Oxbridge students has also been under attack. Half of Oxbridge students come from public schools, but the* number of students from state schools is rising and ethnic minorities are also well represented. Social background still matters and class is a major determinant of educational achievement.

There is no denying that the function of the Oxbridge system is the preservation of elite power. It has an image of academic excellence and remains unequalled in terms of prestige. But, the competitive atmosphere of Oxbridge can cause clinical depression and eating disorders and some students even *drop out.

Access to higher education remains unequal on account of underfunding. The tuition fees for British universities are high and participation in higher education by socio-economic groups D and E is still less than half that of groups A to C. In spite of the availability of *grants and loans, students from poorer backgrounds continue to be seriously under-represented in higher education. If most full-time undergraduate students resident in the UK received their higher education tuition free of charge from 1989 to 1995, in further education many part-time students are charged a fee which covers a quarter of the costs of the course.

The Blair government has announced a series of measures to promote meritocracy in British higher education, thanks to non-repayable bursaries for mature students and increased loans for maintenance related to parental income. The funding of students will enable all students to develop their full intellectual and personal potential.

Nevertheless the recruitment of students in British higher education has become more meritocratic in the past twenty years and the number of students has risen. If the students of British universities are more likely to have been educated in British public-schools, there are also some overseas students from Hong Kong and Malaysia, as well as from China. Ethnic minorities have made striking educational advances in higher education. Young Asian and black people make up 12% of all full-time students aged 16 to 25, although they represent 8% of this age group. More students from ethnic minorities are now applying and entering higher education and achieving degree-level qualifications. In 1997, they made up 12.8% of all first year students in UK universities.

The platform for 2001 drafted by David Blunkett was definitely aiming at excellence from primary school to higher education. The government has insisted on the value of lifelong education and on the improvement brought about by the introduction of the web in open universities. Higher education should strike a balance between elitism and meritocracy. As Tony Blair pointed out "Higher education is the best economic policy there is. And it is in the marriage of education and technology that the future lies."

# MORE ABOUT...
## ...OPEN UNIVERSITIES

### A FILM REVIEW
### EDUCATING RITA

The film *Educating Rita* was produced in 1983 by Lewis Gilbert after the play by Willy Russell. The setting of the play was in a university in the North of England in the 1980s, at a time when the Open University was developing and making higher education available via radio and television to hundreds and thousands of people who had previously imagined that such an education belonged exclusively to an elite. It showed the transformation of a barely educated hairdresser into an articulate graduate and portrays the excitement of someone making her first contact with the world of ideas and literature.

The film is a comedy verging on drama, and a character-study of a twenty-seven year old middle-class hairdresser and housewife and an older literature professor who suffers from low self-esteem and is a whisky addict. Much to the annoyance of her husband, before having children, Rita would like to escape mediocrity and improve her condition through learning, "to change from the inside" as she keeps repeating. She enrolls on an Open University literature course and every night after work goes to College to meet her tutor Frank. Gradually Rita is transformed from a naïve, ignorant, ordinary girl to a devoted, conscientious, learned student able to advise even criticize her tutor at the end of the film. All along her journey through knowledge, the spectator experiences her determination, her enthusiasm, and follows her progress to self-achievement. Whenever she discovers something new, she reacts with her unflinching common sense, or is overbrimming with uncontrolled joy. For instance, an assonance is "to get the rhyme wrong", discovering *Macbeth* at the theatre is a source of exhilaration, till the day when poetry, Blake's *Songs of Innocence* and *Songs of Experience* in particular, have no mystery for her, to Frank's amazement. Her struggle is a long fight against her tutor who first refuses to coach her, then against her husband who goes as far as burning her books. Gradually the girl who was laughed at imposes herself. The hairdresser becomes a barmaid in a bistro to be in contact with interesting people who can "talk about what matters instead of irrelevant rubbish". She changes her name back to Susan to sound more proper and she also tries to change her look, in order to have what "they" have. Her route through education has led her from nothingness to self-fulfilment, in her true belief that culture is a "stepladder to the stars". She finally passes her degree with distinction. In her quest for self-respect she has made difficult choices, found values to live by, proved to herself and to others who she was.

The film is a tribute to the Open University which has worked a miracle on an ordinary girl. Both can be proud of themselves as she concludes, when she sees Frank off at the airport.

The cinematographic devices are in keeping with the plot, simple, relevant and telling. The film opens up in a conventional, stuffy atmosphere enlightened by lively music and ends on the wide open horizon of an airport hall which can anticipate the boundless opportunities of her future. It quivers with life and the scenery sets off the locations which must look like paradise in the eyes of Rita. The beauty of Trinity College, Dublin, where the film was shot is enhanced by the round-the-season rhythm: summers flow in full bloom, winters ebb under the snow in a romantic atmosphere pervading the whole campus, meant to contrast with the dull, dreary and grimy streets of the city. It is just as if culture wafted magic to alleviate the gloom of life. The contrast is also emphasized by the low-angle shots often used to show the almighty professor and the high-angle shots used to show Rita, overwhelmed by the situation, as if she were the underdog crushed by the superiority of the *academics. The situation gradually reverses and both Susan and Frank are shown on an equal footing at the end. Susan has gained the dignity of a woman who has made her choices with a will and mastered her own fate. On the contrary, the professor yields to his own passion, alcohol, and he is his own victim. He is finally sacked and sent to Australia.

The whole film is another illustration of Pygmalion as the professor transforms his student who in the end excels him and even despises him, as her words testify: "You might have started reforming yourself". His is a bookish knowledge which does not help him understand humanity or express his feelings; hers is a knowledge about life and herself. Learning has freed her, enabled her to help other victims of society and made her able to "sing a better song", through the relationship between a pupil and her teacher and the pupil's development from dependence to independence. Wider issues are raised about social class, lifestyle, women's rights, educational opportunity and the quality of education.

The film was previewed at the Open University on April 29th, 1983.

# 12 Sports in Britain

*Sophie Loussouarn*

Sport plays a very important part in the social, political and economic life of Britain. Sports clubs exist at the very heart of middle-class and working-class communities and there are now about 150,000 in Britain. Britain is involved in the Olympic Games and in the Commonwealth Games and there are numerous competitions such as the Wimbledon lawn tennis championships and the Grand National steeplechase which attract foreign athletes. There are also other sporting events such as the famous Boat Race, as well as Henley Regatta and Royal Ascot which are part of the season. In the 19th century, sport was part and parcel of the public-school curriculum (rowing, rugby), to teach discipline and excellence in keeping with tradition, but *games were only formally introduced in state schools in 1944 (football).

## The various types of sport

Sport has always been linked to class and class background has an impact on the kinds of sport people pursue. It was originally a leisure activity for gentlemen, later on, in the 1920s, women took to it as a means of keeping *fit.

Fox-hunting and shooting have always been an aristocratic sport which became organized and commercial in the eighteenth-century. It was a way of life and adventurous and energetic gentlemen liked this past-time. It was mainly fox-hunting: a Georgian invention. But recently, fox-hunting has been criticised by public opinion for its cruelty. It is even threatened by the law, the House of Commons have banned it, taking advantage of the outbreak of foot-and-mouth disease. Nevertheless the Lords oppose the ban.

Some sports were invented by the British.

Angling is one of the most popular British sports and there are numerous fishing clubs in England, Wales, Scotland and Northern Ireland.

Badminton was named after the country home of the Duke of Beaufort, Badminton House, where the sport was first played in the nineteenth century. Badminton today is the home of three-day eventing.

British bowls, whether it be lawn or indoor bowls, is very popular in international championships.

The rules of boxing were established by the Marquess of Queensberry in 1865 and it has become both an amateur and professional sport.

Cricket is a British institution and is part of the English boy's curriculum, but it is also played at girls' schools and in colleges and universities. It is based on rules laid down by the Marylebone Cricket Club (MCC) which was founded in 1787. In the eighteenth century, cricket was played by aristocrats. The three great matches of Eton vs Harrow, Oxford vs Cambridge and Gentlemen vs Players have become annual events. Playing roles were divided into professional bowlers (mostly working class) and amateur batsmen (gentlemen players).

Rowing is very dependent on class and is still associated with Oxford and Cambridge as well as Eton. The boats are single, pairs, fours and eights. The University Boat Race takes place on the Thames between eight-*oared *crews from Oxford and Cambridge. The Henley Regatta attracts crews from all over the world each July.

Rugby was named after the public school of Rugby where it originated in the first half of the 19th century. The professional game is governed by the Rugby Football League, while the amateur game is governed by the British Amateur Rugby League Association.

Squash was invented at Harrow school in the 1850s and about 2 million people play squash in the UK.

Swimming appeared as a competitive sport in the eighteenth century and has become the most popular sport, ever since. King George III's children were taken to the seaside by their governesses every summer. The Amateur Swimming Association co-ordinates the selection of teams.

Lawn Tennis was introduced from France ("longue paume") but the modern game of tennis dates back to 1873. It became a sport for ladies and gentlemen alike which enabled sociable mixed play. It was played in boys' boarding-schools and in girls' boarding-schools. For tennis, Wimbledon, which dates back to 1877, is the most exclusive club competition.

But working-class sport flourished in the nineteenth century. Cycling developed as a non-competitive sport.

Road and track racing, motocross and mountain bikes, together with soccer and snooker are working-class sports par excellence as they are cheap and easy to practise. Pigeon and grey-hound racing should also be mentioned, and the Queen herself has a stable of racing-pigeons.

### Sport and violence

Football is often associated with violence on the pitches. So restrictions on the use of violence were introduced as early as the late 19th century and sports rules decreased the violent content of sports. But certain sports remained violent, such as hockey, basketball and football.

Football hooliganism developed in the 1960s and it is known as the English disease. The term became applied to soccer fans after a series of incidents which took place in English and Scottish soccer stadiums. It is nothing new since it originated in 1921 when fans of Arsenal and Tottenham Hotspur tried to kill the referee. In the 1930s, the public disapproved of the invasion of the soccer field and of attacks on players and the police. Then violence calmed down from 1945 to 1960. Hooliganism seems particularly prevalent in England because of local rivalry between fans of opposing football teams.

Hooliganism was localized in Britain at first and it was exported by the groups of fans following

British teams. But hooliganism became militarized in the 1980s. As a consequence, there was a ban on alcohol in football stadiums in 1985.

The main reason which accounts for violence in sport is that more money began to circulate in British soccer. This money mainly came from satellite TV rights or lottery funding which had a great impact on cash-starved British sports. Furthermore, there is a *knock-on effect between the observation of aggression on the soccer field and hostility on the part of the spectators. Many youngsters are satisfying their need for stimulation through fan violence.

### *Sport as a means of integration*

Sport has been used as a means of social integration. Sports such as cycling and rambling were proposed as a means of social reform at the end of the 19th century. Various sports were also organized by the working classes from 1920 onwards as the number of working hours decreased. Football and cricket were means of integrating the working classes and turning them into healthy people.

Furthermore, sport is also a means of integrating ethnic minorities. Many athletes from the British Commonwealth have taken part in national as well as international sporting events and have won medals in the Olympic Games as well as at the national level in football, cricket, boxing and athletics. The Blair government has tried to ban racism from football grounds and has encouraged more Asian players into the game. In cricket, numerous players from Commonwealth countries such as Viv Richards, Imran Khan and Brian Lara have taken part in competitions.

Age, ethnic background and region are criteria in the access to sport. Sport has been used as a unifying force at the local and at the national level. But British sport has also played a part in the development of sport at the international level. Several sporting events have taken place in Britain, ranging from the British Open in golf to the Wimbledon Championships. Sports played a part in cementing the Empire before 1945 and afterwards were important for the Commonwealth with the organization of the Commonwealth Games.

# VOCABULARY

| | |
|---|---|
| available | disponible |
| bid (to) | faire une offre |
| breed (to) | engendrer, entrainer |
| bribery | corruption |
| bring (to) about | causer, entraîner |
| bung (slang) | bakchich |
| coaching | entraînement |
| conviction | condamnation |
| compel (to) | contraindre, obliger |
| compulsion | contrainte |
| crew | équipage |
| damage (to) | endommager, ternir |
| disabled people | handicapés |
| excel (to) oneself | se surpasser |
| fairness | impartialité, équité, justice |
| keep (to) fit | garder la forme |
| forefront | premier plan |
| games | les sports |
| horse-riding | équitation |
| incentive | encouragement, stimulation |
| induce | persuader |
| knock-on effect | répercussions |
| oar | rame, aviron |
| pave (to) the way for/to | préparer le terrain, ouvrir la voie |
| pitch | terrain (football) |
| pool | billard |
| prevail (to) over | l'emporter sur, prévaloir |
| rambling | randonnée |
| resort (to) | recourir à |
| rowing | aviron |
| rugger | rugby |
| ruthlessness | détermination |
| self-esteem | amour propre, respect de soi |
| single-mindedness | résolution, constance |
| snooker | billard |
| solidify (to) | consolider, forger |
| be (to) at stake | être en jeu |
| steeplechase | course d'obstacles |
| supersede (to) | supplanter, remplacer |
| training | entraînement, formation |
| trial | procès |
| urge | incitation |
| wheelchair | chaise roulante |

# Focus...

| | |
|---|---|
| 1751 | Foundation of the Jockey Club |
| 1787 | Foundation of the Marylebone Cricket Club |
| 1857 | Foundation of the Alpine Club |
| 1885 | Foundation of the Football Association (FA) |
| 1871 | Foundation of the Rugby Football Union |
| 1875 | Formation of the Yacht Racing Association |
| 1879 | Formation of the Irish Rugby Union |
| 1881 | Formation of the Welsh Football Union |
| 1893 | Foundation of the Ladies' Golf Union |
| 1907 | Ladies' Alpine Club founded |
| 1948 | The Olympic Games held in London |
| 1969 | Foundation of the Women's Football Association |
| 1975 | The first Cricket World Cup |
| 1986 | Foundation of the Women's Amateur Rugby League Association |

◆ **Participation in the most popular sports in Great Britain in 1996 (people aged over 16)**

| | Men | Women |
|---|---|---|
| Walking | 49 % | 41 % |
| *Snooker/*pool | 20 % | 4 % |
| Cycling | 15 % | 8 % |
| Indoor swimming | 11 % | 15 % |
| Soccer | 10 % | |
| Keeping fit/Yoga | | 17 % |

A **"Sports Cabinet"** was created in 1998 to identify priorities for sport, headed by the Secretary of State for Culture, Media and Sport; it concerns England, Wales, Scotland and Northern Ireland. Its objective is to:
- improve access to facilities and to better *coaching
- achieve better health through sport

Civilisation britannique

- improve sporting performance
- maximise the potential of sport in order to create wealth and employment.

All distributing bodies of Lottery funding are to ensure that applicants incorporate access and availability for *disabled people.

The Government also wishes to improve facilities for disabled spectators (*wheelchair spaces offering an unobstructed view of the *pitch).

After the Hillsborough Stadium disaster in 1989, when 96 spectators died, the Taylor Report required all clubs in the Premier League and those in the First Division of the Football League to have all-seater grounds, to complete the safety work required.

**Wembley Stadium** in London is to be relocated into a new 90,000 capacity all-seater national stadium for football, rugby league and athletics. It will cost around £475 million, £120 million of which will be provided from Lottery funding. It will bid to host the 2006 football World Cup and other major sporting events.

**An Ethics and Anti-Doping Directorate** coordinates a drug-testing programme and an education programme aimed at changing attitudes to drug misuse. UK Sport provides a Drug Information Line to allow athletes to check whether a medication is permitted or banned. The UK is at the forefront of work to establish a new Internatonal Anti-Doping Agency.

# Essay

Comment upon the following sentence:

"Money is the most apparent of extrinsic rewards and as sports have become increasingly professional, so hard currency has become more important as a motivating force."

*The development of professional sport in the late nineteenth century introduced extrinsic motivations. Yet throughout the twentieth century, most players were in the game not for the love of the game, but for the love of money that it \*breeds. Professional sportsmen and women are unquestionably motivated by money. All the players in major professional sports are relatively well-paid. Money may keep on providing a stimulus for aspiring athletes, but other kinds of reward structures must be found.*

*Money is a great \*incentive for players. Sports athletes are rewarded by huge sums of money and money arouses their enthusiasm and their persistence to stick to a gruelling training programme. The extrinsic reward of sportsmen is the tangible dividends made \*available by sports organisations. At the beginning of his career, a sportsman wishes to earn money to satisfy his needs, once he has satisfied his need for security with a multimillion dollar contract, he will be motivated by the \*compulsion to win on and on and the \*urge of \*self-esteem.*

*But there are other motivating forces. Relatives of sportsmen play an essential part in the motivation of athletes. Indeed the desire for recognition and adulation plays an important part. Personal accomplishment \*compelling an athlete to \*excel himself is a strong motivation as well.*

*This is what is illustrated in the Oscar-winning film* Chariots of Fire *(1981). It introduces the spectator to two British athletes training for the 1924 Summer Olympics. One is a Jewish student at Oxford who considers that sport is a way of building and \*solidifying character. The other one is a Scottish working-class Christian who runs for the greater glory of God. A third competitor is the portrait of the vanishing English gentleman-amateur who doesn't show any \*single-mindedness or \*ruthlessness and shares his time between \*training and champagne. The Jewish student heralds a new type of athlete: the amateur who defies the amateur ethos disclosing his ambition when he avows that if he can't win, he won't run.*

*Sport is also full of stories of great athletes motivated by seemingly inhuman desires to succeed. Let us remember the idealistic notion of Pierre de Coubertin, founder of the modern Olympic Games: "the main thing is not to have won, but to have fought well". "Citius, altius, fortius" might \*induce athletes to reach the limits of human performance, \*resorting to drugs to go beyond, to reach out for the "pot of gold". \*Fairness is then at \*stake, cheating has corrupted the very practice of sport, in order to make more and more money out of sport, and so business transactions have gradually \*superseded the ideal of sport. Market norms now \*prevail over the rules, and \*bribery might guide competitors, coaches and managers as well, leading to the subversion of rules in trading players or negotiating contracts. Thus suspicions of misconduct in soccer's official Premier League led to a "\*bung" inquiry in September 1997, followed by a report which concluded that "bungs" had been offered but sport itself was not corrupt... The inquiry was followed by the \*trial of three players without any \*conviction ensuing, the players continued to play and the case \*paved the way for players to negotiate previously unheard-of salaries. Satellite contracts and merchandising as well as the importance of high-tech and high-cost science-based training programmes explain the fact that the amateur athlete can no longer compete on the same level as the professional as he could in the past owing to the lack of facilities. This explains tumbling world record performances.*

*Yet when athletes have reached their limits, they may lose their hunger and their motivation and run the risk of defeat and humiliation. But after all, sport implies the longing for victory together with the acceptance of defeat in a fair-play attitude.*

# 13 The eccentric – an English beast?

*Sarah Loom*

Any discussion of eccentricity of course begs the question: what exactly can be deemed "eccentric"? Let's put aside those habits, traits or traditions which any English person who travels abroad soon learns are the mockery of other countries (driving on the left or Englishmen who mow their lawn dressed in a smart shirt and tie etc) and instead look only at what the English *themselves* deem eccentric or strange, singular, capricious, curious, *quaint, *cranky, *kinky, *quirky, *queer, bizarre, *barmy, *bonkers, *weird, peculiar, odd, outlandish, idiosyncratic, anomalous, uncommon, unconventional, remarkable, *whimsical or *Pythonesque, to put it another way.

## First identify your subspecies

If we *peer through the bars, there are two main *exhibits in the eccentric zoo – the *retiring eccentric and his flamboyant cousin. The former, by definition a more difficult species to observe, manifests his rejection of norms in a number of ways. We could quote, for instance, the archetypal figure of the *shabbily-dressed English Lord in his *dingy uniform of *handed-down tweed and well-worn *brogues. Numerous stories (doubtless apocryphal) tell of naive American houseguests mistaking His Lordship for the gardener or the *odd-job man and haughtily ordering him to carry their suitcases…

Newspaper stories also abound of outwardly normal-looking little old ladies who break non-stop *hopscotch records in their free time, *stuffy bank managers who participate in the annual Maldon Mud Race and *staid solicitors who triumph in the World Bog-Snorkelling Championships. No-one in England is surprised when whole villages get together to roll cheeses, eat *nettles or stir up the biggest Christmas pudding in the world. The English don't so much as *bat an eyelid at the tradition of the Dunmow Flitch (mentioned in Chaucer, no less) – a side of bacon awarded every summer to the married couple who can convince a specially convened court that not a single *cross word has passed between them for a whole year.

If England is the home of the eccentric, then there's nothing more eccentric than an Englishman's home. If you're not convinced, then visit the modest Oxford terrace with a 25-foot fibreglass shark embedded in the roof, or even spend a weekend in the giant pineapple built in 1761. And if the Englishman's home is his castle (or fruit salad), then his garage can also be his aquarium – don't be shocked if you bump into Phil Vincent, who has transformed his Morris Minor into a massive pink lobster whose claws snap as he zooms along. You could always sit down and recover on Ed China's motorised armchair – with a pizza for a steering wheel and a top speed of 79mph. So many examples which prove that even outwardly conservative, *humdrum Englishmen often have an eccentric secret life. So why do they do it? Could it be, as John Stuart Mill claimed, that "the amount of eccentricity in a society has generally been proportional to the amount of genius, mental vigour and moral courage which it contained"?

## "I am not a number – I am a free man!"

The peculiar *antics of ostensibly "normal" citizens are perhaps typical of a wider tradition in England – that of freely expressing one's opinions, however bizarre, in public. Speakers' Corner in Hyde Park, where every Sunday *orange-box orators address, *harangue or simply bore anyone who cares to listen, typifies the tolerance traditionally extended by British law to opinions of every hue. In 1670, a jury refused to convict Quakers William Penn and William Mead for preaching ideas which went against state orthodoxy. More recently, a High Court judge overturned the 1997 conviction of two street-corner Christian Fundamentalist preachers, saying "The irritating, the *contentious, the eccentric, the heretical, the unwelcome and provocative have a right to be heard."

This tolerance extends to the way the English dress, and perhaps explains why England has traditionally been associated with numerous eccentric yet influential fashion styles. In the early seventies, Vivienne Westwood, Malcolm McLaren, the Sex Pistols and other leading lights of the nascent punk scene scandalised England's *chattering classes with their provocative clothes and aggressively anti-establishment brand of rock. In fact, the uniform of punk – shredded denim, slashed leather, ripped fishnets, safety pins and studs, coupled with a red, green or blue Mohican – actually became so standardised and easily recognisable that many English punks rejected the look as no longer being shocking enough. Pockets of punkdom remain to this day, particularly on the continent, but overseas tourists search London's Carnaby Street in vain for the "genuine article".

Punk style continues to influence British fashion designers in the 21st century, however, and fashion's resident eccentric, John Galliano, recently turned stuffy Christian Dior upside down with his ripped 'n zipped, *frayed 'n shredded haute couture reworking of punk. Such fashion flamboyance – the antithesis of the classic, cashmere good taste and silky sophistication of the French – is actually nothing new in the pantheon of English eccentricity. The image of the outrageously dressed Englishman is actually something of a tradition, from Oscar *"One should either be a work of art or wear a work of art"* Wilde via the Edwardian *dandy to Laurence Llewelyn-Bowen (the pink-suited presenter of the current hit TV decorating programme "Fantasy Rooms"). Even Winston Churchill had a velvet zoot suit!

"The dangerous and delightful desire of being different from others" (dixit Oscar Wilde) notwithstanding, such extravagant eccentricity is often more than mere affectation or ostentation. It can also be the materialisation of a deep-rooted desire to challenge people's preconceptions. Witness the late Quentin Crisp, who styled himself "England's stately homo" and is perhaps best known in England for his role as Elizabeth I in the film *Orlando*. Crisp's provocatively *foppish *attire was doubtless part of a calculated *bid to affirm and defend his homosexuality in staid post-war Britain. On another level Damien Hirst and Tracey Emin, those much-hyped darlings of the modern art scene, have attempted to confound bourgeois conceptions of art with their novel and iconoclastic works (overflowing *Brobdingnagian ash trays and dead sheep suspended in formaldehyde). Eccentricity can even be found in the *hallowed halls of Westminster around election time – see "Portrait of an English Eccentric", page 136.

### Literary wild canons

However, eccentricity in England is nowhere more at home than in the established tradition of nonsense literature, as typified by Edward Lear's rhymes and Lewis Carroll's *Jabberwocky*. In *Through the Looking Glass*, Alice discovers a strange poem entitled *Jabberwocky* which is written in "looking-glass language" [i.e. you have to hold the words up to a mirror in order to read them] and declares it "*rather* hard to understand". Luckily Humpty Dumpty (the egg-shaped nursery rhyme character who falls off a wall – but that's another story…) is on hand to explain the tricky words like "rath" (a sort of green pig), "brillig" (four o'-clock in the afternoon, of course) and "toves" (creatures something like *badgers, something like lizards and something like corkscrews?!). Although nonsense is often classified as children's literature, certain nonsense neologisms have entered mainstream English, and postmodernist authors such as James Joyce and T. S. Eliot certainly owe a debt to the tradition. Modern literary eccentrics include the humorist, poet and actor Spike Milligan whose rhymes in the pure nonsense tradition are much loved by English children and ex-children, also known as "adults".

### Mad dogs and Englishmen…

*Ludicrousness and absurdity have filtered down from 19th-century nonsense literature to the world of comedy – we could quote the world-famous Monty Python team or Rowan Atkinson's ubiquitous "Mr Bean" as classic examples of self-mocking English eccentricity. Much less well-known but arguably more influential were The Goons, whose silliness and facetious wit had post-war Britain in stitches. Unfortunately, such humour is not easily appreciated by anyone who is not a citizen of Her Majesty. Or to quote the English dictum "You don't have to be mad to live here, but it helps."

# VOCABULARY

| | |
|---|---|
| barmy, bonkers, cranky, outlandish, quaint, queer, quirky, weird, whimsical etc. | tous plus ou moins synonymes de bizarre ou excentrique |
| antics | bouffonneries, singeries |
| attire | les habits |
| badger | un blaireau |
| bat an eyelid (to) | broncher, sourciller |
| bid | une tentative |
| Brobdingnagian (adj.) | énorme, démesuré (de **Gulliver's Travels**, Jonathan Swift, 1735) |
| brogues | chaussures d'homme de style traditionnel |
| "chattering classes" | « intellos » |
| contentious | contesté, litigieux |
| cross/to have a cross word | fâché ; se fâcher, se disputer |
| the cut and thrust | les choses sérieuses, la réalité |
| dandy (from "jack-a-dandy"? C18th) | « dandy » (homme excessivement préoccupé par sa tenue vestimentaire) |
| deposit (hence a "deposit-loser") | le cautionnement à verser pour faire acte de candidature (une somme de £150, augmentée à £500 en partie à cause des Loonies !) |
| dingy | miteux |
| drab | terne, fade |
| exhibit | un objet exposé |
| foppish | dandy (de) |
| frayed | effiloché |
| fringe (adj.)/"lunatic fringe" | en marge ; les enragés, les cinglés du monde politique |
| hallowed | saint, sacré |
| handed-down/hand down (to)/ "hand-me-down" | vêtements d'occasion, récupérés des parents ou des frères ou sœurs aînés |
| harangue (to) | sermonner, haranguer |
| hopscotch | jeu d'enfant, similaire au jeu de la marelle |
| humdrum | monotone, banal |
| (raving) loony cf. the Monster Raving Loony Party | un fou (furieux) |
| ludicrous/ludicrousness | absurde ; l'absurdité |
| nettles | orties |
| odd-job man | homme à tout faire |
| orange-box orator | orateur amateur |
| peer (to) | regarder attentivement, scruter |
| Pythonesque | absurde (cf. les Monty Python) |
| retiring (adj.) | réservé |
| shabby/shabbily-dressed | pauvrement vêtu |
| staid/stuffy | sérieux, collet monté |

Civilisation britannique

# FOCUS...

## ◆ Examples of nonsense literature

**Lewis Carroll (1832 – 1898)**
***Jabberwocky* (first stanza)**
'Twas brillig, and the slithy toves
Did gyre and gimble in the wabe;
All mimsy were the borogoves,
And the mome raths outgrabe.

**Frank L. Warrin's translation**
***Le Jaseroque***
Il brilgue : les tôves lubricilleux
Se gyrent en vrillant dans le guave.
Enmîmés sont les gougebosqueux
Et le mômerade horsgrave.

**Edward Lear (1812 – 1888)**
**Limericks from *A Book of Nonsense* (1846)**

There was an Old Man of New York,
Who murdered himself with a fork.
But nobody cried,
– Though he very soon died -
For that silly Old Man of New York.

There was an Old Man with a beard,
Who said "It is just as I feared!
Two owls and a hen,
Four larks and a wren,
Have all built their nests in my beard."

**The Beatles (lyrics: John Lennon)**
***I am the walrus* (extract)**
Yellow matter custard dripping from a dead dog's eye.
Crabalocker fishwife pornographic
priestess boy you been a naughty girl,
you let your knickers down.
I am the eggman oh, they are the eggmen –
Oh I am the walrus. GOO GOO G'JOOB

**Spike Milligan (1918 – )**
***On the Ning Nang Nong***
On the Ning Nang Nong
Where the cows go Bong!
And the monkeys all say Boo!
There's a Nong Nang Ning
Where the trees go Ping!
And the teapots Jibber Jabber Joo.
On the Nong Ning Nang
All the mice go Clang!
And you just can't catch 'em when they do!
So it's Ning Nang Nong
Cows go Bong!
Nong Nang Ning
Trees go Ping!
Nong Ning Nang
The mice go Clang!
What a noisy place to belong,
Is the Ning Nang Ning Nang Nong!

***Hamlet***
Said Hamlet to Ophelia,
"I'll do a sketch of thee,
What kind of pencil shall I use,
2B or not 2B?"

***Rain***
There are holes in the sky
Where the rain gets in,
But they're ever so small
That's why rain is thin.

Civilisation britannique

# Essay

## Portrait of an Eccentric

Perennial *deposit-losers in British elections since the 1970s, the "Monster Raving *Loony Party" was led by the flamboyant figure of "Screaming Lord Sutch" until his death in 1998. The self-styled "Lord" Sutch, with his manic grin and customary leopard-skin top hat, stood for parliament 39 times and forfeited almost £100,000 in lost deposits and campaign expenses in the process. Sceptics may dismiss such a colourful figure as an irrelevant eccentric or, worse, as an out and out lunatic, but Sutch and his party did in fact arguably influence British politics. In May 1990, for instance, the Loonies polled 418 votes compared the Social Democrats' 155 votes. Sutch's offer of a Loony – Social Democrat merger was never taken up, but this result undeniably forced the Soc Dem leader, Dr David Owen, to acknowledge that his party had no political future. Similarly, in the 1997 Uxbridge by-election the Loonies' score was ten times that of the UK independence party. Admittedly we are dealing with the barmy *fringe of politics rather than with the *cut and thrust of actual government, but the Monster Raving Loony Party is without doubt part of the British political landscape.

In addition to his political coups, Sutch also liked to claim that he was responsible for the introduction of votes at 18, the abolition of the 11-plus exam and the decision to award MBE's to the Beatles. He will go down in history for witticisms like "Why is there only one Monopolies and Mergers Commission?" and the campaign slogan "Vote Loony – you know it makes sense!" Above all, Sutch was a typical exponent of the English tradition of heterodoxy, never letting politicians forget that everyone has the right to voice an opinion, constantly reminding the great and the good that they mustn't take themselves too seriously. Past centuries have also given rise to notable religious and political nonconformists – Daniel Defoe (1660-1731), John Bunyan (1628-1688), William Blake (1757-1827) and so on.

It remains to be seen how Lord Sutch's replacement, Alan Hope, who now leads the party jointly with his cat Mandu, will fare in the twenty-first century. It's just possible that as well as brightening up the *drab conformity of election-night coverage, the Loonies and their policies (which include Britain becoming the 52nd state of America and replacing the euro with the loono) may well be victorious yet!

# 14 Home Sweet Home

*Sophie Loussouarn*

Home Sweet Home: how ironical an exclamation in a period when homelessness is a *scourge of society. Home plays a great part in the everyday life of the British. Home provides shelter from the elements, an essential base for social life and reflects the status and social standing of the household in the community. It is associated with material conditions and standards, privacy, space, control, personal warmth, comfort, stability, safety, security and physical well-being.

It is therefore an essential element in a human being's life.

A foreigner travelling through the United Kingdom will be struck by the rich architecture of the houses and the decoration contributing to the soul of the house. The notion of home has evolved over the centuries. Since the Industrial Revolution, when people started *commuting from one place to the other, the home and the workplace have been clearly separated. The home *stands for a unit where the population can reproduce and a location for social relations within the family. In the twentieth century, people laid *claim to social advancement, material comfort and general improvement in the house. Since 1945, owner occupation has been encouraged, but there is still a huge gap between the residences of the *affluent and the poor, and the two nations still remain in the 20th century.

## The various types of home

The home reflects the social structure together with individual tastes. On the one hand, there are *stately homes or country houses which were the private homes of the aristocracy until the early nineteenth century. They are the symbols of aristocratic wealth and privilege. The past outlives in the present with castles, palaces and country seats. Blenheim which is the *seat of the Duke of Marlborough and Chatsworth which is the seat of the Duke and Duchess of Devonshire remain *outstanding examples of such stately homes. They contribute to tourism in Great Britain, whoever they belong to. As a matter of fact a lot of mansions are being sold to new aristocrats in blue jeans when the original family can no longer *maintain them. Some privately-owned stately homes which do not belong to the landed gentry are not listed on the tourist circuit. Others are managed by the National Trust.

On the other hand, after World War II, many *semi-detached or *terraced houses were built to *accommodate people whose houses had been bombed down.

## Housing policy

After the Second World War, there was a housing problem characterised by the housing shortage and the poor conditions of remaining houses.

Post-war British politics was based on a moderate consensus to use the state for economic reconstruction and social redistribution. The three main parties had the same *commltment: reconstructing Britain with the same efforts the war had *demanded. The Greater London Plan proposed to accommodate 383,000 people in new satellite towns beyond the Green Belt: so in March 1945, Stevenage (Herts) was designed as the first new town experiment. Abercrombie's plan was a success at the time. The period from the 1950s to the 1980s proved to be one of sustained expansion for town planning, which transformed the face of Britain's towns and cities. In 1998-1999, the number of dwellings in the UK was estimated at 25 million and the number of *households in England is projected to increase from 20.2 million in 1996 to 24 million in 2021. The increase varies across England, it ranges from 25% in the South-East and the South-West to under 10% in the North-East. Builders will no longer be allowed to develop homes similar to the tower blocks built in the 1960s, the preference goes to terraced houses with gardens.

There has been a huge shift of the residential structure of England from renting to owning. Before 1914, 90% of households in Britain rented their accommodation from a private landlord and only 10% of householders owned their own homes. More than half of British families were owner-occupiers in 1970, while the others rented their homes, mainly from district councils. There are still about 3 million rented *council homes provided by local authorities at below market rent. Allocations for 2000-01 amount to £2.1 billion – about 50% more than in 1999-2000. Nowadays, more and more British families own their homes. By the end of 1998, 68% of the population owned their homes. There are more home-owners in the South East and in the East, whereas there are fewer in Wales and Northern Ireland. At the end of 1998, 21% of all homes were rented to *tenants by public sector and non-profit making bodies in England. A relatively high proportion of homes are *purchased with a *mortgage from a high street bank or building society, using the property as *security.

In England, the Secretary of State for the Environment, Transport and the Regions has responsibility for determining housing policy and supervising the housing programme. In July 2000, the Government announced an additional £1.8 billion for investment in housing.

There are numerous schemes which aim to increase low-cost home ownership. In England, these include the Right to Buy, Right to Acquire and Voluntary Purchase Grants, which offer tenants in social housing a discount against the market value of the home they rent if they choose to buy it. Government spending on social housing is provided by subsidies to local authorities to help pay for the costs of over 3 million rented council homes. Most social housing in England is provided by local housing strategies.

Improving existing housing is among the major features of housing policy. Subsidies are spent to renovate and improve existing council housing. Local authorities in England are entitled to help home owners and tenants to improve the worst quality housing.

## *Homelessness*

*Slum clearance and regeneration have been major features of housing policy in urban areas. Local authorities offer relocation grants to help overcome home loss, they also help those in need to buy a home in or close to the same area. Home improvement agencies provide advice and assistance to elderly people, the disabled or those on low incomes who can't *carry out repairs. They also have legal duties to provide assistance for vulnerable people in need, especially households with dependent children, pregnant women, old aged pensioners or the mentally or physically ill. In 1999, 243,600 *applicants were *eligible under the homeless provisions of the 1985 and 1986 Housing Acts.

The Government's target is to reduce the number of those *sleeping rough in England to as close to zero as possible. The Rough Sleepers Unit has a budget of £160 million for London over 3 years. A Government strategy for homelessness in England, *Coming in from the Cold* was published in 1999. It proposed a new approach: helping vulnerable rough sleepers off the streets, preventing new rough sleepers, and rebuilding the lives of former rough sleepers.

Bad living conditions have a damaging effect on the education of children. Furthermore, homelessness has an effect on health. People sleeping rough experience the worst health of all. They are more likely to have chest problems, skin complaints and muscular problems. Furthermore, many homeless people *take to alcohol or other drugs which leads them to depression and mental illness. In the 1960s, there was a marked and continuous increase in homelessness in London and other parts of the country. Since the 1960s, homelessness outside the capital has increased faster than in London. The average annual rate of increase in homelessness for England as a whole was about 50% higher than for London.

There are regional differences in the rates of homelessness. Heads of household *currently living in urban areas are over two and a half times more likely to have experienced homelessness. The housing problem is concentrated in London and in northern cities where the amount of working class people is higher. Glasgow, Birmingham, Liverpool and Manchester are towns which have been severely hit by the economic crisis. The collapse of the car and manufacturing industries and the economic crisis have increased the rate of unemployment causing social problems.

The Urban Task Force was formed in April 1998 to examine the causes of urban decline and encourage people to return to urban neighbourhoods. Home Zones are to be set up, aiming at improving the quality of life in residential areas.

# Vocabulary

| | |
|---:|:---|
| abode/no fixed abode | demeure, domicile ; sans domicile fixe |
| accommodate (to) | loger |
| affluent | riche |
| applicant | candidat, demandeur |
| carry out (to) | exécuter, effectuer |
| claim (to)/lay claim to (to) | revendiquer |
| commitment | engagement |
| commute (to) | faire le trajet |
| commuter | banlieusard |
| council home | HLM |
| currently | actuellement |
| demand (to) | exiger |
| dereliction | abandon |
| domesticity | vie de famille, attachement au foyer |
| down and out | sans le sou |
| dwelling | domicile |
| eligible | ayant droit, acceptable |
| epitomize (to) | incarner, être le parfait exemple |
| focus on (to) | se concentrer sur |
| household | ménage, foyer |
| maintain (to) | entretenir |
| mansion | manoir, hôtel particulier |
| mortgage loan | emprunt hypothécaire |
| outstanding | remarquable, exceptionnel |
| purchase (to) | acheter |
| sleeping rough | coucher à la dure, sans abri |
| scourge | fléau |
| seat | château, siège |
| security | sûreté, garantie |
| semi-detached house | maison jumelée |
| slum clearance | suppression des taudis |
| soup kitchen | soupe populaire |
| stand for (to) | signifier, vouloir dire |
| stately home | château |
| state room | chambre d'apparat |
| take to (to) | s'adonner à |
| tenant | locataire |
| tenure | occupation (locaux) |
| terraced houses | rangée de maisons attenantes |

# Focus...

There was a stock of 25 million *dwellings in the UK at the end of 1998.

Britain is a country of houses rather than flats.

The Housing Minister has announced that 39,000 new homes a year will be built in 2001.

In April 2000, a Housing Green Paper was published: "Quality and Choice: a Decent Home for All", its objectives were:
- to help key workers on lower incomes into home ownership, in high-demand areas (£250 million will be provided over 2001-04)
- to help unemployed people back to work, with housing costs
- to prevent landlords neglecting their responsibilities
- to help homeowners with maintenance and modernisation
- to improve efficiency and fairness of the rent systems and reduce fraud
- to raise the standard of social housing
- to provide assistance for homeless people aged 16-17

◆ **Tenure of Dwellings in the UK, in 1998 (in per cent)**

|  | Owner-occupied | from local authority | Rented registered social landlord |
|---|---|---|---|
| England | 68 | 17 | 5 |
| Wales | 71 | 16 | 4 |
| Scotland | 61 | 27 | 5 |
| Northern Ireland | 71 | 22 | 3 |

◆ **Average sale price in England, in 1999 (£)**

|  | Detached Houses | Semi-detached | Terraced houses | Flats |
|---|---|---|---|---|
| North East | 101,214 | 50,044 | 42,124 | 44,124 |
| North West | 116,972 | 60,735 | 39,787 | 57,776 |
| East Midlands | 101,609 | 54,105 | 43,840 | 47,215 |
| West Midlands | 126,302 | 69,941 | 50,350 | 51,622 |
| London | 284,789 | 168,159 | 151,204 | 131,375 |
| South East | 196,487 | 106,101 | 84,186 | 69,910 |
| South West | 134,592 | 78,734 | 65,118 | 65,623 |

Civilisation britannique

The chart above shows that the closer the location to London and its area, the more expensive prices are.

The South is also more expensive than the North, as there are more jobs, more resources, and more competition.

◆ **Public help for beggars on the streets**

To end the "*soup kitchen culture" measures are to be taken.

The Government's Rough Sleepers Unit recommends the public to give beggars help or advice instead of giving them money or food. The Unit will call for an army of homeless helpers to recruit rough sleepers to work in shelters, and encourage them to do community work, in order to get them to participate in the wider community, instead of excluding them.

◆ **An example of a successful city: Ipswich**

The Suffolk town's Wet Dock, built in 1840, was the biggest in Europe at the time. It fell into *dereliction in the 1980s with the decline of sea-borne trade, but it now has a future as a social centre with offices, pubs, restaurants and a marina. It follows today's trend in city living which is becoming increasingly visible and which goes against the traditional middle class culture.

# Essay

**Comment upon the first stanza of the traditional song written by John H. Payne**

> Mid pleasures and palaces
> Though we may roam,
> Be it ever so humble,
> There's no place like home.

*This traditional song written by John H. Payne (1791-1852) underlines the importance of the home in Britain: "Home, home, sweet sweet home, There's no place like home, There's no place like home". It \*epitomizes the English love of \*domesticity.*

*The song focuses on the pleasures and the security of a home, however wealthy it may be.*

*It opposes rich dwellings to humble homes and stresses the need to have a fixed place of \*abode. Palaces are valued as places of comfort and convenience for their owners, they are the link between generations and between the past and the future. The concept of privacy began to develop in the eighteenth century and has lived on.*

*As Lord Salisbury said at the time of the 1932 Town and Country Planning Act: an Englishman's home is his castle. Happiness and moral comfort don't depend on the size, or on the luxury of the home, but home rather stands as a protection from the outer world, a feeling of safety for its inhabitants, a centre of exchange. This is a place where a man's roots are, where his identity is forged, where a sense of belonging grows from.*

*The aristocracy still lives in country houses which have always been power centres and showplaces for the display of authority. In country houses, the nobility were their own masters, their authority being dependent upon their ability to display opulence and offer hospitality. The \*state rooms provided opportunities for entertainment on a generous scale. At Houghton Hall, for instance, Sir Robert Walpole held open house towards the commencement of the shooting season; this went on for six or eight weeks.*

*The estates acted as centres of hospitality, which were partly a way to display generosity and authority to the villagers, partly a function of sociability: a shared experience between hosts and guests and partly a way to create useful political or matrimonial contacts. Visiting consisted essentially of two kinds: short-term when hosts and guests were constantly together and long-term when life resumed its normal pattern and the guests were treated as part of the family. It is obvious from correspondence, diaries and novels of the time that it was very common for relatives and friends of the family to pay* extended visits, lasting from a few weeks to a few months. The aristocrat's palace thus became a residence. For instance, in the 18th century, the Devonshires used to entertain the whole of political England, at Burlington House, and when the season was over in London, they would move, with the whole family, to Chatsworth for the summer. Palaces could boast of a splendid architecture contrived by the best architects of the time and are the best legacy of the artistic, architectural and literary heritage of England. Country houses witnessed the great events of the country and welcomed the greatest people, such as Turner who was frequently welcomed at Petworth where lots of his paintings can still be seen.

Owners handed down the estate to their heirs. All the milestones in the life of the family were celebrated in the house. Until the nineteenth century, girls would even be brought up by governesses on the very estate, whereas their brothers would be sent to boarding-schools. The mansion was often the heart of the political life of the county and, as paintings by Hogarth testify, politicians would meet there to prepare their election campaigns.

Humbler people lived in cottages and smaller houses. Their lives lacked the lustre of that of the aristocracy, theirs was a busy life. For tradesmen and craftsmen, the home could even be a place where they could work. The shop was often part of tradesmen's houses, just as the workshop was the home of craftsmen. They used to spend their free time around the hearth sharing long evening hours with the family.

Nowadays, many of the major country houses have become part of the national heritage, with their traditional owners remaining in situ as custodians or trustees. They attract more and more visitors from all over the world longing to share a family experience or a slice of the history which has built up the nation. The country house remains the quintessence of the English home. It is a landmark for the nation and a treasure to be protected, admired and emulated.

What remains of a house when its inhabitants have gone? This is the question raised in the novel by Ishiguro, The Remains of the Day, which relates the glorious past of a stately home which secretly presided over the destiny of the nation before the Second World War. At the time, German and British politicians met there to debate over the future of Europe. After the ruined landowner had sold it to a rich American, though the way of life changed, its soul lived on through the wistful memories of the butler who still cared for the estate. This is also what curators from cottages to *mansions open to the public try to bring back to life: a home not a house.

# 15 Preservation of Nature

*Florence Binard*

The British are notorious animal and nature lovers, a reputation which is well founded. They have been world pioneers in many animal welfare and environmental issues.

Historically, concern over animal welfare and the environment are linked to the Enlightenment of the eighteenth century. The new appraisal of man's place in the order of creation which emerged entailed a challenge of the anthropocentric view that placed human beings at the centre of all things. Darwin's theory of evolution further reinforced the view that man was but a link in the chain.

## *Ethical treatment and protection of animals*

"...*The question is not, can they reason? Nor can they talk? But can they suffer?*" Jeremy Bentham (1789)

The fact that animals cannot claim their rights does not entail that they should not be entitled to rights and that we don't owe them moral obligations.

The world's first ever anti-cruelty law was introduced in 1822 by Richard Martin MP; it *outlawed cruelty to cattle, horses and sheep. The purpose of this first Animal Protection Act was to ensure better treatment of farm animals. Cruelty to domestic and captive animals became a legal matter nearly a century later, in 1911. In Britain, most animal protection laws have been the result of often virulent *campaigns undertaken by animal rights groups who have played an essential role in public awareness. They have won a number of victories – the criminalisation of cruelty to animals, the ban on fur farming, on cosmetic testing, regulations on intensive animal farming, live exports and hunting. It is interesting to note that some of the most popular UK animal charities today were actually formed in the nineteenth century. For instance, the oldest animal welfare organisation in the world, The Royal Society for the Prevention of Cruelty to Animals (RSPCA) was founded in 1824. Other *pressure groups focusing on specific aspects of the mistreatment of animals were also formed in the nineteenth century. Thus, the world's leading anti-vivisection *campaigning organisation, The British Union for the Abolition of Vivisection (BUAV), was created in 1898.

## *Vegetarianism*

Concern over animal welfare is sometimes associated with vegetarianism and there is no denying that there is a definite vegetarian tradition in Britain. It is claimed that the first English vegetarian cookery book appeared in 1812. Thirty-five years later, in 1847, the oldest vegetarian association in the world was founded in England – The Vegetarian Society.

As evidence of the importance of vegetarianism in England, during the Second World War, the Vegetarian Society won concessions for vegetarians: for example, in 1941, they were granted an extra ration of cheese.

In the fifties and sixties, due to active campaigns, the general public became increasingly aware of what intensive factory farming meant and many started to turn vegetarian. It is estimated that there are around four million vegetarians in Britain today.

If vegetarianism goes hand in hand with animal welfare, it is also seen as part of the process of change and *conservation of resources.

## Environmental concern at home

Vegetarians are obviously not the sole defendants of nature, and awareness of the degradation of environmental systems has involved people from all walks of life. The fact that industrialisation, uncontrolled development and the introduction of modern farming techniques were not only threatening scenery but wildlife and the wider environment became a source of concern in the nineteenth century. Among the earliest organisations was the Commons Preservation Society (CPS) whose aim was to fight against *enclosures. The existence of such parks as Hampstead Heath or Epping Forest in London, are the results of campaigns that were fought by the CPS in the 1860s.

After the First World War, the development of urbanisation led to the creation in 1926 of the Council for the Protection of Rural England (CPRE).

But the most famous and the largest *conservation charity in England is the National Trust which was launched in 1893. As Octavia Hill, one of the founding members of the Trust, put it, the aim of the Trust was to provide "open-air sitting rooms" for ordinary people. Ever since its creation, the goal of the Trust has been to acquire and conserve buildings of historical interest, to protect the threatened *coastline and countryside throughout Britain. Completely independent of government, the National Trust, which counts 2.6 million members, relies entirely on donations and *subscriptions.

### *Activism

Non-violent direct action tactics are a traditional feature of British activism. In the nineteenth century, radical environmentalists often resorted to civil disobedience to achieve their goal and make themselves heard. The building of railways and enclosures were major environmental causes. There were often clashes between estate owners who wanted to enclose waste and common land and anti-enclosure campaigners who were fighting for the preservation of open spaces.

Today, the situation is similar, except that the number of causes has increased substantially and the number of direct action groups has soared. Many believe that the only way to alert public opinion is by attracting media attention and they have often been proved right. In 1994, faced with the growing number of "eco-terrorist" demonstrations, the Government introduced the Criminal Justice and Public Order Act which created the new *offence of "aggravated trespass". This new law is, however, most controversial as many Britons share the view of Lord Justice Hoffman who declared: "*Civil disobedience on grounds of conscience is an honourable tradition in this country and those who take part in it may in the end be vindicated by history.*"

## Globalisation

The British are not solely concerned with what happens in their country, they are also staunch supporters of such organisations as WWF or Greenpeace. They are also the founders of Friends of the Earth (1971) which is the largest international network of environmental *pressure groups. FoE is represented in 52 countries and aims "to protect the environment by promoting rational and *sustainable use of Earth's resources".

Ecological issues such as the development of nuclear energy, the *greenhouse effect or *global warming have led to many demonstrations on British soil.

## Conclusion

Perhaps the most telling evidence of the British population's commitment to animal welfare and environmental issues lies in the fact that the "Big Five" (the five supermarket chains which dominate the British market) all provide ranges of "animal-friendly", vegetarian, organic or "*environmentally-friendly" products. They have adopted or developed a variety of logos which testify that their products have not been tested on animals or that they come from animals whose welfare has been *safeguarded throughout their lives. These supermarkets regularly publish leaflets to inform their customers about their policies with regards to animal welfare or environmental issues. For example, in 2000, Sainsbury's issued a brochure entitled "living *landscape" in which they presented the company's commitment to environmentally-responsible farming and especially Integrated Crop Management (ICM) which relies on crop rotation and whereby "natural" methods are used, whenever possible, to control disease and pests. Tesco's "freedom food" leaflet informs the customer that they offer animal products that meet hygiene, environmental and animal welfare standards, which are open to supervision by the RSPCA.

# Vocabulary

| | |
|---|---|
| activism | militantisme |
| address an issue (to) | aborder un problème |
| back (to) | soutenir |
| backlash | retour de bâton |
| bloodsports | sports sanguinaires |
| break the law (to) | violer la loi |
| campaign for (to) | faire campagne pour |
| coastline | littoral |
| conservation | protection |
| contaminate (to) | contaminer |
| damage (to) | endommager |
| dispose of (to) | se débarrasser de |
| enclosures | le fait de clôturer |
| endangered species | espèces en voie de disparition |
| environmentally-friendly | qui ne détruit pas l'environnement |
| field sports | pêche et chasse |
| footpath | sentier |
| global warming | réchauffement de la planète |
| globalisation | mondialisation |
| greenhouse effect | effet de serre |
| irradiate (to) | irradier |
| landscapes | paysages |
| national conservancy | équivalent de l'Office des Eaux et Forêts |
| noxious | nocif |
| nuclear power station | centrale nucléaire |
| offence | un délit |
| organic | bio |
| outcry | tollé, levée de boucliers |
| outdoor activities | activités de plein air |
| outlaw (to) | proscrire |
| ozone layer | la couche d'ozone |
| ozone-depleting | qui épuise l'ozone |
| pollute (to) | polluer |
| pressure group | groupe de pression |
| sab | saboteur |
| safeguard (to) | sauvegarder |
| species | espèce |
| stir public opinion (to) | agiter l'opinion publique |
| subscriptions | cotisations |
| sustainable | durable |
| vegan | végétalien |
| waste disposal plant | usine de traitement des ordures |

# Focus...

75% of British population live in urban areas.

**Preservation** means maintaining the state of nature exactly as it was or might have been.

***Conservation** is the management of natural resources in such a way as to integrate the requirements of the local human population with those of the animals, plants, or the habitat being *conserved.

In 1949, the ***Nature Conservancy** was established. Its purpose is to identify and establish National Nature Reserves.

**The National Trust**, which is independent of government, cares for over 248,000 hectares of countryside, 600 miles of *coastline and more than 200 buildings and gardens.

**English Heritage** was established in 1983 and is the Government's leading body for the historic environment in England.

**Chlorofluorocarbons** (CFCs) which were invented in the 1930s, are evidence of the danger of human interference with ecological processes. They are responsible for the *greenhouse effect and the depletion of atmospheric *ozone.

**Intensive Factory Farming** is a method of production which aims at minimising the cost of breeding animals while maximising the profit margin.

**The Royal Society for the Prevention of Cruelty to Animals** (RSPCA) employs 328 inspectors who investigate 100,000 cruelty complaints a year in England. The RSPCA treats over 270,000 animals a year. This charity receives no State or lottery aid and relies totally on voluntary donations. The running costs are over £60 million a year.

◆ **Anti-vivisection**

> In the nineteenth century, feminist and animal activist Frances Power Cobbe played an important role against vivisection. She presented the first anti-vivisection bill in history to the House of Lords and founded the Victoria Street Society, a group specifically devoted to the cause of anti-vivisection.

The Cruelty to Animals Act (1876) aimed at regulating the use of animals in experiments and established yearly licensing requirements for all experimenters.

◆ **The Vegetarian Society symbol**

It was first used in 1969.

*The Vegetarian* has been the mouthpiece of The Vegetarian Society since 1848.

In 1991, National Vegetarian Day was first organised and the experience proved so popular that it has now grown into National Vegetarian Week. The event is important for the UK food industry as it is estimated that the vegetarian food market is worth £11.1 billion per year. It is believed that between 3,000 and 5,000 people become vegetarian each week in Britain.

◆ **Swampy the Mole-Man**

It is the nickname given to an eco-protester who made the headlines in 1998. In an attempt to hinder the building of a motorway, he hid in a series of burrows dug under the path of the controversial motorway and it took the police more than a week to find him. What was amazing was the fact that he attracted the sympathy of people from all walks of life and all political leanings. He was regarded as a hero and it is argued that thanks to him direct action protesters are less seen as anarchic eco-terrorists.

# Essay

**Environmental issues, animal welfare and the clash of cultures in Britain: the example of fox-hunting.**

*Britain has seen in recent years the development of raging debates around environmental and animal welfare issues. The latest and possibly most burning of all has been the controversy over fox-hunting. Some commentators even go as far as to compare it with America's anti-abortion campaigns, so passionate, heated and unfortunately sometimes violent the whole question is.*

*It is estimated that about 200,000 people take part in fox-hunting in the UK. The pro-hunting lobby argue that fox hunting is a worthwhile \*field sport which contributes to agricultural pest management while supporting the local rural economy. According to them, foxes \*damage crops and cause harm to lambs, poultry and game birds. It is, therefore, essential to control their population. They also believe that thanks to fox hunting a substantial number of jobs can be maintained in rural areas.*

*On the other hand, anti-hunting protesters claim that fox hunting is not only unnecessary but cruel. They concede that foxes sometimes kill livestock, but minimise the issue. They argue that foxes are valuable in that they eat rodents and that anyway, they only account for 1% of lamb deaths. They add that when tracking their prey, foxhounds and horses create far more havoc to crops or fences than the foxes themselves. Most of all, they reproach hunters with deriving pleasure and entertainment from chasing animals who suffer stress and a painfully slow death as they are inevitably torn to pieces by a pack of dogs.*

*Both sides claim to defend nature and the environment and have organised actions to make themselves heard.*

*The anti-hunting campaign really started in 1924 with the establishment of the League Against Cruel Sports (LACS). As they felt they were not heard, the opponents of "\*bloodsports" have resorted to non violent direct actions in order to save foxes but also to attract media attention. The Hunt Saboteurs Association which is the most active anti-hunting group seeks to distract hounds by shouting, blowing hunting horns to confuse the hounds and by laying false trails. They often find themselves in situations of direct confrontation with the huntsmen which can lead to verbal abuse and even physical violence. People have been seriously injured on both sides.*

*What fuelled the conflict was the decision of the Labour Government to introduce a Bill to \*outlaw fox hunting.*

*In an effort to make the Government go back on its decision, the British Field Sports Society and the pro-hunting lobby organised rallies throughout the country as well as a massive demonstration in London. The 2000 Boxing Day gathering in London was, according to the press, one of the largest demonstrations in the history of British social protests.*

*It is felt that the conflict has divided England or rather that it has highlighted the gap between town and country and some would also say between social classes. The stereotyped image of the saboteur or "\*sab" is that of a left-wing \*vegan animal rights activist with an urban upbringing. Fox-hunting, on the other hand is seen as the symbol of arrogance and exclusivity displayed by red-coated huntsmen who perpetuate a 300 year-old aristocratic tradition. Is it not a fact that most members of the Royal family enjoy field sports?*

*Conservative MPs and peers accuse the Labour Government of turning the fox-hunting question into an election issue. Some even claim that for New Labour, the campaign against hunting is "the image of class war without its price".*

*It is estimated that three quarters of people in Britain are in favour of a ban of fox hunting. There is therefore little doubt as to the eventual defeat of the hunting world.*

# 16 The British Media

*Florence Binard*

## The press

*A short history*

The first English "newspaper" was published in London in 1621 and was called the *Weekly Newes*. But the development of the press as such really dates back to the early eighteenth century when the Licensing Act of 1662 was allowed to lapse in 1695. With the end of direct state censorship, the number of English newspapers began to rise and access to a relatively free press was definitely achieved for the *well-to-do. However, in 1712 the first Stamp Act was introduced. The aim was to regulate the press by imposing a stamp duty on newspapers and the advertisements they printed, which probably resulted in a slower expansion of the press.

The real boom took place in the second half of the nineteenth century when education became compulsory for all. As a matter of fact, not only did the growth of popular literacy pave the way for mass communication but it led to new developments in the content of newspapers which so far had been mainly political. The expansion in readership meant that newspapers were no longer the privilege of a wealthy, educated minority and thus opened up the way to new and broader interests such as crime, romance, scandal and sport.

At the same time, advertising and stamp duties were abolished. The result was that by the end of the 19th century the main source of revenue for the newspaper industry came from advertising. The true cost of papers being subsidised by advertising, their cover prices could be reduced.

Until the advent of television after the Second World War, newspapers held a safe and prominent position as the main source of information for the general public.

The decline started when in the fifties, TV superseded the press as the dominant means of communication. The consequence was a decrease in *circulation but even more threatening was the *competition with television for advertising which meant a fall in revenue. Competition between newspapers became harsher than ever.

In the provinces, the decline of local press was fostered by the development of a new kind of paper the "free sheet", or free newspaper, which is entirely subsidised by advertising.

On the national scene, polarisation has been between the popular and the quality press. The seventies saw the rise of the *tabloid press notably with the success of *The Sun* with its famous page three featuring a topless woman. The *gutter press as it is often called deals with "junk journalism" and is easily recognisable with its large *headlines, wide columns and plethora of pictures.

In the mid-eighties, as the total average sales of newspapers started to drop considerably, two press *tycoons, Rupert Murdoch and Robert Maxwell, launched a price war which benefited the readers.

But more importantly, taking advantage of the support of the Conservative government of Margaret Thatcher, Rupert Murdoch seized the opportunity to transfer his newspapers to Wapping in the London Docklands. He was soon followed by others. This departure from Fleet Street meant the end of an era for the print unions who then lost many of the privileges they had acquired over the years, such as high wage settlements, closed shop agreements.

Another ill-effect of the circulation wars was that the tabloids went even further down market than they already had been and were criticised for encroaching on the private lives of people. Attempts to introduce statutory regulation that would protect the rights of the individual while upholding the public's right to information were unsuccessful. However, the newspaper and magazine industry adopted a self-regulatory regime operated through the Press Complaints Commission (PCC) and a *Code of practice for the Press was introduced in 1997 after the death of Princess Diana – it was alleged that the paparazzi were involved in her death.

### Television and Radio

The British *Broadcasting Corporation was set up in 1922 as a commercial enterprise but it soon became a public owned institution. Unlike other media industries, the BBC developed as a public service funded by a *licence fee payable by radio *listeners initially and subsequently by TV owners. Until the fifties the BBC held the monopoly over radio and TV broadcasting

But as television boomed in the fifties (between 1950 and 1960 the number of TV owners rose from 4% to 80% of the adult population) pressure for commercial radio and TV intensified.

Demand for the end of the monopoly of the BBC mainly came from companies who saw juicy profits from advertising on a commercial channel. They enjoyed the support of a large part of the population who were dissatisfied with the way the BBC failed to be impartial in its reporting of news, especially when it came to dealing with Government policies. The campaign eventually led to the 1954 Television Act which resulted in the creation of the first private TV *network, the ITV network (Independent Television).

The BBC nonetheless enjoyed a safe and secure place until the mid-eighties when the Conservative government started to challenge the need for public service broadcasting and paved the way for a further development of commercial TV. The Broadcasting Act of 1990 laid the foundations for a more competitive and efficient broadcasting framework in Britain.

### Media development and issues of concern

Pressure groups such as the Campaign for Press and Broadcasting Freedom (CPBF) who work "for a diverse, democratic and accountable media with positive public service obligations" have expressed concern over *cross-media ownership and the development of media conglomerates (the fact that a company has a significant stake within or both within *and* across different media, for example, ownership of several newspapers as well as *TV channels). According to them, the danger is that if too many media companies were in the same hands, diversity and plurality would no longer be ensured. Also, the quality of the programmes would suffer greatly as the primary target of these large companies would be to ensure their commercial success and growth. If media conglomerates were allowed to develop, it has been argued that the "tabloidisation" of TV would necessarily ensue. Indeed, to improve their *audience ratings they would produce programmes focusing on the royal family, celebrities, gossip, sex and sport, soaps etc which are popular with a large section of the population.

In response to these fears and to avoid the concentration of the media in the hands of a few conglomerates, the government passed the Broadcasting Act of 1996. For instance, the act makes it illegal for a company that controls more than 20% of national newspaper circulation to have more than a 20% stake in an independent television. Another restriction is that no commercial TV company may have more than 15% of the total TV audience.

## New media and the future

With the rapid development of cable TV, satellite and the Internet, the British Government has come to review its policy with regards to large media conglomerates. They now believe that despite the dangers of monopoly, British media companies should be allowed to expand so as to be able to *compete internationally.

The new media which are threatening to replace the terrestrial-led broadcasting systems are also revolutionising mass communication. Indeed, instant transmission of images simultaneously to all parts of the planet, the ability for people to interact with the media, and the information superhighway are evidence that the media are entering a new era. We are witnessing the formation of a global culture as nationally based media are being replaced by international media.

The question is how to ensure that the people's best interests are protected? What does the future hold, freedom or Big Brother?

## Vocabulary

| | |
|---:|:---|
| accuracy | respect des faits, de la vérité |
| audience rating | audimat |
| broadcast (to) | diffuser |
| broadsheet (newspaper) | journal plein format (synonyme de qualité) |
| circulation | tirage |
| code of practice | code de déontologie |
| competition | concurrence |
| cover an event (to) | couvrir un événement |
| cross-media conglomerates | conglomérats multi-média |
| daily newspaper | quotidien |
| disclose (to) | divulguer |
| distorted reports | informations erronées |
| editor (newspaper) | rédacteur en chef |
| gutter press | presse à scandale |
| headlines | gros titres |
| invasion of privacy | atteinte à la vie privée |
| infringe privacy (to) | attenter à la vie privée des personnes |
| issue | numéro |
| leading article | article de fond |
| licence fee | redevance |
| listeners | auditeurs |
| media accountability | responsabilité morale des média envers le public |
| mould opinions (to) | façonner les opinions |
| network | réseau |
| online provider | fournisseur d'accès à internet |
| press cutting | coupure de presse |
| prime time | heure de pointe |
| publisher | éditeur |
| review | critique |
| screen | écran |
| serial | feuilleton |
| series | série télévisée |
| subscribers | abonnés |
| supersede (to) | remplacer |
| survey | étude, enquête |
| tabloid | quotidien populaire de demi-format |
| tv channel | chaîne de télévision |
| tv viewers | téléspectateurs |
| tycoon | magnat |
| weekly (newspaper) | hebdomadaire |
| watchdog (committee) | comité de surveillance, garde-fou |
| well-to-do | aisé, riche |

# FOCUS...

### ◆ The written press

1896: *The Daily Mail*, the first popular mass circulation *daily newspaper was launched.

There are three main sectors: the "quality" "middle" and "popular" press. All the popular papers are now tabloids and most of the quality papers are *broadsheet papers. (The broadsheet format originated as a response to the stamp duty on papers; the tax concerned the number of pages not the size.)

About 60% of British people read a national daily paper.

About 70% of British people read a national Sunday paper.

The total sales of national daily newspapers is of 14 million.

The total sales of national Sunday newspapers is of 15 million.

The best-selling titles have a circulation of between 1 and 4 million.

The national press is dominated by four companies which account for about 90 % of sales. The most important being Rupert Murdoch's company, News Corporation, which publishes four national newspapers: *The Sun, The Times, The News of the World* and *The Sunday Times* and which together make up more than 20% of the market.

### ◆ The audio-visual media

#### *The radio*
• British radio started in the 1920s and now operates national networks, regional services and local stations. The market is equally divided between commercial radios which are funded by advertising and sponsorship and the BBC which is funded by the TV licence and therefore does not *broadcast adverts.

#### *Television*
• 1936: the first British television service started in November.

• 1955: introduction of commercial TV.

• BBC1 and BBC2 are publicly owned and funded by a licence fee and do not carry advertising. BBC1 offers a diverse range of popular programmes and news whereas BBC2 is meant to be more culture oriented and offers a diversity of programmes including news programmes, drama, educational and arts programmes.

• ITV (independent television) is split into different regional companies which broadcast national programmes at *prime time and their own programmes at other times. They rely on advertising for their revenue.

- Channel 4 is a hybrid public, minority interest service which also raises revenue through advertising sales. Channel 4 is mainly a broadcaster rather than a programme maker.
- Channel 5 is a national commercial channel.
- BskyB satellite TV is controlled by Rupert Murdoch's News International.

◆ **British soap operas**

A soap opera is a popular television or radio drama *serial about the daily lives and problems of the same group of people. The name comes from the fact that these serials were frequently sponsored by soap manufacturers.

British soap operas are possibly one of the most interesting features of British TV and radio. They differ greatly from American soaps in so far as they do not deal with the melodramatic or sentimental tangled interpersonal situations of rich people. British soap operas are usually set around a small community of ordinary people. They are geographically and culturally specific in their setting – Manchester for *Coronation Street*, the Yorkshire dales for *Emmerdale* or London for *East-Enders*. Social verisimilitude is a key element. The audience witness the evolution of the characters through the years as they adapt to the changes of society. Also, as a testimony to societal developments, new characters are introduced – all soaps have now included ethnic minority characters or gays and lesbians for example.

***The most famous British soaps***

*The Archers* is a radio soap set in a rural community and centres around the life of the Archer family. Initially, it was meant as propaganda for agricultural reform after the Second World War. It is the most popular radio programme in the UK.

*Coronation Street* is the longest running TV soap in the UK. It deals with the lives of a Manchester community of working-class people who live in the same street, Coronation Street. This soap which has been running for forty years is by far the best known programme on British television. In 1999, it achieved the top audience rating of nearly 20 million viewers whereas the Champions' league final reached 15.6 million.

◆ *The Economist*

This paper was founded in 1843 to support the cause of free trade. It is a weekly international news and business publication in a magazine format mainly "written for an audience of senior business, political and financial decision-makers".

# Essay

**Should the media be left to their own devices or should the Government intervene and regulate the industry?**

*The media have been dubbed the "Fourth Estate" and it is generally agreed that they play an essential role in the democratic functioning of British society. However people are also aware of the power of the media and fear that in the wrong hands they would be a most powerful weapon of social control.*

*With the advent of information technology and the development of the globalisation of the media industry, the question of regulation has had to be re-evaluated and is a most controversial issue.*

## Censorship & regulations: who decides when a piece of news or programme is not suitable for release?

*Existing regulatory bodies*

• *There is no statutory regulation of the British press, however, in the wake of Princess Diana's death, the press decided to issue its own ethical \*code of practice which is operated by the Press Complaints Commission (PCC). The PCC is an independent body which deals with burning issues such as inaccuracy, \*infringement of privacy, misrepresentation and harassment.*

• *Unlike the press, British radio and television are regulated by the law. Three organisations are responsible for the protection of the citizen and consumer: the Broadcasting Standards Commission, the Independent Television Commission and the Radio Authority.*

### Is regulation an absolute necessity?

*So far it has been agreed that if left uncontrolled the media could easily be used to manipulate and \*mould public opinion.*

*It is a well-known fact that television has become an essential instrument used by politicians, that the latter and their policies are sold to the electorate in the same way as commercial products. In the 1992 election, seven of the eleven daily papers were pro-Conservative, three Labour, and one neutral, and when the Tories won the election,* The Sun *proudly blazed the headline "It's* The Sun *wot won it".*

*Many people also blame the media for their adverse influence on the young generations. It is argued that TV in particular – through its portrayal of sex and violence – is responsible for the collapse of moral standards in Britain. What is more, it is feared that the development* *of digitalisation and the proliferation of commercial channels will dumb down the quality of TV as is the supposed case in America. It is believed that if the state does not interfere and if the market alone determines what people see on their screens, standards will be diluted. Another important aspect is that of the free access to national media events. Since 1996, many major sporting occasions are no longer broadcast free by the BBC or ITV but are sold to \*subscribers of satellite and cable TV. (The Labour government in power intends to review and extend the list of protected national sporting events.)*

*So far, all terrestrial broadcasters have had public service obligations of varying degrees, for instance they must broadcast news, religious or arts programmes. The aim is to ensure that the public have access to a diverse range of "voices". At the same time, controls on religious advertising and the ban on political advertising safeguard the public from manipulation by political or religious groups.*

*It is however felt essential that the media should remain independent of the State. Newspaper and broadcasting organisations were sued in 1999 by the City of London Police when they refused to hand over video material, photographs and reporters' notes taken during an anti-capitalist demonstration in the City. The police claimed that under the Police and Criminal Evidence Act, the media should hand over their riot footage to the police, to which the media refused to comply, arguing that it should not be and must not be seen to be the job of journalists to gather material for the police. They insisted that they did not want the media to be above the law, but they were adamant that they should be independent of it. The prosecution accused the journalists of attempting to put the media above the law, of hindering the police in their investigations and of helping law-breakers to escape arrest. However, the Old Bailey ruled in favour of the media.*

*Since the mid-eighties, British political parties have favoured the expansion of market forces into broadcasting. The Broadcasting Acts of 1990 and 1996 have forced the BBC to act more like a commercial operator and regulation of commercial TV has weakened. According to the Communications White Paper published in January 2001, Labour plans for the future are for even fewer restrictions on conglomerates and media cross-ownership. However, the trend is not for de-regulation but for self-regulation. The government have come to realise that devising legislation that would cover all the media from the Internet to the BBC is an impossible task. They are also aware that if such regulation existed it could not be easily enforced, if at all possible – for instance, pornography on the net.*

# 17 British Cinema

*Florence Binard*

The history of the British *film industry is one of ups and downs. British cinema has always suffered from American competition and the fact that America and Britain share the same language is partly responsible for this phenomenon. However, contrary to what is often claimed, a common language does not account on its own for the failure of British cinema to impose itself on the international scene.

## From the beginnings to the *heyday of British cinema

In 1912, the British Board of Film Censors was founded. Initially it was meant to ensure that films showing nudity or portrayals of Jesus Christ should be banned. But within a year of its creation, the number of rules concerning the propriety of films was largely extended. The purpose of the Board was clearly to control the production of films and to classify them according to the public targeted. (It was then that the *certificates U, for universal, and A, for adult, were introduced.) However, to a large extent, the Board was also a tool with which to limit the importation of foreign films, mainly American films, on account of "unsuitability".

Despite these efforts to promote British films, the British public still favoured American films and in the early twenties, the British film industry was on the verge of disappearing completely. By then, the Establishment had come to realise that British films could provide publicity for Britain and serve as a tool for propaganda. Thus, in 1927, Parliament came to the rescue of the British film industry and brought in the Cinematographers Trade Bill whose aim was to ensure a guaranteed home market for British films by imposing a minimum quota of British films to be shown in cinemas. The question was how to define a British film. It was decided that to be registered as a British film, a film had to satisfy three criteria: the *script writer had to be a British subject, the studio scenes had to be shot within the British Empire and at least 70% of the labour costs should be paid to British citizens.

The bill was a success in that many British films were produced in the thirties, however, the films produced were of such poor quality that the public ignored them. These films have been dubbed the *shoddy "*quota quickies".

British film-maker, Alexander Korda stood as an exception. He was the symbol of the success of British cinema and introduced a tradition of historical dramas and adaptations of the classics. His greatest box office success was the Oscar winning *Private Life of Henry VIII* in 1933.

Taking advantage of the loopholes in the Cinematographers Trade Bill, a number of American companies moved into the UK to make quality British films!

Civilisation britannique

The forties and fifties were the golden years for British cinema. During the Second World War, there was a surge of public interest in British films and it is believed that some of the best British films were then produced – *Henry V, Millions Like Us, The Life and Times of Colonel Blimp* to name but a few.

The most successful British films were produced by the Ealing Studios. Initially, the studios produced films that were reminiscent of *documentaries in that they associated fiction and social realism. But soon after the war, the studios turned to comedy and are now mainly remembered for this genre. It was in the late fifties that the first *Carry On* films were made.

### The decline

Many of the American companies which had left Britain at the outbreak of the war did not return as Hollywood was becoming more attractive. And, despite the help of the government which had created the National Film Finance Corporation (1948) and introduced the Eady Levy (1950) as a means of raising finance for film production, the British Film industry was not producing enough quality films and the public were again turning to American productions.

By the mid-fifties, competition from television had become so harsh that many cinemas were shutting down and were being turned into ballrooms or Bingo halls. From then on till the mid-eighties, *attendance and the number of cinemas never ceased to decrease. It is estimated that between 1955 and 1984, the number of cinemas dropped from about 4,500 to 650.

British cinema has nonetheless managed to survive with its ups and downs. In the late fifties and early sixties, the Free Cinema movement which was committed to realism and social issues left its imprint. The *release of the film *Room at the Top*, in 1959, is regarded as being a turning point in the development of post-war British cinema. It is thought that by granting the film a certificate, the British Board of Film Censors opened the way to a radical change in attitude towards *censorship, particularly with regards to portraying sex and sexuality. A number of daring films addressing taboo subjects such as homosexuality, abortion and other social issues were subsequently produced. These are known as the "kitchen sink dramas".

Another important element was the arrival in England of American *film-makers such as Carl Foreman, Joseph Losey, Stanley Kubrick and others who were escaping from McCarthyism in America.

The eighties, when between only 30 and 50 films were made each year, were the lowest point ever in British film production. It was then that financial support for British cinema through the NFFC and the Eady Fund (the tax on cinema *admission, the revenue from which was reinvested in British production) was withdrawn by government. The NFFC was privatised and replaced by the British Screen Finance Consortium which failed in boosting British cinema. Paradoxically, however, Margaret Thatcher is thought to have been "the catalyst that sparked a British film renaissance" by giving it its subject matter. A number of socially committed films which explicitly or implicitly criticised her policies hit the *box-office.

What is more, if in the fifties television was to blame for the decline of British cinema, in the eighties, television undoubtedly contributed to its revival. The creation of Channel Four led to the production of *low budget films which unexpectedly met with great success – Stephen Frears's *My Beautiful Launderette* being the first of a long series. In the nineties the trend carried on with films such as *Trainspotting, Brassed Off, Elizabeth, The Full Monty, Secrets and Lies* to name but a few. People even talk of a renaissance in British film making.

### *The present situation*

The growing relationship between TV and cinema, the advent of the video cassette recorder (VCR) resulted in many people watching films at home rather than at the cinema. Yet, it seems that due to the development of multiplex cinemas – out-of-town cinemas with five or more screens – there is a revival of cinema going in Britain.

The problem, however, is that most of the films shown in these modern cinemas are *big budget American productions and, therefore, are most unlikely to contribute to the expansion of British cinema. Compared with America, the British home market is small and does not generate as much profit. In order to ensure an effective promotion of their films the British film industry cannot afford to invest in advertising the vast amounts of money that their American counterparts spend.

Another issue is that a lot of seemingly British films are financed and produced in America; that is the case for instance of *Shadowlands, Sense and Sensibility* and *The English Patient.* As a consequence, it is feared that the definition of a British film may soon simply be that it has been shot in Britain and/or relates to a British subject matter.

It is also argued that Britain belongs more to the European than to the American film community and that the Tories should not have pulled Britain out of the Eurimages co-production fund in 1995. It is through a strong European cinema that the further development of a global monopoly at the expense of national diversity may be avoided.

Finally, most of the recent successful British productions have been *low-budget films, starring little-known actors – *The Crying Game, Trainspotting, Four Weddings and a Funeral* or *The Full Monty*. The fact that these films were not designed to gain large audience figures corresponds to British culture and the British way of doing things. Recent studies have shown that "film audiences make hits or *flops... not by revealing preferences they already have, but by discovering what they like". It is thought to be unwise that British film-makers should be encouraged to compete with Hollywood by making *blockbusters as this does not concur with the British tradition of film-making.

# VOCABULARY

| | |
|---|---|
| admission | entrée |
| attendance | assistance |
| award a prize (to) | décerner un prix |
| "B"film | film a faible budget durant environ une heure et presenté en première partie d'un long métrage. |
| big/low budget film | film à gros/petit budget |
| blockbuster | film à succès |
| box office | guichet |
| cast (and credits) | distribution, générique |
| censorship | censure |
| certificate | certificat d'exploitation |
| close-up | gros plan |
| director/film-maker | réalisateur |
| documentary | film documentaire |
| feature (to) | figurer, jouer dans |
| feature film | long métrage |
| film industry | industrie cinématographique |
| flop | four |
| go to the cinema/pictures (uk) movies (US) | aller au cinéma |
| heyday | heure de gloire |
| leading role/part | rôle principal |
| period film | film d'époque |
| producer | producteur |
| quota quicky | film qui a été produit à la va-vite afin de remplir des quotas |
| release of a film | sortie d'un film |
| review | critique |
| script | scénario |
| scriptwriter, scenarist | scénariste |
| shoddy film | film de mauvaise qualité |
| shoot a film (to) | tourner un film |
| silent film | film muet |
| slapstick comedy | comédie bouffonne |
| soundtrack | bande son |
| supporting/minor role | second/petit rôle |
| talkie | film parlant |
| thriller | film à suspense |
| U film | film tous publics |
| warts and all | sans aucun embellissement, fidèle à la réalité |
| win an oscar (to) | gagner un Oscar |
| X rated film | film à caractère pornographique |

# Focus...

◆ **UK Cinema Admissions**
- The 1940s to the mid-fifties witnessed a peak in cinema *admissions with between 1,000 million and 1,500 million admissions a year.
- From the mid-fifties to the mid-eighties there was a sharp decline in cinema attendance; the lowest ever seen, being 1984 with only 54 million admissions.
- Since the mid-eighties there has been a steady rise. The average for the nineties was 120 million admissions, with about 140 million admissions in 1999.

◆ **Number of Cinemas in Britain**
- In 1955 there were 4,500 cinemas in Britain, whereas by 1984 the number had dropped to only 660.
- It is thought that the development of multiplex cinemas since the mid-eighties has contributed to the rise in cinema attendance in Britain.

◆ **UK Box Office**
- Out of the top ten films ever at the UK box office only two are British, the rest are mainly American films!

*The Full Monty* was the top British film in 1997 (£52 million at the UK box-office)

*Notting Hill* was the top British film of 1999 (£30 million at the UK box-office)

- The all time top five British films at the UK box office are:

*The Full Monty, Notting Hill, Chicken Run, The World is not Enough* and *Four Weddings and a Funeral*. Only the latter is entirely British, all four others were produced with the help of American investment.

◆ **British films fall into three main categories**

***Comedies and *slapstick***
The *Carry On* films (the longest series in film history), the *Monty Python* films, *Mr Bean*.

****Period films and adaptations of the classics***
Kenneth Branagh's adaptations of Shakespeare's plays, *The Wings of the Dove, The English Patient, Sense and Sensibility, Pride and Prejudice, Tess* etc. A number of these costume dramas are set in England and deal with an English subject matter, however because

Civilisation britannique

they are financed thanks to American investments they are often classified as American films.

### *Social films*
A tradition which has its roots in the Free Cinema Movement of the sixties and which is much alive in the films of Mike Leigh, Stephen Frears and Ken Loach. *The Full Monty* and *Billy Elliot* are the latest successes in this category.

◆ **Famous British film directors**

**Alfred Hitchcock** (1899-1980): he is known as the "master of suspense". With his great sense of humour he revolutionised the *thriller genre. Although he was British born, he spent a great part of his life in America. When he died in 1980, he was dubbed "Britain's most famous export to America". Among his most famous films are: *Vertigo* (1957), *Psycho* (1958) and *The Birds* (1963).

**David Lean** (1908-1991): he is best remembered for his epic adaptations *The Bridge on the River Kwai* (1957), *Lawrence of Arabia* (1962), *Doctor Zhivago* (1965). Some claim he is the best British film director so far.

**Tony Richardson** (1928-1994): like Anderson, he was a leading figure of the "new wave" of the sixties. *A Taste of Honey* (1961), *The Loneliness of the Long Distance Runner* (1962).

**Stephen Frears** (1941-): *My Beautiful Launderette* (1985), *The Snapper* (1993), *The Van* (1996).

**Mike Leigh** (1943-): he is famous for his satiric depiction of Thatcherite Britain. *High Hopes* (1989), *Life is Sweet* (1990), *Secrets and Lies* (1995).

**Ken Loach** (1936-): he began his career as a television filmmaker and attracted attention with his fictionalised documentaries. He is famous for his social commitment and he is thought to be the most radical voice in British cinema. *Kes* (1969), *Raining Stones* (1993), *My Name is Joe* (1998).

◆ **Actors and actresses**

The most renowned British film actors and actresses are mostly associated with the theatre. That is the case for instance of John Gielgud, Alec Guiness, Lawrence Olivier, Vanessa Redgrave and Judi Dench.

Laurence Olivier is often considered as the greatest British actor of all time. His most famous performance was that of Hamlet in the 1948 Mankievicz film production of *Hamlet*.

# Essay

**British cinema and social realism**

*British cinema has long had a tradition of social films. Emerging from the Free Cinema Movement, the New Wave realism of the sixties led to the production of a number of socially committed films starting with* Room at the Top. *During the seventies, very few British films were made. The eighties, however, were the starting point of a revival of British cinema. And there is no denying that social films have played an important part in this renaissance. The creation of Channel Four and the decision of the channel to invest in cinematographic films were decisive. It was the unexpected success of Stephen Frears's* My Beautiful Launderette *at the Edinburgh film festival in 1985 that led to the film's release in cinemas and that comforted Channel Four in its policy of subsidising cinema productions.* My Beautiful Launderette *is a love story between two inner-city men, a white man and a Pakistani who set up their own business: a launderette. Set against a backdrop of social deprivation, their plans are thwarted by racism and homophobic sentiment.*

*This film, like many others in the same vein, is a criticism of Thatcherite England. The breaking down of the social fabric with an emphasis on the fact that society is ridden with inequalities and that the victimisation of the working-class poor are its underlying themes. But, however bleak and depressing the subject matter, what characterises many of these films, is that they are a mixture of comedy and socially conscious drama. They are set in alienating urban inner-city areas – mostly in the industrial North – and deal with the lives of ordinary people whose social background make them "losers". The films are political statements but ask more questions than they supply answers. They are not dogmatic on the whole, with perhaps the exception of Mark Herman's* Brassed Off *(1997). The film is overtly pro-Labour and is an indictment of Margaret Thatcher's policies. The story is set in a Yorkshire mining town in 1992. An amateur brass band serves as the focus to the conflicts which arise between the inhabitants when the century-old mine is threatened with closure due to government cutbacks. The film shows how the community struggles to keep united in the face of economic repression.*

*My Name is Joe (1998) by Ken Loach centres not so much around a community but around individuals. The setting is a tough housing estate near Glasgow. Joe is an unemployed former alcoholic who falls in love with Sarah, a community health worker. As has been pointed out,* My Name is Joe *is "a film in which the complexities of social issues are explored to reveal unpalatable truths. It seems that some people can find themselves in situations in which all their choices are wrong ones!"*

*But what is particularly interesting about these films is that they are not just about the impact of Thatcherism and the decline of heavy manufacturing. They are not simplistically anti-Thatcher. As Mike Leigh puts it, these films portray ordinary people who are depicted, as they truly are, "*warts and all". Thus, some of the darker sides of these communities and especially their traditional macho view of society are shown.*

*Peter Cattaneo's* Full Monty *(1997) and Steven Daldry's* Billy Elliot *(2000) are good illustrations of this point.* The Full Monty *is set in Sheffield where redundant steelworkers imagine a striptease boys-band type of show as a means to earn some money to make ends meet. These men who are not by any standards handsome men turn themselves into sexual objects just as women turn to prostitution in desperation.* The Full Monty *is a testimony to a changing society where men's position as family breadwinners is destroyed.*

Billy Elliot *which is set in a Durham coal mining community is also a social film in so far as the secondary plot deals with the struggles of the coal miners to defend their jobs and obtain fair wages and benefits. However, the main plot relates the story of a young boy who wants to become a ballet dancer against his father and brother's wishes. The film is therefore primarily an illustration of how a gender-ordered society is being challenged as well as a plea for the deconstruction of masculine identity which restricts men to allegedly virile roles.*

# 18 Religion in Britain

*Sophie Loussouarn*

There has been a marked decline in the membership of the main Christian denominations and in *church attendance since the Second World War. By the end of the 1960s, a profound and irreversible revolution in social and sexual attitudes had taken place. The Church of England was challenged on every front, but it remains an integral part of a far from secular state. In spite of the changes in religious practice, religion still plays an important part in defining the lives of British people. The main religions practiced are the Christian, *Muslim, Sikh, Hindu and *Jewish. Although the Church of England is the established Church, Britain is a multi-faith society and enjoys freedom of *worship. Apart from the main state Church of England, the Anglican Church includes the Church in Wales, the Episcopal Church of Scotland and the Church of Ireland. In Scotland, the national church remains an obvious focus of Scottish nationhood, whereas there is no equivalent in Wales.

## The Church of England

The Church of England came into being in rather dubious circumstances at the time of the English Reformation, which *severed the links between England and Rome in the reign of Henry VIII. After he divorced his first wife, Catherine of Aragon, Henry VIII took total control over the Church of England in 1534 with the Act of Supremacy. In 1536, the Act against the Pope's authority threw off England's allegiance to Rome. The position of the Church of England was consolidated under the Elizabethan settlement, an arrangement which rejected servility to Rome. The Church of England simplified the liturgy and the Book of Common Prayer gave the people of England a pattern of worship.

The Monarch is the Supreme Governor of the Church of England and appoints *archbishops, *bishops and deans of cathedrals on the advice of the Prime Minister. The Head of the Church of England has to fulfil two qualifications: to be the Head of State and to be Protestant.

The Church of England has a historic relationship with the State. Establishment involves one church within one country of the United Kingdom, but Establishment does not mean that the Church of England is identified with the state. It does however signify a special relationship between the church and the political order. The established nature of the Church of England confers certain rights and privileges upon one and only one church within the UK. 26 Church of England bishops for instance have the right to sit in the House of Lords. This means that the State will want to maintain control in the appointment of bishops. The advantage of a seat in the House of Lords has to be weighed against

Civilisation britannique

the restriction embodied in the appointments system.

The links between the church and the state concern a set of connections at the centre of government. The apex of this system lies in the General Synod of the Church of England.

The synodical structure represents the more active section of the Church of England rather than its wider membership. It provides a *lay voice at every level of ecclesiastical debate. The established nature of the Church of England requires that the decisions of the General Synod are themselves subject to approval by Parliament. The General Synod is taking increasing responsibility for Church of England affairs. But the ultimate authority continues to lie not in Parliament but with the Crown, for the monarch has to give royal assent to the canons enacted. Indeed it is in the person of the monarch that the relationship between the church and the state reaches its apogee. The Coronation Oath requires that the Supreme Governor shall uphold the Protestant Reformed religion established by law and shall maintain inviolably the settlement of the Church of England, and the doctrine, worship, and discipline established in England.

Its parochial structure continues to give the Church of England a unique *foothold in English society. It has held the Church of England both geographically and socially in every section of English society. There are 13,000 Church of England *clerics in the United Kingdom. The Church of England is divided into two provinces, led by the Archbishop of Canterbury, Dr George Carey and the Archbishop of York, Dr David Hope.

To be baptized in the Church of England provides a criterion used in the *ascription of membership, which accounts for more than 80% of the Anglican membership and amounts to 25 million members in England today.

## *A multi-faith society*

Significant changes have led to religious plurality in Britain but immigration is the main cause of religious diversity. It started with the large flow of Irish who were Roman Catholics. Then came the *Jews, fleeing from the Russian anti-semitic policy and later from the Nazis; however, relatively few came to Britain after 1945, so that Britain has only the fifth largest Jewish community in the world with about 330,000 members.

After the Second World War, immigration from the New Commonwealth brought about waves of black Christians, Muslims, Sikhs and Hindus.

The Roman Catholic community is relatively young and working class and it accounts for 11% of the adult population in England and Wales (5.6 million members). There has been a decline in mass attendance but 40% of first-generation Catholic immigrants attend church weekly.

The orthodox community remains small and is mainly represented in England with 500,000 members. Nevertheless, the *congregation is growing.

The largest non-Christian minority in Britain is made up of Muslims, coming from the Indian subcontinent, notably Pakistan and Bangladesh. There were as many as 1.1 million members in 1995 and the Muslim community is a very active one. One hundred new mosques are being built to house Britain's fastest growing religion.

The 400,000 Hindus and the slightly larger group of 600,000 Sikhs are the other religious minorities living in Britain. The former live in Greater London and the cities of the Midlands, while the latter mostly live in Southall and Gravesend.

## The future of the established Church

The established nature of the Church of England is either regarded as wholly right or wholly wrong.

On the one hand, there are several arguments in favour of *disestablishment.

According to some critics, the present system is no longer tenable in contemporary society, for it discriminates against religious minorities which are an essential part of British life. Current diversity within society makes many people outside the Church of England feel uneasy with that institution.

Some argue that the involvement of the Church of England in public life is inappropriate and that the churches' business is not of this world.

Others argue that the relationship between the church and the state cannot be ignored in this controversy. Can an established church obliged to undertake a pastoral role combine with it an effective critical role with respect to the government of the day?

Finally, the Church of England is seen as the arm of English isolationism in Europe. But there is very little interest in what might replace the present system.

On the other hand, the defenders of the Church of England are aware that it is far from a perfect institution but it is useful in a pluralist society and above all flexible. The Church of England is a member of the Churches' Commission for Inter Faith Relations and works to build good relations between the communities of all the major faiths in Britain. Besides, it is a decentralized institution with 43 dioceses in England. Moreover, disestablishing the Church of England would have the result of marginalizing the Church of England in contemporary society and of pushing to one side all those who take faith seriously. Finally, the Church of England still meets the spiritual needs of a substantial proportion of the English people and it has a major involvement in education, health care, the prison service and civic life.

Britain is a multireligious society, but religious minorities are not evenly spread throughout Britain and there are wide differences depending on the regions. The pattern of religious life is changing. *Churchgoing has decreased, but it remains strong in rural areas which are sparsely populated and within religious minorities who encourage a continuity of religious practice.

# VOCABULARY

| | |
|---|---|
| allegiance | fidélité, obéissance |
| archbishop | archevêque |
| archdeacon | archidiacre |
| ascription | attribution |
| belief | croyance |
| bishop | évêque |
| Buddhism | Bouddhisme |
| calling | vocation |
| chaplain | aumônier |
| Christendom | chrétienté |
| church attendance | pratique religieuse ; pratiquant |
| churchgoing/churchgoer | pratique religieuse/pratiquant |
| churchman | ecclésiastique (n) |
| cleric | ecclésiastique (n) |
| congregation | assemblée des fidèles |
| creed | principes |
| curate | vicaire |
| dean | doyen |
| disestablishment | séparation de l'Église et de l'État |
| dissent (religious) | dissidence |
| foothold | prise |
| have (to) a grip on | avoir prise sur |
| Hinduism | hindouisme |
| infringe (to) | transgresser |
| Jew/Jewish (adj.) | juif |
| laity | laïcs |
| layman/lay preacher | laïque ; prédicateur laïque |
| Muslim | musulman |
| non-stipendiary | ecclésiastique sans appointements |
| parochialism | esprit de clocher |
| persuasion | confession, religion |
| secularism | laïcité |
| secularization | laïcisation |
| see | siège épiscopal, évêché |
| sever (to) the links | rompre les liens |
| be (to) spread | être répandu, être étendu |
| upheaval | agitation, bouleversement |
| uphold (to) a religion | faire observer une religion |
| vicar | pasteur, curé |
| worship (freedom of) | liberté de culte |
| worship (places of) | lieux de culte |

# Focus...

Less than 10% of people in Britain attend church. Church-goers tend to be women (51%). 25% are under 15 and 24% are aged 45-64.

Even though Catholics account for one-fifth of the members of the Anglican Church, there are more Catholic worshippers attending Mass than Anglicans.

There are 1,702 women priests and 11,273 men priests in the Church of England today.

◆ **Religious dissent**

Religious *dissent from the Church of England came with social and political upheavals in the seventeenth century.

**The Baptist Church** was founded in 1611 and the Baptists believed that Christ's death was for all men and not only for the elect. Baptists were influential in the religious and political life of Britain during the nineteenth century, but their membership declined after World War I.

**Methodism** originated from John Wesley's revival preaching in 1739. It meant to reform the Church of England from within and became an autonomous church in 1795, four years after Wesley's death. The difference between Methodists and Anglicans is not in doctrines but in emphases. Methodism insists on the power of the Holy Spirit to confirm the faith of the believer and transform his personal life, on the personal relationship with God. The Methodist church has a strong interest in social issues, ranging from poverty and the betterment of social conditions, to education and peace.

**Presbyterianism** existed in England in the 16th and 17th centuries but it was revived by Scots who began to settle in Britain in the 18th century. The merger of the United Presbyterian Church and Scottish Presbyterian congregations in England led to the organization of the Presbyterian Church of England in 1876. In 1972, it was merged into the United Reformed Church in England and Wales.

◆ **The acceptance of women priests**

Women who have long been the greatest number of members, attenders and activists of the Church of England were long denied the right to do what clergymen did. The Methodist Church allowed women preachers, but the Church of England long held onto the Roman Catholic idea that the priesthood was a distinct *calling and that men had a monopoly on the Anglican priesthood. After decades of pressure from women within the Church, in 1992, the 574-member General Synod of the Church of England approved the measure which allows women to become priests. Today, there is one woman *archdeacon, there are 11 women cathedral ministers, 426 women *vicars, 433 women assistant *curates, 233 women *chaplains and 598 women *non-stipendiaries in the Church of England.

# Commentary of a Text

*Concours de classement, ENA, mars 1999*

"Faith, Hope And Political Meddling" By William REES-MOGG (*The Times*, April 13, 1998).

On Good Friday, *The Times* published a major interview with David Hope, the Archbishop of York. David Hope is a celibate priest and an Anglo-Catholic. That makes it the more remarkable that he has raised the issue of disestablishment. He is himself in favour of retaining links between the Church of England and the State, but considers that the whole of the relationship needs to be reviewed.

In England state authority has recently been imposed over the appointment of James Jones, previously the Bishop of Hull, to be Bishop of Liverpool. In England, the State still claims an unlimited right to appoint bishops.

However the convention has been that two names should be submitted by the Church to the Prime Minister and that he or she should choose one of them. Two names were, indeed submitted for the *See of Liverpool. The Prime Minister, possibly correctly, thought that neither would meet Liverpool's special needs; so he decided to select the Bishop of Hull. Perhaps Bishop Jones had the support of John Prescott, who is a Member of Parliament for Hull, and would have seen Bishop Jones's pastoral work in another large and impoverished industrial port.

Tony Blair broke a convention which had been observed even by Margaret Thatcher. He had the constitutional right to do so, but he broke the custom and practice which has great force in England's unwritten constitutional arrangements. It is, after all, an English matter; Mr Blair holds office by virtue of his majority in the Parliament of the United Kingdom. It was, in its mild way, an act of constitutional aggression in which the State imposed its will on the Church. The Prime Minister may have been right on the merits of the appointment, but he has made a counter-challenge to his use of the State's power almost inevitable.

There are now three choices open to the Church of England. The first is complete disestablishment, which is already the situation of the Episcopal churches in Scotland, Wales and Ireland. The Queen is the Supreme Governor of the Church of England, but her ministers in London have no power over these parallel churches. The second is that the Church of England should remain the established Church, but it should become completely self-governing. That would make the synod independent of Parliament, and would give it, under whatever new statutes might be adopted, the power of making its own appointments.

The third option is the status quo; the government of the day would continue to have the ultimate power over appointments, parliament would retain the ultimate power to legislate for the Church. The original Tudor settlement would remain in force.

Complete disestablishment would, however, deprive the Church of England of its special role and would reduce the remaining Christian influence on national life. No Christian, whether Anglican or not, would want that. It may not matter whether bishops continue to sit in the House of Lords – many people favour a wholly elected body, it does matter that the Church of England should not lose its relationship to the nation. That naturally suggests that the link to the Queen should remain the same, but that she should be advised on all ecclesiastical matters by her archbishops, bishops and synod and not by her Prime Minister, ministers and Parliament. Political matters are for political people; Church matters are for church people, even when they make mistakes.

The next years are, in any case, likely to see a debate on the structure as well as the role of the Church of England; the Archbishop of York should be congratulated on having had the courage to open this debate. The role of the Prime Minister in church appointments seems no longer to be defensible; the politicians need to be taken out of the Church's chain of authority. As individuals, they may or may not hold religious views, but they have no qualifications to take church decisions or to make church appointments.

*In a leading article of the daily paper,* The Times, *the former editor of the broadsheet deals with the complicated links between the Church of England and the State.*

*Recently, the appointment of the bishop of Liverpool was evidence of the important part played by the Prime Minister whose role is criticised by the journalist. Indeed, Tony Blair \*infringed the unwritten constitutional arrangements for the appointments of bishops which says that they should be chosen out of two names put forward by the Church.*

*This leads the journalist to focus on the implications of the three options left to the Church of England. First of all, like the churches in Scotland, Wales and Ireland, the Church of England could be disestablished. Secondly, the Church of England could remain established, but the synod would be entitled to appoint bishops and the State would no longer have a say on church matters. Thirdly, the relationship between the Church and the State could be maintained after Henry VIII's Act of Settlement.*

*The article reveals Rees-Mogg's attachment to the established Church of England thus having a \*grip on the nation and retaining a special link with the royal family. It also tackles the controversial issue of the Prime Minister's role in church matters and church appointments which should be altered.*

# 19 Ethnic Minorities

*Sophie Loussouarn*

Numerous groups have *settled in Britain (Irish, Jewish, Polish, Chinese), but a new *pattern of immigration was established after 1945. The end of World War II brought about new flows of immigrants coming from the New Commonwealth (India, a few African countries, the West Indies) and from Pakistan. The Commonwealth had taken part in the war and soldiers had fought under the *Union Jack with the British troops, and the UK seemed all the more welcoming in its role of mother country as there was a high rate of unemployment in the Commonwealth countries.

From the very beginning, just after the war, ethnic minorities first came from the *Caribbean and then from the Indian sub-continent, until about 1960. But, from 1962 onwards public attitudes towards ethnic minorities have gradually deteriorated. Legislation was introduced to cut down immigration and to promote equal opportunities for ethnic minority communities.

3.3 million Britons are now from an ethnic minority which *accounts for 5.5% of the population, but there are numerous differences between the groups in their standards of living, access to opportunities such as jobs, education or housing, as well as in their belief systems, likes and dislikes.

## The main ethnic minority groups

The post-war era was determined by the relationships established during the colonial period. On the one hand, the political and cultural links between the UK and former colonies encouraged migration to Britain. On the other hand, Britain's attempts to rebuild its *shattered economy and the demands for a cheap labour supply in the 1940s and 1950s drew many more workers from the former British Empire.

The British Nationality Act of 1948 allowed citizens of the Commonwealth to settle in Britain and facilitated a new era in which most of the migrants were "coloured" people.

The mass migrations of the 1950s and 1960s produced close *networks of *related migrants from particular regions of origin. New Commonwealth immigrants formed numerous ethnic groups based on common language, religion and race. Distinctions are made between the Afro-Caribbean and Asian communities, but far greater diversity exists than is *implied by this *two-fold categorisation.

The first Afro-Caribbeans arrived in 1948 to work in public transport, manufacturing and the National Health Service. According to the Office for National Statistics figures for 1999, the 900,000 members of all-Black groups now make up 1.5% of the population.

Their aspirations to integrate ensured more contact with the white community than was experienced by the Asian community.

The Asian community is composed of several groups based on 7 main languages further divided into numerous dialects. Some groups have to *resort to a second language, such as English, in order to integrate. The Asian community is further divided by several religions, values, cultural practices and castes, as well as by the political tensions found in the politics of the Indian subcontinent. According to the Office for National Statistics figures for 1999, the Asian community was made up of 900,000 Indians (1.5% of the population), 600,000 Pakistanis (1%), 200,000 Bangladeshis (0.3%) and 200,000 Chinese (0.3%).

Some Indians, Pakistanis and Bangladeshis have come to work in the textile and other industries while others have set up their own businesses, opening corner shops and restaurants in towns. They work hard and have strong family values. They have left their homeland with high motivation to succeed materially and to improve but they also have strong warnings about the danger of moral corruption in the West, hence an increased awareness of values and behaviours, and a reappraisal of ethnic identity. The *assessment of difference depends in large part on their position in the residential, employment and social structure. In the 1970s and 1980s, Hong Kong Chinese and refugees from Vietnam came over to Britain to work in the *catering business. The Asians' detached attitude towards the host community *insulates them to some extent. They also have entirely separate cultural traditions which provide a strong sense of identity.

## Anti-discriminatory policies

Even though ethnic minorities have added to the British economy through enterprise and job creation, they were not always welcome and sometimes faced discrimination and violence. Policy-makers thus passed race relations laws in 1965, 1968 and 1976. The 1965 Race Relations Act enunciated the principle of ending discrimination against black immigrants on the grounds of race and *outlawed discrimination in "places of public *resort". The 1968 Race Relations Act extended the 1965 Act to include employment and housing and set up the Community Relations Commission "to promote harmonious community relations". Yet, the 1976 Race Relations was the most important step in tackling racial discrimination and promoting equal opportunities. It introduced the notion of indirect discrimination, based on the American model of affirmative action and outlawed racial discrimination in employment and education and in the *provision of goods and services. It set up the Commission for Racial Equality (CRE) with its wide powers to carry out formal *investigations and to issue notices against *unlawful discrimination.

During the 1997 election campaign, the Labour manifesto claimed to "seek the end of unjustifiable discrimination wherever it exists in society or at work".

The Blair government is committed to working towards equality in employment and the New Deal programme should promote equal opportunities. The Department for Education and Employment has adopted a Race Equality Strategy in its employment policy and develops action plans to meet the *needs of ethnic minorities. The *civil service has decided to increase its minority ethnic staff. The Foreign and Commonwealth Office has encouraged recruitment of ethnic minorities in junior and senior posts and the government aims to recruit 8,000 black and Asian police officers over the next ten years. Furthermore, the Army launched an equal opportunities plan in 1997 and the plan means to *increase the number of black and Asian soldiers fivefold to 5.2%.

## The lifestyles of ethnic minorities

Ethnic minorities have contributed to British culture and politics and they have their own newspapers and political organizations. Weekly newspapers include the *Caribbean Times, Asian Times,* and *Amar Deep Hindi.* The Standing Conference of Afro-Caribbean and Asian Councillors, the Black Against State Harassment and Repression Groups and the Muslim parliament are the main ethnic organizations. There are about 650 ethnic minority councillors in England and Wales (3.1% of the 21,498 local councillors in 1998), but in the House of Commons there are only nine black or Asian MPs and in the House of Lords there are 10 black or Asian life peers. Ethnic minorities are *worse off than the British community, especially Pakistani and Bangladeshi families. In 1997, 82% of Pakistani *households and 84% of Bangladeshi households had an income below half the national average, owing to high rates of male unemployment, low rates of women's economic activity, low wages and large households. Furthermore, the unemployment rate for black (Caribbean, African and other) and Pakistani/Bangladeshi male workers was three times higher than the rate of white workers. And in 1997, black men earned 82% of the white median rate of pay while Pakistani/Bangladeshi men earned only 55% of the white hourly median.

In spite of the improving living conditions in Britain, ethnic minorities are over-represented among the homeless and housing conditions may be poor for some groups with overcrowding in *inner-cities and lack of *amenities such as central heating. But while 25% of Chinese live in rented housing, 80% of the Indian population and 75% of the Pakistani are owner occupiers.

Since the arrival of the first Afro-Caribbeans in 1948, British race relations have had some *bleak moments. There were the Notting Hill riots of 1958, Enoch Powell's Birmingham speech in 1968 calling for a halt to black immigration, and the Brixton *riots of 1981 leading to the Scarman Report. Discrimination in housing and employment is now illegal, but racial *prejudice and violence still exist. If racial prejudice endures, ethnic minorities have managed to integrate and some of them have succeeded in business, politics, music and *entertainment.

# Vocabulary

| | |
|---:|:---|
| account (to) for | représenter |
| amenities | aménagements |
| assessment | estimation, évaluation |
| bleak | triste |
| breed (to) | engendrer |
| the Caribbean | les Antilles |
| catering business | restauration |
| civil service | fonction publique |
| condone (to) | excuser |
| entertainment | divertissement |
| to some extent | jusqu'à un certain point |
| flock (to) | s'assembler |
| greed | envie |
| household | famille, ménage |
| imply (to) | impliquer |
| imprint | empreinte |
| increase (to) fivefold/twofold | multiplier par cinq ; doubler |
| inner cities | banlieues |
| insulate (to) | isoler |
| carry (to) out an investigation | procéder à une enquête |
| mug (to) | agresser |
| the needs of | besoins |
| network | réseau |
| outlaw (to) | proscrire, bannir |
| outstanding | remarquable |
| pattern | modèle, motif |
| prejudice | préjugé |
| be (to) prompted by | être animé par |
| provision | fourniture |
| related | apparenté |
| resort (to) to | recourir à |
| places of public resort | lieux public |
| riot | émeute |
| shattered | bouleversé |
| settle (to) | s'installer |
| steady | progressif |
| thrive (to) | prospérer |
| the Union Jack | drapeau britannique |
| unlawful | illégal, illicite |
| worse off | plus pauvre |

# Focus...

Black and Asian people make up 5.6% of the population, although in some inner-city areas, it goes up to 40 or 50%.

The GDP of ethnic minorities in the UK totals £37 billion and they have a combined disposable income of some £10 billion.

The number of immigrants now entering Britain from non-European countries has declined and 69,800 people were accepted for settlement in the UK in 1998.

In the 1997 general election, 84% of black and Asian voters supported Labour.

◆ **Roy Jenkins's definition of integration in his 1966 speech**

"I define integration not as a flattering process of assimilation but as equal opportunity, accompanied by cultural diversity, in an atmosphere of mutual tolerance. This is the goal. […] In the present circumstances we are bound, as almost everyone now recognizes, to contain the flow of immigrants within the economic and social capacity of the country to absorb them – the social capacity being for the moment, more restrictive than the economic."

◆ **Enoch Powell's Birmingham speech in 1968**

The Conservative MP delivered this racist speech at the time of the second Commonwealth Immigrants Act of 1968, in Birmingham where there was an anti-immigration lobby. He used rhetorical devices and resorted to Latin quotations in order to express his ideas.

"As I look ahead, I am filled with foreboding. Like the Roman, I seem to see "the River Tiber foaming with much blood"; that tragic and intractable phenomenon which we watch with horror on the other side of the Atlantic but which there is interwoven with the history and existence of the States itself, is coming upon us here by our own volition and our own neglect. Indeed, it has all but come. In numerical terms, it will be of American proportions long before the end of the century. Only resolute and urgent action will avert it now."

### ◆ The Brixton disorders

The Brixton disorders of April 10th, 1981 were scenes of violence, in which the ethnic minorities attacked the police with stones, bricks, iron bars and petrol bombs. As a result, 280 policemen were injured. Among the causes of the disorders were the oppressive policing over a period of years and the protest against society by people deeply frustrated and deprived.

An inquiry was launched and the Scarman Report of 1981 called for a co-ordinated and government-led policy against racial disadvantage. The Report emphasized the need for tight immigration controls.

# Essay

**Is Britain A Multicultural Society?**

*Is Britain today a multicultural society? Such a question raises complex, difficult and controversial issues. Invasion, expansion, Empire and Commonwealth brought about new flows of immigrants at various stages of British history. The Irish in the eighteenth and nineteenth century, the Jews from 1880 onwards, the Afro-Caribbeans and Asians in the post-war period \*flocked to Britain and have created a mixture of traditions, customs and religions. This wide range of cultures has had an impact on the food the British eat, the music they listen to and the clothes they wear. The ethnic minorities with their cultural identities and heritage add value to contemporary Britain. But there are downsides to it, and multiculturalism also appears as a threat to British identity.*

*Britain is a multilingual country where Punjabi is spoken by 52% of British Asians, Urdu by 32% of British Asians, Hindi by 27% of British Asians, Gujarati by 25% of British Asians, not to mention Bengali and Sylheti, Cantonese, Mandarin, Hakka, Vietnamese and Caribbean Creole. Turkish, Spanish and Greek are also spoken.*

*It is also a multi-faith society with Christians, Muslims, Sikhs, Hindus, Jews and Buddhists.*

*The various ethnic groups living in Britain have created a culture of diversity and have influenced the arts and food and play a prominent part in British sports and fashion.*

*Ethnic minorities have brought new forms of art, new talents and new ways of performing. Artists belonging to ethnic minorities are supported by the National Black Arts Network, Asian Art Access, the British Chinese Arts Association and ArtBlackLive, which are funded by the Arts Council. British popular music has been influenced by black music and black musicians have become role models for all young people. Black music such as reggae, soul and rap as well as jazz has had a great impact on British music. New sounds have appeared, mixing traditional Asian, black American and electronic music and giving birth to bhangra which has left an \*imprint on British pop music and has fostered new cross-over styles. Some music groups such as Shiva Nova, Black Voices, Croydon Clocktower and Tomorrow's Warriors now have a wider audience than ethnic minorities owing to the promotion of the Asian, African and Caribbean Music Circuits of the Arts Council.*

*Furthermore, ethnic minority artists are increasingly involved in video and film production and novelist and scriptwriter Hanif*

*Kureishi prides himself on the writing rights of Stephen Frears's* My Beautiful Laundrette *(1985). Ethnic minorities have also contributed to the British theatre and companies such as Talama, Kuumba, Tara Arts, Black Theatre Co-op and Black Mime Theatre Company have won national and international reputations. Besides, contemporary British literature reckons award winning writers such as Ben Okri and performance poets such as Benjamin Zephaniah.*

*Apart from music, film-making, drama and dance, food and eating in Britain have been enriched by the ethnic minorities who thrive in the catering industry. A wide range of food from around the world is now available, especially curry, chow mein, pasta and pizza. Among the most popular types of ethnic food, Chinese comes first before Indian, Italian and Greek cuisine.*

*Ethnic minorities have also contributed to British sport and some have achieved worldwide recognition in football, cricket, boxing and athletics. 25% of British professional footballers are black and the most renowned are John Barnes, Ian Wright and Paul Ince. \*Outstanding sportsmen from Commonwealth countries also play a prominent part in English cricket, especially British Caribbean-Asians Mark Ramprakash and Nasser Hussein.*

*If multiculturalism has played an important part in renewing British culture, it is also potentially the source of social problems. The image of inner city areas becoming black enclaves where "British" law and order cannot be easily enforced has led to a fear of emergence of alien values which have been seen as a potential threat to the way of life and culture of white residents. Many claim that white Britons have a duty to preserve British culture and to object to non-Christian religions being taught in schools.*

*Moreover, clashes between ethnic cultures \*breed racism between the various communities. Asians are often targeted by Afro-Caribbeans, because they are more successful than blacks; consequently, Asians are occasionally \*mugged in the streets and their cars are sometimes smashed up. Many of these muggings have nothing to do with culture or religion but are \*prompted by \*greed. On the other hand, 30% of Asians and Jews are reluctant to \*condone interethnic marriages with the Afro-Caribbean community and Muslims are also against marrying out of the community.*

*Pluralism in Britain should not be exaggerated. Multiculturalism is an urban phenomenon and differs from region to region. Large tracts of the country, especially the more rural areas, remain uncompromisingly mono-cultural. But according to recent forecasts, white people will account for less than 50% of Britain's population by 2100.*

# 20 Feminism in Great Britain

*Florence Binard*

*"I myself have never been able to find out precisely what feminism is: I only know that people call me a feminist whenever I express sentiments that differentiate me from a \*doormat..."* Rebecca West

## The precursors of feminism

Feminism, which is both a doctrine and a movement aiming at \*equal rights and opportunities for women, is often described as a 19th century phenomenon. There were a number of women who voiced feminist ideas long before women started to organise collective actions but these voices were sparse and isolated.

The first major feminist work, the landmark in feminist theory, was *A Vindication of the Rights of Women*, written by Mary Wollstonecraft and published in 1792. The book is a plea for a change in society's perceptions and treatment of women. Education, marriage and property laws are among the topics she addresses and which were of concern to early feminists. Girls were not educated and upon marrying a woman *forfeited her rights and property to her husband.

Another important figure in the history of British feminism is John Stuart Mill. His *Subjection of Women,* 1869, was a harsh criticism of the marriage establishment which he saw as the key to women's oppression and degradation. On 20th May, 1867, he initiated the first debate in the House of Commons on women's suffrage. His insistence that it was through the legislative sphere that women's lot would be improved contributed to the formation of the suffrage movement which was soon to become a primary goal of feminist activities.

Other feminist issues were never totally forgotten but it was argued that with the vote women would have the power to influence and even take part in government decisions. The vote would be the weapon women would use to force the government to set up and improve laws in favour of women.

**Militant political action** among women really started in 1903 when Emmeline Pankhurst founded the Women's Social and Political Union (WSPU). A few years after its creation faced with government indifference, the WSPU embarked on a civil disobedience campaign which involved window smashing, boycotts, bombings, picketing, hunger strikes etc.

On the eve of the First World War, the vote was still to be achieved. But, with the advent of the war, many feminists decided it was their duty as citizens to take part in the war effort. Women's services were organised and soon women were replacing men in factories, on farms and in non-combat tasks as ambulance drivers or nurses for instance. This earned them recognition by the government and in 1918 women aged thirty and

Civilisation britannique

above were enfranchised. It took another ten years of action for them to be granted the vote on an equal footing with men.

**During the inter-war period** and until the late fifties, feminists remained active but the strength of their actions did not compare with pre-war militancy. They adopted a "woman centred approach" and fought for birth control and the protection of the mother and child within the family unit. Some advances were made, for instance, in 1923 the Matrimonial Causes Act enabled wives to sue for divorce on the basis of adultery, a right that men had had since 1857. But on the whole, this period is not seen as one of major advancement for women and the place of women beyond mothering was barely challenged. In fact, feminists of the next generation reproached them for being genteel middle-class ladies who represented the interests of women as dependants.

**The sixties and seventies** saw a resurgence of militant feminism with the *Women's Liberation Movement, better known as "Women's Lib". This second wave of active feminism was more of a social than a political movement; sexual liberation ("Our Bodies, Our Selves") and equity in the workplace were the cornerstones of the battles that were fought. Throughout the country women formed "consciousness raising groups" which were discussion groups whose purpose was to make women aware of their common disadvantages. Having recognised and identified the source of their oppression – a capitalistic *patriarchal society – women would then be able to free themselves from their own self-oppression and *fight for their rights. Thus, the starting point of the battle was the individual woman and the home, although their aim was clearly to disrupt and revolutionise society. Many women embarked on a demystification of the hypocritical prevailing image of femininity: the myth of the "Eternal Feminine" which transformed women into *sex-objects. They did not accept the idea that a woman's primary duty was to her family and demanded that men should share the housekeeping duties. Interestingly, the one demand that was completely new, that is to say that had not been the subject of campaigns since the nineteenth century, was the demand for 24 hour *nurseries (a demand that has yet to be met).

Nonetheless, thanks to the Women's Liberation Movement, a number of important battles were then won, as the *Sex Discrimination Act, the Equal Pay Act and the Abortion Act testify.

The seventies also saw major changes in feminist ideology. Divisions between feminists emerged, in particular between socialist feminists and *radical feminists. And women started reproaching the women's movement for being exclusive in political, ethnic and class terms, in a nutshell for being a white middle-class organisation. Thus, pacifist women, ethnic minority women, lesbians started setting up their own feminist splinter groups so as to address the issues that dealt with their own specific needs and concerns.

**In the eighties and early nineties** a *backlash emerged and feminist militancy lost its potency. For instance, in 1990, the 1967 Abortion Act was amended and the period of time before a termination was reduced from 28 to 24 weeks.

Ironically, this happened when for the first time in British history a woman was Prime Minister. Margaret Thatcher who was nicknamed the "Iron Lady" and described as the best "man" for the job held strong conservative views on the place of women in society.

In reality, ever since the seventies, however much women have distanced themselves from Women's Lib they have never ceased to fight for their rights. Paradoxically, while rejecting feminism many women have made feminist claims their own. From a minority cause, feminism has gradually become a majority cause. Many women who today would not call themselves feminists have integrated feminist ideas and regard equality between the sexes as their due.

### *The present situation*

Although pay differentials for comparable work are theoretically illegal, women earn on average 20% less than men. Inequities in career advancement, the existence of a "*glass ceiling" and the fact that they are grossly under-represented in the political arena have led women to take actions to redress the injustice.

Under the pressure of women's lobbies, the New Labour Government of Tony Blair has had to include women's issues in their agenda. They *claim to aim at parity in all sectors between men and women and also recognise the huge unpaid contribution that women make to the maintenance of civil society – it is estimated that unpaid carers (mostly women) save the country £30 billion a year. But "respect, recognition and representation" for women are still to be achieved.

### *The National Alliance of Women's Organisations and the EWL*

Not only has feminism become plural but it is international. The National Alliance of Women's Organisations (NAWO) which is a British umbrella organisation regrouping 200 smaller organisations is also the co-ordinating body for the European Women's Lobby (EWL) in England. Such organisations play a vital role at national and international level. Representatives of the EWL argue that throughout Europe women are faced with the same discrimination and that to redress the injustice it is essential that women should be represented at the highest political levels.

They pay close attention to law-making and reforming through a policy of mainstreaming. In other words, they do not only deal with subjects that obviously and solely concern women. Their aim is to ensure that each law whatever its subject takes into account women's *equal opportunities so as to prevent *discrimination where it may not be manifest. They are also in favour of the introduction of quotas; to make a difference to policy and business organisation more women must hold decision-making positions but without some kind of positive discrimination decades will be necessary for women to hold these positions.

# VOCABULARY

| | |
|---:|:---|
| activist | militant (e) |
| backlash | retour de bâton |
| claim (to)/claim | revendiquer ; revendication |
| compete (to) | rivaliser |
| discriminate (to) | établir une discrimination |
| discriminatory attitudes | attitudes discriminatoires |
| domestic violence | violence conjugale |
| doormat | paillasson, quelqu'un de faible, qui se laisse marcher sur les pieds |
| eco-feminism | écoféminisme |
| equal opportunities | égalité des chances |
| equal pay for equal work | à travail égal salaire égal |
| essentialist | essentialiste |
| fair sex | beau sexe |
| fight for (to) | se battre pour |
| forfeit (to) | renoncer à |
| fulfil oneself (to) | se réaliser |
| full-time/part-time job | un travail à temps complet ; à temps partiel |
| gender | genre |
| glass ceiling | plafond de verre |
| hold top jobs (to) | occuper des postes importants |
| household chores | corvées ménagères |
| male chauvinism | phallocratie |
| male dominated fields | domaines réservés aux hommes |
| nurseries | crêches |
| patriarchy | patriarchie |
| playgroup | une garderie |
| radical feminism | féminisme radical |
| sex discrimination | discrimination sexuelle |
| sex object | objet sexuel |
| sexism | sexisme |
| sexual harassment | harcèlement sexuel |
| sisterhood | solidarité féminine |
| struggle (to)/struggle | lutter, lutte |
| suffragist, suffragette | suffragette (le terme « suffragette » fut initialement employé de façon dérogatoire) |
| take up a career (to) | embrasser une carrière |
| weaker sex | sexe faible |
| women's lib movement | Mouvement de Libération des Femmes (MLF) |
| women's rights | droits des femmes |

# Focus...

## ◆ Major Feminist Writings

Although British feminism has its own specificity, there is no denying that the theory of feminism is international and widely influenced by notably, French, American and English authors.

1953    *The Second Sex* by Simone de Beauvoir "*One is not born, but rather becomes, a woman.*"

1963    *The Feminine Mystique* by Betty Friedan. The "feminine mystique" is the myth whereby women could only achieve happiness in life through marriage and motherhood.

1969    *Sexual Politics* by Kate Millett. Sex has a political aspect, in a patriarchal society, men dominate women in sex, as they do in most aspects of life.

1970    *The Female Eunuch* by Germaine Greer. "*She (woman) could begin not by changing the world, but by re-assessing herself.*" "*Women have very little idea of how much men hate them.*"

1991    *Backlash* by Susan Faludi. Women's hard-won feminist victories are insidiously threatened.

## ◆ Important dates

1870    The Married Women's Property Act gave married women the right to their own earnings.

1918    Vote for women over 30.

1928    Vote for women over 21 (equality with men).

1923    Matrimonial Causes Act enabled wives to sue for divorce on the basis of adultery.

1954    Equal pay for men and women in the civil service.

1961    The contraceptive pill became available and free on the National Health.

1968    The Abortion Act allowed for legal abortion if two physicians agreed that pregnancy was dangerous for mental or physical health of woman.

1975    Sex Discrimination Act and Equal Pay Act.

## ◆ Women in politics

- Despite the influx of women in Parliament in 1997, women remain widely under-represented: they only make up 18% of MPs.

- Only 16% of the members of the reformed House of Lords are women.
- Only a quarter of Britain's local councillors are women.

◆ **Women and work at the turn of the 21st century**
- In the early 70s women made up over a third of the workforce, in the late 90s women's share of employment rose to about 50%.
- A quarter of all jobs are *part-time jobs. Out of the 7 million people in part time employment, about 5.5 million are women.
- Nearly 45% of women in employment work part-time.
- Fewer than 20% of managers in business are women.
- Women in full-time work are paid, on average, just 81% of the hourly wage of their male counterparts.
- Women working part-time fare even worse, receiving just 58% of the hourly earnings of men in full-time work

◆ **A lifetime of inequality**

|  | Mid-skilled man with or without children | Mid-skilled woman with no children | Mid-skilled woman with two children |
| --- | --- | --- | --- |
| Lifetime earnings | £ 891,000 | £ 650,000 | £ 510,000 |
|  |  | Price paid for being a woman: £ 241,000 | Price paid for being a woman and a mum: £ 361,000 |

◆ **Women and education**

Education is the most important factor determining a woman's earnings over her lifetime.
- Since the early 80s, the number of females in Further Education has been higher than that of males.
- In engineering there are six times as many men as women graduates; in maths and computing three times as many and in physical science twice as many.
- About 90% of those starting apprenticeships in childcare, hairdressing and floristry are women.

◆ **Family life and household chores**
- Single parents head about 25% of families with children, three times as many as in the early 70s. The overwhelming majority of single parents are women. Four out of ten lone parents are on incomes below 40% of the average.
- About 45% of all violent crimes experienced by women are cases of *domestic violence.

# Essay

## Millennial feminism: post-feminism or third wave feminism?

*On the one hand we hear that the future is female, that women have won their battle, that not only are they men's equals but they are overtaking them in many fields and that it is just a matter of time before they hold the reins of power. On the other hand, we are told that women are growing dissatisfied with their lot. Some are faced with a reality which shows them that equality between the sexes is a myth whereas some others feel that they have been wronged by feminism. Have we come to the end of feminism or a revival of it?*

*Feminism and feminists have always been rather unpopular, but it seems that they are more unpopular than ever. The word is used by many as a derogatory term and many women go out of their way to make it clear that they do not see themselves as feminists. Other women who see themselves as feminists are reluctant to admit it for fear of the reactions they may encounter. Only a few feel confident enough to shout out loud that they are feminists.*

*This is partly due to the stereotypical views of the seventies feminists that are engraved in people's minds. That is to say an image of women who are aggressive and hate men.*

*Another point put forward is that feminism has become a dated concept since women now hold the same rights as men. It is even argued that in some fields where women have overtaken men, positive discrimination measures should be taken in favour of the latter. This is the case, for instance, in education, where girls are outdoing boys.*

*But the truth is that reality does not match the law. The assumption that the feminist conflict is over and that all can leave the battlefield is more than premature, it is dangerous. If there is no denying that this generation of women is much freer than the previous, figures show that they are still poorer and less powerful than men. Moreover, the sad truth is that too many men still think of women's bodies as commodities offered for their consumption. The figures for domestic violence are horrifying. It is estimated that more than 1 in 4 British women experience domestic violence at some time during their lives.*

*Women have not won parity, they have only achieved equality on paper. The reason for this is twofold. Firstly, equality has been interpreted in a conservative fashion, that is to say as equality of opportunity rather than of result. Secondly, much of the inequality is institutionalised and requires action at the heart of the government where women are largely under-represented. Therefore, unless women hold positions of power at the core of institutions, the necessary reforms will never be implemented.*

*Also, millennial feminists have learnt from the past and they have come to acknowledge that feminism is no longer a minority movement, that feminists are diverse, that they can be all sorts of women; white women, black women, lesbians, heterosexual, bisexual, fat women, working-class women, managers, right wing, left wing etc. New feminists are more diverse than their elders, they are less utopian, they no longer believe in a united \*sisterhood. They are more aware of the importance of money and recognise that power is the key to effectual changes.*

*But most importantly, they have come to realise that their goals may be antagonistic. For instance, some argue that the image of women conveyed by the consumerist women's press and advertising are often degrading and sexist and teach women to despise their bodies by encouraging unrealistic expectations. While others disagree with this point of view and even approve of cosmetic surgery claiming that being able to do what one wishes with ones body is a feminist victory.*

*To conclude, it can safely be said that even if few women might call themselves feminists most take feminist views for granted, albeit without knowing it.*

*Margaret Thatcher once said: "there is no such thing as society, there are only individual men and women and there are families" but women have come to realise that "no woman is an I land". And if there is no denying that difference is a core component of third wave feminism, women must unite to be in a position to ignite the structural changes without which* de facto *equality may never be achieved.*

# 21 *Gays and lesbians in England

*Florence Binard*

Homosexuality is not a twentieth century phenomenon; sexual intercourse between individuals of the same sex has always existed and will always exist. Among the earliest and most frequently quoted texts as evidence that homosexuality is universal, are the Bible with the Sodom and Gomorrah episodes and the Fragments of Sappho which were written in the 6th century BC. In recent years, forgotten texts mentioning homosexuality have been recovered and the corpus of material is ever growing.

Gay and lesbian identity, however is not universal but ideological. The perception people have of homosexuality varies from one historical period to another, from culture to culture, and even from one person to another.

## *Homosexuality: a crime*

Up to the mid-nineteenth century, homosexuality was not regarded as a collective phenomenon concerning a group of individuals. The gay man was seen as a "sodomite" and the lesbian as a *tribade.

In England, from 1533 to the mid-nineteenth century those charged with sodomy or *buggery were liable to a death sentence. In 1861, the maximum penalty was reduced to life imprisonment. Homosexual men were actually targeted as such for the first time in British history in 1885, when the Criminal Law Amendment Act was amended by the Labouchère Amendment. The new law made acts of "*gross indecency" between two men liable to up to two years imprisonment with *hard labour.

Oscar Wilde was the most celebrated victim of the Labouchère Amendment. In 1895, he was prosecuted on a charge of sodomy and sentenced to the maximum penalty of two years' imprisonment with hard labour. The treatment he underwent in jail no doubt led to his premature death in 1900. At the time, the *trial caused a great stir among the general public and for many people, even decades after, the name and works of Oscar Wilde remained synonymous with disgrace. Amongst the homosexual community Oscar Wilde has gradually come to be seen as a martyr to the cause.

Contrary to male homosexuality, lesbianism was never punished by the law in England. In 1921, there was an attempt at introducing a clause similar to the Labouchère Amendment concerning acts of indecency between women, however, the Lords rejected the bill on the grounds that it would do more damage than good in the prevention of lesbianism. One of the most fervent opponents argued that the overwhelming majority of English women had never heard of the "vice" and that if the bill were passed knowledge of its existence would then be widely spread. Aware of female homosexuality, women might start indulging! Thus, instead of curbing the "crime" the law would in fact encourage it.

## Homosexuality: a disease

In the first half of the twentieth century, as the works of Sigmund Freud and Havelock Ellis were becoming better known, more and more people were beginning to view homosexuality from a medical rather than from a criminal angle. The main theory was that of *inversion. Homosexuals or *inverts, as they were called, suffered from a congenital defect that affected their sexual drive. Male inverts were described as women trapped inside men's bodies and female inverts as men trapped inside women's bodies. Inversion being congenital, inverts should not be deemed responsible for what they were and instead of blaming them, people should pity them for their plight. Such was the message that Radclyffe Hall wanted to convey when in 1928 she published *The Well of Loneliness*. The book which relates the story of Stephen Gordon, a female invert, was the first novel ever written to openly defend the cause of gays and lesbians. Several novels had been written on the subject before, but none of them had taken a non-condemning stance, let alone a positive one. Soon after its publication however, *The Well* was banned in England as the novel and its content were judged "obscene".

## The decriminalisation of homosexuality

After the Second World War the number of prosecutions for homosexual offences increased considerably: a number of famous people were tried. Historians even refer to the period as the homosexual witch-hunt. However, under the pressure of the intelligentsia and surprisingly the Church of England, in 1954, the Government decided to set up the Departmental Committee on Homosexual Offences and Prostitution which was chaired by John Wolfenden. The conclusions of the Committee were published in a Report on September 4th, 1957 and recommended that homosexual behaviour in private between consenting adults (21 and over) should be decriminalised.

The Wolfenden report led to the creation of the Homosexual Law Reform Society whose aim was the decriminalisation of homosexuality.

Opponents to legalising homosexual acts between men claimed that a change in the law would damage the moral fabric of society, that it would "open the floodgates" and result in unbridled licence and indicate State condonation. The debate lasted ten years until 1967 when the Sexual Offences Act decriminalised homosexual acts in private between consenting men over 21 years of age.

## Gay pride

The 60s and 70s saw a major shift in the attitudes and demands of homosexuals which was symbolised by the adoption of the word "gay". This new militant approach was developed in the Gay Liberation Front (GLF) Manifesto of 1971. It was the starting point of a battle for the civil rights which gay people were denied. What they wanted was not just reforms but a revolutionary change in society: *"the long-term goal of Gay Liberation is to rid society of the gender-role system which is at the root of our oppression."* This meant a rejection of the "masculine" and "feminine" roles imposed by society. The GLF emphasised the need for gay people to free themselves from self oppression which entailed an open lifestyle. Apologetic pleas for tolerance were to give way to an affirmative stance. Gays and lesbians were to stop being ashamed of their *gayness and *come out of the closet: "*we must root out the idea that homosexuality is bad, sick or immoral, and develop a gay pride*". The London Gay Pride, which first took place in 1972, has been a yearly highlight of the active campaign against discrimination against gays and lesbians ever since.

### *Backlash and the new impetus

The eighties saw a backlash. Taking advantage of the AIDS crisis which stigmatised the gay community in the eyes of public opinion, the Conservative Government of Margaret Thatcher introduced Clause 28 of the Local Government Act of 1988 which prohibits the promotion of homosexuality by teaching or by publishing material. Thus, in English schools, it is illegal to refer to homosexuality from a favourable angle and the study of works by gay or lesbian authors is theoretically forbidden.

Paradoxically, this anti-gay climate gave gays and lesbians a new impetus. In response to the AIDS crisis "Act Up London" was founded in 1989 and "Stonewall" which regroups gay lobbies was created in 1988.

During the nineties the battle intensified and saw the emergence of controversial direct action groups, such as "OutRage!" in 1990 and "Lesbian Avengers" in 1993, whose strategy is to attract public attention through provocative actions like public kiss-ins or the *outing of prominent public figures.

British gays and lesbians regard progress towards legal equality as shamefully slow and homophobic crimes are still commonplace, as the bombing of the Admiral Duncan pub in the London gay quarter in 1999 testifies. However, gay and lesbian activism has helped change people's attitudes and thinking.

There are numerous gay and lesbian organisations and lobbies in all domains – gay business lobbies, political groups, legal action committees, and their campaigns are bearing fruit. In 2000, the British government lifted the ban on gays and lesbians serving in the armed forces and the *age of consent for gay men was lowered to 16.

There are TV and radio programmes specifically targeted at gays and lesbians, most TV and radio soaps feature an openly gay character, and a number of prominent politicians and business people are now openly out.

Despite these undeniable advances, there are still issues to be addressed and in the near future it would seem that the *repeal of Section 28 and the fight for the legal recognition of same-sex partnerships are top of the agenda.

# Vocabulary

| | |
|---:|:---|
| activist | militant |
| age of consent | âge de la maturité sexuelle (terme juridique) |
| backlash | retour de bâton |
| buggery | sodomie |
| butch | lesbienne d'apparence masculine |
| come out (of the closet) (to) | révéler son homosexualité, sortir du placard |
| drag king/queen | femme (**drag king**) ou homme (**drag queen**) qui se « déguise » de façon extravagante, soit en homme, soit en femme |
| dyke | lesbienne, gouine |
| faggot | pédé |
| gay-friendly | favorable aux gays |
| gay icon | symbole gay |
| gayness | homosexualité (il n'existe pas de traduction en français, il s'agit d'un néologisme marquant la différence entre homosexualité qui fait référence à la seule sexualité et le fait d'être gay qui englobe sexualité et identité) |
| gender behaviour | attitude qui consiste à se conformer aux modèles de féminité et masculinité construits par la société (construction sociale et culturelle de la différence des sexes) |
| gross indecency | outrage aux mœurs |
| hard labour | travaux forcés |
| inversion | inversion (terme employé au XIX$^e$ siècle et début du XX$^e$ pour désigner l'homosexualité) |
| invert | inverti(e) |
| mardi gras (US) | carnaval |
| out (to) | révéler l'homosexualité de qqn (sans le consentement de la personne concernée) |
| queen | folle |
| queer (to be) | homo, pédé, gouine |
| queer bashing | chasse aux pédés |
| rainbow | arc-en-ciel |
| repeal | abrogation |
| straight | hétéro |
| transgender | qui transcende la notion de masculinité et féminité, transgenre |
| trial | procès |
| tribade | tridade (du grec **tribein** qui signifie « frotter » mot couramment employé jusqu'au XIX$^e$ siècle pour désigner une lesbienne) |
| unnatural offence | crime contre nature (sodomie) |

# Focus...

◆ **Symbols**

• The Pink Triangle which was first used in Nazi Germany to identify gay men in concentration camps became a gay icon in the 70s and 80s. Lesbians have adopted a black triangle, which was the identification symbol given to some lesbians imprisoned by the Nazis for "anti-social behaviour".

• The *Rainbow Flag was designed in 1978 by Gilbert Baker of San Francisco and has been adopted as a symbol of gay and lesbian community pride.

◆ **Organisations**

• **ActUp** (AIDS Coalition to Unleash Power) "Act up" also means to misbehave. The organisation encourages acts of civil disobedience to make themselves heard.

• **OutRage!** The name of the organisation plays on the polysemy of the word "outrage" which depending on the context means indignation or atrocity, scandal but also on "out" as in "being open about one's sexuality" and "rage" which expresses anger or fury.

• **Stonewall** is a lobbying organisation which derives its name from the Stonewall Rebellion which took place in New York after the police had molested the patrons of the Stonewall Inn, a gay bar in 1969. The Stonewall riots are regarded as the landmark of the gay and lesbian movement.

◆ **Pride**

The First Gay Pride in England took place on July 1st, 1972 and gathered about 2,000 lesbians and gays who marched down Oxford Street to Hyde Park.

From the 70s to the early 80s the attendance at the London Gay pride rarely exceeded 1,000 participants.

However, in 1988 when Section 28 became law, about 40,000 people attended the London Pride Mardi Gras Gay Festival.

In July 2000 there were over 100,000 participants.

It is interesting to note that "Pride" changed its name over the years. It was first called "The Gay Pride", then in the mid-eighties, it became "The Lesbian and Gay Pride" and in 1996, the name was altered to "The Lesbian, Gay, Bisexual, and Transgender Pride".

### ◆ Oscar Wilde

Although Queen Elizabeth still refuses to rehabilitate the "eccentric genius", Oscar Wilde is more fashionable than ever. A number of biographies of the playwright and novelist have been recently published, his plays are being performed in many theatres, a film about his life was made in 1998 and a remake of *The Picture of Dorian Gray* is to be released in 2001. What is more, a statue to his memory was unveiled in London in 1998 and the British Library has set up an exhibition to celebrate the 100th anniversary of his death.

### ◆ Radclyffe Hall

Radclyffe Hall's tomb was restored in 1994. Two biographies of Radclyffe Hall were written in the late 1990s; one was published in 1997 and the other in 1998. *The Well of Loneliness* that has been dubbed the "Lesbian Bible", is a landmark novel which has sold millions of copies since its first publication in 1928. Even to this day it remains a best seller.

### ◆ Essentialism and Social Construction

According to essentialists, one does not become homosexual, one is born homosexual and the essence of homosexuality is universal. Homosexuality is therefore transhistorical and transcultural.

Some "radical" essentialists even claim that there is no such thing as bisexuality. At best, it is a transitional phase towards homosexuality, at worst, it is a refusal to fully accept one's homosexuality. They argue that masculine women and effeminate men have always existed and will always exist.

Constructionists challenge the binary gender theory. Sexual identities are not fixed and do not determine who we are. Their ultimate goal is the dissolution of sexual consciousness – be it gay, *straight, bisexual or other – in favour of "polymorphous sexuality". According to them the root of the problem is that heterosexuality is seen as superior to homosexuality. When equality is achieved, gender nonconformity will be the rule and the differences between the sexualities will lose their significance.

# Essay

## The Female Husband

*The document is the cover of a book published in 1746 entitled* The Female Husband. *The book which relates the true story of a woman, Mary Hamilton, who was charged with marrying another woman, was written by Henry Fielding but was initially published anonymously on account of its improper and shocking subject matter. As Fielding's opening lines to* The Female Husband *show, his aim was to denounce "monstrous and unnatural lusts". His opinion – which remained the predominant view until a few decades if not a few years ago– was that nature and morals dictated that men and women complement each other in order to ensure the survival of the human race.*

Dated as it may be, this mid-eighteenth century document is interesting on several accounts. It testifies to the universality of lesbianism and transgenderism – contrary to what is sometimes claimed, in the past, women did have sex with other women.

This publication is also evidence that the conspiracy of silence that surrounded female homosexuality was not always total in past centuries. It must be emphasised, though, that only a tiny minority of people knew about this "monstrous vice". There is no doubt that until the second half of the twentieth century the vast majority of people were unaware of the existence of lesbianism. Queen Victoria is even said to have declared that sex between two women was impossible. As a result, acts of indecency between women were not introduced in the Labouchère clause in 1885.

But, if lesbian sexual practices remained taboo, the inappropriate *gender behaviour of these women was deemed unnatural and shocking. What people did at home in private could be ignored. The way people dressed and behaved, on the other hand, was visible and therefore a matter of public concern. Thus, although cross-dressing was not illegal for women in England, masquerading as a man or behaving in what was regarded as a masculine way was looked down upon and stigmatised. Mary Hamilton was a freak because she had sex with another woman but what was even more monstrous was that she transgressed the law and assumed a male identity.

Until recently, the predominant image of the lesbian has been that of a masculine woman, the "*butch-*dyke". This vision is largely due to the fact that the lesbians that were visible and identifiable were those who adopted sexual roles mimicking the masculine and feminine stereotypes of straight society. This butch/femme role-playing which concerned gay men as much as lesbians was criticised and is still frowned upon by gays and lesbians who challenge the binary gender theory. According to them, such attitudes were and are the result of gender brainwashing whereby people are expected to conform to established pseudo male and female roles. Detractors of the butch/femme role-playing also claim that such behaviour reinforces the belief that male is superior to female and that heterosexuality is superior to homosexuality.

The title of this document, The Female Husband, is an oxymoron, a contradiction in terms in so far as it evokes a situation where a woman has assumed a male identity by marrying another woman. She has not only transgressed established roles by taking the place of a man but she has committed the crime of desecrating the marriage institution.

Now, if marriage between people of the same sex was unthinkable until the most recent past, it is clearly no longer the case. In the seventies, gays and lesbians rejected the marriage institution and the family unit on the grounds that they were at the root of their oppression. But recent developments have shown that things are changing. The number of gay and lesbian couples with children is constantly increasing. Also, partly due to the AIDS crisis that left many gays destitute upon their partner's death, there has been a growing demand for the legal recognition of same sex-partnerships. Gays and lesbians are now campaigning for the Government to introduce new laws to ensure that homosexual couples could benefit from the same protection regarding financial and property rights as married couples. Some argue in favour of gay marriages whereas others support the idea of civil unions. Whatever happens though, "male wives" and "female husbands" are not on the agenda – these terms refer to dated notions that no longer reflect the fabric of twenty-first century British society.

# Civilisation américaine

# Introduction to the United States

When studying the civilization of the United States, one feels that the country is both close to us (it became a democracy at the same time as France made its revolution, its culture and moral tenets are deeply rooted in European tradition and on both sides of the Atlantic, lifestyles tend to be increasingly similar), and fairly distant in its approach to many issues such as individual freedom, capital punishment, accountability of public figures or reassessment of past history.

The United States was founded by people with ideals in mind. The Puritans who set up the first colonies left their hallmark on public and private life; they also inspired the role played by religion in a country with record numbers of churchgoers among western democracies. The men who wrote the Constitution carefully chose the kind of society they wanted to live in: freedom of enterprise was from the outset the guiding principle for the American form of government.

The word freedom alone seems to be identified with the country. But what is meant by freedom is often significantly different from its European definition. There is probably more free speech in America than in most other countries, yet foreigners find it hard to admit that, for example, the right to bear arms – which accounts for a high rate of gun violence – must be kept in the name of the freedom of American people.

Contrary to European tradition, political parties are little more than electoral machines. Political activism is essentially carried out through lobbying which can be extremely efficient at shaping government decisions.

What sets the United States apart is not just the ideals on which it was built, but it is also the bounty of a vast, almost uninhabited territory, whose natural resources and limitless possibilities offered European immigrants undreamt of opportunities.

The talent for entrepreneurship, based on individualism and risk-taking – eminently core American values – could only flourish in the land of opportunity. Throughout its relatively short history, the United States has kept setting the pace with countless innovations and a level of business acumen envied by other countries.

The United States is different in yet another regard. Its population came from other parts of the world. This has been both a blessing and a tragedy. A blessing because all the wretched and the oppressed of the earth, from

19th-century European immigrants to today's Latinos and Asian newcomers, have benefited from the opportunities they were barred from at home, and have contributed to the country's diversity and dynamism. A tragedy because the importation of black slaves from Africa in colonial times created a discrimination which belied the ideals defined by the Founding Fathers.

Only recently has America taken action to eradicate discrimination against its black citizens. But so many generations of Americans lived in the belief that blacks – and non-whites in general – ought to remain second-class citizens that it is hard today to erase the past, even with the toughest legislation. For the past forty years, all administrations have striven to penalize racial discrimination, sometimes with controversial legislation. But changing people's prejudices takes more than an intricate set of laws.

The 60s rebellion and the Civil Rights movement set forth new attitudes aiming at changing the way people view minorities. It took on the awkward form of political correctness – a trend which has now invaded the Old Continent, but to a lesser degree – and later gave rise to multiculturalism, a new approach to race relations.

Today, the United States stands as the only super-power in the world. Its economic might gives it a competitive edge in the new economy as well as in world trade affairs. In the 90s, the country enjoyed a period of unprecedented prosperity, resulting in great optimism for the future of the nation. Unfortunately not all Americans benefited from the booming economy: the new restrictions on welfare passed during the boom years may reverse the downward trend of poverty if boom turns to bust.

Because of its leading position worldwide, the United States is often put in the dock abroad, first as the main beneficiary of globalization, but also because of its self-proclaimed role as a global policeman. No matter how one feels about it, one must bear in mind that in most cases the United States meets little resistance or opposition from the rest of the world, in particular from the European Union.

The major criticisms leveled at the United States today concern its refusal to abolish the death penalty and its inability to control the use of guns. Such issues can be understood only with regard to the historical and cultural context of the country. America is also blamed for its cultural imperialism through its film industry – another example of its economic domination.

But America is readier than most western democracies to acknowledge its own mistakes. It is probably the only country today where a president can be impeached for lying to the people and where the government's secret dealings can create a scandal. The war in Vietnam, undoubtedly the most painful episode in the past few decades, has now risen to the status of American experience – unsuccessful though it may be – with a memorial in Washington and a series of films which aim at telling things as they really were. The United States has a tremendous capacity to reassess its errors, to confess its wrongdoings – and to move on.

As the biggest power in the world, confident in its superiority, the United States may often sound irritating and overpowering. But it has not got everything wrong – far from it.

## 1 – Population

Evolution:

| | |
|---|---|
| 1790 | 3,929,214 |
| 1800 | 5,308,483 |
| 1900 | 76,212,168 |
| 2000 | 281,421,906 |

*Population according to the 2000 census*

The American population has increased by 13.2 percent since 1990 – a higher figure than expected. Another 2.5 million inhabitants were added each year over the last decade of the twentieth century. This is largely due to the constant flow of immigrants. The chart below shows the evolution of each ethnic group over the 1990-2000 period. Hispanics and Asians account for a large part of the population increase and are currently the fastest-growing groups. It is estimated that by 2010, Latinos will outpace blacks as the largest minority group; by 2020, the number of Asians will double to 20 million people. By 2050, whites might be only 50 percent of the total population.

*Population according to ethnic origin*

| ethnic group | 2000 population | percentage change 1990-2000 |
|---|---|---|
| whites | 196,659,000 | + 4% |
| blacks | 33,476,000 | + 14% |
| Hispanics | 32,440,000 | + 45% |
| Asians & Pacific Islanders | 10,504,000 | + 50% |
| Indians, Eskimo | 2,050,000 | + 14% |

*The share of immigrants*

In 1999 more than 26 million immigrants (9.7 percent of the population) lived in the United States. More than 50 percent came from Latin America, 27 percent from Asia, 16 percent from Europe and 6 percent from other parts of the world.

*Where people live*

Population growth is fastest in the South-West – where most immigrants from Latin America settle.

Over the same ten-year period, Nevada's population increased by 50.6 percent, Arizona's by 30.4 percent. Other fast-growing states are Colorado, Utah, Idaho, Oregon, Washington, Texas, Georgia, Florida and North Carolina.

## 2 – The wealth of a nation

The United States is by far the wealthiest nation in the world. In 2000, its total Gross Domestic Product (GDP) was 9,299 billion dollars.

The country has enjoyed exceptional prosperity since 1992 thanks to investment in new technologies in particular; 22 million jobs were created between 1992 and 2000. The budget surplus for the years 2002 to 2011 is currently estimated 5,610 billion dollars, allowing for generous tax cuts – if all goes well, that is.

*Prosperity has benefited Americans in various degrees*

The number of millionnaires and billionnaires has soared. As a rule all income brackets have been affected by prosperity but all experts agree that higher incomes have benefited far more than the rest of the population and that income inequality has been rising over the past decade.

The top 20 percent of households saw their income rise by $17,870 during the 1990s; the top 5 percent enjoyed an average $50,000 increase (the figures do not include capital gains so the real ones are probably much higher). Over the same period, families with incomes in the bottom 20 percent only earned $100 more on average.

*Median income and poverty line*

From 1998 to 1999, median household income increased 2.7 percent to $40,800 – the highest level ever measured.

Similarly, the poverty rate fell for the third consecutive year to 11.8 percent in 1999 – the lowest poverty rate since 1979. The number of poor people dropped from 34.5 million in 1998 to 32.3 million in 1999.

The poverty threshold in 1999 was $17,029 for a family of four. Children are overrepresented among the poor: while making up 26 percent of the total population, they account for 38 percent of the poor.

Typically, poverty affects single-parent families, disabled people, families with many dependent children. Blacks and Hispanics are disproportionately represented in this category. Many American households living under the poverty line include adults who have a job. They are called the working poor, who scrape by with low-paid jobs.

### Today's American way of life

Nearly 70 percent of Americans are home owners. 50 percent of Americans use the Internet regularly; 22 percent have stock – stock options have been soaring in recent years; 83 percent have health insurance (usually paid for by their employer).

## 3 – Federal Government

### 1 – The Executive Branch

The President is the Chief Executive. He and the Vice-President are elected by the electoral college for a four-year term (the 22nd amendment limits the President to two terms).

Powers of the President

The President has a legislative role: he can veto a bill passed by Congress – unless a two-thirds vote in each house overrrides the veto. In his annual message to Congress, he can propose legislation. He has the power to call Congress into special session to examine the legislation.

The President appoints Supreme Court judges and federal judges – these are subject to confirmation by the Senate.

He can grant a pardon to anyone convicted of breaking a federal law.

As head of the executive branch, the President can issue executive orders which have the force of law.

The President is Commander in Chief of the armed forces. In times of war, Congress may grant the President more power to protect the nation.

He chooses the heads of all executive departments and agencies as well as top federal officials.

He appoints ambassadors – subject to confirmation by the Senate; he is in charge of relations with other nations, and manages relations with other governments aided by the Secretary of State.

## The Cabinet

Various departments, created by Congress, are in charge of specific areas of national or international affairs. The heads of the departments form the President's Cabinet.

| Department | Head of Department | Year of creation |
|---|---|---|
| State | Secretary of State | 1789 |
| Treasury | Secretary of the Treasury | 1789 |
| Defense | Secretary of Defense | 1949 |
| Justice | Attorney General | 1870 |
| Interior | Secretary of the Interior | 1849 |
| Agriculture | Secretary of Agriculture | 1889 |
| Commerce | Secretary of Commerce | 1913 |
| Labor | Secretary of Labor | 1913 |
| Health and Human Services | Secretary of Health and Human Services | 1979 |
| Housing and Urban development | Secretary of Housing and Urban development | 1965 |
| Transportation | Secretary of Transportation | 1966 |
| Energy | Secretary of energy | 1977 |
| Education | Secretary of Education | 1979 |
| Veteran Affairs | Secretary of Veteran Affairs | 1988 |

In addition to the Departments, many other independent agencies perform various tasks under the responsibility of the federal government. Here are the most often quoted:

- The Securities and Exchange Commission (SEC) protects investors who buy stocks, can punish fraud in the sale of securities and has power to regulate stock exchanges.
- The Federal Reserve System supervises the private banking system.
- The National Aeronautics and Space Administration (NASA) is in charge of US space programs.
- The Food and Drugs Administration (FDA) plays a major role in public health protection.
- The United States Information Agency (USIA) provides information on the United States for foreigners and informs the US government on foreign opinion about US policies.

## 2 – The Legislative Branch

Congress is composed of the Senate, with two seats for each state and the House of Representatives. Membership in the House of Representatives is based on the size of the population in each state. Senators are elected for six years – every two years, one-third of the Senate stands for election. Representatives serve for two years.

Each house of Congress has the power to introduce legislation except tax bills which must be introduced by the House of Representatives. If a bill is passed by a majority of votes in the House of Representatives and in the Senate, it goes to the President. He may sign it and make it a law or veto it. If vetoed, the bill goes back to the house where it was introduced. If it gets a two-thirds vote in the House of Representatives, it goes to the Senate. If the bill wins a two-thirds vote there, it then becomes a law without the president's signature.

Both houses are helped by a number of committees which specialize in various areas of legislation.

Congress has the power to investigate and gather information on future legislation or on the effectiveness of laws, or to inquire into the qualifications of officials of the other branches. Committees usually carry on the investigations.

## 3 – The Judicial Branch

The federal court system is headed by the Supreme Court whose judges are appointed for life by the President. It has appellate juridiction over decisions made in lower courts; it also has the power of judicial review.

The courts of appeal review the decisions of the district courts in their own areas. There are 11 appeals regions.

The district courts sit in each of the 89 districts.

The federal courts have power to judge criminal cases, civil cases and cases of equity. All crimes are tried by jury.

In addition to the federal courts, each state has its own court system with local courts.

Both federal and state judicial systems are constructed like a pyramid with the US Supreme Court and state supreme courts at the top of each.

## 4 – State and Local Government

The structure and powers of state government were inherited from the colonial period when the thirteen colonies were governed separately by the King of England. After independence, each had an autonomous government. The constitution defines the rights of the federal and state governments.

Each state has the three branches of government (legislative, executive and judicial). The state legislature is divided into the state senate and the state assembly. The chief executive of the state is the governor, elected by popular vote. He is endowed with the power of administration, appointment and veto.

Each state has a constitution which follows the pattern of the federal constitution but details the operation of businesses, banks and public utilities. States have their own codes of civil and criminal law. They have the power to levy taxes, to maintain hospitals and clinics, to set curriculum standards in the public school systems, to maintain institutions of higher education. Most states have a state police force and a state highway patrol.

State governments control welfare programs for the needy. They provide training services for workers.

In cooperation with the federal government, the state governments are in charge of the conservation of natural resources and the environment.

City governments directly serve the needs of citizens in terms of police and fire protection, health regulations, public transportation, education. There are several types of city government: usually there is an elected council and either a mayor or a commission of several elected officials acting as the executive body. Managing a city has become so complex that some cities have opted for the city manager, a highly experienced professional paid to work under the control of the elected council.

## 5 – Elections and political parties

*Congress*

Congress is divided into two chambers, the Senate and the House of Representatives.

Senators must be at least 30 years old, US citizens for at least nine years, and residents of the state where they are elected. Representatives must be at least 25, US citizens for at least seven years and residents of the state which elects them.

Each state is entitled to two senators and a number of representatives proportional to the state's population – the seats are redistributed every ten years according to population shifts, when census data are released.

Representatives are elected for a two-year term, senators for a six-year term. Every two years, one-third of the Senate stands for election.

## The Presidency

The President is elected every four years. The Vice-President may succeed the President should the President be incapacitated and is the presiding officer of the Senate.

The President must be a native-born American citizen and must be at least 35 years old. He is first nominated by his party's convention and elected by the electoral college. As this institution came into prominence after the muddle of the 2000 election, it may be useful to explain how it works.

Every four years, on election day (in November) voters go to the polls to vote for their Congressmen, a number of local officials, and the President and Vice-President of their choice. The total number of votes for the President is called the popular vote. But the President is not elected by the people; instead he is elected by the electoral college – a body composed of people chosen by the two parties to perform the single task of electing the President.

Each state has a number of electors (members of the electoral college) equivalent to the total number of Congressmen they have. The number of representatives being directly proportional to the state's population, it varies from one to over forty; but the number of senators – two by state – disproportionately favors sparsely-populated states (they outnumber the states with a high density of population). Moreover, if a majority of, say, 51 percent of votes goes to one presidential candidate in one state, the candidate's party wins all the electors alloted to the state.

This "winner-take-all" system has been criticized in a variety of ways since the 2000 election as undemocratic and outdated. In fact, when the Constitution was written, it was deliberately conceived as a means of mitigating the uncertainties of the popular vote. The Founding Fathers were wary of granting too much power directly to the people.

## Political parties

Political parties in America differ broadly from their European counterparts. Ideology is almost non-existent, party discipline an unknown thing, and citizens will readily shift their votes from one party to the other according to the personality of the candidate – in particular for presidential elections.

In Congress, party lines are frequently broken in fights on legislation. It is not uncommon for Congressmen to vote with the Senators or Representatives of the other party. Two conservative judges in the Supreme Court, Antonin Scalia and Clarence Thomas, were nominated by Republican presidents and approved by a Democratic majority Senate. Similarly, a

Republican president may appoint a Democrat to a federal office or a Democratic state governor will ally himself with a Republican senator on state policies.

The United States has developed a two-party system ensuring great stability in political life. In fact, both Democrats and Republicans share the same values of free enterprise and individual freedom, both appear as responsible and equally reliable politicians. No matter who is elected President (most presidents are elected by a very short margin), political life at home and abroad will be dictated by the neccessities of the day rather than by any political platform.

This feature is rooted in the framing of the Constitution with the absence of proportional representation, exacerbated by the winner-take-all system and the division of power between the nation and the states. Moreover the difficulty of getting elected and the high cost of election campaigns has all but eliminated "third" parties.

Third parties occasionally appear on the political scene and have sometimes managed to draw attention to the situation of specific groups of citizens. But they do not function as political parties the way Democrats and Republicans do. Rather, they function as pressure groups or interest groups. Ralph Nader, the long-time consumer activist and founder of an active consumer lobby, ran as candidate for the Green party in 2000. He was definitely seen as the troublemaker, the media boycotted his candidacy and he was the butt of harsh Democratic attacks as he took votes from the Democratic candidate.

Political parties are essentially broad-based associations aimed at forging a majority coalition in view of elections. The Democratic and Republican parties exist permanently on a local or state basis only as electoral machines wielding influence through the distribution of patronage, that is, granting public offices to those who supported the elected candidate.

Both have to compromise between conflicting interests; both have to appeal to different social groups, to different religious communities and to ethnic minorities as well. Depending on the concerns of the local population, state Democrats and Republicans may adopt very different political lines so that it is hard to make out one single national policy supported by each party.

The Presidential nominating convention which takes place in the summer preceding the November election is the only occasion when parties display some kind of unity around the candidate's platform. But the point is to win the electoral contest rather than push for political changes. After the presidential election the "spoils system" consists in granting offices to those who supported the winning candidate. Nearly 20% of federal positions in Washington are reserved for the friends of the President.

### Democrats and Republicans

At the time of the writing of the Constitution, there was strong opposition between the Federalists – led by Alexander Hamilton – who were in favor of a strong federal government and the anti-Federalists – led by Thomas Jefferson – who wanted to preserve the rights of the states against the prerogatives of a federal government.

The Democratic party comes from the party founded by Jefferson in 1801 and adopted its present name in 1829. It was the dominant party during the first half of the 19th century but lost its influence after the Civil War. The former slave states later became a Democratic stronghold and the South in general kept voting for the Democrats throughout most of the 20th century.

Democrats triumphantly came back to power with Franklin D. Roosevelt who launched the major reform wave of the New Deal. From then on, Democrats have often been associated with vast reform programs like John F. Kennedy's "New Frontier" and Lyndon B. Johnson's "Great Society" in the 60s: both programs aimed at fighting poverty and racial discrimination and improving education. More recently, the Clinton administration unsuccessfully tried in the 90s to set up a national social security program similar to the European systems.

Democratic voters tend to be urban, female, minority. Traditionally – since the 30s at least – labor votes for the Democrats and so do the vast majority of blacks who won the Civil Rights under a Democratic administration. Similarly ethnic groups vote for the Democrats who support affirmative action measures. More women have recently opted for the Democrats who support the right to abortion and restrictive measures on the use of guns.

As a rule, Democrats are associated today with welfare measures, more regulation on business and more foreign involvement. As they were accused in the past of being big tax-spenders they now insist that they, too, are for lower taxes.

The Republican party, also called the Grand Old Party, or GOP, comes from the Federalists founded in 1787 by Alexander Hamilton. It is the party of George Washington and Abraham Lincoln. In the second half of the 20th century, most presidents were Republican but only recently did Republicans seize control of Congress (in 1994 and for the first time in 40 years).

Among the traditional supporters of Republicans are the rural parts of the country, corporations and small businesses. The Republican party favors limitation of the Federal government intervention and under the Reagan administration amplified deregulation of business.

The Reagan years (1980-88) marked a turning point in American political life. Many Americans had been upset by the Great Disruption of the 60s and 70s which they thought was the cause of rising crime rates, illegitimate births and drug addiction. Many Democratic voters deserted for the Republican candidate. Reagan stood for religion, patriotism, authority and traditional family values.

He called for a return to the pioneer spirit of free entreprise and risk-taking – opposed to the "slavery" of welfare programs. This is when Christian conservatives (the "moral majority") started influencing the ranks of the Republican party. Meanwhile, the gun lobby went political and courted Republican Congressmen.

Today Republicans are still associated with anti gun-control groups, anti-abortion (pro-life) associations and locally with Christian fundamentalists. They are often seen as white, male, middle class and opposed to minority rights and welfare programs. Yet this is hardly a truthful picture of the party. Many Republican women are pro-choice, i.e., support abortion rights. Middle-class blacks, Asians and Hispanics increasingly vote Republican. Republican President George W. Bush is set on fighting poverty and poor education standards with "compassionate conservatism".

Compassionate conservatism is a typical example of American politics crossing party lines with an acceptable compromise. By transferring the burden of helping the poor to religious organizations, it both keeps the advantages of welfare programs (so far run by government agencies) and offers conservative voters an acceptable answer to fighting poverty. It also shows that Republicans feel as concerned as Democrats about how to eradicate the lingering problem of poverty.

In the US media, the two parties are often represented by a donkey for the Democrats and an elephant for the Republicans. Thomas Nast, a 19th-century cartoonist in *Harper's Weekly*, had used the two animals to caricature the political parties. It became so popular that each party has kept the symbol.

# 6 – Chronology

| | |
|---|---|
| 1620 | The Pilgrim Fathers found the colony of Plymouth (near Boston). |
| 1776 | Declaration of Independence – War against the king of England. |
| 1783 | The thirteen former colonies (Massachussets, New Hampshire, Connecticut, Pennsylvania, Rhode Island, New York, New Jersey, Delaware, Maryland, Virginia, North Carolina, South Carolina, Georgia become the United States of America). |
| 1787 | The Constitution is drawn up by the Founding Fathers at the Philadelphia Convention. |
| 1791 | The Bill of Rights is adopted. |
| 1803 | Louisiana purchase – The United States buys from France a vast, largely unexplored territory, expanding from New-Orleans to the Canadian border. It opens the move westward. |
| 1823 | President Monroe opposes European colonization on any part of North and South America: this is known as the Monroe doctrine. |
| 1820-1838 | Deportation of the Indians to the territories west of the Mississippi. |
| 1845-1848 | Congress annexes Texas. War with Mexico. Mexico sells California and New-Mexico to the United States. Britain sells the Oregon territory. |
| 1840-1860 | First great wave of immigrants – mostly Irish and Germans. About five million Europeans leave their homelands each year. |
| 1861-1865 | Civil War between the southern slave-holding states and northern states. Slavery is abolished. President Lincoln is assassinated in 1865. |
| 1867 | Alaska is bought from Russia. |
| 1881-1893 | Four transcontinental railroads are completed. |
| 1880-1900 | Second wave of immigrants, first from Ireland, England, Germany and Scandinavia, then from southern and eastern Europe (Italians and Jews). |
| | The Gilded Age. Trusts and monopolies come into being. Huge fortunes are made. |
| 1890 | Closing of the Frontier. |

|  |  |
|---|---|
|  | First anti-trust legislation (the Sherman Act). |
| 1896 | Segregation in the South is upheld by the Supreme Court. |
| 1898 | Annexation of Hawaii. War with Spain over the independence of Cuba. Spain gives the United States Puerto-Rico, Guam and the Philippines. Cuba becomes independent. The United States has a right of intervention on the Island. |
| 1898-1913 | The United States emerges as the biggest economic power in the world. |
| 1914 | Opening of the Panama Canal. |
| 1917 | The United States enters WWI. |
| 1920-1929 | Birth of air traffic. Electricity reaches all parts of the country. 50 percent of households own a car. |
|  | Prohibition is not really enforced. |
|  | Quota policies for immigration come into effect. Ban on Japanese immigration. |
| 1929 | Wall Street crash – beginning of the Great Depression. |
| 1933-1939 | New Deal policies under the Roosevelt administration. |
| 1941 | The United States enters WWII after the Japanese attack on Pearl Harbor on December 7. |
| 1945 | Yalta conference with Roosevelt, Churchill and Stalin. |
|  | Bombing of Hiroshima and Nagasaki. |
| 1947 | President Truman launches the "containment policy" aimed at curbing Soviet influence abroad. |
| 1948 | An Executive Order bans segregation in the Army and government agencies. |
| 1950-1953 | War in Korea. |
| 1950-1954 | McCarthyism. |
| 1954 | The Supreme Court bans segregation in schools. |
| 1963 | Assassination of President Kennedy. |
|  | Beginning of the War in Vietnam – it ends in 1973. |
| 1964 | President Johnson launches the Great Society program. |
|  | The Civil Rights Acts put an end to segregation. |
| 1965 | Change in immigration quotas favors an influx of immigrants from Asia and Latin America |
| 1968 | President Nixon is elected with the support of the "silent majority". |
| 1969 | Apollo 11 lands on the Moon. |
| 1972 | Watergate scandal. |

| | |
|---|---|
| 1974 | President Nixon resigns from office. |
| 1980-1988 | The Reagan years, marked by tax cuts, deregulation, economic recovery. "Reaganomics" seemed to work but left a huge budget deficit. Adoption of the Strategic Defense Initiative, known as "Star Wars". |
| 1991 | The Gulf War. |
| | Recession hits hard with job losses and rising inequality between rich and poor. |
| 1992-2000 | The Clinton years, marked by economic recovery, the boom in the "new economy" and budget surpluses. The gap between rich and poor keeps widening. |
| | With the collapse of the Soviet Union, The United States has become the only super-power in the world. |

### *Recommended further reading:*

- Paul Johnson, *A History of the American People*, 1997, HarperCollins Publisher.

   British historian Paul Johnson makes a challenging and extremely well-documented survey of the United States. He sheds light on forgotten or less well-known aspects of American history, those which are often overlooked in other similar books. With the critical view of a European, he helps us understand a nation that both fascinates and frightens so many of us.

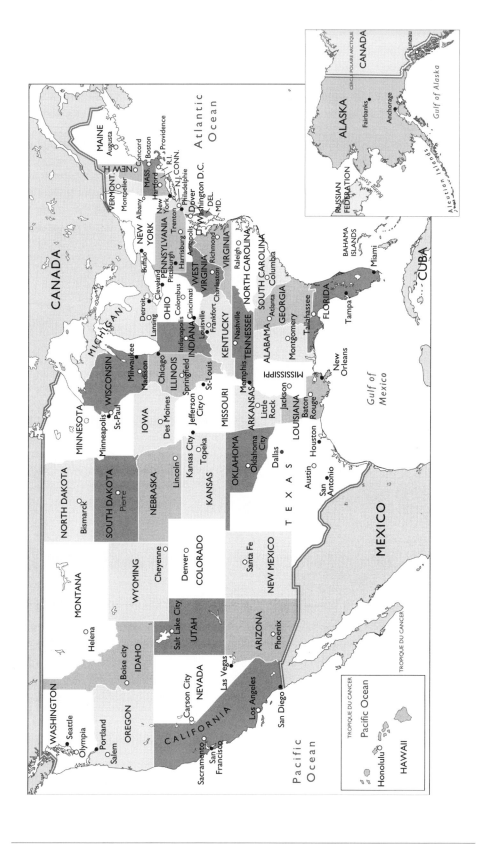

# 1 The Constitution

*Monique Chéron-Vaudrey*

The American constitution is often viewed today as extremely ingenious and effective work. The fact is that the United States has kept the same founding document since 1787, altering it 17 times only with *Amendments (in addition to the first ten, called the *Bill of Rights). The secret of such stability can probably be credited with two features: adaptability and flexibility. The words used in writing the Constitution – and the ideas which sustained these words – were both precise and flexible enough to be clearly understood by everybody and to adapt to a changing society as well.

## From independence to the making of a nation

Oddly enough, the idea of writing a constitution came only as an afterthought after the first years of independence. In 1781, the states had first adopted the Articles of Confederation, which was only a loose association and soon appeared as weak and inadequate: there was no executive and no possibility to *enforce the laws, no national court to interpret them, no provision for *levying taxes for the federal government. The legislative congress had no power over the various states. Some started disputes over boundaries, engaged in negotiations with foreign states for their own purposes; there was no single currency, and tariffs were laid on all goods imported either from Europe or from the neighbor states.

In addition to political and economic chaos, the diverging traditions and interests of the various states raised another difficulty. The former English colonies had been granted a charter by the King of England and had developed a kind of self-government long before the war of independence; they had started writing their own constitutions and voting their own laws and were not ready to relinquish their power to a federal government – many even questioned the validity of such a prospect.

## The guiding lines

The *Founding Fathers had been convinced that a central government was called for, but they were also aware that a compromise had to be reached with the states. So they devised a two-level system of government, the Federal government and the state governments, carefully sharing out the rights and obligations of each. Above all, they were wary of a return of tyranny and they meticulously worked out a system that would prevent any of the governing bodies from having too much power – the system of *checks and balances.

The spirit of the Constitution reflects the American society of its time. The vast majority of Americans were thriving in the land of plenty. Even in the 18th century, when many were still newcomers, it was possible over a lifetime to acquire property. Increasing opportunities afforded by the new land made people think in terms of how much money they could earn and how fast. Already the words of the Declaration of Independence "life, liberty and the pursuit of happiness" had made it clear: liberty was not just liberty from the tyranny of the King of England, it was also liberty of enterprise, and the pursuit of happiness meant the pursuit of wealth.

## The Constitution

Experts have often noted that the Constitution makes no reference to democracy. This was not in fact a priority. Even the fundamental individual liberties were later added as several states had protested, before ratifying the Constitution, that there was no mention of them. Ten amendments defining those rights were added in 1791 and formed the Bill of Rights. Not surprisingly, Negro slaves were not meant to benefit from liberty – they were merely counted as three-fifths of a man; Indians counted as foreigners.

The Constitution is divided into three parts: the preamble, the main body and the Amendments.

The preamble both reaffirmed the ideals of the Founding Fathers and established the need for a strong central government.

The main body is made up of seven articles which define the federal government with its three branches, the legislative body called *Congress, with the *House of Representatives and the *Senate; the executive body represented by the President, and the *judiciary, with the federal courts and the *Supreme Court.

The principle of federalism establishes a hierarchy: the Constitution is the *law of the land to which all other laws must conform. It defines how power is shared between national government and state government. The power of each is limited by reservation or delegation of some powers to the other level of government. Any other powers are the powers of the people (see Amendment X, p. 228).

## The separation of powers

The checks and balances system ensures that the power of each branch should be balanced by the power of the other two and that each branch should be able to check the excesses of the other two branches.

Thus the President appoints Supreme Court *justices, federal judges and several high federal officers, but the Senate must confirm the appointment. The President can veto legislation passed by Congress but a two-thirds majority in both houses can *override the veto. Congress may impeach the President, Vice-President or civil officers. Hardly more than a dozen officials have effectively been impeached since the Constitution was written. A congressman may be expelled by a two-thirds vote of his House.

Congress has the power to raise taxes and allocate the money for government programs, but the Executive branch controls the way the money is used. To top it all, citizens can curb the powers of the legislative body: if a citizen challenges an *Act of Congress or a presidential Executive Order, the Supreme Court may, after examination, declare it unconstitutional.

## The possibility of change

The great quality of the Constitution was that it provided for the possibility of introducing changes whenever needed. The Founding Fathers were aware that they were building a new country which was very likely to expand and to meet new challenges.

The Constitution can be changed through amendments. An amendment can be initiated in two different manners: through Congress by a two-thirds vote in each house, or the legislatures of two-thirds of the states may ask Congress to call a national convention to draft amendments. An Amendment must be ratified by three-fourths of the states' legislatures or by special conventions in three-fourths of the states.

This careful provision was meant to avoid amendments which would not have approval from a large majority of elected officials. At the same time, it makes it possible to introduce changes whenever necessary. It is interesting to note that throughout the course of its history, the United States has adopted – and sometimes repealed- amendments according to the prevailing problems of the times. This was the case for slavery (see p. 283) and for Prohibition, instituted in 1919 and repealed in 1933. Voting rights for women were added in 1920 (19th Amendment); the voting age was lowered to 18 in 1971 (26th Amendment).

## The Supreme Court

The Constitution is made flexible through another means: the Supreme Court. The nine judges are the interpreters of the Constitution. Their major role is to decide whether executive and congressional acts are in keeping with the Constitution. This is called the power of *judicial review. Otherwise, they examine court decisions challenged by citizens. They may either *uphold or *strike down decisions made by lower courts. For each session, they examine a few dozen cases out of the hundreds submitted to them.

This power is highly sensitive as the Supreme Court Justices are *appointed by the President – for life. It was established progressively and confirmed after the Civil War: the idea was to *implement federal *law throughout the country. Today the decisions of the Court are often criticized as judicial activism, opponents arguing that the Court is making decisions which ought to be left to the elected bodies. Some of them call for an opposite course of action, judicial restraint where the justices would limit their *rulings to a strict application of what is clearly stated or implied in the Constitution and *Acts of Congress.

# Vocabulary

| | |
|---:|:---|
| act | loi définitivement adoptée |
| amendment | amendement |
| appoint a judge (to) | désigner un juge |
| ballot initiative | référendum |
| bill | projet de loi |
| Bill of Rights | Déclaration des Droits |
| checks and balances | système d'équilibre des pouvoirs |
| common law | droit commun |
| Congress | Congrès |
| dock (to put in the) | faire le procès de |
| due process of law | procédure légale régulière |
| elector | grand électeur |
| enforce the law (to) | faire appliquer la loi |
| Founding Fathers | Pères fondateurs (auteurs de la Constitution) |
| House of Representatives | Chambre des Représentants |
| House Republican | représentant républicain |
| hubris | excès d'orgueil |
| impeachment | mise en accusation, en vue d'une destitution |
| implement the Constitution (to) | appliquer la constitution |
| issue a warrant (to) | délivrer un mandat |
| judicial review | vérification de la constitutionnalité des lois |
| judiciary (the) | le pouvoir judiciaire |
| justice | juge |
| law | la loi (en général) |
| law of the land (the) | loi suprême du pays |
| levy taxes (to) | percevoir des impôts |
| nominate (to) | désigner un candidat |
| override (to) | annuler |
| poll/go to the polls (to) | scrutin ; aller voter |
| redress of grievances | réparation des torts subis |
| register (to) | s'inscrire (sur une liste électorale) |
| ruling | décision |
| searches and seizures | perquisitions et saisies |
| Senate | Sénat |
| Supreme Court | Cour Suprême |
| strike down a decision (to) | casser une décision |
| term | mandat |
| uphold a decision (to) | soutenir, confirmer une décision |
| voter | électeur |

# Focus...

◆ **Ratification by the states**

Three compromises were necessary to obtain ratification by the states:

***The Great Compromise***
While large states wanted representation according to population, small states favored equal representation for each. In order to satisfy every state, Congress was divided into the House of Representatives, with a number of representatives determined by the population of each state, and the Senate, with two senators per state regardless of its population.

***The Three-Fifths Compromise***
The South had a large population of slaves who did not count as citizens. But the whites argued that they would be under-represented if slaves were left out. It was thus decided that a slave would count as three-fifths of a man for representation in Congress.

***The Commercial Compromise***
To satisfy both southern plantation owners and northern manufacturers and traders, it was decided that Congress would tax imports but not exports.

◆ **Local government**

In many fields, states may have their own laws, ranging from traffic regulations, to education… or abortion rights and capital punishment. They also have their elected legislature and governor. Other laws are applied throughout the country, as is the case for the Constitution, and are thus called the law of the land.

◆ ***Ballot initiatives**

Ballot initiatives are proposed by citizens and are placed on the ballot. They are passed if enough *voters sign the petition for the initiative. They often deal with the kind of issues that candidates shy away from supporting or combating, like doctor-assisted suicide, background checks for gun purchases or homosexual rights. Several states have recently ended affirmative action policies after such initiatives received a majority of votes.

◆ ***Impeachment**

"The President, Vice-President and all civil officers of the United States shall be removed from office on impeachment for, and convicton of treason, bribery or other high crimes and misdemeanors (article II or the Constitution). The House of Representatives must vote a *bill of impeachment. The official is then tried in the Senate. Hardly more than a dozen officials have effectively been impeached since the Constitution was written. President Nixon got away by resigning from office; President Clinton was acquitted.

◆ **Some landmark Supreme Court decisions**

*Marbury v. Madison (1803)*
The Supreme Court decided it had power to review the acts of Congress and invalidate them when they conflict with the Constitution. This gave the Court considerable power which has since then repeatedly been criticized. The power of judicial review allows the Court to strike down decisions made in Congress, in addition to the decisions made by lower courts.

*Plessy v. Ferguson (1886)*
The Court declared constitutional "separate but equal" development in the South – in other words, segregation.

*Brown v. Board of Education (1954)*
Probably the most momentous decision ever, it declared school segregation unconstitutional as it violated the "equal protection" clause of the 14th amendment. It was the first step on the long road to major changes in race relations in the country.

*Engel v. Vitale (1962)*
The ruling forbade prayers in public schools, in accordance with a strict separation of the church and the state.

*Miranda v. Arizona (1966)*
This is a familiar feature of American movies and TV series. It requires the police to inform suspects in custody of their right to remain silent, that anything they say may be used against them and that they have a right to representation by a lawyer before interrogation.

*Roe v. Wade (1973)*
The decision made abortion legal in the country. After much debate and opposition nationwide, the decision was nearly overruled in 1989 but later confirmed as law of the land in 1992. This ruling is the most likely to come under siege in the coming years.

**Further reading**
- *La Constitution américaine et les institutions*, Jean-Eric Branaa, 144 pages, 1999, Ellipses – useful for a detailed analysis of the subject.

Related chapter: see p.206-210.

# Essay

F.D. Roosevelt complained in 1937 that "the Court (...) has improperly set itself up as (...) a superlegislature (...) reading into the Constitution words and implications which are not there." Comment. Does this remark still apply today?

*President Roosevelt blamed the Supreme Court for setting itself up as a superlegislature when Court rulings systematically annihilated all the federal government's efforts to put the country back on its feet again. Because the Judges were conservatives opposed to the New Deal policy, they took advantage of their power to oppose the decisions of a government supported by the majority of the country.*

*Today many experts also level the same accusation, and call the Court a superlegislature. One critic said the defining characteristic of this Court is \*hubris. Others contend that the Court prefers to follow conventional opinion rather than challenge it. There seems to be little consensus on the relevance of Court rulings, and the media echo a flurry of complaints about those who make the final decisions.*

*Indeed, when a Court ruling affects questions of public policy or has consequences on people's private lives, it is bound to create discontent among those citizens who disagree. Under the stewardship of conservative Chief Justice Rehnquist, the Court recently upheld the right to abortion, reaffirmed the Miranda decision, and confirmed that organizing prayers before football games in schools is unconstitutional. The same Court decided that a Boy Scout organization has the right to expel an adult Scout leader because he is gay; that the Food and Drug Administration has no right to regulate tobacco products; or that federal money can be used to buy computers for a parochial school.*

*It would be hard today to identify Court decisions with political guerilla warfare against the administration. Obviously, though conservative Judges are in a majority, the Supreme Court is divided over most issues. In fact, the Court is identified with a superlegislature because it makes decisions which ought to be voted in Congress. So the question is rather, why is that so?*

*The answer is twofold: first, the Supreme Court is one piece in the puzzle of the checks and balances system. Its role is seen as a safeguard against tyranny of the majority. If Congress is too one-sided or shows too much hubris, the Court may counterbalance its decisions. On the other hand, Congressmen are often prisoners of* *their own voters. With an election system that sends voters to the \*polls every two years anyway, candidates are prone to avoiding any controversial issue that might cost them reelection. This is a familiar feature in our democracies. So much so that decisions on important issues often escape the scope of the legislative body in the United States and find their way either through ballot initiatives or through Supreme Court rulings.*

*Roosevelt noted that the Judges were "reading into the Constitution words and implications which are not there". Indeed, the Constitution was written for a country in the making, and the words carefully chosen to adapt to any new situation. It is the Court's duty to rightly interpret those words – and it is no easy task. Sometimes they do follow conventional opinion, sometimes they make courageous choices that Congress proves unable to make (for school desegregation, for the right to abortion), and sometimes they follow their own biases.*

*In the vast majority of cases, the Supreme Court Justices try to speak the voice of wisdom – and this is possible because they are submitted to nobody's pressure. Sometimes they fail to do so – we can arguably wonder why no Court ruling in the recent years has ever tried to question capital punishment or to limit gun ownership, despite growing unease about the two subjects. Many disgruntled Americans protested at the Court's ruling, by a 5-4 vote, handing victory to George W. Bush, the popular-vote loser in the 2000 presidential election. This, more than other controversial decisions, is likely to put the Supreme Court in the \*dock in the near future. But here again, is the Supreme Court to blame, or is the American system of government just as imperfect as other democratic systems?*

*(686 words)*

## MORE ABOUT...
### ...FOUNDING DOCUMENTS

EXTRACTS FROM THE DECLARATION OF INDEPENDENCE
4 JULY 1776

"We hold these truths to be self-evident: That all men are created equal; that they are endowed by their Creator with certain unalienable rights; that among these are life, liberty and the pursuit of happiness; that, to secure these rights, governments are instituted among men, deriving their just powers from the consent of the governed; that whenever any form of government becomes destructive of these ends, it is the right of the people to alter or to abolish it, and to institute new government, laying its foundation on such principles, and organize its powers in such form, as to them shall seem most likely to effect their safety and happiness. (...)

The history of the present King of Great Britain is history of repeated injuries and usurpations, all having in direct object the establishment of an absolute tyranny over these states. (...)

He has refused his assent to laws, the most wholesome and necessary for the public good. (...)

He has dissolved representative houses repeatedly, for opposing, with manly firmness, his invasions on the rights of the people. (...)

He has obstructed the administration of justice. (...) He has made judges dependent on his will alone." (...)

The declaration further mentions the more recent causes for discontent:

"For quartering large bodies of armed troops among us; for protecting them from punishment for any murders they should commit (...)

For cutting off our trade with all parts of the world;

For imposing taxes on us without our consent; (...)

For taking away our charters (...)

We, therefore, the representatives of the United States of America, in General Congress assembled, appealing to the Supreme Judge of the world for the rectitude of our intentions, do, in the name and by the authority of the good people of these colonies, solemnly publish and declare, that these United Colonies are, and of right ought to be, FREE AND INDEPENDENT STATES; (...)

And for the support of this declaration, with a firm reliance on the protection of Divine Providence, we mutually pledge to each other our lives, our fortunes, and our sacred honor."

John Hancock and fifty others

## THE BILL OF RIGHTS

Amendment I — Congress shall make no law respecting an establishment of religion, or prohibiting the free exercise thereof; or abridging the freedom of speech, or of the press; or the right of the people peaceably to assemble, and to petition the government for a *redress of grievances.

Amendment II — A well-regulated militia being necessary to the security of a free State, the right of the people to keep and bear arms shall not be infringed.

Amendment III — No soldier shall, in time of peace, be quartered in any house without the consent of the owner, nor in time of war, but in a manner to be prescribed by law.

Amendment IV — The right of the people to be secure in their persons, houses, papers, and effects, against unreasonable *searches and seizures, shall not be violated, and no warrants shall *issue but upon probable cause, supported by oath or affirmation, and particularly described, the place to be searched, and the persons or things to be seized.

Amendment V — No person shall be held to answer for a capital, or otherwise infamous crime, unless on a presentment or indictment of a grand jury, except in cases arising in the land or naval forces, or in the militia, when in actual service in time of war or public danger; nor shall any person be subject for the same offense to be twice put in jeopardy of life or limb; nor shall be compelled in any criminal case to be a witness against himself, nor be deprived of life, liberty, or property, without *due process of law; nor shall private property be taken for public use without just compensation.

Amendment VI — In all criminal prosecutions, the accused shall enjoy the right to a speedy and public trial, by an impartial jury of the State and district wherin the crime shall have been committed, which district shall have been previously ascertained by law, and to be informed of the nature and cause of the accusation; to be confronted with the witnesses against him; to have compulsory process for obtaining witnesses in his favor, and to have the assistance of counsel for his defense.

Amendment VII — In suits at *common law, where the value in controversy shall exceed twenty dollars, the right of trial by jury shall be preserved, and no fact tried by a jury shall be otherwise reexamined in any court of the United States than according to the rules of the common law.

Amendment VIII — Excessive bail shall not be required, nor excessive fines imposed, nor cruel and unusual punishments inflicted.

Amendment IX — The enumeration in the constitution of certain rights shall not be construed to deny or disparage others retained by the people.

Amendment X — The powers not delegated to the Unites States by the constitution, nor prohibited by it to the states, are reserved to the states respectively, or to the people.

# 2   Lobbying

*Monique Chéron-Vaudrey*

### What is lobbying?

Lobbying consists in trying to influence legislators so that they will pass laws favorable to an *interest group representing a category of citizens. The *lobby is the large hall adjacent to the assembly hall of a legislature; it is open to the public. As this is where the first efforts to influence legislators took place, it gave its name to the activity.

In order to be effective lobbyists must present legislators with a full array of arguments likely to convince them of how they should vote and they will use all means at their disposal to win over those who make decisions.

### Not just an American phenomenon

Many aspects of lobbying in the United States correspond to pure political activism in Europe. Americans concentrate more readily on specific issues in which they have a *vested interest, regardless of the divisions along party lines. Problems subjected to a lot of lobbying are often called nonpartisan issues when they find supporters *across the political spectrum; others whose advocates are essentially in one political camp are partisan issues (the gun lobby, for instance, has close links with the Republicans).

Moreover, Europeans may be clever at influencing their own legislators, and no doubt some lobbies on this side of the Atlantic are just as active and effective as their American counterparts, but lobbying is a *derogatory word in Europe and a great deal of its activities are kept underhanded.

### Who are the lobbyists?

Lobbying is widespread and systematic in the United States, with many government decisions directly influenced by interest groups. Lobbying may affect absolutely every aspect of American life. Corporations are great lobbyists indeed, but so are trade-unions, ethnic groups, civil rights activists, lawyers, gays, the medical profession, farmers, environmentalists, consumer groups, members of thousands of communities...

Having your message *conveyed to legislators is no easy business. It is time-consuming and requires a lot of expertise. So the job will best be performed by professionals. Lobbying firms are found everywhere in the country, as lobbying has become a flourishing industry comprising a wide range of activities. Not just lawyers, but public relations consultants, publicists, former members of Congress, former White House staffers and all sorts of professionals and experts are on the *payroll of those firms.

### Fund-raising

The most traditional way of lobbying was – and still is – pouring money into the legislators' pockets. For a long time the rules were lax and you could give any amount of money without the judges even blinking an eyelid. In the 70s, rules became stricter. Federal and state governments regulated the fund-raising for a candidate, and the amount of political donations was strictly *capped. Regulated money came to be called "*hard money".

But soon after lobbies found indirect ways of getting round limitations. They started multiplying independent groups (like Political Action Committees) centered on specific issues. The contributions of such groups are tax-deductible and parties do not have to disclose who the real contributors are. Provided they are not directly advocating a vote for a specific candidate and are not directly controlled by a candidate, there is no limit to the money independent groups can spend to influence a campaign. This kind of money was coined "*soft money".

Several cases of abuse were brought to court but the judiciary has always upheld the rights of those groups to collect money in order to voice their views, on the basis of the First Amendment's right to free speech. Since the early 90s, there has been a surge in "soft money" which can be used for influencing decision-makers in many ways.

### What money can do

*Issue advocacy ranks first among them these days. It consists in setting up communication to promote a set of ideas rather than a particular candidate or party. It takes the form of advertising, especially with TV commercials, called *issue-ads or public advocacy ads, and sounds like public education campaigns. The content and timing of the message are carefully *monitored so as to influence large audiences. TV-viewers may be urged to send mail to their Representative, or to call a *toll-free 800 number for more information, or to join a group of concerned citizens. People are usually unaware that the ad campaign is financed by an interest group and many unknowingly follow the advice given.

*Grassroots activism consists in organizing groups of citizens around a particular issue – sometimes in the wake of advocacy ads. Web sites, direct mail services and 800 numbers are familiar tools. The point is to create enough *momentum among the population to convince legislators they cannot act against citizens' wills. The National Smokers Alliance is one such group – funded by Philip Morris. Various senior citizen groups are funded by the pharmaceutical and insurance industries.

Putting direct pressure on legislators can also be achieved through monitoring information. Legislators need an ever increasing amount of information on ever more complex issues. Lobbies will gather up-to-date information, hire experts, create independent study groups and *think tanks to provide decision-makers with just what they need. The same think tanks may also provide the public with *biased information thus making sure that from grassroot voters to Congressmen everybody will hear the same story.

Legislators rely on such information and are grateful to those who provide it. In exchange, they will inform lobbyists on the *intricacies of the legislative process and on the development of government policies so that lobbies can adapt their tactics.

Lobbying firms are of all kinds. The most prestigious whose activities range far and wide have their headquarters in Washington, D.C., but many limit the scope of their activities to state legislatures and local interests. They provide interest groups with a variety of services, depending on the *stakes they have in an issue.

Having a problem putting the message across? You will be given advice on how to frame your policy options. Want to get access to a member of Congress? A firm will give you the right services.

Need some grassroots action to support your view? A public relations firm will place interviews and stories in the newspapers, organize a mail service, run a toll-free phone number.

Want to make your point but have limited means and little time to spare? A firm in Washington will help any group organize picketing in front of the White House, provide the banners, and even the picketers if the client cannot take the trip. They will duly send photographs of the picketing, too.

Most often, effective lobbying will defeat legislation, obtain *subsidies, *tax exemptions for the interest group. Forty-one major corporations not only do not pay taxes but also receive subsidies. All this, indeed, at the expense of other taxpayers.

### Has lobbying gone too far?

The amount of money spent these past decades has reached mind-boggling figures, and one might reasonably ask, is it really worth the trouble? The answer is, yes. In many fields, important changes have been or are on the *agenda like health care and telecommunications reform. The stakes are such that money is no object for lobbyists.

In the process, free speech has been perverted into freedom for some to spend millions on *shaping the balance of power. There is at the moment increasing protest that money can buy everything when it comes to policy decisions. While lobbying is accessible to all, from trade-unions and consumer groups to big corporations, it has never been so true that the more money you have the louder you can speak. For obvious reasons many lobbies cannot compete with major industries in their lobbying efforts. Advocates of gun control legislation, victims of tobacco, patients who cannot bear the high cost of prescription drugs simply cannot afford to keep up with the campaigns funded by gun manufacturers, tobacco companies or the pharmaceutical industry.

In the name of freedom of speech, lobbying is an unrestricted activity – so unrestricted indeed that a majority of citizens may be misled or silenced by a minority with powerful financial means.

# VOCABULARY

| | |
|---|---|
| across the political spectrum | (qui affecte) toutes les tendances politiques |
| advance one's position (to) | faire avancer son point de vue |
| agenda (on the)/political agenda | à l'ordre du jour ; décisions politiques à prendre |
| biased information | information tendancieuse/non objective |
| burnish one's image (to) | améliorer son image |
| cap (to) | limiter |
| commission polls (to) | commander des sondages |
| contribute to charities (to) | faire des dons à des organisations humanitaires |
| convey a message (to) | faire passer un message |
| derogatory | péjoratif |
| grassroots (the) | les gens de la base |
| harbinger | présage |
| hard money | contributions électorales contrôlées par la loi |
| hefty contribution | contribution importante |
| hold in check (to) | contrôler |
| interest group | groupement d'intérêts |
| intricacy | complication |
| issue advertizing | publicité sur un problème politique |
| issue advocacy | campagne sur un problème politique |
| limelight (to be in the) | être en vedette, être au premier plan |
| lobby | lobby, groupe de pression |
| make one's case (to) | défendre son point de vue |
| momentum (to create) | créer une dynamique |
| monitor (to) | contrôler |
| payroll (to be on the) | être payé par |
| relax restrictions (to) | alléger les restrictions |
| run ads (to) | faire paraître des publicités |
| serve one's own goals (to) | servir ses propres intérêts |
| shape the balance of power (to) | façonner l'équilibre des forces |
| soft money | contributions électorales non contrôlées par la loi |
| stake (to have a) | avoir un intérêt financier |
| subsidy | subvention |
| tax-exemption | exemption fiscale |
| think tank | groupe d'experts |
| toll-free 800 number | numéro vert |
| underwriter | garant financier |
| vested interest (to have a) | être directement intéressé |

## Focus...

In policy battles, the capacity to obtain information and control its dissemination is the most important political power of all (in *The Sound of Money* – see reference below).

The tobacco industry – though under severe attack – is still the main beneficiary of subsidies for agriculture.

The gun lobby has so far managed to defeat any serious legislation on gun control despite growing momentum on the side of gun-control advocates.

Across the country, there is a growing feeling that corporations can have the upper hand in political decisions. 70% of American citizens feel they have too much influence over legislators.

"Public Citizen" was founded by Ralph Nader in 1971. It is a 150,000-member organization representing consumer interests through lobbying, litigation, research and public education. It is active in Congress, the courts, governmental agencies and the media. For all its activism, it could not prevent Nader from being silenced in the 2000 campaign.

◆ **Partisan money**

*Some of the major donors and how they shared their money in the 2000 presidential election*

Those who gave most of their contributions to the Republicans:

car manufacturers, oil and gas, various manufacturing and distributing companies, electric utilities, retired people, general contractors, the pharmaceutical industry.

Those who gave most of their contributions to the Democrats:

industrial unions, building trade unions, public sector unions, transportation unions, lawyers, the TV and movie industry.

Those who shared their contributions between the two parties:

computers and Internet, business services, lobbyists, civil servants, telecom services, construction services, hospitals, casinos.

How much does it take to contribute to an election campaign?

Political fundraising is definitely on the increase; soft money, which is not subject to government control, is absorbing an ever bigger share of the pie. The figures below are in millions:

|      | House | Senate | Presidential | hard money | soft money |
|------|-------|--------|--------------|------------|------------|
| 1992 | $207  | $161   | $106         | $219       | $46        |
| 1996 | $271  | $158   | $230         | $392       | $149       |
| 2000 | $393  | $259   | $335         | $391       | $255       |

### ◆ Growing unease about the power of money

"There's something quite disturbing about watching the world's richest man trying to buy his way out of trouble with Uncle Sam. One of the most deep-seated principles in American jurisprudence is that nobody should be above the law. Another is that judicial decisions should be free from political interference. By defying both these values, Gates's actions undermine the legal system itself."

(A commentary on Bill Gates's political contributions in the 2000 election campaign – *Business Week*, April 24, 2000)

"Campaign spending has divided Americans into two groups: first- and second-class citizens. This is what happens if they are in the latter group:

They pick up a disproportionate share of America's tax bill. They pay higher prices for a broad range of products, from peanuts to prescription drugs. They pay taxes that others in a similar situation have been excused from paying."

(*Time* magazine, February 7, 2000 – special report, "Big Money & Politics")

"Campaign finance is a confusing topic in many ways. But it is money which, arguably, determines the very basics of our democracy: who runs, who wins, and how they govern."

(Dan Fromkin in *The Washington Post*, Sept. 4,1998.)

### *Further reading*

- Literature on lobbying abounds. For further, up-to-date information, you can read *The Sound of Money,* by Darrel M. West & Burdett A. Loomis – W.W. Norton & Company, New York – 1998.

# Essay

**Is money in politics a threat to American democracy?**

*It would no doubt be naïve or utopian to contend that politics should be free from moneyed interests. All candidates need funds for their electoral campaigns. In politics as in other fields in America, big money is the hallmark of success, and the ability to raise large sums may appear as proof of voters' support for a candidate. Except that the most \*hefty contributions usually come from a handful of interest groups – not from the grassroots.*

*Recent developments have shown that powerful special interest groups can mobilize all sorts of so-called citizens' groups, hire experts and run campaigns that will shape public debate and influence legislators. The pharmaceutical and tobacco industries – to quote just a couple – can work wonders in fighting for their own interests. To face such giants, what can ordinary citizens do if they want to lobby for their own interests as victims of tobacco or as prescription drug users?*

*Even getting objective information is becoming harder. Concerned citizens who want to learn about an environmental issue will read reports and comments released by a foundation or a think tank sponsored by oil companies, car manufacturers or the logging industry. Senior citizens wary of the high cost of prescription drugs will receive mail or phone calls from a front group funded by the pharmaceutical industry and end up joining a so-called grassroots organization mainly devoted to barring Congress from regulating the prices of expensive drugs.*

*Access to information is free for all in the United States indeed. But when new issues arise, such as global warming (about which not all experts agree), or when major reforms such as health care are on the agenda, information is extremely hard to obtain. It may take a lot of expertise and commitment for public interest groups to gather information and form a definite opinion on new and complex issues.*

*What is freedom of speech worth when millions or billions of dollars are necessary to have your message aired on TV? How can you voice your opinion to contradict those who set no limits to their expenses in order to preserve their interests? And how can citizens make a fair choice if they are overwhelmed by a torrent of issue-*

*advertizing from one side of the debate while the other side can offer hardly more than a trickle of information?*

*Is free speech really protected when the only experts who speak on the pros and cons of limiting greenhouse gases are on the payroll of think tanks funded by the oil industry?*

*It may be argued that a large number of lobbies whose actions focus on civil rights or ethical issues also pour money – and a good deal of grassroots activism, too – into the public debate. Women's groups, gay rights activists, environmentalists have all come under the \*limelight recently; so have pro- and anti-abortion activists. Their activism has had its ebb and flow but their viewpoints are now familiar to the public. And in many regards their lobbying has enjoyed some success. But their policy options do not jeopardize big money interests.*

*Not surprisingly, many in America feel that business has too much power over too many aspects of American life (1). Freedom of speech is being thwarted by the power of money and the rule of the majority, which is the basic tenet of democracy, is in many cases being twisted to serve the interest of the few.*

(1) 72% exactly, according to a Business Week/Harris Poll conducted in August 2000. In the same poll 95% said they agreed with the following statement:

"US corporations should have more than one purpose. They also owe something to their workers and the communities in which they operate, and they should sometimes sacrifice some profit for the sake of making things better for their workers and communities."

## MORE ABOUT...

### ...AN OVERVIEW OF RECENT BIG TIME LOBBYING

#### NAFTA

The North American Free Trade Agreement signaled the emergence of interest-group politics. It was signed by the United States, Canada and Mexico in December 1992. It proposed to abolish trade barriers among the three countries with a prospective market of $6.5 trillion. It had to be approved by the legislative body of each nation. Unexpectedly NAFTA found strong opposition in the US, with former presidential candidate Ross Perot launching "infomercials" on TV claiming the treaty would cost nearly 6 million jobs to the United States. He was soon followed by the AFL-CIO labor federation whose advertizing campaign exposed the lack of protection for American workers. The public were informed on NAFTA mostly through this negative advertizing and about 60% of Americans thought it would cost jobs to the country. President Clinton had to send cabinet secretaries all over the country to explain why NAFTA was good for America. The treaty was eventually approved in November 1993 by a short margin.

#### CLINTON'S HEALTH CARE PLAN

NAFTA was only a *harbinger of more serious problems to come. After his election in 1992, with a Democratic majority in Congress and opinion polls showing a strong support for health care reform, Clinton hoped to set up a landmark reform with universal health care coverage. This was the first of several large-scale policy changes in the 1990s, qualified as a "trillion-dollar pot of gold" by the Welfare Secretary, affecting the interests of hospitals, nursing homes, doctors, the pharmaceutical industry and insurers. Those interest groups staged a war against the Clinton plan, taking full advantage of the new communications technologies with issue ads and 800 numbers. Thousands of stories about health care were published in the media or aired on TV and radio stations. Academic studies, focus groups and foundations received money to carry out research on health care and "inform" the public. It is estimated that 650 organisations worked on the anti-health care plan campaign, spending $100 million to influence the debate. The arguments centered around fear of too much government control in health care, fear of lower quality and loss of choice, and a threat of higher costs for the taxpayer. As the issues were complex, citizens failed to understand what was really at stake. The reform was eventually defeated. For the first time interest-group tactics had managed to shape public debate and to influence the vote in Congress.

## THE TELECOMMUNICATIONS ACT OF 1996

The Telecommunications reform, involving telephone companies, cable operators, TV networks and Internet providers involved one seventh of the GDP. It gave rise to a major wave of lobbying with ad wars and competing narratives in support of the different interests.

After the reform was passed telephone companies kept lobbying to *relax the restrictions they are submitted to. Broadcasters have propositions that would kill a plan to issue new licenses to hundreds of low-power FM stations, and they want to relax the law that keeps them from having control over more than 35% of the television market. Said an official of Consumers Union (a lobbying group for consumers), "It is AT&T seeking to protect its cable profits. It's the Bell telephone companies seeking millions of dollars from Internet providers and their customers who use the Internet. It's the broadcasters trying to block community radio stations to enhance their dominant position in the market. And it's cable companies seeking taxpayer support to provide local channels in the communities that they are already supposed to wire." (quoted in *The Washington Post*, Oct. 24, 2000).

## BIG TOBACCO

In 1997, when they received their first major blow, tobacco companies were the top "soft money" contributors to the Republicans and Democrats for a total of nearly $2 million. The tobacco industry has long relied on sponsorship of sporting events and cultural activities and contributed to philanthropic causes to enhance its public image. Philip Morris has been *running ads showing the company is devoted to making the world a better place; the company is also a major *underwriter of operas and theater productions. Yet the cost of tobacco in health care expenses kept rising and the industry came under fire. The major setback was the $246 billion legal settlement granting 46 states compensation for the cost of treating sick smokers. States have started pocketing the money and will do so for 25 years. California and New York State will get more than $1 billion a year on average. The states are consequently likely to lobby the federal government to prevent any course of action that would cut off the money flowing into their coffers. Many indeed will be able to do things they would never have dreamed of. Big Tobacco has paid a high price, but hopes to keep the business going for some time – with the support of 46 states!

# 3 The Land of the Free

*Monique Chéron-Vaudrey*

Americans fought the war of independence in the name of freedom. As the Pilgrim Fathers had meant to set up a model society blessed by God, the Founding Fathers who wrote the Constitution were aware that their new nation, "conceived in liberty", would serve as a model of freedom. In the late 18th century, freedom essentially meant two things: freedom from tyranny and freedom to own property.

The Constitution explicitly limited the powers of government with the checks and balances system and protected the rights of individuals with the Bill of Rights (see p. 228). Freedom of property was something new in those days. In Europe most people could not own property if they had no birth right to it, but in colonial America it was common for free men to become propertied. Many had already made a fortune at the time of independence. From the outset, the new nation asserted the principle of *free enterprise, the right for individuals to develop their farming, trading or industrial activities free from government interference. What attracted ever larger numbers of immigrants from Europe was not just the abundance of the land, it was also the legal *framework which made *entrepreneurship a more meaninglul and more fruitful word than on the old continent.

### Freedom for some only

Freedom indeed was not the privilege of everybody. In the thirteen English colonies, the community of English and Dutch settlers were the main beneficiaries of freedom. After independence things remained much the same. Voting rights were reserved for men who had property. Women were excluded from voting rights – even though some had already started voicing their protest at male domination. Black slaves would have to wait for another century before emancipation – and yet another one for their civil rights. From independence to World War II, the United States kept excluding whole categories of its inhabitants from the full benefits of freedom (see p. 303 – Multiculturalism).

### The *huddled masses *yearning to breathe free

In the century that followed independence, liberty attracted the oppressed masses from Europe and more recently it has attracted millions of people from all over the world. As Emma Lazarus rightly said, all of them came to America because they were "yearning to breathe free".

It can be argued that what immigrants experience when they set foot in the land of the free bears little resemblance to freedom. Today, as in the 19th century, recent immigrants get menial jobs, are the butt of racism, often live in ghettos. Despite the authorities' efforts to *curb illegal immigration, undocumented workers with shockingly low hourly wages account for a considerable part of California's, Texas's or New Mexico's economy.

Yet they keep coming in in large numbers. Why? The pattern is simple – and *speaks volumes. They experience slave labor conditions for about ten years – but meanwhile they can support a family and send their children to school. Later on, they can move on to better jobs, start a business of their own – and become US citizens.

The gap may be widening between rich and poor in the US but as long as being poor in the US is a more enviable condition than being middle-class in the Philippines, Mexico, Haiti and a hundred other countries in the world, they will keep coming.

### *Yearning young \*upstarts*

Over the past few years, a new breed of immigrants has been flocking to the United States. They are young computer scientists from India, graduates from French engineering schools, nurses from Britain, who are seeking better jobs, better conditions to pursue a career in research, or better opportunities to set up their own businesses. And as the country is badly in need of highly-qualified workers to meet the demands of the new economy, they are given special visas and enjoy the status of middle-class Americans as soon as they arrive.

### *Freedom for the oppressed*

In all the *troubled spots of the world, where dictatorship, civil war or political *unrest prevail, young people who cannot hope for a better tomorrow in their home country, have only one dream, going to America in order to be free. And the dream comes true for those who can make it. In addition to better living standards, they can also enjoy the fundamental freedoms of speech and worship and nobody minds if they speak broken English and keep using their own language. The success of the Cuban community in Florida has done more to undermine the Cuban regime than all the failed attempts of the various administrations to eliminate Fidel Castro.

### *Changing notions of freedom in today's world*

The shock of WWII initiated a new approach to the rights of human beings. Already during the war, President Roosevelt had started including people of all races and *creeds in the beneficiaries of freedom – an *omen of the changes to come. The Universal Declaration of Human Rights in 1948 outlined the new definitions of freedom for mankind. In the US, the changes took the form of the historical decision to end segregation in schools, itself a springboard for the Civil Rights movement. The notions of exclusion on which Americans had so long relied to build a free community tailored for WASPs was definitively abandoned.

The 60s rebellion contributed to the shaping of new freedoms. Freedom for minorities and women were followed by freedom to organize one's own private life according to one's liking. Traditionally, America had been a refuge for religious communities eager to live according to the principles of their creed. More recently the gay community has been able to carve out new *havens in cities with a long-standing tradition of tolerance, like San Francisco or Atlanta. New freedoms centered on individual fulfilment have been defined, including choice of *attire, food, medicine, lifestyle, etc. This may sound naive or utopian these days, but it took hold in America, giving rise to innumerable associations which make up the "counter-culture" of the country. Some have become environmentalists, others have founded New-Age communities, many get mobilized on a number of issues ranging from the right to abortion to the World Trade Organization.

### *Freedom of speech lives on*

Americans probably enjoy more freedom of expression than most democracies. This is due both to the definitions of freedom enshrined in the Bill of Rights and to the limitations of government interference in the rights of individuals. Freedom of speech became an issue in the 20th century only. Groups of citizens like black people and industrial workers started claiming rights they were deprived of. At the same time, participation in WWI was marked with the first restrictions on freedom of speech. The *Cold War in the 1950s remains as a unique episode in American history when an *all-out assault on freedom of speech swept the country (see p.247).

But as a rule, all philosophical, religious or political opinions can benefit from absolute freedom of expression in the country. The Supreme Court, whose job it is to interpret the First Amendment, has had to rule on cases affecting art, entertainment, pornography, racist opinions, and has established four exceptions to free speech: speech posing danger of imminent violence or lawlessness, disclosures threatening national security, obscenity, *fighting words that would provoke a reasonable person to an imminent, violent response. Even those restrictions are subject to different interpretations.

With the exception of the Cold War episode when the administration unashamedly strangled free speech, restrictions on First Amendment freedom usually come from groups of citizens who, in the puritanical tradition, want to impose on others their own interpretation of what is right: the 1930s censors who imposed decency codes on Hollywood productions, the pro-life activists who murder abortion-clinic doctors in the name of the right to life, political-correctness fundamentalists who impose their speech codes on campuses or white supremacists who call for a deportation of non-whites.

- Related chapters: Multiculturalism, the Land of Opportunity, Religion, Hollywood.

# VOCABULARY

| | |
|---|---|
| accountability | responsabilité |
| all-out assault | attaque en règle |
| attire | vêtements, accoutrement |
| censorship/censor (to) | censure ; censurer |
| classified document | document classé secret |
| Cold War | Guerre froide |
| creed | croyance religieuse |
| curb illegal immigration (to) | restreindre l'immigration clandestine |
| dabble in (to) | faire quelque chose en amateur |
| due process | procédure légale |
| entrepreneurship | esprit d'entreprise |
| fighting words | discours incitant à la haine |
| flag | drapeau |
| framework (legal) | cadre (juridique) |
| free enterprise | liberté d'entreprendre |
| gloomy | sombre, lugubre |
| haven | abri, refuge |
| huddled | blotti, recroquevillé |
| investigative journalism | journalisme d'investigation |
| mistake the forest for the trees (to) | c'est l'arbre qui cache la forêt |
| omen | signe annonciateur |
| outcry | tollé général |
| relish (to) | se délecter de |
| rugged individualism | individualisme acharné |
| scrutiny (to be under) | être sous surveillance |
| self-reliance | indépendance |
| smugness | suffisance |
| speak volumes (to) | être éloquent |
| stave off (to) | écarter |
| troubled spot | point névralgique |
| unpalatable | désagréable au goût, désagréable à entendre |
| unrest | instabilité |
| upstart | arriviste |
| weirdo | loufoque |
| wield influence (to) | exercer une influence |
| witch hunt | chasse aux sorcières |
| yearn to be free (to) | aspirer à la liberté |

# Focus...

### ◆ Amendments and Freedom

In 1868, the XIVth Amendment gave birthright citizenship and equal rights for all Americans. This was meant not just for blacks, but also for the people who would flock to the country. Children of Asian immigrants barred from US citizenship would thus be American citizens.

The XVth Amendment added in 1870 barred the states from making race a qualification for voting.

### ◆ WWI and the fight for freedom

President Wilson's speeches defined the US as the land of liberty, fighting alongside "a concert of free people." Democracy and freedom were used as ideological weapons opposed to German authoritarianism. Meanwhile freedom of speech came under severe restriction. The Sedition Act criminalized spoken or printed statements intended to "cast contempt, scorn, contumely or disrepute" on the "form of government". The deportation of anarchist aliens was authorized. People served jail sentences for their opinions, publications of foreign-language newspapers were denied use of US mail. This was followed by the Red Scare of 1919-1920 which was a response to the massive strike wave that followed the war.

### ◆ WWII and the Four Freedoms

In his January 6, 1941 State of the Union Address, President Roosevelt spoke of a world founded on four essential freedoms: freedom of speech, freedom of worship, freedom from want, and freedom from fear. The Four Freedoms were to be pictured by the famous illustrator Norman Rockwell. The United States entered the war a few months later. From then on, the definition of freedom has taken on new dimensions. Roosevelt later urged American citizens to "defend the great freedoms against the encroachment and attack of the dark forces of despotism". In the following years, especially after the war, America defined itself as the beacon of the free world while the Soviet Union in the Reagan years became the "evil empire".

In a 1942 radio address, Roosevelt declared the Four Freedoms embodied the "rights of men of every creed and every race, wherever they live". For the first time non-whites were officially included among the beneficiaries of freedom.

Civilisation *américaine*

◆ **Extract from the Universal Declaration of Human Rights (1948)**

*Article 2 says,*

"Everyone is entitled to all the rights and freedoms set forth in this Declaration, without distinction of any kind, such as race, color, sex, language, religion, political or other opinion, national or social origin, property, birth or other status."

◆ **Brown vs. Board of Education**

The 1954 landmark Supreme Court decision outlawing segregation in public schools says:

"Although the court has not assumed to define "liberty" with any great precision, (...) it cannot be restricted except for a proper governmental objective. Segregation in public education (...) constitutes an arbitrary deprivation of [Negro children's] liberty in violation of the *Due Process clause."

◆ **The Fourth Estate**

The power of the media is nowhere as influential as in the United States. This is why they are called the "Fourth Estate" exerting their power after the law, government and religion. The American press especially demonstrated its influence in two celebrated cases: the Watergate scandal (see p. 355) and the Pentagon Papers. In 1971, President Nixon tried to stop the publication of a document which surveyed American involvement in Vietnam. It was *classified "top secret" and the White House argued that its publication would endanger national security. The publication was delayed 12 days, until a Supreme Court decision ruled against the government.

*Further reading:*

- Eric Foner, *The Story of American Freedom* – W.W. Norton & Company, 1998.

   The author is a Professor of History at Columbia University. This book surveys the central theme of freedom in the American identity and underlines the conflicts which have arisen from the different interpretations of the notion in the course of history. It is a highly commendable analysis of the innumerable fights waged in the name of freedom and provides the reader with precious information on the United States past and present.

   Eric Foner's articles are sometimes translated in the French media.

# Essay

Discuss the following assertion :

Americans have more freedom to think what we will and say what we think than any other people on earth. We can denounce politicians in uninhibited language. We can read books banned in Britain or Israel. We can even burn our *flag, as a political protest, without fear of punishment.

"*Staving Off the Silencers", Anthony Lewis, *The New York Times*, December 1, 1991 – an article published for the 200th anniversary of the Bill of Rights.

*This statement may sound like yet another example of American *smugness in the never-ending vein, "we have more and we are better." Yet one has to admit that the words of the First Amendment, "Congress shall make no law (...) abridging the freedom of speech, or of the press" are fully implemented in America. Few democracies indeed would allow public exposure of their Head of State as was the case with Nixon or, more recently, in "Monicagate", a questionable replica of Watergate, where Clinton had to admit he had lied about his relationship with the White House intern. France in particular is an example to the contrary these days as *accountability of our public figures has become a highly controversial issue.*

*Similarly, few democracies would consider flag-burning as a political protest a right protected by freedom of speech, as was ruled by the Supreme Court in two cases a decade ago. And the United States singles itself out in asserting the right to free speech of the Ku-Klux-Klan declaring that "the nigger should be returned to Africa, the Jew returned to Israel", or in upholding the right of cable-TV operators to carry sexually explicit channels during the daytime. Racial discrimination or sexual harrassment are punished by law, but racist words are considered as an opinion protected by the Bill of Rights; so are sexually explicit movies and many other forms of expression.*

*Such decisions would raise public *outcry in other countries with a call for *censorship. The American conception of freedom accepts that those ideas we do not *relish should be expressed freely. It is based on the assumption that individuals are free to choose the speech they want to hear, and free to make opinions on their own. Nothing hurts the American mind as the possibility that one's preferences and life choices should be regulated by laws and government control.*

*There might be \*unpalatable hate groups and all sorts of \*weirdos in America, but let us not \*mistake the forest for the trees. This is the price to pay for genuine freedom of speech. If \*investigative journalism is still a reality in the United States, if government officials feel they are permanently under public \*scrutiny, it is because today the country is capable of "staving off the silencers". Indeed, this has not always been the case and intolerance has not spared America in the past. But many countries could certainly take inspiration from the American model of free speech.*

# MORE ABOUT...
## ...FREEDOM UNDER SIEGE

### THE COLD WAR

As in other democracies, the United States has experienced periods when freedom underwent some severe restrictions. This was the case during WWI with the passing of the Espionage Act in 1917 restricting freedom of speech, and the Sedition Act in 1918 which made it a crime to deliver statements considered to be scornful of the form of government of the country. But the Cold War is remembered as one of the *gloomiest episodes of US history. The end of WWII had left two major victors, the United States and the Soviet Union. In 1947, the Truman administration set out to contain the influence of the Soviet Union – at home and abroad. On the world scene, it resulted in dubious military adventures and awkward alliances with dictatorships. The Cold War dominated international relationships for almost fifty years till the collapse of the Soviet Union.

At home, it generated hysteria about communism – the most severe assault on freedom of speech the country has ever known. It was orchestrated by a demagogue, Republican Senator Joseph McCarthy of Wisconsin. He started his campaign in 1950 drawing lists of workers in the State Department who, he claimed, were communists. Soon all government employees were checked for their political beliefs. Some were accused of sending *classified documents to Moscow in the 30s, others were declared guilty of betraying atomic secrets to the Soviet Union. Among them, Julius and Ethel Rosenberg refused to cooperate, contrary to the other accused; they were sentenced to death and executed in 1953. The Rosenbergs became a "cause célèbre" all over the world. The *witch hunt extended to corporations, universities, Hollywood. In a manner reminiscent of the Salem witch hunt and of the Moscow trials in the 30s, the accused were urged to give the names of their "communist" colleagues, to inform the government of un-American activities and to make public confessions. People who refused to cooperate lost their jobs and were blacklisted. Some committed suicide, many served jail sentences. Just among federal government employees, 1,400 were "purged" because they were just left-wing... or gay.

In fact there were very few communists in the country – from 60,000 to 80,000 members in 1945. No wonder. The communist ideology is so alien to the American tradition of *self-reliance, *rugged individualism and distrust of government intervention, that it never won much support – though it may have attracted a handful of idealists and adventurers who occasionally *dabbled in spying activities. Thanks to access to KGB archives, historians have recently discovered that Moscow had indeed infiltrated the Roosevelt administration, and that the Rosenbergs very likely were "red spies". But at the time, nobody knew for sure.

McCarthyism was also targeting liberal-minded Americans, those who had supported Roosevelt's New Deal, and who came in much larger numbers. The fight against communism became a means to oppose a series of issues which had little to do with Soviet influence, like union rights or civil rights for blacks.

The McCarthy hysteria ended as rapidly as it had started. Suddenly in 1954, the Senate censured him on grounds that he had brought "dishonor and disrepute" to the legislative body; he was soon deserted by his supporters and lost all the influence he had *wielded previously.

There were few reactions in the country – people were scared at the idea of losing their jobs and often readily cooperated with this new political police. Many renowned academics gave "loyalty oaths" and filmmakers secured a career after giving names or making public statements against communism. Few resisted the assault. Some filmmakers chose exile – among them, the most prestigious of all, British-born Charlie Chaplin.

## THE AMERICAN CIVIL LIBERTIES UNION

The ACLU was founded in 1917 after anti-war protesters had been arrested under the Espionage and Sedition Acts. It was first a small coalition of pacifists, lawyers and Progressives like Roger Baldwin who had a deep distrust of governmental power and was an ardent supporter of free speech. The ACLU supports the principles of the Bill of Rights; in many regards, it has helped shape the notion of individual rights developed throughout the twentieth century.

Over the years, the ACLU has been at the forefront of civil liberties, taking diverse stands influenced by the dominant mood of the day. For instance it refused to support jailed Communist leaders in the 50s, defended the right to free speech of Klan members and Black Panther activists as well. More recently, it opposed "English only" legislation because it is contrary to the spirit of tolerance and diversity embodied in the Constitution. It also opposed President Bush's decision to fund religious organizations' participation in social service programs.

The ACLU regularly supports fights to stop discrimination against gays, women and minorities. It denounces the execution of mentally-impaired convicts. It has engaged in the defense of cyber-rights as well. The ACLU has affiliates and chapters in every state, files lawsuits on any civil rights issue, issues reports and studies, gives advice to Congress. It is a powerful lobby to be reckoned with.

# 4 The Land of Opportunity

*Guy Richard*

### Social mobility:
### "If I were a rich man..."

Whatever their motivations, all immigrants did not necessarily want to make a fortune, but at least to start a new life. They hoped their children would be able to *work their way up, to *climb up the social ladder and the poor immigrant who gets rich thanks to hard work and determination became a stock character in the US psyche. Horatio Alger, a popular writer at the turn of the 19th century, contributed to spreading the archetype of the poor deserving young man who works his way up thanks to sheer will-power, integrity and industriousness. Besides, real life self-made men amply demonstrated that real opportunities to make a fortune did exist in America. The reason why such entrepreneurs became emblematic of the country itself is easy to understand: they came to embody Mr. Everyman who could also "*strike it rich". They started from scratch and managed to build an empire owing to qualities which became associated with the Americans' pioneering spirit such as will-power, industry, ingenuity and rugged individualism. "Rags to riches" novel characters found their real life counterparts in people like Levi, Rockefeller, Mellon, Vanderbilt or Carnegie. (cf. Focus, p. 253). But some critics would object this happened a long time ago.

### Geographical mobility:
### "go west, young man..."

19th century America must have looked like a boundless continent of wide, open spaces, with plenty of natural resources and opportunities to be taken, provided pioneers had the drive to go west and start a new life. In this respect, the Frontier played a decisive role, both economically, socially and psychologically, since it provided an outlet for the discontented in territories where at least until 1890 the law of the jungle, the "struggle for life", was stronger than the rule of law. Cheap land could be bought (or taken from the Indians), communication was made easier with the completion of the first transcontinental railroad, all the more so as westward expansion had taken a further dimension a few decades earlier with the Gold Rush to California and the arrival of the "forty niners", people who came to California in 1849 in search of gold.

But the dream of "*making it" did not come true for everyone and many were bound to feel disillusioned.

### The Frontier Tradition:
### from reality to myth?
### Whose reality, anyway?

The end of the Frontier in 1890 came as a shock to the Americans since they realised their country had been settled and wherever they went, they would have to answer for their acts since the rule of law had replaced the so-called "Wild West". But migrants kept moving west, in search of new horizons and new challenges to take up.

It is no coincidence J.F. Kennedy called his 1960 platform "the New Frontier". By so doing, he meant to build a bridge between past and present and wanted to channel his fellow-citizens' energies in two different directions: opportunities were opening up in the field of space conquest and in the war on poverty. Thus he wanted the US to focus on an outer frontier and on a more domestic one. Even though the former could only be accessible to a happy few, it was rapidly romanticised and the whole country felt mobilised: the technological competitive edge had to be regained over the USSR which had managed to launch its first artificial satellite three years before.

Remaining pockets of the Frontier also enabled highly skilled workers to land a rough but well-paid job during the construction of the trans-Alaskan pipeline in the 1970s, while a less dramatic but steady phenomenon was also taking place in the "lower 48" (US states from the US-Canadian border to the US-Mexican border): westward migration, especially to the South and the South-West. This is a constant shift westwards of the population recorded by the Census Bureau every time a census is taken in the US. The Sunbelt is an area stretching from the Carolinas to Southern California, including states like Georgia, Texas, Arizona and New Mexico. Such a move from the North-East's manufacturing Rustbelt is a typically middle-class phenomenon of a generation in search of new opportunities in a sunnier, safer and perhaps saner environment. Although it now seems to be slowing a bit, it is a reminder, as much psychological as geographical, of the Founding Fathers' pledge: the pursuit of happiness.

Such a quest is encapsulated in California, the ultimate Frontier, the *crucible of so many social experiments and the place where opportunities are *up for grabs. New blood is being infused into the country in Silicon Valley, a mecca for high tech businesses and venture capitalists. But such dynamism can also apply to the West coast as a whole and, in this respect, the violent demonstrations during the World Trade Organisation summit in Seattle in November 1999 epitomised the big issues our western societies are being confronted with, since Seattle is also home to Boeing and Microsoft.

Gone are the days when hippies and beatniks went West in search of a new way of life and of themselves, California is now a laboratory in new high tech fields. High achievers come from all over the world and drain Europe and Third World countries of the much needed talents of engineers, software designers, e-business and dot.com whizz kids.

The saga of Hewlett and Packard starting their business from their basement garage still endures and Bill Gates, Steve Case and Jeff Bezos are all in their own way the worthy heirs to the famed entrepreneurs of the 19th century. The digital age has replaced traditional manufacturing sectors, but the unskilled, those who can't adapt, are left behind or only get menial jobs.

In such a world of winners, where success, money and prestige are the ultimate achievements, those who can't make it are often depicted as lazy and undeserving and this new version of social Darwinism can have far-reaching consequences in a country whose safety net does not care for those who are out of the rat-race. Such an outlook is an application of Darwin's theories about evolution to society and justifies inequalities since only the fittest can adapt to their environment.

Competition breeds selfishness, greed and heartlessness, there are still opportunities, but not for all. Millions are left out in the cold, without the protection of a social safety net (cf. chapter on "Welfare", p. 363).

### Pulling the welcome mat.

No one knows what the future holds for venture capitalists and e-business moguls, but the Mexican peasant willing to take his chance and get into the US illegally every night has more mundane preoccupations: to make ends meet and earn a living wage for his large family back home. Though he is well aware he may be exploited, resented, scorned or even discriminated against, a day's work in "El Norte" is worth twice or three times as much as what he would get south of the border – provided he is lucky enough to get hired. The 2,000-mile U.S-Mexican border is *porous, US border patrols are overwhelmed and feel powerless. They feel their efforts to stem the flood of immigrants are as futile as putting one's fingers into a dike to keep water from rushing in. "Wetbacks", "braceros", "illegals" used to *swim across rivers, scale fences or *sneak into the desert but there is now a more efficient – and dangerous – way to cross the border illegally: gate crashing.

Instead of avoiding check points on the border in Southern California, illegal immigrants now overwhelm them: after a signal given by smugglers, scores of illegals run past Mexican and American guards into the oncoming traffic of the freeway. They are generally successful because border patrols are reluctant to pursue them on the highway. However, it is a risky venture and dozens of immigrants have been hit and killed on the highway in the past few years. US authorities claim chasing them would only make the situation more dangerous. Moreover, they are an easy prey for all kinds of unscrupulous bosses, farmers and smugglers in the border states.

If those people are ready to risk being fatally injured while running along the highway, it is out of economic necessity and those who are caught will try elsewhere, the next evening or even the same night, until they can make it. It is more a revolving door than a watertight dam indeed. Many plans designed to stem the flood of "undocumented" Central and South Americans have failed so far. This will be true as long as developing countries cannot provide for their own populations. Therefore, the "Tortilla Curtain" exemplifies the economic divide between North and South.

The US is still a land of opportunity, even though the dream may become a nightmare.

# Vocabulary

| | |
|---|---|
| be in search of/in quest of (to) | être à la recherche, en quête de |
| beacon of hope | phare, symbole d'espoir |
| buy up a firm (to) | racheter une entreprise |
| climb up the social ladder (to) | gravir l'échelle sociale |
| crucible/melting-pot | creuset |
| dictator/dictatorship | dictateur ; dictature |
| discriminated against (to be) | être victime de discrimination |
| economic/social ladder | échelle sociale |
| flee (fled, fled) (to)/be in flight from (to) | fuir |
| free speech/freedom of speech | liberté d'expression |
| freedom of worship | liberté de culte |
| fulfil one's hopes (to) | réaliser ses espoirs |
| have a snowball effect (to) /snowball into success (to) | avoir un effet boule de neige |
| look for (to)/search for (to) | rechercher |
| lured by (to be)/lure | être attiré par ; miroir aux alouettes |
| mainstream America | l'Amérique profonde |
| make it (to)/strike (to) it rich | réussir, faire fortune, « décrocher le gros lot » |
| makeshift raft | radeau de fortune |
| merger/merge (to) | fusion ; fusionner |
| porous border | frontière poreuse, perméable |
| repatriate (to)/repatriation | rapatrier ; rapatriement |
| rung | barreau |
| savvy (to be business) | avoir le sens des affaires |
| second-class citizen | citoyen de seconde zone |
| set up a business (to) | créer une entreprise |
| sneak across the border (to) | franchir la frontière clandestinement |
| sweat, sweat sb. (to)/sweatshop | suer ; exploiter qqn ; atelier clandestin |
| swim across a river (to) | traverser une rivière, un fleuve à la nage |
| undocumented (the)/the illegals | immigrés illégaux |
| up for grabs (to be) | à saisir (opportunité) |
| upward social mobility | promotion sociale |
| work one's way up (to) | assurer son ascension sociale (par son travail) |

# Focus...

◆ **Two Self-Made Men**

*Levi Strauss*

When he arrived in California, Levi Strauss, a Bavarian immigrant, was empty-handed except for a roll of canvas he had brought along with him. He thought miners would buy it in order to make tents. But the idea proved wrong and he decided to take another chance: miners' trousers were not sturdy enough for their tough working conditions and he hired a tailor to cut trousers from his canvas. Word spread and "those pants of Levi's" (hence "Levi's") became more and more popular: this was the beginning of a world-famous industry which was to *snowball into success. Clothes originally designed for work became a fashionable piece of clothing all over the world, emblematic of the active, out-of-doors, adventurous life that Americans consider theirs.

*Andrew Carnegie*

The same "rags-to-riches" story was also exemplified by Andrew Carnegie. Born in Dumferline, Scotland, young Andrew arrived in the US with his family when he was a 13-year-old boy. He started at the bottom of the economic ladder and, through sheer work and determination, he managed to work his way out of poverty. He first worked as a bobbin boy in a Pittsburgh mill and borrowed books from the local library to study during his free time. He then got hired in the newly-created telegraph office, where he taught himself the Morse alphabet. He then went on to become an assistant to the director of the Pennsylvania Railroad. When he was presented with a model of a car for night travelling, an innovative idea at the time, he created a company with a partner. He would subsequently set up a bridge-building firm and later on, a steel company. After oil was discovered in Pennsylvania in 1859, he bought a farm on which... oil was found four years later. Not only was he a born businessman, he was business-*savvy too.

In 1901, he sold out and became a philanthropist, founding libraries and universities, granting deserving students scholarships to enable them to work their own way up. He went down in History as one of America's iconic self-made men, a theme which was to be harped on for the benefit of generations of would-be billionaires.

◆ **Cuban immigration**

Together with Puerto-Ricans, Mexicans and other Central and South Americans, Cuban-Americans belong to a fast-growing, assertive group, the Hispanics. The history of Cuban immigration to the US mirrors the tense relations the US has had with its Caribbean neighbour in the last forty years.

In the early 1960s, 650,000 Cubans fled their homeland in the wake of Fidel Castro's takeover in January 1959. They were granted political asylum by the American Administration which was only too happy to show the US was still a land of opportunity and the exodus was exploited for propaganda purposes in the tense context of the Cold War.

In May and June 1980, the Carter Administration was confronted with an unprecedented event: as some Cubans had taken refuge in the grounds of the Peruvian Embassy in Havana, Castro unexpectedly gave people permission to leave the island, an opportunity 135,000 Cubans took. Most of them settled in Florida and joined relatives already in the US since the 1960s. The latter organised a boatlift, chartering a flotilla of small craft to take their families over from Mariel, a harbour on Cuba's northern coast (hence their names "Marielitos"). US authorities found it hard to screen them as Castro had also decided to get rid of common criminals and lunatics whom he had promptly embarked on the Marielitos' craft as well.

President Carter's "open arms policy" found a sympathetic audience in the US since it was still at odds with the USSR.

When in 1994, Cuban would-be escapees started crossing the Straits of Florida on *makeshift rafts (hence their name in Spanish: "balseros"), the Clinton Administration was first reluctant to let them in since they were alleged to be coming over for economic reasons. The Berlin Wall had fallen a few years before, the Soviet Union had disintegrated and such refugees were no longer needed as propaganda ploy... But the Cuban-American lobby was strong and vocal enough to make itself heard and to soften the Administration's "get tough" policy.

More recently, in 1999/2000, little Elian Rodriguez's odyssey was exploited politically both by Florida's Cuban-American community and the Castro regime: should Elian be given the opportunity to stay in the US or should he be sent back to his father's home in Cuba?

The different waves of Cuban immigrants have contributed to Florida's prosperity. The Mayor of Dade County, where Miami is located, is a 36-year old Cuban-American and Miami is now a gateway to business ventures in Latin America. First and second-generation Cuban-American and their American-born children dominate everything from local politics and the law to business, education, the media and the entertainment world. They are now shaping pop culture whose Latino (and Latina) icons youngsters try to emulate. Their dream lives on too.

# Essay

In *A Nation of Immigrants*, J.F. Kennedy wrote:

"In the community he had left, the immigrant had a fixed place [...]. In the New World, it was the future and not the past to which he was compelled to address himself [...]. A continent lay before him."

Would you say such a promise still holds true nowadays? Give specific examples to make your point.

*Although his father was a multimillionaire, J.F. Kennedy did not forget his roots and remembered his own family had fled rural Ireland to come to the US in search of a better life. His ancestors may never have heard of the Declaration of Independence, but they somehow responded to its pledge, as millions of others were to do.*

*In his own way, Kennedy demonstrated the US was a land of opportunity since he was the first Roman Catholic to be elected President, which showed the sky was the limit, provided Americans had determination, doggedness and the money to fulfil their hopes. The US has always been synonymous with enterprise, success and upward social mobility. Examples are legion in history and nowadays, Bill Gates has replaced Rockefeller and Carnegie in the pantheon of self-made men whom people admire and want to emulate. But now, opportunities have moved west and can be symbolised by Silicon Valley where tomorrow's world is being shaped thanks to high tech, venture capitalism and entrepreneurship. Therefore, the myth of success still endures and though it may not be within everyone's reach, it is a dream many poor people from the western hemisphere are still lured by. If they cannot get resident status, they sneak into the US by any means at hand.*

*Kennedy's quotation is also reminiscent of the Frontier and it brings to mind the image of the cowboy riding out towards a future filled with undreamt-of opportunities.*

*Kennedy's "New Frontier" was also to revive the dream and the Sunbelt is the modern-day version of a westward search for new opportunities. Mobility – both geographical and social – on which the US was built, is still alive and many Americans are under the (false?) impression they can go anywhere and do anything their talents enable them.*

*Critics would argue the dream often turns sour and that many are bound to be disappointed. Yet, there is no denying immigrants keep pouring into the US and it is hard to keep them out. The myth endures and it is no use trying to deter them from coming, whatever hardships they may have to encounter. Thus, they do believe the dream of boundless opportunity is worth \*sweating for.*

# MORE ABOUT...
## ...A BRIGHT PROSPECT FOR THE NEW MILLENNIUM?

### SILICON VALLEY AS THE ULTIMATE SOCIAL LABORATORY

In its issue dated Sept.18 2000, *Newsweek*, the American weekly magazine, gives a few mind-boggling statistics about what lies ahead for the US in the years to come, with special attention devoted to California, namely:

- Silicon Valley's influx of hyper-achieving techno-immigrants, along with a swelling Hispanic population, creates a microcosm of the future.
- The ethnic make-up of California's population as a whole is mirrored in Silicon Valley's:
- percentage of Whites: Sil. Valley: 49.9%; Cal: 49%
- percentage of Hispanics: Sil. Valley: 30 %; Cal: 24%
- percentage of Asians: Sil. Valley: 23 %; Cal: 12%...

Mobility and opportunities are key notions Americans of all descriptions have always responded to and illegal immigration is bound to continue as the US is likely to be viewed as THE land of opportunity and promise by the world's dispossessed. Denying would-be (im)migrants – whether they be legal or not – is a tough proposition and may be a losing battle in the decades to come. In their own way, they all want to "keep the dream alive". The journalist ended his article with a reflection which may show the way to the future:

> "The Valley's challenge now is to apply all its diverse brainpower to create more opportunity for the sons and daughters of East Palo Alto° to live the dream too."

*Note*: East Palo Alto is an economically depressed neighborhood next to a high tech, computer-oriented district.

# 5. The Land of the Big

*Monique Chéron-Vaudrey*

For the first-time visitor, everything in the United States looks *larger than life – Manhattan's skyscrapers, cars, bath tubs, burgers, Sunday papers... The country itself seems to outdo in size all the other countries in the world. Even Nature seems bigger with countless open spaces, vast mountain ranges, gigantic rivers and lakes. Several natural sites feature among the longest, largest or highest in the world: the Mississipi, the Grand Canyon, the sequoias of the West coast.

In fact the creation of the United States benefited from exceptional circumstances. It was a sparsely populated continent when the first European settlers set foot on its shores. They found a vast expanse of fertile land, rich in all sorts of natural resources. For the first settlers, prosperity was instant. And the land was so vast and so generous that for more than a century it could welcome a continuous flow of immigrants and provide them with enough space and opportunities to allow them to support a family and make a good living.

## Easy access to land ownership

Soon after Independence, the United States acquired or won vast territories which could be controlled only if more American citizens settled there. What happened during the immigration waves of the 19th century is a unique phenomenon in history. With the Homestead Act, the US government transferred millions of acres of federal land to settlers for a nominal sum. Now for the impoverished farmers of Europe, even for better-off immigrants, this was something unheard of. At the time in Europe land ownership was often the privilege of the aristocracy, or when land could be bought, it was so scarce that few had access to it anyway. Yet here was a country where ordinary people could become landowners, provided they were ready to work hard and show their talent. The pioneers crossed the Appalachians, settled the Mississippi Valley and the Great Plains, then they crossed the Rocky Mountains until they reached the Pacific Ocean – and as they moved westward they found more fertile land, with large deposits of coal, copper, iron and oil. Indeed the enterprise was likely to forge a new spirit, characteristic of the American mindset, defined in the myth of the Frontier. It fostered the feeling that space and resources were limitless, that America was the land of plenty.

## The benefits of early industrialization

In the 19th century, while Europe was trying to adapt to the modern world with railroads and road networks, America was never impeded by crowded cities or private farmlands. It jumped several of the stages Europe had been going through and from nothing built railroads, roads and bridges,

Civilisation *américaine*

large cities crowned by skyscrapers.

The settling of virgin lands in the West would not have really contributed to the amazing prosperity of the country if the most advanced technologies had not supported the development of farming. Again, the size of the country required vast operations. Started in the 1860s, the building of the railroads, for which the government gave 24 million acres of public land – thus contributing to the building of huge private fortunes – allowed fast and safe transportation of cattle, farm produce and manufactured goods. Meanwhile, McCormick rolled its first monster *reaping machines onto the vast fields of the Mid-West.

Cities, too, were transformed by the latest technologies. New York and Chicago became the first symbols of the outsized city. Skyscrapers emerged, thanks to new building techniques like steel framing and the development of the elevator. Besides, tall buildings in commercial and business city centers were likely to turn out a higher profit than scattered smaller ones. Today in each American city, the skyscraper stands erect as a triumphant symbol of success and limitless possibilities, as if proclaiming that the sky is the limit.

### The urban sprawl

The frontier was closed in the late 19th century but territorial expansion has kept reaching ever new areas. The idea of freedom is closely linked to the idea of moving in the American mind. As space still seems to be limitless, middle-class Americans keep moving away from city centers for quieter places in the suburbs and *exurbs, often at the cost of long hours wasted in *commuting. For a long time, in pure pioneer tradition, people moved from the East coast to the West. Now that California has become as crowded – and as expensive – as New Jersey or Massachussets, Americans are discovering new havens in the South and South-West. The two fastest-growing states today are Nevada with a 66 percent population growth over the last decade, and Arizona with a 40 percent rate. Las Vegas, the city which was built from nothing in the middle of nowhere hardly more than half-a-century ago, is now home to 1.4 million inhabitants and adds 70,000 people each year to its population. In fact, it is the new suburbs, built several miles away from the city center, which attract most new residents.

Another example of urban sprawl is Atlanta, Georgia, whose population has doubled over the past three decades and spread out very far away from the center, making it just as bad as Los Angeles for *commuter traffic. Plans for some kind of public transportation have been vigorously opposed by the inhabitants of the new residential communities. A rail link or a bus line would attract unwelcome, lower-class residents. In pure pioneer spirit, space and distance are still the surest ways of preserving one's own privacy and freedom.

### A country of car drivers

When Henry Ford automated his production line and put his model T on the market – a cheap car that Ford workers could afford, he initiated more than yet another technological revolution. As more families were able to buy a car, they could also move to the suburbs – which is how urban sprawl started. By the mid 1920s, more than half American households owned a car – cheap home-produced steel and oil helped a lot in making the car accessible to all.

Today the country seems to have been shaped for car-driving citizens requiring big parking lots for companies, schools, libraries, clinics, etc. Indeed it gave rise to big shopping malls so far away from home that when you go shopping you fill your trolley to the brim and come back with big bulging shopping bags.

## The mecca of the consumer society

Some historians date the birth of the consumer society back to the early 19th century when manufactured products and fine goods were sold to ordinary people. The prosperity of the 1920s gave a huge impetus to mass consumption and so did the the period following WWII. While Europe and many other parts of the world were slowly recovering from the wounds of war, the United States stood as a real exception with its abundance of goods and opportunities. Buying big cars, living in spacious two-garage homes, piling up large quantities of food in fridges as big as a linen closet became the hallmark of American prosperity – never mind that it helped create a nation of overweight people.

This often strikes foreigners as odd – after all the consumer society has long spread to the other advanced countries in the world but nowhere else can one find such a frenzy for consumption in large quantities. The one-pound steak, the half-gallon ice-cream cup, the *king-size bed and the *SUV are the cherished privileges of American consumers.

Let us bear in mind that Americans are the grand-children of people who experienced poverty and deprivation – and many of the more recent immigrants have left part of their family in poverty-ridden parts of the world. Some have a consumer definition of freedom, with unlimited access to the *cornucopia of goods available thanks to the American way of life.

## The biggest power in the world

Above all, Americans are acutely aware that their country is the biggest power in the world. Already in the mid-19th century, it had become the wealthiest country. It took another fifty years – and participation in two World Wars for the United States to achieve this prominent status. It does not just dominate the world through its economic might, it does so through its international influence as well.

It may not be surprising then that many Americans should be proud of being the best or the biggest or whichever superlative comes to mind. More often than not, it is true!

# VOCABULARY

In this list are some commonly-used expressions of bigness:

| | |
|---:|:---|
| behemoth | animal monstrueux, énorme (terme biblique) |
| Big Apple | surnom donné à New York |
| Big Blue | IBM |
| Big Oil | grandes compagnies pétrolières |
| Big Tobacco | grandes sociétés de tabac |
| Big Three | General Motors, Ford, Chrysler |
| big game hunting | chasse au gros gibier |
| big government | interventionnisme de l'État |
| big money | capitaux importants, « grosse galette » |
| big player | grosse pointure |
| big science | grands projets scientifiques |
| big time | réussite, gloire, cour des grands |
| billionaire | milliardaire |
| blockbuster | film à gros budget et à gros bénéfices |
| commute (to)/commuter | faire le trajet domicile-travail ; celui qui fait ce trajet |
| cornucopia | corne d'abondance |
| extra-large, or XXL | très grande taille (pour les vêtements en particulier) |
| exurb | banlieue très éloignée du centre |
| hype | battage publicitaire |
| juggernaut | poids lourd énorme, puissance écrasante |
| jumbo | géant (nom aussi donné à l'éléphant) |
| king-size | géant (cf. **king-size bed**) |
| larger than life (to be) | être hors normes |
| make it big | avoir beaucoup de succès |
| mega bucks | beaucoup d'argent |
| mega deal | super-contrat |
| mega trend | tendance très forte |
| megaplex | très grand multiplex |
| millionnaire | millionnaire, milliardaire |
| reaping machine | moissonneuse |
| stretch limo | limousine dont la carrosserie a été retravaillée et étirée en longueur |
| Super Bowl | finale du championnat de football américain |
| super jumbo | encore plus grand que grand |
| SUV or Sports Utility Vehicle | gros 4x4 |
| use big words (to) | parler en utilisant des mots longs et recherchés |
| whopper (car/ burger/ lie) | énorme (voiture, burger, mensonge) |
| zillion | néologisme récent : somme tellement importante qu'on ne peut plus vraiment compter... |
| zillionnaire | encore plus riche que le milliardaire |

# Focus...

◆ **How New York became "the \*Big Apple"**

There is no certainty about its origin. Researchers have found two references: one in a book "The Wayfarer in New York" (1909); the author Edward Martin commented about the Midwest attitude, saying, "Kansas is apt to see in New York a greedy city... It inclines to think that the big apple gets a disproportionate share of the national sap". In a 1924 issue of The New York Morning Telegraph, a turf writer wrote, "There's only one Big Apple. That's New York".
In the 30s, it became the name of a Harlem night-club.

◆ **The Homestead Act**

The 1862 Homestead Act offered a farmer 160 acres (64 hectares) of public land. The law later extended the acreage to 640 acres (a square mile) for cattle raising. The farmer could become owner of the land after six months on paying $1.50 an acre, or for nothing after five years' residence.

◆ **The Manifest Destiny**

The term "manifest destiny" was first used in 1845 with reference to the already familiar notion that the US had been selected by God for the achievement of liberty. Then expanding to the rest of the North-American continent was considered the means to satisfy God's will. The divine mission indeed justified the taking over of Indian lands for the benefit of the chosen people. The notion of "manifest destiny" was later used for international purposes.

◆ **The myth of the Frontier**

It was shaped in 1893 by historian Frederick Jackson Turner who said that what made American development distinctive (from European history) was the exploration of the free land in the West. The pioneers who settled the vast territories developed the American values of individualism, hard work, love of freedom, innovation, optimism and patriotism. On the frontier "barbarism" collided with "civilization". The frontier was declared "closed" in 1890 but the myth has lived on. Until recently California had been the place where people went when they wanted to have their dream come true. Only skyrocketing housing prices are driving people off back East again, to the South-West in particular.

◆ **Town planners did it on a large scale**

Quantity and size do not just characterize the making of the country, they also show in people's daily lives: Americans live in spacious houses and display a special bias in favor of big cars. They may have an excuse for that. The large-scale means used to tame a huge continent were reflected in town planning. Most towns and cities were built a little more than a century ago. But town planners had foreseen the influx of new inhabitants and decided that street-width ought to be larger than in Europe. New York's streets in the early 19th century had to be at least 60 feet wide, avenues 100 feet or more. While going west, the standards would expand, with a record 132 feet street-width for Salt Lake City – yet another city built in the middle of nowhere.

◆ **Presidential quotations**

"Like all Americans, I like big things: big prairies, big forests and mountains, big wheat fields, railroads – and herds of cattle too – big factories and steamboats and everything else. But we must keep steadily in mind that no people were ever yet benefited by riches if their prosperity corrupted their virtue. […] We have fallen heirs to the most glorious heritage a people ever received and each of us must do his part if we wish to show that this nation is worthy of its good fortune."

President Theodore Roosevelt

"America doesn't need small. America needs big."
President Clinton in 1996.

◆ **When small is beautiful**

The Wilson administration first introduced "big government "policies on the eve of WWI and after, establishing the Federal Reserve system and the Federal Trade Commission. But the New Deal era inaugurated massive government intervention – a policy which has since then been criticized by Republicans as "big government".

In the 2000 presidential campaign, even Democratic candidate Al Gore adopted the new gospel:

"I'm opposed to big government. I'm for a smaller, smarter government that serves people better, but offers real change and gives more choices to our families. A return to big government would be as wrong for our economy as a return to big tax cuts for the wealthy."

## Compréhension de texte

### Épreuve d'expression du concours IENA 1999 – LV1

#### From Trust Busters to Trust Trusters

Theodore Roosevelt plotted the beginning of the end of John D. Rockefeller's oil empire at a secret meeting at the White House on a summer night in 1906. Surrounded by his attorney general and other key cabinet members, he mapped out the antitrust suit against Standard Oil. It took five years for Roosevelt's case to be won in the Supreme Court, breaking up Standard Oil into 34 companies. And for the better part of the next 70 years, Washington's economic agenda was dominated by the high-stakes politics of curbing the power of big enterprises.

But something has changed in Washington in the past decade or so, something that has taken the issue that Woodrow Wilson called "these vast aggregations of capital" off the country's political agenda.

Last week, when two of the biggest remaining parts of the old Rockefeller empire, Exxon and Mobil, were recombined in the world's largest merger, Washington yawned. House Minority leader Dick Gephardt, the pro-union, pro-consumer voice of the Democratic party's left wing, spent the day complaining loudly – about the Clinton impeachment inquiry, and he has yet to say anything about the deal, according to his office. In fact, scarcely a politician of any stripe headed for the cameras to question whether the $75 billion deal was good for the country, for workers or for consumers.

The same silence greeted the deal that created Citigroup, which was the largest financial services company for a few minutes until Deutsche Bank bought Bankers trust Corp., earlier this month.

Less than a decade ago, when Japanese corporations snapped up New York's Rockefeller Center and two Hollywood studios, many in Congress were in an uproar over the sale of American icons to foreigners. But these days, with the Dow bobbing at record levels and analysts declaring the triumph of American-style capitalism, neither the Deutsche Bank acquisition nor Daimler-Benz's purchase of Chrysler Corp. last spring has yielded a similar furor.

Many theories have been offered to explain this new passivity about the evils of Big Everything: the pace of technological change, or the realities of borderless competition in a year of global tumult, or the confusing business currents that at once celebrate the global reach of US-based multinationals and the entrepreneurial spirit of small businesses.

And perhaps it's just temporary – if prices start going up again at the pump, or if the US economy falters, there could be a renewed clamor to rein in corporations viewed as too big, too powerful or too heartless. Sen. Paul Wellstone, D-Minn., is among the few in Congress still exercised about the concentration of corporate power. "Whatever the reason," he noted, "once upon a time this was a burning issue, and now it's not even on the table."

Civilisation américaine

At a rare high-profile hearing this year on the long-term effects of mergers, Federal reserve Chairman Alan Greenspan argued that the government was inept at determining in advance those mergers that would create competitive problems and would be wiser to wait and see.

Greenspan's view was challenged at the hearing, chiefly by Joel Klein, the assistant attorney general in charge of antitrust, and Robert Pitofsky, the chairman of the Federal Trade Commission. Pitofsky noted that undoing the damage after employees of an acquired company have been fired, after its plants have been closed and after top management has moved on, "is enormously expensive."

But the fact remains that few lawmakers dare to venture deep into this territory, even though it sustained generations of their predecessors. "The biggest reason is the mix of money and politics", says Wellstone. "For both parties, these are the heavy hitters, the monied interests who have a huge impact on the tenure of people in Congress. Not too many people want to challenge them."

Of course, that was also true in Roosevelt's day. But Wellstone notes a second reason: the quiet arrival in Washington of "a set of shared assumptions about what is necessary these days for survival in a global economy".

The first is that while bigger is not always better, it may be the only way to extend one's reach abroad. "The ability to be a global player and to be competitive anywhere in the world has become more important as all the traditional walls of regulation, state ownership and time barriers have come down," said Daniel Yergin, chairman of Cambridge Energy Research Associates.

The second assumption is that technology moves faster than antitrust cases. When the government began its push against IBM in the late 60s, the microprocessor had just been invented. By the time the case was abandoned thirteen years later, the microprocessor was revolutionizing the computer industry, and IBM was missing the boat. It caught up, but market dominance was no longer an issue.

*The New York Times* – December 6, 1998

**1 – Explain what the following sentence means:**

**"Whatever the reason," he noted, "once upon a time this was a burning issue, and now it's not even on the table." (100 mots + ou – 10 %)**

> *After considering various factors for Americans' passivity about big enterprises, the article quotes one senator who is not sure about the reason for the absence of debate on recent mergers and acquisitions by foreign corporations. He emphasizes the sudden change of mood with the expression "once upon a time", the traditional opening phrase of fairy tales set in a remote past – except that the last public debates over similar acquisitions took place less*

*than a decade ago. The antitrust crusading of Theodore Roosevelt's days is history and recent mega-mergers have hardly raised an eyebrow – as if Americans were convinced that to compete in a global market, "bigger is better".*

**2 – Explain what the following sentence means:**

**The first is that while bigger is not always better, it may be the only way to extend one's reach abroad. (100 mots + ou – 10 %)**

*That "bigger is not always better" always comes as a paradox for the American mindset. The United States is where "big is beautiful" and in many aspects people see nothing wrong with what is big. But Americans have also learned that too big corporate power can be harmful for the consumer and the taxpayer. This is why antitrust legislation was passed as early as 1890. Though ackowledging this piece of popular wisdom, the article argues that "bigger" may be a necessary evil to extend business abroad – at a time of global competition, only the biggest survive.*

**3 – In your opinion, to what degree is big business beneficial to consumers, the economy, and society in general? (300 mots + ou – 10 %)**

*The purpose of business is to make a profit. Everybody knows that. So when someone wonders whether business is beneficial to individuals or to society in general, it must be clearly established that the benefits to people are incidental – though not negligible – to the main purpose which is to make a profit and obtain shareholder satisfaction.*

*In today's globalized economy, powerful corporations have engaged in mergers and grown even bigger. Can society and individuals benefit from it? The answer indeed is twofold.*

*On the dark side, we may point to the dangers of corporations which can easily take unfair advantage of their power. It is common practice, through lobbying activities, for corporations to influence legislation in their favor. In other countries, though the means are different, the ends are the same. Mergers also result in eliminating redundant personnel – a consequence American workers readily accept as long as the booming economy keeps creating new jobs, but in Europe layoffs are felt as an insult and a threat to workers' future. And in order to keep costs as low as possible, manufacturing jobs have been relocated in poor countries with a cheap labor force. Tales of Pakistani children working for famous sportswear brands have revealed the seamy side of globalization.*

*On the other hand, bigness is the key to producing more and better. Everyone praises the merits of today's technological prowess in many fields. The consumer society has provided practically every household with affordable, convenient and good-quality commodities. None of this would have been possible without the rise of big business and the merging of companies into ever bigger ones. The cost of investing in Research and Development is a luxury that only major corporations can afford – yet it is the key to making safer cars, inventing more efficient drugs, developing information technologies a few steps further.*

*So big business may be the necessary evil to keep our society going. The only question is, if corporations can monitor our lives, how can citizens control corporations?*

*(334 words)*

# The changing face of *entrepreneurship

*Sarah Loom*

The English word "entrepreneur" is derived from the French term *entreprendre*, meaning to undertake. Despite the term's morbid undertones in other contexts, in the world of business "entrepreneur" is very much a *buzz-word. The entrepreneur is an individual who undertakes to manage and assume the risks of a business, and in a broader sense someone who seizes business opportunities and applies innovative solutions to uncertain situations. Generally speaking, an entrepreneur possesses the characteristics of personal initiative, self-reliance, risk-taking, *competitiveness, *drive, opportunistic behaviour, and the ability to learn from mistakes.

Interestingly, *The Oxford English Dictionary* defines an entrepreneur as "**a.** The director or manager of a public musical institution. **b.** One who gets up entertainments. **c.** Pol. Econ. A contractor acting as an intermediary between *capital and labour, 1885." Only the third definition has anything in common with the modern breed of entrepreneur, who, since the 1980s, has emerged as a focus of attention for academics, economists and business students around the globe. The recognition of entrepreneurs in any modern sense would appear to date back to 18th-century France, when it was associated with "risk-bearing" activity in the economic sector.

The entrepreneur also played a key role in England during the Industrial Revolution. More recent definitions are closely linked with notions of *free enterprise in a capitalist context:

*"Entrepreneurship consists in doing things that are not generally done in the ordinary course of business routine; it is essentially a phenomenom that comes under the wider aspect of leadership"* (Schumpeter).

*"Entrepreneurship is the dynamic process of creating incremental wealth. This wealth is created by individuals who assume the major risks in terms of *equity, time and/or career commitment [...] The product or service itself may or may not be new or unique but value must somehow be infused by the entrepreneur"* (Ronstadt).

### Entrepreneurship in the US

Exact definitions aside, it is true that entrepreneurs are the heroes of contemporary American economic development. *Entrepreneurial business *ventures are frequently snapped up by major corporations looking for a slice of the entrepreneurial pie, and the term "intrapreneurship" has been coined to refer to entrepreneurial activity within large companies. However, by and large, entrepreneurs flourish within a small *firms environment. In the States, small firms make up over 90% of businesses and are thus directly linked to employment *growth. Federal Government support for individuals wishing to set up small businesses is highly developed and publicised, and takes a number of forms – deregulation and tax *incentives, rigorous *patent laws, easy access to *venture capital and so forth.

Through a network of *MDIs (microenterprise development institutions) the US government aims at fostering economic activity at a local, community-based level. These non-profit organisations help in a number of ways. On the one hand, "credit-led" MDIs provide *microloans (normally loans of less than $25,000) to people who may be unable to access traditional sources of venture capital. On the other hand, "training-led" MDIs focus on facilitating small-scale economic activity via technical assistance for *fledgling businesses. Would-be entrepreneurs can benefit from experienced advice on *book-keeping, business planning, *cash flow and tax questions, marketing strategies and so on. In Washington State, for example, the Seattle Chamber of Commerce has set up an "angel *investor" network. Local people with an interest in reinvesting some of the wealth they earned as early employees of Microsoft or other successful high-tech companies are put in touch with entrepreneurs looking for private capital sources.

Such initiatives go some way to explaining why the USA has a flourishing entrepreneurial culture, and are at the same time a reflection of core American values. As a culture that encourages risk-taking, individualism and effort over social class, America confers a high social status on entrepreneurs (as opposed to, say, politicians or bureaucrats). "WASP" values of hard work, wealth accumulation, confident self-reliance and upward mobility are without doubt conducive to an entrepreneurial culture.

## Celebrity entrepreneurs

We have already stated that an entrepreneur needs to be *adept at risk-taking and creative problem solving. If we look at a couple of recent high-profile examples, we shall also see that entrepreneurs (while undoubtedly associated with a capitalist business culture) are not necessarily devoid of a social conscience. The crucial entrepreneurial quality of being able to learn from one's mistakes is perhaps best illustrated by the company 3M, which invented the ubiquitous "Post-it" notes. Rather than throwing away a new glue which was not sticky enough for its original intended purpose, the company concentrated on finding an innovative use for it – the "Post-it" (and with it a multi-million dollar industry) was born.

Another famous multi-million business was started in a converted petrol station in rural Vermont. The ice-cream company "Ben & Jerry's Homemade" was founded in 1978 by Ben Cohen and Jerry Greenfield, who had only a couple of thousand dollars to their name. The two childhood friends, whose hairy faces smiled out from tubs of ice-cream bearing funky names like "Pulp Addiction" or "Chunky Monkey", sold ice-cream with a social conscience – they vowed to donate 7.5% of their total pre-tax *earnings to community projects, to use only natural ingredients and to provide a fantastic working environment for their employees. The Ben and Jerry's headquarters became an overnight tourist attraction and the hairy, hippie entrepreneurs became household names. American consumers saw Ben and Jerry's as more than a mere ice-cream brand – it came to represent a statement of social protest, epitomised by the burgeoning anti-globalisation movement which claims that America's soul is being gobbled up by multinationals. When Ben and Jerry's was bought up in 2000 by Unilever (one of the largest consumer products companies in the world) fans fought the decision to sell the company under the banner "Multi-Flavours not Multinationals"!

### *Revenge of the nerd*

Entrepreneurs seem to have become the heroes of contemporary American business culture. In the 1970s, entrepreneurship courses were taught in a mere handful of North American universities, whereas today the figure stands at over 500. Various schools of thought have emerged, and many best-selling books have been published which chart the journeys of entrepreneurs from obscurity and poverty to fame and fortune. Despite this abundant literature, the actual qualities which are necessary to be a successful entrepreneur remain fairly difficult to pin down. The US economist Israel Kirzner claims that what he labels "entrepreneurial *alertness", while being nigh-impossible to quantify, plays as important a role in the American economy as land, labour or capital. As such, entrepreneurial alertness contradicts the first law of accountancy, which states that "*if you can't measure, it can't be all that important*". It is perhaps easier to conclude by defining what an entrepreneur is not, and by dispelling one or two of the most common myths surrounding entrepreneurship.

First of all, the idea that entrepreneurs are born and not made, that the characteristics of entrepreneurs cannot be either taught or learnt is slowly being erased. The acceptance of entrepreneurship as a discipline with its models, processes and case studies is now prevalent, as the large number of university programmes shows. The myth that entrepreneurs are inventors, *gamblers, "thinkers not doers" also unfairly minimises the actual amount of planning and hard work that goes into being a successful entrepreneur. Last but not least, the modern entrepreneur finally seems to be losing his image as an academic and social misfit. This reputation was the result of certain well-known entrepreneurs having started up successful businesses after dropping out of school or leaving a job. Nowadays, the misfit is a hero – it is as if the "nerd" of the class just turned up to the High School reunion in a Ferrari...

# Vocabulary

| | |
|---:|:---|
| adept (adj.) | expert |
| alert/alertness | vif, éveillé ; la vivacité |
| book-keeping | comptabilité |
| buzz word | mot à la mode |
| capital | capitaux, fonds |
| capital expenditure | dépenses en capital |
| capital gains tax | impôt sur les plus-values |
| cash flow | *cash-flow*, trésorerie |
| competitiveness | esprit de compétition |
| corporation (US) | société à responsabilité limitée |
| decline/drop | baisse |
| drive | dynamisme |
| DTI | **Department of Trade and Industry (GB)** |
| e-business | monde des affaires sur internet |
| earnings | profits, bénéfices |
| entrepreneurial (adj.) | entreprenant |
| entrepreneurship | esprit d'entreprise |
| equity | équité |
| figures | chiffres, statistiques |
| firm/company | compagnie ; société |
| fledgling/a "fledgling" business | débutant ; une jeune entreprise |
| free enterprise | libre entreprise |
| free enterprise economy | économie de marché |
| gamble/gambler/gamble (to) | affaire risquée ; personne qui prend des risques ; jouer, prendre des risques |
| growth | croissance |
| hike | hausse |
| incentive/tax incentive | incitation (fiscale) |
| investor/to invest/investment | actionnaire ; placer de l'argent ; placement, investissement |
| loan/loan (to) (US)/lend (to) (GB) | prêt, emprunt ; prêter |
| loan capital | capital-obligations, capital d'emprunt |
| MDI (microenterprise development institution) | organisation d'aide à la création de petites entreprises |
| microenterprise/small business | petite entreprise |
| microloan | prêt modeste |
| patent | brevet |
| patentee/patent-holder | breveté ; détenteur d'un brevet |
| patent laws | lois gouvernant la propriété industrielle |
| venture | entreprise, tentative commerciale |
| venture capital/venture capital funds | capital-risque |
| venture capitalist | spécialiste du capital risque |

# Focus...

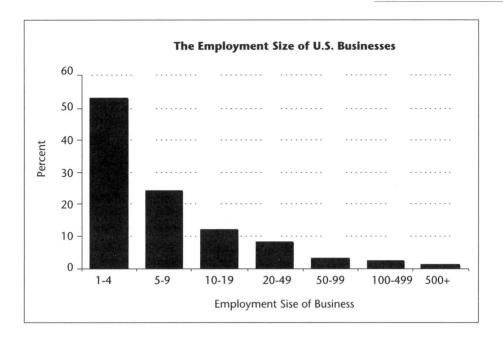

As we have already mentioned above, small firms make up the vast majority of businesses in the United States. Obviously this *figure depends entirely on the definition of the term "small", but as we can see from the first graph, more than half of all American businesses employ fewer than five people. More importantly, over 90% of companies have fewer than 20 employees and over seven million Americans work for themselves. Despite the rhetoric of the anti-globalisation movement, huge corporations are actually far from being the dominant business model in the US, with only 15,000 firms (out of some 21 million businesses in existence) employing 500 or more people.

The impact of small firms on the American economy is particularly crucial in the area of employment growth. According to statistics, small-scale entrepreneurship has been creating a steady supply of net new jobs since the 1960s. The sectors which experts predict will be the fastest-growing up to 2005 are those dominated by small firms – residential care, for instance, or data processing, health and legal services, and nursing and personal care facilities. The following graph illustrates the fact that the smallest businesses create the most new jobs, by comparing the employment share of small businesses and the net number of new jobs which they create:

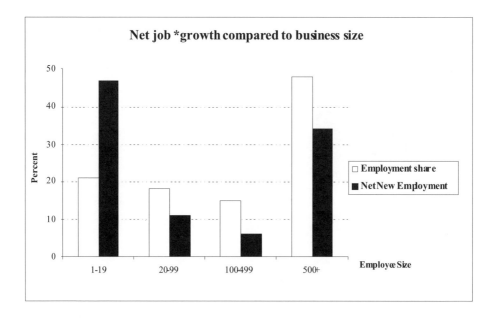

# Essay

## Compare attitudes to entrepreneurship in the UK and the US

- *To set up a business in the United States takes about three weeks and a couple of hundred dollars. In certain European Union countries, if an entrepreneur is lucky, it will take him anything up to three months.*

- *A 1999* Financial Times *review of the world's **top 50 business schools** sent a clear message to politicians and entrepreneurs alike – out of the leading 22 business schools, all but three were American.*

- *The latest report from the **Global Entrepreneurship Monitor** shows that in the domain of entrepreneurial activity the UK and France are lagging way behind the USA, Canada and Israel.*

*Can it merely be the differences in attitude and culture towards entrepreneurship in these countries which set them apart in the global business market place? Since the late nineties, British politicians have been speaking out against other disparities and more concrete barriers to business, in an attempt to generate within Europe the sort of entrepreneurial dynamism that is common in the States.*

## Tony's cronies

*For instance, the British Trade Secretary, Stephen Byers, has called on the EU to adopt a charter for small businesses: "Europe is lagging behind its global competitors. We struggle to generate the entrepreneurial dynamism which has helped to put the US economy on top of the world. Part of the solution must be to shift our focus to innovation, knowledge and enterprise."*

*He also advocates a more flexible approach to business: "There must be a recognition that regulation can be a barrier to economic growth and job creation. We need to create a business culture and tax environment which actually rewards risk. We need a single European venture capital market, providing better access to finance for small firms and high growth companies".*

*Speaking at an enterprise awards ceremony in June 2000, Tony Blair's ambitiously-titled Minister for Competitiveness, Helen Liddell, echoed these sentiments, warning that commercial ideas will be developed in the US or Japan if European governments fail to pay enough attention to the needs of entrepreneurs: "We need to give people the confidence to take a chance. In America, if you set up a business, you are regarded as get-up-and-go. In the UK you are regarded as being crazy."*

*Recent Labour initiatives have attempted to put an end to this attitude, which is perceived as a significant handicap to British entrepreneurs. Although politicians acknowledge that the challenge of establishing an entrepreneurial culture will not be met overnight, they have overseen the launch of ambitious initiatives like the "Business Environment Simplification Taskforce", the catchy-sounding "Phoenix Fund" or the DTI's £5.5 million "Internet Monitoring Initiative". The UK can now boast its first ever "e-Minister" in the form of Patricia Hewitt MP, minister for e-Commerce, another of the infamous "Blair's babes". In the March 2000 budget, the Chancellor of the Exchequer announced £50 million of new funding to support small business development.*

## L'entente cordiale?

*On a wider European level too, we have witnessed attempts over the past two or three years to cut through the miles of red tape, the armies of inspectors and the bureaucratic restrictions on small businesses in Europe. In March 1998, Tony Blair and Lionel Jospin set up the grandly-named joint Ministerial Task Force on Entrepreneurship in order to formalise* ad hoc *business links between France and GB. In June 2000, amid much media hype, The European Council (which is made up of the EU Prime Ministers) signed a charter for SMEs (small and medium enterprises). On the one hand, the report contained the usual load of sound-bites and Euro-speak, with platitudes such as "small enterprises are the backbone of the European economy" and the vacuous "Europe's efforts to usher in the new economy will only succeed if small business is brought to the top of the agenda". However, the report also figured an action plan containing a number of concrete proposals which, if successfully implemented across the EU, will go a long way to boosting entrepreneurship in Europe. The report suggests, for example, that tax systems should reward business success and encourage expansion by small firms, that governments should favour the creation of pan-European venture capital sources and that business training schemes should be much more widespread. More ambitiously, a further aim of the charter is to make the EU the cheapest place in the world to set up a business...*

*If the rhetoric sounds ambitious, it's only in line with the considerable stakes of entrepreneurship and small businesses in terms of revenue, employment growth and so on. In both France and the UK, a vast majority of businesses fall into the small and medium sized category. They represent a major source of private sector employment (12 million jobs in France and 10m in GB) 50% of which is in the beleaguered manufacturing sector, as well as being the main source of employment growth in recent years. Many market pundits claim that the euro will accelerate the globalisation of markets and has the potential to put the EU at the forefront of trade in the 21st century. The greatest challenge doubtless lies in transforming these words into deeds, metamorphosing today's ugly duckling of European entrepreneurship into tomorrow's swan.*

# 7 A Nation of Immigrants

*Odile Gouget-Escobar*

*"Give me your poor, your tired, your huddled masses yearning to breathe free..."*

The following synopsis will necessarily be an oversimplification of overlapping factors. For instance, immigrants of Anglo-Saxon stock continued to arrive in the US well into the mid-19th century, at the time when immigrants from Central and Southern Europe started pouring in. People could be driven by a combination of two motivations, political AND economic reasons, for example. Therefore only general trends will be highlighted. Besides, blacks will not be mentioned since they were shipped to America and had no choice. The US was definitely not a land of opportunity for them...

**1607** and **1620** were famous landmarks in US history. Most of the first settlers who arrived in the New World were of Anglo-Saxon stock and adjusting to the New World must have been easy for them since the WASPs (White, Anglo-Saxon Protestants) had a common background as far as language, religion and customs were concerned.

**In the 1850s**, 1.5 million Irish people had to leave their country because of the Great Famine; most of them sailed to the US. They were to face discrimination and suspicion because they were Catholics, but theirs was an economic reason too.

**From 1848 onwards**, in the wake of "the Spring of Nations" throughout Europe, many people who had supported the abortive revolutions had to flee their countries (especially in Central Europe) not to be jailed or executed. Their motivations were both political and economic. Besides, there were recurrent waves of anti-Semitism and pogroms in Russia which drove many Jews out of Russia and other neighbouring states. All these people formed the Slavic wave of immigration, were generally discriminated against and had to fight their way in the New World.

**1890** marked the beginning of immigration from Latin countries because of starvation and overpopulation, i.e. for an economic reason. Many WASPs felt threatened and pressured Congress to pass restrictive laws. They argued the WASP majority would soon be outnumbered and claimed it was getting more and more difficult for new entrants to adjust, as their languages, religions and ways of life were different from the WASPs' and some asserted they would be unassimilable. President Coolidge declared "America must be kept American". A wave of xenophobia engulfed the US. Sacco and Vanzetti were tried, sentenced to death and executed.

**In 1921 and 1924**, two sets of "quota laws" curbed immigration and favoured arrivals of Anglo-Saxon origin.

**Between 1892 and 1954**, 17 million immigrants were processed

Civilisation américaine

at Ellis Island (cf. chapter on "Sites of memory").

In **1965**, the quota laws were abolished and replaced by ceilings, meant to make family reunion easier and giving preferential treatment to immigrants with much needed skills. More and more Asian and Latino immigrants are expected to apply in the next decades.

The concept of the US as a land of opportunity has always mirrored world events, and especially the Cold War. As the US wanted to project an image as a champion of freedom, it was only too glad to welcome some 400,000 people from Eastern Europe in the wake of World War II and 38,000 Hungarians after the Budapest uprising in 1956.

There were also two waves of Cuban immigrants, in the early 1960s and in mid-May 1980 (cf. Focus, p. 279) and the American Administration really granted them political asylum, at least until 1994.

After the collapse of the US-backed South Vietnamese regime and the fall of Saigon in **1975**, (cf. chapter on "the Vietnam War and the American Psyche"), 135,000 South Vietnamese fled their country and were airlifted to the US. As they had either worked for the Americans or had supported the regime, they were also admitted as political refugees. Later, in the 1980s, it was to be more difficult for other Vietnamese immigrants to enter the US. The "boat people" were admitted more selectively as the American administration claimed they came more for an economic reason than for a political one. They stayed in overcrowded refugee camps in South East Asia and many of them were forcibly repatriated to Vietnam.

## A) *Hispanics*

The Hispanic community started emerging as an ethnic minority in the early seventies. This community is growing fast and is likely to *outnumber blacks in the 21st century. It is far from being a monolithic entity. Indeed, in spite of their common languages, cultural roots and religion, they belong to at least eighteen different nationalities, have different races, economic and social backgrounds.

The first Puerto Ricans arrived in New York after 1917, once Puerto Rico had become an American territory. Congress thus granted Puerto Ricans the same rights as American citizens.

As they have American passports, Puerto Ricans are free to come and go as they like. They are usually regarded as an underclass among Hispanics. They are unskilled workers and therefore condemned to accept *menial jobs. The unemployment rate is very high in Puerto Rico, which is why a lot of adults prefer to emigrate.

Dominican immigrants leave their island for economic reasons. Their integration is difficult and their presence is resented by earlier immigrants who blame them for creating the stereotype of the Dominican-Yorker, who is supposedly undisciplined and attracted by easy money.

The difficult economic situation in Mexico urges people to leave. The US needs a cheap labor force. That's why thousands of Mexicans cross the border every year, often illegally.

The Border Patrol in the USA keeps recruiting agents to watch the border, but "it's like shoveling sand against the tide": illegal immigration will go on as long as there are higher-paying jobs in the USA and employers willing to hire undocumented aliens.

There are also Central American immigrants who come from Nicaragua, El Salvador and Guatemala to flee political unrest.

### B) Carribean immigrants (who are not Hispanics)

A great deal of Jamaicans have settled in New York in the past thirty-five years. Most of them think the whites in America treat them with more respect than they treat black Americans. They do not want to be mistaken for black Americans as they do feel superior to them. That's why black Americans resent their presence: they compete for the same jobs and housing.

Political repression and economic exploitation have been *part and parcel of life in Haiti for a long time. Consequently people have tried to leave the political chaos at home in order to come and settle in the States. Their integration is difficult and their poor knowledge of English is a *hindrance.

### C) Asians

Well-off people in Hong Kong chose to leave before the *handover of Hong Kong to China in 1997. They left and transferred their money to American banks, thus helping to modernize the American "Chinatowns".

There are also a lot of poor illegal Chinese immigrants who are desperate to leave China and are the victims of unscrupulous *smugglers nicknamed "snakeheads". They work illegally in New York *sweatshops and it takes them years to refund their smuggling fees.

There are also Korean immigrants. Many of them belong to the middle class and are Protestant. They are highly qualified but rarely work in their field: medicine, law, banking. Indeed not speaking English fluently is the main obstacle. But as they have money, they are able to run successful businesses.

As for Indians, they leave home for economic reasons. They have degrees and therefore contribute to the development of the American economy.

### D) Africans

They are for the most part English-speaking immigrants with a very good education. They come from Nigeria, Ethiopia, Ghana, Kenya and the Cape Verde islands. When they arrive in the States, they usually work as taxi drivers, waiters, tailors and *peddlers. There are also quite a few professors, doctors, businessmen and accountants.

### E) Europeans

They are far less numerous than in former times and mostly come from Eastern Europe, looking forward to *starting from scratch. A few scientists from Western Europe tend to go and settle in the States in order to carry out their research work in better conditions. It is the "brain drain" phenomenon.

# Vocabulary

| | |
|---:|:---|
| allot (to) | attribuer |
| apron | tablier |
| ban (to) | interdire |
| bar (to) | exclure |
| barefooted | aux pieds nus |
| beacon of hope | phare, symbole d'espoir |
| cart | carriole |
| Civil War | guerre de Sécession |
| crack down on (to) | sévir contre |
| curb/curb (to) | frein ; freiner |
| degree | diplôme universitaire |
| discriminated against (to be) | être victime de discrimination |
| dropout | élève qui abandonne ses études |
| executive order | décret présidentiel |
| handover | rétrocession |
| hindrance | obstacle |
| log cabin | cabane en rondins |
| Manifest Destiny | destinée manifeste (au XIX$^e$ siècle, les Américains considéraient que c'était pour eux une mission divine d'étendre leur territoire et leur influence sur tout le continent nord-américain) |
| menial | subalterne |
| outnumber (to) | dépasser en nombre |
| part and parcel of (to be) | faire partie intégrante |
| pauper | indigent |
| peddler (US) | vendeur ambulant |
| pole | hampe |
| shovel (to) | pelleter |
| slaughter (to) | massacrer |
| smuggler | passeur de clandestins |
| Star-Spangled Banner | bannière étoilée |
| start from scratch (to) | partir de zéro |
| sweatshop | atelier clandestin |
| strive (to) | s'efforcer, faire son possible |
| toned down | édulcoré |
| triangular trade | commerce triangulaire |
| undocumented alien | étranger sans papiers |
| unwillingly | à contre-cœur, contre son gré |
| urge (to) | pousser, inciter |

# Focus...

More than 40% of the total Puerto Rican population live in the USA.

15,000 Dominicans settle in New York every year.

In New York alone there are 6,000 clothing workshops employing 20,000 Chinese workers.

Africans only make up 2.5% of the total number of immigrants.

The rate of naturalization is very high among Africans: 44%.

Minorities make up one fifth of the total population.

◆ **A few landmarks concerning immigration laws**

1882   The Chinese Exclusion Act is voted on the grounds that Chinese labour takes jobs away from Americans.

1892   Ellis Island opens as the new Federal Bureau of Immigration: it is said to accomodate two ships at a time and up to 7,000 new arrivals per day.

1907   President Theodore Roosevelt issues an *executive order directing that Chinese, Korean and Japanese immigrants must be refused entry unless they can prove they are not labourers.

1910   Congress amends Immigration Act of 1907 to *bar entry into the USA of *paupers, criminals, anarchists and diseased people.

1917   Congress passes an Immigration Act: Asian workers other than Japanese will be barred from the USA and all other immigrants must pass a literacy test.

1921   Congress passes the Emergency Quota Act which sets a limit of 358,000 immigrants per year.

1924   Congress passes the Johnson Reed Act which establishes more severe limitations and regulation of immigration. Quotas based on the population of each ethnic group present in 1890 cut the maximum number of European immigrants to 164,000 per year. Asian immigration is completely barred.

1952    The Immigration and Naturalization Act restricts and restructures immigration. It establishes quotas based on natural origin percentages as of 1920. Visas will be *allotted with priority given to foreigners with "high education, technical training, specialized experience, or exceptional ability."

1965    President Johnson signs the Immigration Bill which ends most national *curbs. It raises the annual ceiling to 120,000 western hemisphere immigrants a year and 170,000 from the rest of the world, with a limit of 20,000 from any one nation.

1986    President Reagan signs the Immigration Reform and Control Act (IRCA) which *bans the hiring of illegal aliens and also offers legal status to immigrants who can prove that they have lived in the USA continuously since January 1st, 1982. There are an estimated 3 million illegal aliens.

1996    The Illegal Immigrant Reform and Immigrant Responsibility Act is passed to *crack down on people who are in the USA illegally: anybody in the USA illegally for the last 180 days is barred from obtaining legal status for three years. If illegal imigrants stay after April 1st, 1998, they are barred for ten years.

# Essay 1

*This etching is entitled The Building of America. It represents five characters lifting the American flag called either the Stars and Stripes or the \*Star-Spangled Banner. It is made up of thirteen stripes which represent the first English colonies on the East coast: New Hampshire, Massachusetts, Rhode Island, Connecticut, New York, New Jersey, Pennsylvania, Delaware, Maryland, Virginia, Georgia, North and South Carolina. The fifty stars represent the fifty states.*

Americans are very fond of their flag. There are flags everywhere in America, including in churches. It symbolizes the independence and the freedom of America. The Americans consider they had to fight in order to have every piece of land they now own.

On the right-hand side we can see a native American (an Indian) who is making a very strong effort so as to put the flag up. He is nearly touching the ground with his right knee. We must bear in mind that the native Americans were the very first inhabitants of America. They had a very special relationship with Mother Earth and lived in very close contact with nature. They respected their natural environment which was for them a present from the Great Spirit. They were later driven away from their territories by the white men who *slaughtered them and their buffalo.

There is quite a big gap between the native American and the next character who is obviously a 17th century man. He could very well be one of the Pilgrim Fathers who came from England on the Mayflower in order to escape religious persecution. The Pilgrim Fathers were Puritans who disagreed with the established Church in England and therefore built New England with religious motivations, thinking they could recreate a Garden of Eden in this new Promised Land.

*Then there is a woman who seems to be \*barefooted. She is wearing a long dress and a white \*apron. She must be a pioneer. Like thousands of pioneers, she and her husband must have travelled in a \*cart while going west to explore new territories, she must have slept and lived in a \*log cabin and she must have feared for her life whenever they happened to meet Indians. Women did play a part in the building of America.*

*Behind her, we can make out a black woman who is half-naked. She is of course a slave who, like millions of Africans, were brought from Africa to America \*unwillingly as early as the seventeenth century as part of the \*triangular trade. Slaves were unpaid and the economy of the South was based on this "peculiar institution". They worked on plantations in often bad conditions until slavery was at last abolished after the \*Civil War.*

*The last character is not easy to define, but he probably came to America at the time of the new immigration wave, at the turn of the century. What is striking is that he cannot reach the \*pole. This symbolizes the fact that there is no more room for the newer immigrants. Indeed the immigrants who arrived in America at the end of the 19th century and beginning of the 20th century mostly came from Southern, Central and Western Europe and the Far East. Some politicians were afraid the ethnic unity of America might be threatened. Xenophobia was growing and strict quota laws were passed to limit the arrival of non-WASPs.*

*The general movement of the picture is an upward movement, synonymous with hope and enthusiasm. The flag was down and all the characters are trying to put it up. Their legs are bent to show the strength of their effort. The artist's goal is to insist on the fact that no matter how different all these characters may be, their aim is the same: building America. Nevertheless the expression "melting pot" may not be the best to define the reality of America today with the clashes that repeatedly occur between the different communities who often still live in ghettos. Today's America is a \*toned-down version of this etching.*

*And yet there is a touch of irony when we see that the character who \*strives most to lift the flag is the native American. Indeed in spite of all their eagerness to help the white men (hence Thanksgiving), the native Americans were parked on reservations, deported to places where they did not belong and steadily dispossessed of their ancestors' land. They were thus deprived of their tribal unity and ethnic identity, and all this in the name of God since politicians believed it was America's \*Manifest Destiny to serve as model of democracy to the Indian savages.*

# 8. The Case of the Black Community

*Monique Chéron-Vaudrey*

The black community is a case apart in multicultural America: black people are the only ones whose ancestors did not come to the land of freedom out of their own free will. Though blacks were not the sole victims of discrimination in the making of the country, for over 350 years they were submitted to regulations which deprived them of the rights enjoyed by other Americans. Since *Civil Rights legislation was passed in the 60s, dramatic changes have taken place. Yet, race relations remain one of the most contentious issues in today's America – and one that nobody can ignore.

## Revolution but no Abolition

The question of the status of slaves first arose publicly at the time of the American Revolution. Though the Founding Fathers, who were steeped in the philosophy of their time, condemned slavery as morally wrong, the question was ignored in the writing of the Constitution: the southern states would never have agreed on any restriction to a system which made their wealth. Worse, in order to get slave states to ratify the Constitution, the "three-fifths" compromise was passed (see p. 223).

The society the young republic was intent on developing was based on "life, liberty and the pursuit of happiness" – for whites only. Such a prominent figure as Jefferson, who served two terms as President, had openly condemned slavery before independence, but was a slaveowner himself. Rather than granting black people the status of American citizens, he believed the solution was to deport them outside the United States, possibly to Africa – a solution later envisaged by Lincoln, too.

## Abolition but no Emancipation

The Civil War broke out on whether the new territories to the West would be slave states or free states. The defeat of the South resulted in the abolition of slavery in 1865 under president Lincoln. Congress immediately modified the Constitution with the 13th Amendment banning slavery, the 14th which gave black people birthright citizenship and equal protection under the law, and the 15th which forbade *disenfranchisement of former slaves for reason of race or previous servitude.

What ensued was one long century of fierce resistance among southern whites and rampant racism against blacks in the rest of the country while the federal government, unable to enforce its own legislation, became indifferent and tried to forget about the predicament of black citizens.

Southern whites had considered blacks as a little less than humans. Now that the law put them on an equal footing, they started hating them. The Ku Klux Klan, a secret society founded right after the Civil War, terrorized blacks, organizing racial *lynchings while local authorities looked the other way.

Soon, common agreement was found in the South to deprive black people of their newly acquired citizens' rights. Everywhere, special rules known as the "Black Codes" or "Jim Crow laws" reduced blacks to the status of second-class citizens. Segregation seeped into every aspect of social life. The government in Washington, utterly unable to resist the tide, eventually gave up. Segregation was officialized by a Supreme Court decision in 1886 (see p. 224).

When blacks started moving to the North during and after WWI, their conditions were hardly better. Labor unions were hostile to a new labor force competing with whites for the same jobs. In several cities whites *rioted against blacks who were invading their housing districts. Thus the ghetto came into existence – the 100 percent black district which developed in all major cities after 1940 when ever greater numbers of blacks migrated to the North.

### The Paths to Freedom

Black resistance to persistent discrimination and violation of the law has been a permanent feature among the black community from Abolition to the present day. It has taken on many different aspects, from which two major trends emerge.

On the one hand, some advocated *separate development, within or outside the white community. In the early days of segregation, Booker T. Washington claimed emancipation would be achieved through economic autonomy. This was later taken up in the rhetoric of black nationalists in favor of separate economic and cultural development; in the late 60s, they launched the slogan "Black is Beautiful".

In the 1920s, Marcus Garvey, making his own the suggestion of Jefferson and Lincoln, advocated going back to Africa, while the Black Muslims championed separatism and demanded that several states in the South be given to the black community.

On the other hand, the current for racial integration and equality whose official birthdate was 1909 with the creation of the National Association for the Advancement of Colored People (NAACP) strove to use every legal means to put an end to discrimination and repeatedly pressured the government to enforce its own laws. In a landmark decision in 1954, the Supreme Court had forcefully condemned segregation in schools (see p. 224), but it took the mass movement for Civil Rights to complete the move.

At last, in 1964, a century after the abolition of slavery, the federal government took action to end what had become a serious embarrassment on the international scene for the country which claimed to be the leader of the free world. Both government determination and black activism contributed to the dramatic changes in the fate of American blacks.

### Two worlds apart

More than three decades after the passing of the Civil Rights legislation, optimists insist that black people's conditions have undergone huge changes. The end of segregation and affirmative action measures have opened the doors of colleges, provided black people with opportunities undreamed of before.

Less than half a century ago the vast majority of black people lived in poverty, had practically no access to qualified jobs. Today, it is estimated that one third of the black community has joined the middle class. There are countless black city mayors, elected black officials, and an ever-increasing list of black achievements in every aspect of American life.

But this is only part of the story. Pessimists note that another third are still scraping by with low-paid jobs and – more worrying – the remaining third, the black *underclass, are left out in the cold. Not even the booming economy of the past few years has managed to eradicate ghetto life, with the feeling that no matter what you do, you will not make it. Call it despair, lack of confidence, "being cool", the sad truth is that young black males are more likely to end up in jail than in college and the rate of out-of-wedlock births among young black women has been increasing over the past decades – two indicators that the subculture of the ghetto is not on the *wane.

A superficial look at today's America shows a multiracial society where people seem to get along fairly well; yet, all surveys on race relations tell another story of voluntary re-segregation. The government enforced school desegregation in the 70s; today, schools are resegregating again. Not just schools but also neighborhoods, churches, sports facilities, are increasingly predominantly white, or black or Hispanic. Baseball is predominantly white, basketball predominantly black.

Advocates of multiculturalism champion whatever sets the black community apart from the rest of the country, from the teaching of African languages to schoolchildren to the glorification of ghetto culture – an attitude which alienates the efforts of open-minded whites.

Many white people keep their prejudices – it is the stare of the security guard when a black person enters a store in a white neighborhood, or the recoiling of a white woman when a black man walks by. There are countless examples of persistent discrimination at the workplace (see p. 301) and of racial bias in local governments, in the police forces, even in the army – one of the most integrated places in America.

Although both communities have come a long way toward understanding each other, the present trends show no sign of reconciliation any time soon.

- Related chapters: Multiculturalism – Affirmative Action – the Constitution – the Land of the Free

# Vocabulary

| | |
|---:|:---|
| acre | unité de surface correspondant à 0,4 hectare |
| bigot/bigotry | raciste ; racisme, intolérance |
| busing | méthode développée dans les années 70, consistant à transporter par car (**school bus**) les enfants des quartiers noirs vers des écoles situées dans les quartiers blancs, et vice versa. |
| civil rights | droits civiques |
| disenfranchisement | privation du droit électoral |
| Ebonics | mot composé de **ebony** et **phonics** – langue parlée dans les ghettos |
| inner city | désigne le ghetto, situé aux États-Unis au cœur des villes |
| low-key | discret |
| lynching | lynchage |
| noose | corde de pendaison |
| racial pride | fierté raciale – notion développée par les nationalistes noirs |
| riot | émeute |
| separate development | doctrine prônée par certains courants noirs |
| separate-but-equal doctrine | euphémisme pour ségrégation |
| showdown | épreuve de force |
| sit-in | occupation |
| two-tier citizenship | citoyenneté à deux vitesses |
| underclass (the) | les déclassés ; population des ghettos, vivant en marge de la société |
| uppity nigger | nègre arrogant ; terme des blancs du Sud pour parler des noirs qui ont réussi |
| urban violence | violences urbaines |
| wane (on the) | sur le déclin |
| whip | fouet |
| white supremacy | doctrine prônant la supériorité de la race blanche |

The words used to refer to black people varied with the course of history. First, "negro" was used to refer to slaves. In the segregationist South, derogatory and insulting words became the rule: "nigger" replaced "negro".

Well into the 20th century, the term "colored" was commonly used, too, as an alternative for "negro" (cf. the NAACP). Today it is still used by older generation southerners, often out of habit. Otherwise, it is now considered as derogatory. In the last part of the 20th century, "black" became all right. Politically correct "African American" has become mainstream but is often replaced by "black American."

# FOCUS...

### ◆ Before the Mayflower

The first slaves from Africa landed in Virginia in 1619, before the Mayflower. Throughout the 17th century and well into the 18th the slave trade expanded to provide plantation agriculture with the workforce it urgently needed. Slaves suffered endless humiliation, were not allowed to learn how to read, could not gather for prayer without a white man being present, were not free to move, were even denied the right to found a family as they could be sold to another planter any time. Most female slaves were sexually exploited by their masters – which rapidly contributed to the whitening of the slave population. Even though they came in close contact with their white masters, slaves were considered not as human beings but as part of the property of the plantation.

The slave trade continued after independence. It was definitively outlawed in 1808.

### ◆ In Jim Crow country

The former slaves were left with nothing but freedom in a ruined South. They asked for "forty *acres and a mule" – a small piece of land to make a living. This modest demand was never fulfilled.

It was a crime for a black person to be idle. Many were forced to work for no wages, often on the plantation of their former master. Local authorities (and ordinary white citizens) were allowed to arrest black people for whatever reason. Freedmen were prohibited from possessing firearms. Various tricks, like literacy tests, were used to disenfranchise black men. They were not allowed in public transport and public places where they could meet white people.

### ◆ The KKK

The most virulent whites got organized in a secret society, the Ku Klux Klan, whose major purpose was to terrorize black people, using the *whip and the *noose, sometimes burning their victims in front of a supportive crowd. Nearly 2,000 blacks were killed by lynch mobs from 1882 to 1903.

A second KKK was founded in Atlanta in 1915 and spread during the 20s, boasting one million members: it found additional targets with Catholics, Jews, whites who indulged in "immoral practices". Today the KKK is reduced to the Bible Belt essentially. Though it keeps burning crosses in front of black people's houses and organizing public rallies, it has become *low-key. Even its present leader says he is opposed to affirmative action, not to black people.

◆ **White supremacists**

*White supremacy is based on the notion that all other races are inferior and threaten the survival of the white race (considered as the chosen people). It developed in the post-Civil War period and has spurred a number of militia-like organizations. Many white-supremacist groups flourish all over the country. Some of their members regularly hit the frontpages of newspapers with tales of gruesome attacks against people of color and homosexuals. They make use of the Internet to spread their gospel of hate. But their audience is limited to a few thousand people.

◆ **The NAACP**

Throughout the 20th century, the NAACP engaged in legal battles to expose crimes against blacks, won several cases before the courts, published data on the economic and sociological status of black people. The NAACP, essentially an elite group, has remained one of the most powerful lobbying forces for the black community.

◆ **Quotes from black figures:**

"I am sorry to have to say that the vast majority of white Americans are racists, either consciously or unconsciously."

Martin Luther King in 1968

"After centuries of greater or lesser racial turmoil, Americans are not terribly optimistic that the problem has a solution... discussions about race have a way of deteriorating into efforts to assign blame, and the search for villains, more often than not, ends at white America's doorstep."

Ellis Cose, *Color-Blind*, (HarperCollins Publishers, 1997)

"They'll let us entertain them. We have always been the best at that. But we don't own teams, we don't own record companies, we don't own movie studios. Now I employ 3,000 black people."

Magic Johnson

After he announced in 1991 he was HIV-positive, the basketball champion turned entrepreneur, with a determination to do things no black man had ever done. He has multiplex theaters in Los Angeles, in Harlem and in several cities across the country, a chain of fitness clubs, a music label. He has taken part in a joint venture with Starbucks to open shops in black neighborhoods. He has also created a foundation for HIV and AIDS awareness.

# Essay

Comment these two quotations:

"Slavery helped to shape the identity, the sense of self, of all Americans. Constituting the most impenetrable boundary of citizenship, slavery rendered blacks all but invisible to those imagining the American community". Eric Foner, *The Story of American Freedom*, 1998, W.W. Norton & C°.

"One ever feels his two-ness – an American, a Negro; two souls, two thoughts, two unreconciled strivings; two warring ideals in one dark body." W.E.B. Du Bois, founder of the NAACP.

*For all the efforts officially made by the American government since the passing of the Civil Rights Acts, for all the politically correct posturings of most Americans, blacks and whites still do not feel comfortable in the company of each other. Even the younger generations, who have not experienced the days when segregation was the rule in the South and open racism a fact of life in the North, seem to perpetuate the prejudices of yesterday.*

*It certainly is not easy to wipe away 350 years of history and Americans have to cope with the burden of a schizophrenic past. Slavery was indeed the negation of every moral tenet of those who fought for independence. The men who claimed in 1776 that "all men are born equal" maintained slavery when they built the first republic of modern times. They could only cope with this contradiction by declaring that Negroes were not really human. It took them one full century to get their constitution right and even then, they let the former slave states set up their own brand of \*two-tier citizenship.*

*Yet another century went by before legislation – and strong official backing – definitively put an end to the discrimination black people had experienced.*

*While immigrants learned to shape their new identity as American citizens, they also learned that the freedom and prodigious opportunities open to them were privileges reserved to whites. During the conquest of the West, blacks were barred from taking a chance in territories where Jim Crow was unknown. The children of those immigrants learned the same lesson, generation after generation.*

*And when being black was not enough to deprive human beings of their rights, it was further argued that they were inferior in intelligence, or not capable of working hard, or that they were lusting for white women.*

*Americans will spin yarns on the advantages of their country, as every foreign visitor knows. Most of what they say is true – but does not apply to the black part of the population. Blacks, indeed, are invisible to many Americans.*

*How can American blacks feel truly American? The feeling of "two-ness" first expressed in the early 20th century by W.E.B. Du Bois is still alive. American citizens can forget about their Irish, Italian, Jewish ancestry. Those who are black are constantly reminded of it, when entering a store, asking for a bank loan, applying for a promotion.*

*Du Bois's quotation expresses a wish for feeling like one individual only, one human being, one American citizen. This wish was later embodied by the civil rights fighters and forcefully worded in Martin Luther King's speech, "I Have a Dream". Today, in an age when the Universal Declaration of Human Rights is celebrated all over the world as the creed of mankind, it seems only natural that people should be judged by the content of their character – not by the color of their skin. But the American experience tells us that the dream, so far, has not come true.*

# MORE ABOUT...
## ...THE CIVIL RIGHTS MOVEMENT

### LITTLE ROCK

On Sept. 25, 1957, nine black students entered Little Rock's Central High School under the protection of federal troops. They had challenged the Arkansas governor's decision to oppose the court-ordered integration of the school. Washington had to intervene in the local *showdown. The event was reported worldwide – putting America in the dock for its racial policy.

### THE BUS BOYCOTT

In 1955, in Montgomery, Alabama, Rosa Parks, a black seamstress and a civil rights activist, was arrested after she refused to surrender her seat on a city bus to a white rider. The incident was the starting point of the mass movement that would lead to the end of segregation. The black community engaged in a one-year boycott of the company's buses before it eventually obtained desegregation of the buses.

In the wake of this first mass action by black people, came anti-segregation sit-ins: in 1960, four students of a Greenboro, North Carolina, black college decided to sit down at the Woolworth whites-only lunch-counter and refused to leave until they were served. They returned the next day, and the following days, with more black people sitting in silence with them. In the following year, 50,000 people, including some whites, participated in *sit-ins.

### FREEDOM RIDES

A year later, "Freedom Rides" involved blacks and whites who traveled together on segregated buses. Two buses left Washington, D.C. on May 4, 1961 for New Orleans but never reached their destination. Riders were beaten, one bus was destroyed by fire. Another freedom ride organized by the Student Nonviolent Coordinating Committee experienced police arrests and bloody beatings by local whites. The federal government did nothing. The FBI observed, but took no action. Such movements became extremely successful and often ended in court decisions forbidding segregation. The fight for civil rights attracted black and white people, students in particular, who, for the first time, worked together at building an integrated society.

### TERROR AGAINST CIVIL RIGHTS ACTIVISTS

Police reaction in the South was extremely violent: black prisoners were severely beaten, police dogs were regularly seen on TV reports attacking black marchers. White supremacists multiplied terrorist attacks on civil rights activists, churches were set on fire, innocent people were killed, like the four little girls who perished in the bombing of a Birmingham church. In 1964, three civil rights workers, one black and two whites, were arrested by the Mississippi police who handed them to the local Klansmen. They were killed and their bodies buried on a Klansman's farm. The case attracted national attention, no doubt because two whites had disappeared, and an FBI investigation led to the arrest of 21 Klansmen, including a County Sheriff. Some served prison terms, others were never charged. The episode inspired the 1988 film *Mississippi Burning* by Alan Parker.

## MARTIN LUTHER KING

The Montgomery bus boycott had been organized by a young black minister, Martin Luther King.

MLK was born in 1929 in Atlanta, Georgia, now home to an impressive museum dedicated to the Civil Rights leader. He studied at a Theological seminary and went on to study at University of Pennsylvania, then Harvard. He was deeply influenced by the American philosopher Henry David Thoreau and Mahatma Gandhi who both inspired his use of nonviolence. Like many black civil rights activists, he found in the church strong support for his fight.

He was a minister in a Montgomery church when Rosa Parks was arrested for refusing to give up her seat to a white bus rider. MLK organized the year-long boycott. The Civil Rights movement kept using nonviolence and passive resistance to force the legislator to repeal unfair laws.

He later came back to Atlanta. In the summer of 1963, he organized a march on Washington, D.C., where a crowd of 250,000 people of all races, ages and creeds gathered at the Lincoln Memorial. This is where he delivered the memorable speech:

*"I have a dream. It is a dream deeply rooted in the American dream. I have a dream that one day this nation will rise up and live out the true meaning of its creed: 'We hold these truths to be self-evident, that all men are created equal.' [...] I have a dream that my four children will one day live in a nation where they will not be judged by the color of their skin but by the content of their character."*

The next year, the Civil Rights Act was passed and MLK was awarded the Nobel Prize for Peace.

In 1965, he led a march in Alabama to demand the right for blacks to register to vote. The march from Selma to Montgomery took five days, it was joined by 25,000 people, and resulted in the Voting Rights Acts passed immediately afterward.

In 1968, MLK prepared another march on Washington, this time to ask for better jobs, better low-cost housing and better welfare plans. But before the march took shape, he was assasinated in Memphis, Tennessee.

His birthday has now been made an official national holiday.

# 9 Affirmative Action

*Monique Chéron-Vaudrey*

The *Civil Rights Act passed in 1964 prohibited discrimination based on race, color, sex or national origin. Conservative southern Democrats who were hostile to the legislation added sex discrimination in the hope that it would confuse things. It officially put an end to the discrimination and segregation black people were still forced to submit to. But the new legislation *fell short of making up for the centuries of inhuman treatment suffered by black people. Further steps appeared necessary to *implement the principle of *equal opportunity for all. The expression *affirmative action was first coined in 1961 in an *Executive order on hiring practices issued by President Kennedy, but not until 1965, under President Johnson, was it made a priority.

## Preferential policies

The new policies have consisted in granting preference to minority people in education, employment, scholarships, financial aid and government contracts. First conceived for the black community – the main victim of discrimination – it soon encompassed all *ethnic minorities, women, Vietnam veterans and people with disabilities as well. Affirmative action at its beginning was set up as a temporary measure to *level the playing field for all Americans. It has been in action for thirty years now and yet not everything has worked according to plan.

## The strong points

There is no denying that thanks to affirmative action black people have been offered school and college admissions, have been promoted to better jobs, and have sometimes achieved outstanding success. Without it, it is doubtful that mainstream America would have readily shared its pie with those who had until then been considered second-class citizens. It has also contributed to changing white America's attitude to the black community. As a new generation of citizens have shared their schooldays and their workplace experience with black people, a lot of the old days' prejudice has been shed. Blacks and whites have learned to live together somehow.

## The weak points

On the other hand affirmative action has *ushered in intricate and rigid legislation and *spawned an overbearing bureaucracy which have given rise to a series of hot public debates and even lawsuits – making it one of the most controversial issues in today's America.

First, the *preferential policies have progressively included so many people that unless you are white, male and healthy, you can now claim access to some kind of *preferment. This indeed is a *far cry from the initial goal of giving black people compensation for the outrage of slavery and segregation.

Civilisation américaine

Moreover, preferential policy has been implemented locally through special favors granted minorities. For instance, many universities have a different admission policy for minority applicants. As a result a white student can be denied admission while a less qualified minority student is admitted. Similarly a white worker cannot be hired or promoted because the company has to watch its diversity policy.

### Mixed feelings

While most Americans admit affirmative action is in general a good thing, they overwhelmingly condemn the quota system which, some people say, leads to reverse discrimination. Over the past twenty years many "*angry white men" – and some women too for that matter – have gone to court for abuse of their constitutional rights when they felt they were victims of affirmative action, and often successfully obtained Supreme Court rulings in their favor.

### Some American values in question

More importantly perhaps, affirmative action which was meant to transform America into a *color-blind society, providing equal opportunity for all regardless of race or gender, has indeed fostered highly *color-conscious attitudes, with people encouraged to see themselves as members of a group rather than as individuals (see the chapter on Political Correctness), and to feel they are victims entitled as such to some kind of preferential treatment. This too is alien to the American tradition of hard work and merit, of *pulling oneself up by one's bootstraps.

The myth of the self-made man – one of the basic tenets of American identity – has been taken over by the notion that you need legal help and public money to go up the social ladder. *Victimization has supplanted self-help.

Conservatives, who are in their overwhelming majority made up of white people, have pointed to the unfairness and absurdities affirmative action can sometimes lead to and have repeatedly tried to tear down preferential policies.

Meanwhile, a growing number of the minority elite, blacks in particular, argue that affirmative action has become counter-productive, convincing minority students that they are not good enough and need special treatment, instead of allowing them to work hard and compete with other students on the basis of merit only. Similarly, in the workplace, race relations have sometimes become poisoned because of the suspicions raised by affirmative action programs.

### Toward a divided society?

In addition we have to bear in mind the impact of new trends within American society revolving around ethnic awareness, group identity, multiculturalism, diversity... Though affirmative action was not meant to favor the division of American people into various competitive groups, it was developed just at a time when it could become a tool in the hands of various lobbies championing these new attitudes. Victimization for instance is the brainchild of such groups rather than that of affirmative action. Many ethnic minorities who never went through the hardships endured by black people may enjoy the benefits of affirmative action. Even the children of the black middle class, who never experienced the discrimination of the pre-Civil Rights period, can qualify for preferential treatment.

On the other hand, as an increasing number of experts point out, poverty, not race or sex, determines how you will succeed in life. Children living in poor neighborhoods are very unlikely to go to college, no matter what color they are.

### Cautious judges

The attitude of the Supreme Court has been prudent on affirmative action. One reason is that the judges themselves are politically divided on the subject, but the whole question is laden with so many complex and thorny implications that even the most conservative judges have usually balked at dismissing the legislation altogether. They have for instance condemned a strict quota policy (the Bakke case) while upholding a modest one as constitutional in other cases. The Court condemned a few cases of reverse discrimination and cases of blatant discrimination against black people as well. As a rule the Supreme Court has supported race and gender preferences on the grounds that it is the only way to remedy past discrimination.

### Uncertain future

It is indeed hard to decide whether affirmative action has been the best way to set right old wrongs. Experts from all over the political spectrum agree that both the strong economy and affirmative action have contributed to building a strong black middle class, accounting for about a third of the whole community. But another third is still shockingly lagging behind – affirmative action or not.

No doubt, American society is far from color-blind – it never has been. But affirmative action contributes to encouraging people to view themselves or their fellow-citizens in terms of race or ethnic group rather than as individuals endowed with merits of their own. This is a sure source of future political strife, and certainly not what the fathers of the new policies had in mind.

- Related chapters: The Case of the Black Community – Multiculturalism – Political Correctness

# VOCABULARY

| | |
|---|---|
| affirmative action | discrimination positive |
| "angry white men" | blancs en colère |
| (after the British expression "angry young men") | |
| Civil Rights Act | loi sur les droits civiques |
| coercion | contrainte, coercition |
| color line | division (invisible) qui sépare les noirs et les blancs |
| color-blind | qui ne tient pas compte de la couleur de la peau |
| color-conscious | qui tient compte de la couleur de la peau |
| die hard (to)/diehard | avoir la vie dure ; jusqu'au-boutiste, réactionnaire |
| equal opportunity | égalité des chances |
| ethnic group | groupe/minorité ethnique |
| ethnicity | appartenance à une minorité ethnique |
| Executive Order | décret-loi |
| fair hiring practices | politique d'embauche fondée sur la justice |
| fall short of (to) | ne pas parvenir à |
| far cry from | très loin de |
| glass ceiling | limite invisible à la promotion des minorités dans l'entreprise |
| government contractor | entreprise qui bénéficie d'un contrat avec le gouvernement |
| hangman's noose | corde de pendu |
| implement the law (to) | faire appliquer la loi |
| level the playing field (to) | effacer les différences, donner les mêmes chances |
| preferential treatment/preferment | variantes de **affirmative action** |
| pull oneself up by one's own bootstraps (to) | se faire tout seul |
| bootstrap | tirant de botte |
| racial prejudice/racial bias | préjugé racial |
| racial slur | diffamation raciale |
| spawn (to) | engendrer |
| termination | licenciement |
| uphold the law (to) | maintenir la loi, confirmer un verdict |
| usher in (to) | introduire |
| victimize (to)/victimization | prendre en victime ; être victime de mauvais traitement |
| vindication of (in) | pour justifier |

# Focus...

Discrimination refers to any kind of unfair treatment based on race, gender, *ethnicity.

Segregation refers to the strict separation of blacks and whites in all aspects of social life. Before the Civil Rights Acts, in the South there were separate schools, buses, hospitals, movie theaters, restaurants for the two races. In public places there were separate lavatories and water fountains. Segregation developed in the southern states after the emancipation of slaves in 1865. The same system was later adopted in South Africa.

◆ **Quotas**

Following the sytem developed in the early 20th century for immigration policies, early affirmative action programs set up quotas according to ethnicity, gender or economic status. Quotas have now been abandoned after several court decisions declaring them unconstitutional.

◆ **Diversity according to the Department of the Interior**

The term "diversity" is used broadly to refer to many demographic variables, including, but not limited to, race, religion, color, gender, national origin, disability, sexual orientation, age, education, geographic origin, and skill characteristics. America's diversity has given this country its unique strength, resilience, and richness.

◆ **Victimization**

Victimization is the attitude partly fostered by affirmative action consisting in positing oneself a victim in order to obtain preferential treatment. Claiming some disability in order to obtain preferment in job opportunities, blaming a hostile environment for failing to achieve success at college are examples of the victimization syndrome.

◆ **Some historical landmarks**

July 2, 1964 – the Civil Rights Act prohibits discrimination of all kinds based on race, color, religion or national origin.

June 4, 1965 – President Johnson delivers a speech asserting that civil rights alone are not enough to put an end to discrimination:

"You do not wipe away the scars of centuries by saying: 'now you are free to go where you want, do as you desire, and choose the leaders you please.' You do not take a man who for years has been hobbled by chains, liberate him, bring him to the starting line of a race, saying, 'you are free to compete with all the others', and still believe you have been completely fair..."

Sept. 24, 1965 *Executive order – *Government contractors are required to take "affirmative action" toward prospective minority employees in all aspects of hiring and employment. In 1967 the order was amended to cover discriminatrion on the basis of gender.

1978 The Supreme Court *upholds Bakke's case: Bakke, a white applicant, had been rejected twice by the University of California Medical School because of the school's strict quota policy. The Court ruled against inflexible quotas while maintaining that race was a legitimate factor in school admissions.

1989 *City of Richmond v. Croson.* The Supreme Court rules against a quota of 30% of city construction funds for black-owned firms stating that "past discrimination in a particular industry cannot justify the use of an unyielding racial quota".

1995 In the Adarand case, similar to the Croson case at the federal level, while two judges advocate a complete ban on affirmative action, the others refer to "the lingering effects of racial discrimination against minority groups in this country" as a reason to maintain preferential policies.

July 19, 1995 – President Clinton calls for the elimination of any program which creates a quota; creates preferences for unqualified individuals; creates reverse discrimination; continues even after its equal opportunity purposes have been achieved.

November 3, 1998 – Proposition 209 banning all forms of affirmative action is passed in California.

A similar initiative is passed in Washington State in 1998.

July 2000 General Motors Corporation, the world's largest company, supports the University of Michigan's affirmative action policies, saying, "Only a well-educated, highly diverse workforce, comprised of people who have learned to work productively and creatively with individuals from a multitude of races and ethnic, religious and cultural histories, can maintain America's global competitiveness in the increasingly diverse and interconnected world economy". Whatever GM's reasons for such a dramatic stance, it is likely to weigh on the issue of affirmative action in the corporate world and on the political scene as well.

# Essay

Opponents to affirmative action claim that *color-conscious remedies violate Martin Luther King's vision of a color-blind society. Discuss.

## In *vindication of affirmative action

One quotation from Martin Luther King's speech "I have a dream", about his four little children who "one day will live in a nation where they will not be judged by the color of their skin but by the content of their character" is frequently used these days by strong opponents of affirmative action who see it as a proof that the great civil rights activist himself was not in favor of the present preferential policies. Martin Luther King has reached such prominent status that the mere mention of his name and words seems to be enough for many to lay claim to their good intentions. No matter that the speech had been delivered at the peak of the fight to end segregation, one year before the historic Civil Rights Act was passed – at a time when black people were indeed still judged only by the color of their skin.

What M.L.K. referred to was an ideal future that could only be reached after a long road of reforms. The same year, he had also called for "discrimination in reverse" as "a sort of national atonement for the sins of the past" – and affirmative action policies were just that. The Federal Government was fully aware that the new legislation could not altogether wipe away three centuries of blatant injustice, that preferential treatments were necessary to put black people on an equal footing with the white majority, that *coercion would be the only way to have companies and universities take on black people.

Of course the paradox of affirmative action is that it conflicts with two basic American principles: the idea that all Americans can enjoy equal opportunities and that hard work and merit, not race or religion or gender, should determine who succeeds and who does not. But that was what slavery and segregation were all about – a denial of equal opportunity and race as a criterion to decide who can succeed and who cannot. If the noble principles have eluded the black community, there is hardly any other solution than stretching the rules to give them priority where it is most needed.

Let us not forget either that affirmative action is the way to keep alive another myth – that of the melting pot. With an increasingly diverse America, affirmative action is a stimulus for people from various origins to feel they have easier access to such highly symbolical opportunities as a college education or a qualified job and thus to speed up their access to the middle class.

*Besides, it is all very well for white conservatives to argue that preferential policies are not fair but things might have been easier if American citizens in their vast majority had been fair and open-minded to the black minority. This has never been so, for obvious reasons.*

*America defined itself as the land of freedom and equality from its very beginning. How could slavery and segregation be justified if not by creating moral and psychological explanations for not treating black people the same way as other citizens? For three hundred years American people had persuaded themselves that black people were not exactly humans, that they did not have the same abilities as white people, so there was no need to give them rights.*

*Entrenched prejudice \*dies hard. A recent study has shown that one in six whites believe blacks fare less well because they lack an "inborn ability to learn".*

*Some people may deplore the slow re-segregation of America, with various ethnic communities choosing to live with their own kind. As President Clinton said, "segregation is no longer the law, but too often, separation is still the rule." This only illustrates how hard it is, three decades after the end of segregation, for American people to come to terms with the idea that they are all part of the same community. Many white Americans still feel a deep-rooted uneasiness with black people, even if it does not show officially.*

*As long as people keep drawing the \*color line in their social and private lives, affirmative action will be needed. Those who oppose it today do not do so on the basis of color-blindness. They are the most vocal in arguing that minorities are having it too good and ought to be asked to prove their merits on the same grounds as non-minority people. It is easy for them to point to the deficiencies of the system: the bureaucracy thriving on preferential programs, the inevitable abuse such programs can lead to. Unfortunately they also keep alive the old stereotype of black people being less intelligent or less hard-working than whites.*

*Affirmative action is no panacea. It apparently contradicts the American values of equality and success based on merit – only if we dismiss past history, though. It certainly has its shortcomings and inevitable abuse or absurdities. But as Civil Rights leader Roger Wilkins put it, "Blacks have a 375-year history on this continent: 245 involving slavery, 100 involving legalized discrimination, and only 30 involving anything else."*

*So maybe Americans should think twice before dismissing affirmative action.*

# MORE ABOUT...
## ...AFFIRMATIVE ACTION IN OPERATION

Thousands of lawsuits are filed each year against companies accused of racial and sexual discrimination. Lobbying groups (essentially black organizations) and unions provide workers victims of discrimination with legal counsel and lawyers. The Equal Employment Opportunity Commission (EEOC), a federal body, is active in enforcing affirmative action policies in the workplace. It examines the charges and often intervenes in those lawsuits. Here are a few recent and significant cases. They illustrate both the scope of the problem, with persistent egregious racial harassment in many places, and the determination of the federal government to end discrimination.

### COCA-COLA

The world-famous soda company agreed to the largest settlement ever in a racial discrimination case in 2000. Coke was accused of leaving its black workers at the bottom of the pay scale – black employees in the company, it was discovered, averaged $26,000 a year less than white employees. The company agreed to pay more than $156 million in compensation: 2,000 current and former black employees will receive an average of $40,000, while four plaintiffs will receive up to $300,000 each. The amount of money seems huge but cannot really hurt a company with $20 billion in sales the year the lawsuit was filed. Coke officials said the settlement was a "business necessity" – minorities buy a disproportionate share of the company's soft drink. So the settlement may be seen as an image-enhancement investment.

More surprising, the settlement also made provision for an outside panel to revise the company's personnel policy for a period of four years at least. The panel, composed of business and civil rights experts, will pay particular attention to the diversity policy of the company and check the wages and promotions of minority workers and women. As a sign of goodwill, the company announced it would tie its executives' salaries to how well diversity goals were met in future. Given the company's reputation, the settlement may have a major impact on other companies.

### RACIAL HARASSMENT IN FLORIDA

Four black workers filed a suit for racial harassment against the Florida citrus grower, Sun Ag, Inc., in 1999. The plaintiffs said that a *hangman's noose was prominently displayed in the company's stockroom. It remained there for several years until a black worker removed it. The worker was later told by a co-worker that the noose was used to hang black people, and that he himself would be hanged one day. Other complaints included *racial slurs and being called "nigger" or "boy" by management and co-workers alike. The four plaintiffs obtained a $250,000 settlement.

### Racially Hostile Work Environment at Lockheed Martin

The giant defense contractor Lockheed is facing two lawsuits for similar complaints which include racial slurs such as "nigger" or "boy", hangman's nooses displayed in the workplace, "Back to Africa" tickets placed at black employees' work stations, leaving KKK graffiti in the company's facilities and subjecting employees who complained about discrimination to intimidation, physical threats and *termination.

### Pending Lawsuits Against Microsoft

Several lawsuits are being filed against the company for racial discrimination in its employment practices. The plaintiffs' lawyer said, "There are *glass ceilings and glass walls in place for African-Americans at Microsoft". Indeed, in 1999, 2.6 percent of the company's employees were black, the figure going down to 1.6 percent for managers. The company's spokeswoman replied that "Microsoft has a zero-tolerance policy toward discrimination in the workplace."

### Gender Discrimination

Women, too, are victims of discrimination. In many companies, they are simply placed in the lower paying jobs, denied promotion opportunities and generally excluded from higher paying positions. This is the "glass ceiling", the invisible limit set by management to the promotion of women.

An industrial plastics manufacturer was recently submitted to a $782,000 settlement in a sex discrimination lawsuit. Swift Transportation, the nation's third largest publicly-held truck carrier, agreed to a $450,000 settlement – the company had been charged with paying six female driver managers less than men in the same job.

# 10 Multiculturalism

*Monique Chéron-Vaudrey*

Today's America is obsessed by race and ethnicity. This is a paradox in a country whose history *epitomizes the futility of racial differenciation. America is and has always been a *multicultural society. From the outset, when European settlers from Spain, Portugal, France, Britain or the Netherlands started colonizing the new territories, a rapid mingling of races was underway. What happened in the thirteen British colonies was similar to the rest of the continent. The Europeans learned to live next to Indian tribes, while many had several slaves brought from Africa, working at home or on their farm. It did not take long before children of mixed blood were born – especially on plantations where white planters thus found a way to increase their valuable slave population at no financial cost.

### A Nation of White Citizens

Yet in some of the thirteen colonies there never was the same fluidity of race barriers as in other settlements. The Pilgrim Fathers had landed on the new continent with a mission: setting up an ideal society which would serve as a model for the rest of the world.

The British settlers, by far the largest group, favored separate development. Contrary to the French and Spaniards who found their *soulmates among the locals, they came with their own women, did not mix with local populations, and imprinted on the country much of their ethics and attitudes to race relations.

When the Constitution was written, it was clear for all that the rules *availed for white people only. Black slaves were not even considered as genuine human beings and Indians were viewed as foreigners for whom the new law could not apply. Very soon the country defined itself as a nation of white people only. The same attitude prevailed throughout the 19th century as the country expanded to the West. Even in the *aftermath of the Civil War, the United States failed to enforce the laws giving former slaves equal rights. The country opened its doors to wave after wave of immigrants, most of whom came from Europe. Only those who came from Asia were *barred from US citizenship!

### The Myth of the *Melting Pot

The great immigration waves helped the nation complete its expansion westward. The *wretched masses were welcome to farm the land and work in manufactures, and to contribute to the expanding wealth of the country. The newcomers were of European stock and shared some common cultural background with those who had arrived earlier. In the general optimism of the time, a myth was born, the myth of the *melting pot: immigrants from different origins would progressively mix their own culture with that of their new country and build up a new identity, eventually becoming truly American citizens. Whether the ideal of the melting pot was ever materialized is a matter of endless debate. Irish, then Italian, then Jewish immigrants were victims of racism before becoming mainstream Americans.

Today in a country which used to set race and ethnic origin as a criterion for citizenship, one can expect *lingering discriminatory attitudes in the population.

## *The trend toward separatism*

Since the United States first developed as a republic of white citizens, those groups which were excluded tried to escape race by building racially pure communities. Indians wanted their own state – they were only allowed to live apart in reservations with a status of colonized people. Blacks, Jefferson and Lincoln thought, would be better off if allowed to go back to Africa. The idea never got hold among the black population (Marcus Garvey's movement advocating a return of black people to Africa in the 1920s first met some success but was short-lived); other nationalists called for a black state, taken out of the western territories.

In the late 19th century, White Supremacy developed the notion of a pure white race to be preserved only by keeping other races separated.

On the other hand, the principle of religious freedom allowed all sorts of communities like the Mormons or the Amish to organize their social lives apart from the rest of the nation – this, too, contributed to giving shape to the notion that a community can opt for separate development.

## *A new era*

Things changed in the 60s with massive immigration from Asia and Latin America (see p. 275). The brutal change in the ethnic composition of the country entailed a resurgence of the 19th-century racist attacks against immigrants. But the new influx took place *hard on the heels of 60s radicalism and the fight for civil rights. Those who were the *butt of racism espoused the political stance of the time: while blacks and Indians popularized *ethnic pride and fought for their rights, Hispanics walked in their footsteps and decided they would keep speaking Spanish – after all, Spanish had been the *vernacular language in Florida, Texas, New Mexico and California until they were added to the United States.

## *The *Salad Bowl*

It started with the desegregation of the country. In a first move, schools and housing districts or residential areas became more integrated. But as blacks kept moving in, whites started moving out. The same pattern has applied to Latinos and Asians. It is illegal – and not politically correct at all – for whites to claim they do not want to send their children to a school with a high proportion of blacks and Hispanics, or to live in a *mixed neighborhood. But there is nothing wrong with moving to residential *lily-white suburbs and exurbs (as distant suburbs, far from the urban core are now called). In the past few years, "*gated communities" with private security guards and locked entry gates have mushroomed throughout the country; most are exclusively white, some are exclusively black; they are the latest way of enjoying life in a neighborhood you feel is your own.

The country is slowly resegregating – this time because people choose to live in ethnic communities, partly to resist animosity and *blatant racism, partly because it allows a more comfortable daily life. Schools, as a result, are also becoming predominantly white or non-white. Children of recent immigrants are given a bilingual education, half in their mother tongue and half in English. But those who grow up in an exclusively Spanish-speaking or Korean-speaking community are bound to have trouble going into higher education.

On the other hand, the federal government's policy of affirmative action has contributed to establishing minorities as legal bodies, with their own rights and *entitlements. Minority lobbies are experts at fighting to keep their status as a group apart in order to obtain favors. The new definition of race in the 2000 census raised protests as it would dilute the power of minorities, with fewer people falling into the black or Asian or American-Indian *slots. Black and minority groups obviously do not believe in a *blurring of ethnic differences and have shifted their policies toward a kind of corporatism – keeping preferential measures forever as they have lost any hope of genuine equality.

### *Drifting apart

The danger with rights and entitlements based on ethnicity is that it favors division, instead of cohesion. Opponents of affirmative action contend that it has developed a policy of victimization with minority people claiming compensation for past wrongs even when they never had to suffer them. And many whites who were not born at the time of segregation – and have never witnessed any kind of egregious racism in their personal experience – are getting tired of the stilted rhetoric of multiculturalists.

The problem is not just ethnic – it is also economic. In fact, when ethnic difference creates inequality in wealth and political power it fosters resentment and racial hatred. Cultural differences would be easier to live with if they did not interfere with social status. But for the time being, ethnic Americans are still disproportionately represented at the bottom of the social ladder.

### A Twist in the Tale?

Several recent surveys predict that some time between 2050 and 2100, the racial composition of the country will undergo a major upheaval: whites will be in a minority. This is already the case in California. Such prospect certainly means no end to multiculturalism but definitely opens the door to yet new attitudes to race relations in America.

- Related chapters: A Nation of Immigrants – the Case of the Black Community – Affirmative Action – Political Correctness

# VOCABULARY

| | |
|---|---|
| aftermath of (in the) | au lendemain de, à la suite de |
| allegation | accusation sans fondement |
| asset | atout |
| avail (to) | valoir, s'appliquer à |
| bar from (to) | exclure de |
| blatant racism | racisme éhonté |
| blur (to) | brouiller (une image) |
| break new ground (to) | innover |
| butt of racism | cible du racisme |
| communitarian | communautaire |
| counterculture | contre culture |
| cultural pluralism | pluralisme culturel |
| drift apart (to) | se détacher progressivement |
| elusiveness | nature insaisissable |
| entitlement | droit (à quelque chose) |
| epitomize (to) | être l'incarnation même de |
| ethnic pride | fierté d'appartenir à un groupe ethnique |
| fumble for (to) | chercher maladroitement à faire |
| gated community | enclave résidentielle privée, généralement ségréguée |
| hard on the heels of | sur les talons de, qui vient juste après |
| lily-white neighborhood | quartier exclusivement habité par des blancs |
| melting pot | creuset, *melting pot* (mélange de cultures) |
| mixed neighborhood | quartier mixe (habité par blancs et non blancs) |
| mulatto | mulâtre |
| multiculturalism | multiculturalisme, communautarisme |
| peasant | paysan |
| salad bowl | salade composée (où les cultures ne se mélangent pas) |
| slot | tranche, catégorie |
| soulmate | âme sœur |
| spawn (to) | engendrer |
| tip the balance (to) | faire basculer l'équilibre |
| unfettered | sans entraves |
| vernacular language | langue vernaculaire |
| wretched | infortuné, misérable |

# Focus...

*E pluribus unum*, the slogan engraved on US coins, means, out of many, one.

WASP is the acronym of White Anglo-Saxon Protestant, the epitome of the American citizen, the one who has had *unfettered access to wealth and power since Independence. Even today, WASPs are overrepresented in state and federal government as well as among corporate executives.

The Naturalization Act of 1790 restricted citizenship to "free white persons".

When California entered the Union in 1850, non-whites were excluded from voting.

Only in 1924 did Congress grant US citizenship to all Indians.

"I believe this government... was made by white men for the benefit of white men... and I am in favor of confining citizenship to white men... instead of conferring it upon negroes, Indians, and other inferior races." Stephen E. Douglas, a leading politician of the 1850s, and Lincoln's opponent.

◆ **The melting pot**
> The expression comes from the title of a sentimental play about immigrants written by an English Jew in 1908. It was extremely popular throughout the country.

◆ **The salad bowl**
> This expression has replaced the melting pot in American mythology. Indeed, in the salad bowl, various ingredients are placed next to one another but they never mix to form a new substance.

◆ ***Elusiveness of ethnic definition**
> What does it mean to be Hispanic? Some are well-to-do middle-class South-Americans, some are poor *peasants from Honduras or Mexico. Some are black, some are white, many have a touch of Indian blood. Except for the language, they often have little in common.
>
> The Asian-American community is a varied mix of very different cultures (Japan, China, Hong-Kong, Korea, Vietnam, Bangladesh, India).
>
> Who is black? Many *mulattos were able to cross the color line and become part of the white society. But if "one drop" of black blood

Civilisation américaine

was found among somebody's ancestors, it was enough to identify him or her as black. To these days, many white Americans who are unsure about their ancestry are obssessed with the "one-drop rule".

◆ **The mathematics of race**

The official five racial categories are: American Indian/Alaskan Native, Asian, African-American, Native Hawaiian/Pacific Islander, white.

In order to allow people to identify themselves as members of more than one race, the 2000 census offered the possibility to check more than one category. There are now 63 racial combinations officially recognized by the federal government. As Hispanics do not count as a race but as an ethnic group, this means 63 combinations for non-Hispanics and 63 combinations for Hispanics.

◆ **Other cultures become un-American**

Participation in WWI resulted in a drive toward Americanization at home. The teaching of foreign languages was restricted in school and German was forbidden in public places. Immigrants who had kept many of their national customs were required to show their patriotism conspicuously. Any sign of sympathy for foreign cultures was immediately stigmatized as "un-American". After the war, a multitude of citizenship education programs were set up to Americanize the masses of recent immigrants, teach them English and American values.

Anti-Semitism and anti-Catholicism were widespread then. The 1921 Immigration Act was meant to keep Jews and the "inferior races of southern Europe" from contaminating the white community. Irish immigrants were commonly called "Negroes turned inside out"; Negroes were labelled "smoked Irish".

◆ **Cultural Pluralism**

Horace Kallen, a progressive who was critical of the Americanization campaign, first coined the phrase "*cultural pluralism" in the 1920s. He insisted that the ethnic and cultural diversity of the country was an *asset; he advocated toleration of difference at a time when official national policy was the standardization of the American mind along the model of the WASP community.

"Segregation is no longer the law, but too often, separation is still the rule (…). Far too many communities are all white, all black, all Latino, all Asian. Indeed, too many Americans of all races have actually begun to give up on the idea of integration and the search for common ground."

President Clinton,
on the 40th anniversary of Little Rock struggle, in 1997

# Essay

**Has multiculturalism solved America's race relations problem?**

*Today, America can be defined as a multicultural society. Though about 70 percent of the population are counted as white, the sheer number of recent immigrants, especially from Asian countries and Latin America, is likely to \*tip the balance in favor of non-white groups a few decades from now.*

*In every aspect of social life today, we are reminded that this is a country of many. When filling a census form, applying for a college admission or asking for promotion, people's ethnic origin is routinely taken into account.*

*Overseas visitors are struck by the diversity of the people they can see on TV, in prominent positions in colleges, hospitals and in Washington. President Clinton \*broke new ground with appointing more diverse public officers, and President George W. Bush's first move was to appoint a black man, Colin Powell, as Secretary of State – a highly symbolical sign that things are changing.*

*Only forty years ago, there were "whites only" signs everywhere in the South, and a black man could be lynched on mere \*allegations of raping a white woman. Americans have come a long way indeed.*

*The culture and history of minority groups have risen to an honorable status. In the past few decades, museums devoted to Indian culture, Mexican art and Asian art have sprouted across the country, reclaiming those heritages from public neglect. Hollywood has followed the trend, too, in particular in the treatment of American Indians. And for all its excesses on campuses, multiculturalism has allowed Americans to become aware of other cultures and to value them.*

*But multiculturalist America also means that ethnic origin will determine where people live, where they shop, go out, which school their children attend, and, too often, how high up the social ladder they are likely to go. Multiculturalism is not just about living apart or enjoying different entertainments, it is also about unequal sharing of the American pie – and this is indeed cause for concern.*

*With its tremendous capacity for invention America is \*fumbling for ways to cope with its diversity. There are comforting examples of togetherness as well as ugly cases of hatred and racial bias. Which road the country will take in future is hard to tell at the moment. The years to come are bound to be ripe for yet new developments as the ethnic breakdown is changing fast.*

# 11 Political Correctness

*Monique Chéron-Vaudrey*

Political correctness arose in the late 1980s, as a byproduct of the activism developed in the rebellious 60s. The new trend spread like wildfire on American campuses, and has come to affect current daily life in America whenever race representation – or diversity in the new speech code – is on the agenda.

It consists of a new set of attitudes aimed at erasing all forms of discrimination against people for reasons of race, gender, economic status, physical condition, etc. It pervades school and college curriculums, court decisions, official appointments and TV programs.

## On the campus

The changing attitudes which gave rise to PC can be traced back to the militancy developed in the wake of the Civil Rights movement. The legislator had seen fit to complement the Civil Rights Act with affirmative action programs to give victims of past wrongs due compensation. Suddenly it was no longer shameful to be non-white. You could even gain opportunities from it.

On the other hand, campuses started reflecting the growing ethnic and racial diversity of the country, while feminism developed a new awareness among female students and academics alike.

In the late 60s and early 70s, American campuses were often transformed into battlegrounds where students embarked on an all-out attack on the American establishment. Opposition to the war in Vietnam was the main reason but not the only one. In many countries students launched an assault on conservatism. In America it took on specific connotations.

## Culture revisited

Political correctness developed "identity politics". Culture, it was argued, reflects groups not individuals; whatever belongs to a group is to be assessed according to the position of the group in the *pecking order of society.

It was decided that the academic world had been unjustly dominated by white Europeans. To redress this wrong, war was declared on Dead White European Males, as the great authors were called. A sonnet by Shakespeare or a novel by Dickens were declared irrelevant because they could only reflect the culture of white males. Notions such as rationalism, humanism and universality were labelled as the hallmark of white culture and as such, condemned to the trash heap of history.

PCers advocated more room on the curriculums for the achievements of women and minorities. This in itself could make sense – helping women understand how they had been treated as inferior beings throughout centuries of western and non-western civilization, inviting a more diverse student body to compare and contrast the traditions of different civilizations.

It did not happen in this way. PC activists claimed rights for each oppressed group. The name of the game was to praise everything identified with the group and to vilify everything coming from its oppressor (white males). All colleges complied with the new order by opening classes of Afro-American studies or Womens' studies whose academic interest has often been questioned. Academics have made a career of developing ethnic studies or gender studies of all kinds.

Students of various ethnic groups are encouraged not just to attend ethnic classes but also to join ethnic clubs and dormitories. The American campus has become a place of voluntary segregation to the point that it is hard for a Hispanic, Asian or black student to socialize with students from other ethnic groups apart from during purely academic activities.

### A new verbal order

PCers decided that changing words would change people's minds. Though there may be good reasons in all languages to avoid words which have become derogatory, PC has *wreaked havoc in the English language.

It became incorrect to *call a spade a spade and all words related to race, sex, age and physical condition were changed for usually much longer expressions. So came into being "Asian American", "African American", "Native American" (for Indians), "Jewish person" (for Jew); "man" became a dirty word so "chairperson" replaced chairman. "Mrs" or "Miss" became sexist and was duly changed for "Ms". "Boy" and "girl" to refer to a college student were dumped in favor of the more formal "man" and "woman".

English is a language based on one-syllable words, so it came as an oddity to shift from the one-syllable "black" to the *sesquipedalian "African-American". Fortunately, Americans are practical people and, except in official documents and academic literature, "black" has come back into fashion again.

### The latest American witch hunt

In order to eradicate all abusive language and behavior, campuses have adopted codes and regulations. "Hate speech" or "hate words" are strictly prohibited. Well, who would object to that? Except that the notion of "hate speech" is so vague that it can be interpreted abusively.

Rape is another big issue. Not because American campuses are crime-ridden places but feminist groups tend to view whatever happens when boy meets girl as rape.

Students using "hate words" have been expelled. Professors mentioning anything vaguely related to sex or race during class can spark off a complaint by students, which may in turn trigger a government investigation and result in the professor's dismissal. As a rule male teachers carefully watch their words and avoid individual contact with female students – except for strictly academic purposes.

School teachers and parents have fallen victim to PC activists. Accusations of child abuse have led innocent adults to jail sentences, the courts often *shying away from checking the allegations, for fear of raising more vehement protest from the accusers.

Sexual harassment has become a major area of the law, too. Female workers are not required to give evidence of the harassment and can file a suit even if the harassment did not prevent their promotion. After several court decisions sentencing employers for staff misbehavior, companies have adopted a strict code of conduct. Like college professors, co-workers have to watch their words, abstain from jokes and compliments (it might be a sexual offense) and keep their eyes on their computer screen.

### *A call for reason*

The worst of the wave may be behind us now: the courts seem to be more cautious about alleged accusations, Americans have come back to traditional language even if some expressions have made their way into the mainstream. Numerous voices have repreatedly called for more sense and insisted on the importance of free speech and unfettered debate for intellectual development. Academics insist on the relevance of the great books even if they were written by "dead white males" for understanding the world we live in. Some regret that defining diversity exclusively by gender, race or class leaves aside different moral and intellectual traditions and narrows the scope of one's vision of the world. But it is feared that the Balkanization of campuses may result in the durable Balkanization of culture, too.

### *Changing words is easier than changing minds*

The lingering question is, has political correctness been effective in changing Americans' attitudes to race and sex? The answer is, no. The main improvements in college admissions and hiring policies for minorities result from the affirmative action policies enforced by federal agencies. But racial tensions in American society are increasing. Women are still repeatedly faced with sexist slurs and discrimination in the workplace. The excesses of PCers have sometimes *pitted groups of Americans against each other. In the conservative camp, the opposite excesses in words – and in deeds – are legion, too.

State and federal policies have duly *paid lip service to political correctness: it is easy to change words and show good intentions in order to be forgiven for past discrimination. How to eradicate this discrimination is still an unsolved problem.

Political correctness is a puzzling phenomenon for Europeans, which can be grasped only in relation with the Puritanical obsession of distinguishing between the saved and the damned. This distinction is a never-ending process in America, recurrently emerging as a bout of fever. Eventually things go back to "normal" – after leaving some casualties, though. Famous comparable 20th-century episodes include Prohibition, the codes of decency imposed on Hollywood and McCarthyism.

- Related chapters: Higher Education – multiculturalism – religion and puritanism

# VOCABULARY

| | |
|---|---|
| call a spade a spade (to) | appeler un chat un chat |
| entrenched euphemism | euphémisme bien établi |
| hanky-panky | polissonneries |
| pay lip service to (to) | se déclarer (du bout des lèvres) en faveur de |
| pecking order | ordre hiérarchique |
| pit somebody against (to) | opposer quelqu'un à |
| sesquipedalian | polysyllabique |
| speak tongue in cheek (to) | plaisanter |
| shy away from (to) | répugner à faire |
| wreak havoc (to) | infliger d'importants dégâts |

Some campus idioms:

| | |
|---|---|
| dead white European males | Dante, Shakespeare, Voltaire, Goethe, etc. |
| Declaration of the Rights of Humanity | Declaration of the Rights of Man |
| dominant culture | mainstream culture |
| ethnocentric | based on one's ethnic group |
| Eurocentric | based on European culture |
| monocultural | white |
| person | man |

Current mainstream expressions (some are perceived as humorous):

| | |
|---|---|
| animal companion | pet |
| diversity education | telling management how to behave with minority staff |
| free-roaming animal | wild animal |
| friendly fire | attack on your own troops |
| full-figured | overweight |
| gender-conscious hiring | hiring of women |
| hearing impaired | deaf |
| homemaker | housewife |
| injury survivor | disabled |
| intellectually challenged | nitwit |
| nonhuman primate | monkey |
| period of economic adjustment | recession |
| physically challenged | disabled |
| quantitatively challenged | hopeless at math |
| senior citizens | the elderly |
| speech impaired | dumb |
| substance abuser | drug addict or alcoholic |
| undocumented worker | illegal alien |
| workforce diversity | hiring of minority people |

# Focus...

◆ **The French are hopelessly politically incorrect**

> In 1992, philosopher Luc Ferry had prepared a speech for a Canadian university entitled "Declaration of the Rights of Man in 1789". The university asked him to change it for "Declaration of the Rights of Humanity". "Only Stalinist or fascist regimes have tried to rewrite history", Ferry commented.
>
> (quoted in a *Time* magazine article – June 13, 1994)

◆ **Living White European Males (unwillingly) inspired PC**

> The intellectual spearhead of student protest was Herbert Marcuse, a Freudian neo-Marxist and an intransigent radical who died in 1979. He unwittingly inspired PC by claiming that the oppressed should be intolerant of those who held power.
>
> Another influence came from the French deconstructivist philosophers Foucault, Lacan and Derrida, who became gurus of the new trend in America. Their claims that words are meaningless and texts have no intrinsic value were adopted by American radicals who never saw that such statements had sometimes been *spoken tongue in cheek.

◆ **Americans have kept a sense of humor**

> In the early 90s, Henry Beard and Christopher Cerf published *The Official Politically Correct Dictionary and Handbook* which listed *entrenched euphemisms as well as short-lived grotesquely warped expressions. Here is their definition of DWEMs: "Dead, white European males, who were not only responsible for creating the vast majority of the irrelevant art, literature and music that still form the core of the modern univesity curriculum, but also conspired to formulate the dominant patriarchal industrial order."

◆ **The Ebonics controversy**

> Ebonics, a word made from ebony and phonics, refers to the substandard form of English poor black people speak, especially in ghettos. In 1996, the school board in Oakland, California, had voted to consider Ebonics as a language rooted in Afro-American culture. Consequently, children speaking Ebonics should not be corrected but, rather, encouraged to learn standard English as a foreign language. The Clinton administration opposed a vigorous no. Reverend Jesse Jackson, a prominent figure of the black community, had to intervene and expose the plan as a "teaching down" of black children.

◆ **History tailored for diversity's sake**

> In the early 90s, a school committee in Brookline, Massachussets, had voted to drop one of the school's most popular courses, Advance Placement European History, because it was incompatible with a multicultural curriculum. Students had to petition to have the course reinstated – they won, provided they also took either a course in African-American history or a course in Northern Ireland, Vietnam and the Middle East which, the school's staff argued, would fulfil the needs of the school's diverse population.

◆ **"Cachez ce sein que je ne saurais voir" – American style**

> Penn State university decided to take down Goya's "Naked Maya" from a classroom wall after a professor had claimed it constituted harassment.

◆ **A kiss is a kiss**

> In 1996, a six-year-old boy from Lexington, North Carolina, was suspended from school for sexual harassment. He had kissed a six-year-old girl on the cheek as a token of friendship. The school board was adamant and maintained that this was inappropriate behavior.

◆ **Mom's photos are \*hanky-panky**

> In 2000, an Ohio woman bus-driver was ordered by the court to undergo reeducation and to destroy the pictures she had taken of her daughter (some showed the little girl naked while having a shower).

◆ **PC on TV**

> Everybody in Europe is familiar with those US TV series whose action takes place in a police department or a hospital. They invariably show a rainbow of ethnic representation. There is at least one black and one woman who is the one in charge: the boss, or the most competent person or the one you can confide in. Does this beautiful set reflect reality? Hardly so. There is persistent discrimination in the police forces in spite of all the efforts made, and women keep complaining of the glass ceiling which bars them from promotion. But TV series abide by PC rules.

*Further reading:*

- Edward Behr, *Une Amérique qui fait peur*, 1995, Plon – collection Pocket.

    The author, an American journalist at *Newsweek* magazine, wrote this book for the French public. He gives interesting reports on the excesses of political correctness in the early 90s.

# QCM de compréhension

## Extrait de l'épreuve CCIP 1991 – LV1

1. When Actor's Equity briefly decided three weeks ago that the part of a Eurasian in the play *Miss Saigon* could not be taken by a European, its board members provided some of the best entertainment seen on Broadway recently. It was not just that they were asserting an Orwellian principle: all races are equal, but some are more equal than others. Nor even that they were threatening to deprive thousands of playgoers of a drama that promised to shed some light on precisely such cross-cultural nuances; nor even that they were more or less ensuring – if the principle were to be applied fairly – that most Asian-American actors would have to sit around in limbo and wait for the next production of *The Mikado*. They were also raising some intriguing questions. How can John Gielgud play Prospero when Doug Henning is at hand? Should future Shakespeares – even future August Wilsons – stock their plays with middle-class whites so as to have the largest pool of actors from which to choose? And next time we stage Moby Dick, will there be cries that the title part be taken by a card-carrying leviathan? (…)

2. The problem with people who keep raising the cry of "racism" is that they would have us see everything in terms of race. They treat minorities as emblems, and everyone as typecast. And in suggesting that a white cannot put himself in the shoes, or soul, of a half-white, or a black, they would impose on us the most stifling form of apartheid, condemning us all to a hopeless rift of mutual incomprehension. Taken to an extreme, this can lead to a litigious nation's equivalent of the tribal vendetta: You did my people wrong, so now I am entitled to do you wrong. A plague on every house.

3. Almost nobody, one suspects, would deny that equal rights are a laudable goal and that extending a hand to the needy is one of the worthiest things we can do. Reserving some places in schools, or companies, or even plays for those who are less privileged seems an admirable way of redressing imbalances. But privilege cannot be interpreted in terms of race without making some damningly racist assumptions. And rectifying the injustices of our grandfathers is no easy task, least of all in a country made up of refugees and immigrants and minorities of one, many of whom have lived through the Holocaust, the Khmer Rouge, the unending atrocities of El Salvador. Sympathy cannot be legislated any more than kindness can.

4. The whole issue, in fact, seems to betray a peculiarly American conundrum: the enjoyment of one freedom means encroachment on another; you can't school all of the people all the time. Older, and less earnest countries like Britain or Japan live relatively easily with racial inequalities. But America, with its evergreen eagerness to do the right thing, tries to remedy the world with an innocence that can become more dangerous than cruelty. All of us, when we make decisions – which is to say, discriminations – judge in part on appearances. All of us treat Savile Row-suited lawyers differently from kids in T-shirts, give preference to the

people that we like – or to the people that are most like us – and make differing assumptions about a Texan and a Yankee. To wish this were not so is natural; to claim it is not so is hypocrisy. (...)

Pico Iyer, TIME, September 3, 1990

**QCM – Choisir parmi les quatre possibilités celle qui vous paraît la mieux adaptée.**

**1.A** – According to the author, the best entertainment available on Broadway lately was offered by
1) Miss Saïgon                2) The Mikado
3) The Actor's Equity Board   4) Moby Dick

**1.B** – The author suggests that – if Actor's Equity had its way – all actors in a production of the Mikado would be
1) white Anglo-Saxons         2) Asian-Americans
3) middle class               4) card-carrying leviathans.

**2.** According to the author the most stifling form of apartheid is imposed by
1) white supremacists         2) half-whites and blacks
3) minorities                 4) people who always talk about racism

**3.** According to the author, "reserving some places in schools or companies for those who are less privileged"
1) must be done               2) would deny equal rights
3) will redress imbalances    4) rests on racist attitudes

**4.A** – According to the author, countries such as Japan and Britain live better than the United States with racial inequalities because
1) they have fewer racial minorities
2) they adopt a more relaxed attitude
3) they try to remedy the world with innocence
4) they are less cruel

**4.B** – The author says all of us treat Savile Row-suited lawyers differently from kids in T-shirts because
1) the two groups look different
2) we prefer lawyers
3) we prefer young people
4) he does not know which group is better

***Answers:***
§1: A3 – B2; §2: 4; §3: 3; §4: A2 – B1

# 12 Higher Education

*Monique Chéron-Vaudrey*

The first institutions of higher education date back to colonial times. The Protestants believed that being educated was the best way to serve God and as such education has always been a major concern for the country. In the early days of independence, it was thought that education would improve the moral standards of the population.

Though the organization differs widely from European systems, the problems are often of the same nature. As everywhere else in the world, only the "right" *degrees obtained from the most selective institutions will secure the best jobs. So competition is high and pressure intense on students and parents alike.

### Preparing for higher education

For some, this may start when the would-be student is only a toddler. Posh *kindergartens have a selective process of admission; highly-paid consultants will get your three-year-old ready for the dreaded test. Things start getting even more serious in high school.

Competition for the *top-notch universities runs high among American teenagers. An average 10 to 15 percent of applicants are admitted to the most prestigious colleges. In order to secure a good chance of getting admitted, senior high school students take several *Advance Placement courses (they offer a bigger challenge to *high-achieving students) and prepare for the *Scholastic Aptitude Test, the SAT, which will largely determine their admission.

Together with extra-curricular activities such as sports and volunteer work, the pressure is so intense that many are in danger of experiencing some form of *burnout. This, too, has created a new business: the independent educational consultant will help families whose anxious teenagers cannot cope with the amount of work and anxiety, while private tutoring and SAT preparation will drill the applicant during evening and weekend sessions.

### The selection process

First, let us bear in mind that 60 percent of higher education institutions admit nearly all those who apply. Selection in fact only affects the *top-tier universities and colleges. Usually the SAT score, the record in units of solid academic courses (English, math, history, science, foreign languages) are determining. When competition is intense, volunteer work, athletic achievement, summer experiences (no holidaying please!) are also considered. There will be an interview with an *alumnus. The essay is often a key factor in the *Ivy League. One college may want musicians, another baseball players, all look for outstanding performers or someone who can make a difference, a minority student, a female engineer, an applicant from Hawaii for example. Last but not least, the child of an alumnus will be given preference. George W. Bush won admission to Yale, not for his academic record, but because his father, former President George Bush, was an alumnus.

## A wide array of higher education institutes

The community college is non selective and keeps students for two years only, either for *vocational training or for the first two years of training at college level. The top students can compete for prestigious private schools. Their strong points rely on small classes, close contact between students and professors, and easy access for minority students.

Four-year colleges are rather small units; they prepare for the *bachelor's degree (BA).

Universities are much larger than colleges. They offer a wide range of studies and are often divided into colleges and schools: engineering schools, law schools, medical schools, business schools.

Some institutes specialize in science and technology like the world-famous MIT (Massachussets Institute of Technology) and Cal-Tech (California Institute of technology).

To all this must be added a number of vocational and technical institutions which prepare students for specific careers.

## Financing higher education

The states finance almost half of the budgets of public colleges and universities but contribute very little to private institutions. The federal government contributes on average 10 percent. Private funds contribute the rest. Higher education does not come free. All students have to pay *tuition fees, including in public universities and colleges. The rates may vary a lot from the community college to Ivy League universities. As a rule, tuition fees are higher in private institutions.

Middle-class families often start saving money for their children's higher education as soon as the child is born. But there are tax breaks if you save for higher education and numerous *scholarships and bank loans which help students finance their college years. Besides, students routinely have part-time jobs or summer jobs.

## A system based on market forces and competition

Universities and colleges, whether public or private, have to rely on their own initiative to raise funds as state and federal money covers at best half of the expenses. Some public universities in rich states benefit from generous funding by the state; this is the case for the University of California which ranks among the best institutions in the country.

The largest part of a university president's job consists of raising funds. Money means you can offer scholarships, open new professorships, fund research and various programs, extend the campus facilities, build new dormitories, etc. Alumni are requested to contribute to the institution's financing, but the corporate world will also generously donate as this money is tax-deductible. Fund-raising campaigns may extend over a period of several years. Harvard recently raised $2.6 billion while Columbia University announced a record figure of $2.74 billion. No wonder a president's salary may compete with that of a CEO. The president of Ivy League University of Pennsylvania received $655,557 in 1998-1999 – the highest salary for a university president.

## *What you can learn*

Probably the most specific feature of college life is that you do not have to choose a major in your *freshman year. Students may choose from a variety of subjects, they can mix mathematics and Asian Art if they like. There are *undergraduate degrees in all sorts of fields. Students will specialize for their B.A. Here again, they can major in one subject and minor in another one. Moreover, there are individually designed programs for those with special interests.

What students usually enjoy most is the *core curriculum which they all take regardless of the other subjects chosen. It is centered on the humanities and may include reading Dante, Shakespeare, Spinoza, Jean-Jacques Rousseau or Goethe. This part of the academic curriculum was under severe attack in the wake of politically correct activism. Classics, it was argued, were tools of cultural imperialism.There was no point in studying DWEM, i.e., dead white European males. Recently, Greek, Latin and West European humanities expanded to reflect other cultures as well.

Another interesting feature is the course in creative writing – an old favorite of American colleges.

## *Diversity in higher education*

All institutions have some kind of diversity policy. In most cases, they abide by the affirmative action rules and reserve places for minorities, women and disabled students. In those states where affirmative action has recently been eliminated, other preferential measures based on merit are given minority students.

The problem is not so much access to higher education for minorities as how minority children get prepared for college. As there is no federal policy for providing all children with the same educational opportunities, it is left to the state and local government to make efforts to offer their young good education. Some states are poor, some have a high proportion of minority citizens, and in some parts of the country, people do not think much of higher education anyway. Some high schools, especially in poor neighborhoods, do not have Advance Placement courses, so their students just cannot compete with others in more affluent neighborhoods. And poor families cannot afford the cost of SAT prep either. The SAT has been condemned for its cultural bias because minority children in general underscore in those standardized tests and are consequently often rejected from better institutions.

- Related chapters: multiculturalism – political correctness

# VOCABULARY

| | |
|---|---|
| academia | monde universitaire |
| academic | universitaire |
| academic achievement | niveau universitaire |
| Advance Placement course | cours suivi au lycée pour se préparer aux études universitaires |
| alumnus, (plural: alumni) | ancien étudiant d'une universtié |
| burn out (to) | s'épuiser au travail, saturer |
| cap and gown | costume universitaire porté lors de la cérémonie de remise des diplômes |
| core curriculum | étude des humanités, commune à tous types d'études |
| degree | diplôme |
| Bachelor of Arts/BA | licence |
| Master of Arts/MA | maîtrise |
| Doctor of Philosophy/PhD | doctorat |
| dormitory, a dorm, a residence hall | résidence universitaire |
| drop out of college (to) | abandonner ses études universitaires |
| endowment | dotation, fondation |
| faculty | le corps professoral |
| freshman | étudiant(e) de première année |
| graduate/graduate (to) | étudiant diplômé, en troisième cycle ; obtenir un diplôme |
| grant | bourse, allocation |
| go into higher education (to) | poursuivre des études supérieures |
| go to college (to) | aller à l'université |
| high achiever | sujet doué |
| Ivy League | universités prestigieuses de la côte Est, datant de l'époque coloniale |
| junior high school, senior high school | collège, lycée |
| kindergarten | jardin d'enfants |
| post-graduate studies | études de troisième cycle |
| SAT (Scholastic Aptitude Test) | test d'entrée à l'université |
| scholarship | bourse |
| sophomore | étudiant(e) de deuxième année |
| TOEFL (Test of English as a Foreign Language) | test d'anglais pour les étudiants étrangers |
| top-notch/top-tier college | établissement d'excellence |
| tuition fees | frais de scolarité |
| undergraduate | étudiant qui n'a pas encore de diplôme |
| vocational training | formation professionnelle (non universitaire) |
| whizz kid | « surdoué » |

# Focus...

There are about 3,500 higher education institutes, half of which are private. This number does no include community colleges.

Nearly 15 million students were registered to attend four-year institutions in 1999. The number is expected to keep increasing over the next ten years.

In OECD countries, entry rates to college education are the highest in the US – but so is the dropout rate (37%). High-school graduation rates – 72% – place the US second to last in 29 nations (figures from 1998).

The Ivy League, so called because of the ivy growing on the walls of the buildings, are prestigious institutions, dating back to colonial times: Harvard, Princeton, Yale, Dartmouth, Cornell, Columbia, University of Pennsylvania, Brown.

On Commencement Day, during the graduation ceremony, all the students dressed in *cap and gown receive their degree. Students' families attend the ceremony, too.

◆ **The SAT**

The SAT first consists of a three-hour test, primarily with multiple-choice questions, measuring verbal and mathematical reasoning abilities. The second part is a one-hour test, mostly multiple-choice, centered on specific subjects and measuring knowledge and the ability to apply it. Many colleges require one or more of these tests for admission.

◆ **Money matters**

For 1998-1999, annual fees for undergraduate tuition, room and board were estimated at $7,000 at public colleges and $19,400 at private colleges. Four years at top-ranked private schools usually exceed $130,000. In California the best public institutions are also the best nationwide; tuition there costs on average $8,600 a year – thanks to taxpayer subsidies.

In OECD countries, the annual expenditure per student on higher education is $7,117 in France, $9,466 in Germany and $17,466 in the United States.

◆ **How many *graduates?**
Over one million bachelor's degrees were conferred in 1996-1997. The largest numbers were conferred in business (227,000), social sciences (125,000) and education (105,000). The largest numbers of master's degrees were conferred in education and business. At doctor's degree level, the most popular fields were education, engineering, biological and life science and physical science.

◆ **Cause for concern**
The recent trends show a significant decline in engineering, computer and information sciences. International students, mainly from Asia, partly fill the gap. Graduates from French institutions are also welcome. Tens of thousands of them have left for the United States.

"The best and most gifted French people are leaving at a rate never seen in France... It is a self-destructive process that no one in France has understood yet." Christian Saint-Etienne, an economist at the University of Paris-Dauphine, quoted in *Business Week*, March 9, 1998.

"The chief aim of school should be not to sort out but to teach as many people as possible as well as possible, equipping them for both work and citizenship." Nicholas Lemann, staff writer with *The New Yorker* and former Harvard student, author of *The Big Test: The Secret History of the American Meritocracy*.

◆ **Those left behind**
The bottom 28 percent economically have a 3 percent representation at elite institutions.

◆ **Programs you can follow in addition to the traditional subjects**
The following is only a sample of various courses offered in different universities:

Afro-American Studies – Women's Studies – Nonverbal Communication

Religion – Death, Dying and Loss – Great Questions of Philosophy

Environmental Studies – Musical Performance – Theater – Dance – Visual Arts – Creative Writing

African Studies – East Asian Studies – European Studies – Hellenic Studies

Applied and Computational Mathematics – Business Ethics – Corporation Finance

# Essay 1

Comment the following assertion:

"Most universities care about having high-median SAT scores, students who can pay their own way, and 'diversity' as measured by race rather than class. (...) Universities admit high-scoring whites and blacks from upper middle class backgrounds and have little incentive to admit or enroll large numbers of working class students of any race." (Richard D. Kahlenberg, The College, the Poor and the SATs, in the *Washington Post*, Sept. 21, 1999). The author wrote *The Remedy: Class, Race and Affirmative Action*.

*The SAT has recently come under fire because it is increasingly obvious that standardized tests favor students who attended the "right" high schools – usually those in middle-class and upper middle-class neighborhoods. Since SAT prep has become a routine for well-off families, even average students from such backgrounds have no difficulty reaching the 1,200 or even 1,600 SAT score required for selective institutions, while the unfortunate students who attended high schools offering the least-common-denominator courses are disadvantaged, no matter how hard they strive to succeed.*

*It is admitted today that the SAT does not test the aptitudes which secure future success such as intellectual curiosity, creativity, social conscience and leadership.*

*Yet most universities keep relying on the SAT for their admissions. Why? It is simply much easier to achieve academic excellence with students who already have the training of hard work and the background that favors success in higher education. Universities compete for the best students because excellence will attract more students, make it easier to raise funds and extend research programs for example. The average SAT score of a university's freshman class is a matter of public record. Who would risk being downgraded, lose high-achieving students and the rest, for the sake of practising some social justice?*

*As the number of middle-class families among minorities has been steadily increasing, it is far more comfortable to show diversity by enrolling minority students who enjoyed the same high school education as better-off whites, than to open the doors for the "working class students of any race", as D. Kahlenberg put it.*

*(267 words)*

Comment the following assertion:

"For every Tiger Woods success story, there are countless other less happy results. Some students participate in programs that take up as much time as school. Fast-track athletic teams compete or practice most days – with weekend consuming road games, and national or international schedules during summers and vacations." (Time Out or Burn Out for the Next Generation – *The New York Times*, Dec. 6, 2000)

> *Tiger Woods, the golfing prodigy, whose total gains were recently estimated at $20 million, must have fostered many dreams of fame and fortune among American teenagers. As being an athlete, or a gifted poet or musician for that matter, may make the difference between acceptance and rejection in many colleges, sport is taking up an increasing portion of high-school students' spare time. Training in athletics is more impressive because it absorbs a lot of time and energy but the same story goes in fact for SAT preparation, sessions with the independent educational consultant, plus indeed the compulsory "voluntary" work every high-school student is supposed to engage in.*
>
> *When students have to add all those pursuits in order to have a chance of being admitted to a prestigious institution, they have little time left for their high-school courses. Time off for family outings and meetings with friends is often out of the question.*
>
> *Are mad schedules an unexpected effect of the American ethic of hard work, or is all this meant to give would-be \*whizz kids a general picture of what is in store for them when they hit the high-paid job? Aren't young athletes victims of their own talents since universities give them preference above all because they are likely to enhance the prestige of the institution – not because of their potential \*academic achievement?*
>
> *Many university officials are now warning families that too much preparation might cause unhappy results with student burnout and underachievement. After all, students in their freshman year are only 17 – they need time to enjoy life and decide what kind of adult they would like to become.*
>
> *Introducing competition is undoubtedly a powerful incentive for people to do their best. But unrestrained competition is sure to leave many casualties. Overworked students are hardly in a position to develop the very aptitudes cherished by academics and companies alike: intellectual curiosity and creativity.*

# MORE ABOUT...
## ...HARVARD UNIVERSITY – CAMBRIDGE, MASSACHUSETTS

Harvard is the oldest institution of higher education in the United States. Though not different in nature from other prestigious universities, whether Ivy League or not, it is also the most famous American university abroad. The information given here is representative of the other top-notch institutions.

Harvard college was founded in 1636, and named after its benefactor, John Harvard of Charleston, a minister who left his library and half his estate to the institution. It followed the English university model and was influenced by the Puritan philosophy prevailing at the time. Many of its early graduates became ministers in various Puritan congregations. In 1650, a charter established the Harvard Corporation – the oldest corporation in the Western Hemisphere – with a seven-member board.

### FUNDING

Harvard is a private university. It relies on endowment funds from alumni, as is the tradition, or from philanthropists – usually corporations which can thus benefit from considerable tax deductions. The university launched a major fund-raising campaign in 1994 which ended in 2000. The money will be used to improve Harvard's computer network and libraries, renovate facilities, create new professorships, enlarge its financial aid program for students who cannot afford full tuition, (about 70 percent of undergraduates receive financial aid) and to support interfaculty initiatives in new areas cutting across traditional disciplines like the environment, health policy, ethics and the caring professions.

### AN EXPENSIVE INSTITUTION OPEN TO THE LESS FINANCIALLY WELL-OFF

Harvard is keen on attracting talented – but often impecunious – students. Tuition at Harvard is more than $30,000 a year – only tuition indeed. In 2000, Laura Spence, a British student from a state school near Newcastle had been rejected from Oxford University. Her interviewer had declared her "outstandingly intelligent" but "low in confidence". Meanwhile, Harvard University admitted her on a $25,000-a-year scholarship. Harvard's Law School recently admitted a white welfare mother who had been denied admission by the University of Washington Law School in Seattle because she would not contribute to the diversity of the class – she may have been a woman, but she was white.

## ACADEMIC EXCELLENCE

Harvard is a world-class research and teaching university; it is proud of recruiting leading scholars and teachers nationwide – and worldwide. It is frequent for reputed scholars from abroad to teach at Harvard, thus adding to the university's prestige. The faculty have counted more than 30 Nobel laureates. Six presidents, including F.D. Roosevelt and J. F. Kennedy, graduated from Harvard.

The selection process of students is as competitive as can be. Barely 13 percent of applicants are admitted. Postgraduate students come from all parts of the world – often on generous grants. Harvard is a powerful magnet and attracts students for continuing education and for summer sessions too, as do other prestigious universities.

## THE STUDENTS

The university claims students come from all regions of the US and more than 100 foreign countries. It is a highly diverse place where all ethnic groups, all religious denominations and all political persuasions are represented. It is also a notoriously politically correct place.

Present enrollment is of 18,000 students. There are also 13,000 students enrolled in one or more courses in the Harvard Extension School. Over 14,000 people work at Harvard, including more than 2,000 faculty.

## WHAT THEY STUDY

Harvard comprises a Faculty of Arts and Sciences, a Graduate School of Design, a Graduate School of Education, a world-famous Business School, a Medical School, a School of Public Health, a Law School, various laboratories and research centers, the Harvard-Smithsonian Center for Astrophysics, the John F. Kennedy School of Government, and a myriad other institutes like the Harvard AIDS Institute, the Civil Rights project, Harvard Forum for Central Asian Studies, Pluralism Project (a research project on religious pluralism in the US), Program on New Approaches to Russian Security, etc.

# 13 Religion and Puritanism

*Monique Chéron-Vaudrey*

Religion plays a more important role in the United States than in the rest of the developed world. 95% of the population believe in God while over 40% *attend a religious service every week. Being religious does not just mean going to church, it also involves a lot of social activities, participation in *charity work, and sometimes political activism (the Civil Rights movement of the 60s was initiated by black *congregations and *ministers.)

Religion is present in official references, in university curriculums, on bookstore shelves, in the workplace, on the airwaves and along the roadsides dotted with churches of all kinds. America is home to a wide array of *denominations reflecting both the diversity of its population and the heritage of the country's Protestant tradition – a tradition which has had *paramount influence in public and private life, much beyond the realm of Protestantism itself.

## Church and State are separated

The First Amendment says that "Congress shall make no law respecting an establishment of religion or prohibit the free exercise thereof" – no religion can be declared the official religion of the country and political power cannot interfere with religious freedom. The religious dissenters, the Puritans, who had fled the corruption of the old world and the oppression of its *established religion founded congregations (an assembly of church members who chose their own minister) which were free of all coercive power (Protestants have no church hierarchy). The pattern has remained much the same today – even in broad-based denominations, local congregations enjoy a high degree of autonomy.

While there is no state interference with religion, religion is invoked in many circumstances in America's public life: Americans see themselves as a religious people and think that the model democracy they have built is somehow the model the early Puritans had in mind, endowed as they were with a divine mission.

## Freedom of religion

Though the majority of *churchgoers are Protestants, religious freedom has not only allowed dissenters of mainstream Protestant denominations to develop churches of their own but also favored the *unfettered development of other religions. With the new influx of immigrants in the past decades, the United States can rightly boast of having practically all the *creeds of the planet represented on its soil. In an increasingly diverse country, religious diversity is felt both as a treasured freedom and as a means of reinforcing the voluntary segregation pervading today's society. In many ways, religious identity is related to social status and ethnicity.

In addition to the rich variety of creeds, countless sects have been mushrooming across the country, some being dissenters of one church or another, others inventing new cults or utopias, and quite a few being bent on developing a profitable business.

## Puritanism and its influence in today's society

### Separatism

American Puritans gave a particular turn to their *faith and left their mark on much of American ethics – and even influenced other creeds.

Paradoxically, one of their first features was intolerance. Each congregation having its own interpretation of religious truth, those who were in disagreement were persecuted, arrested and *disenfranchised. The victims of persecution had but one solution: establish a settlement in another territory. Separation became the door to religious freedom. Interestingly, several of the thirteen colonies were founded on such separatism. Maryland was the refuge of Catholics; Pennsylvania grew as a land of tolerance for Quakers; Rhode Island, which was founded by a dissenter from Massachusetts, granted religious freedom to all.

### Calvinist predestination

The Pilgrim Fathers settled in America with a mission: accomplishing God's will in establishing a model society. "We shall build a city upon a hill" claimed John Winthrop, a major Puritan. In order to achieve such high goals, Puritans put a premium on setting rules in accordance with God's law; they consisted of hard work and discipline as well as a modest lifestyle. In the Calvinist tradition, they thought that God had chosen those who could achieve *salvation. Those who worked hard showed they were eager to please God, and some would be rewarded with worldly success.

### Money as a sign of God's *blessing

In the American context, when it was easy for every free man to get rich quick, it contributed to building an American brand of Puritanism in which material success was encouraged and prosperity considered the sign that one was saved. Such feeling has remained deeply rooted in American society and has fostered attitudes sometimes misunderstood abroad. If money plays such an important role in American values it is not just because Americans are materialistic; it is rather because being rich is the sign of God's blessing. This is why Americans unashamedly brag about how much money they earn. Showing off with oversized cars and the latest status symbols (from the designer watch to the private jet) may look naive or vulgar to many Europeans, but they are just for their happy owners the comforting proof that they acted according to God's will – and have been fairly rewarded.

Similarly, repeated failure or an inability to succeed prove someone is not saved. Those who do not deserve God's blessing should not be helped. Those whose lifestyle is different are not blessed – and those from other creeds are not blessed either. Attitudes may be changing these days as is witnessed by President Bush's "compassionate conservatism" but opponents to welfare benefits and social security for everybody translate this notion into political terms.

### *Eradicating the evil in you

Another tradition was inaugurated with the episode of the Salem *witches in 1692. Two children had had hysterical fits and were urged to confess to being prey of evil forces. It rapidly triggered a witch hunt in Salem. Several people were arrested and tried; those who confessed to using witchcraft were released but 19 others were hanged. The hunt ended as quickly as it had started.

Similar fits of hysteria have occurred in the course of history under various forms, from the McCarthy period to political correctness. The tradition of the public confession of the accused was illustrated with Bill Clinton's TV confession during Monicagate. It also survives with associations meant to support people who have failed or been victims. Women tell publicly of their experience of rape, alcoholics confess about their addiction. Homosexuals today are "coming out" – i.e. they confess publicly their sexual preferences.

### Regulating social life

Protestants in general and especially the Lutherans tried to regulate everyday life, marital duties, entertainment: dancing, drinking and merry-making were disapproved of. Social pleasures brought from the old world were progressively banned, more recent immigrants conforming to the rule. Together with the ethic of hard work, it shaped an austere form of American religious life, and later triggered other bouts of fanaticism with the *temperance league in the 19th century and the short-lived prohibition period, the codes of decency (inspired by Catholics) imposed on Hollywood, and today's codes of conduct on campuses.

### New attitudes

Some people are moving away from church, though not from spiritual fulfillment. The traditional churches and the conservative right usually associated with them have somehow failed to adapt to our modern world. Moreover fundamentalist groups may have a large following in the Bible Belt but have driven many more believers away. The influx of recent immigrants from other parts of the world has fostered interest in religions so far unknown in the United States.

A trend toward *ecumenism has spread even into Congress which recently opened a session with a prayer by a Hindu priest. Spiritual centers cater for citizens in search of a new spiritual life. Prayer breakfasts and spiritual conferences are popular among corporate executives; Bible groups and Buddhist seminars are mushrooming in workplaces across the country. Contrary to the current trends in European countries, interest in religion is growing and affects America's diverse social life in many ways.

- Related chapters: the Constitution – Death Penalty – Political Correctness – the Land of the Free

# VOCABULARY

| | |
|---|---|
| attend service (to) | aller à l'office religieux |
| bless (to)/blessing | bénir ; bénédiction |
| born-again Christian | chrétien qui a retrouvé la foi à l'âge adulte |
| Catholicism/Catholic | catholicisme ; catholique |
| chaplain | chapelain, aumônier |
| charity | œuvre de bienfaisance, bénévolat |
| Christianity/Christian | christianisme ; chrétien |
| churchgoer | fidèle (qui va à l'office religieux) |
| congregation | congrégation (parfois église autonome) |
| creationism | créationnisme |
| creed | croyance |
| denomination | confession |
| devout | devôt |
| disenfranchise (to) | priver du droit de vote |
| ecumenism/ecumenical | œcuménisme ; œcuméniste |
| eradicate (to) | faire disparaître, supprimer |
| established religion | religion d'État, religion officielle |
| faith | foi |
| faithful | fidèles |
| fundamentalism | fondamentalisme, intégrisme |
| God bless America | que Dieu bénisse l'Amérique |
| Islam | Islam |
| Jew/Jewish | Juif (nom) ; juif (adjectif) |
| Judaism | judaisme |
| minister | pasteur |
| Muslim | musulman (nom et adjectif) |
| paramount | suprême |
| popism | papisme |
| preacher | pasteur, prédicateur |
| Protestantism | protestantisme |
| salvation | salut |
| sin/sinfulness | péché ; les péchés (d'une personne) |
| televangelism | prêche télévisé |
| temperance league | ligue anti-alcoolique |
| unfettered | sans entraves |
| wise guy | gros malin |
| witch | sorcière |
| worship (to)/worshipper | vénérer ; fidèle |

# FOCUS...

Protestants, by far the largest group – about 80 million – are divided into a multiplicity of denominations and churches, ranging from the ultra-conservative to the liberal-minded.

Catholics, with 60 million members, are the second largest group; they have been growing fast with the influx of immigrants from Latin America.

Jews are a little more than 4 million.

Islam is a fast-growing group with nearly 6 million members.

Hindus are 1.3 million – and expected to increase their number in future.

Jehovah's witnesses are just above one million.

## ◆ American civil religion

American democracy abstains from supporting any religion but constantly refers to God:

God is invoked in the Declaration of Independence. The words "In God we trust" are engraved on coins. Presidents and political leaders call on God to bless America. Conscientious objection on religious grounds is accepted as a reason not to become a soldier. The military forces pay *chaplains of all faiths and give them a military rank.

Moreover several symbols of American patriotism play the role of a civil religion meant to foster national unity: there is the flag, called the "stars and stripes," flying in many places including people's private yards; the Constitution and the Bill of Rights – a civil Bible used by courts as a reference whenever there is political strife; the Statue of Liberty *worshiped as a Goddess. There is also the Pledge of Allegiance which schoolchildren recite every morning:

"I pledge allegiance to the flag of the United States of America and to the republic for which it stands.

One nation under God, indivisible, with liberty and justice for all."

## ◆ The Bible Belt

The inhabitants of the southern states are by far the most fervent believers. This is where Evangelical religion spread in the early 19th century. Preachers spoke of man's *sinfulness and Christ's redeeming grace. They called for reforming morals, had sessions of "conversion" where one could experience God's grace, and had an emotional approach to the spiritual experience. This conservative form of religion definitively took hold after the Civil War and is still alive today. The Bible Belt is the country of *born-again Christians, of collective baptizing ceremonies, of preachers speaking on street-corners and of fundamentalists who take the Bible literally.

◆ *Creationism

Creationists hold to a literal interpretation of the Bible; in particular they believe that God created the world about 6,000 years ago and that all living things are today the same as they were then. Since Charles Darwin developed the theory of evolution, the story of Adam and Eve has ceased to be considered literally true. But in the Bible Belt, Darwinian views are still not accepted. In 1925 the Butler Act made it illegal to "teach any theory that denies the story of the Divine Creation of man as taught in the Bible." The law was repealed in 1967. Recently, several states – unsuccessfully – proposed similar legislation banning the teaching of evolution as fact.

◆ The religion business

With so many Americans involved in religious pursuits many have come up with new ways of reaching for the *faithful – and their money. In the past few decades, *televangelism has developed into a prosperous – though not always lawful – enterprise. With Hollywood-style TV preach-shows, a *wise guy, Jim Bakker, managed to garner $70 million from gullible TV-viewers. The money, they were told, would serve for their salvation and the construction of a Christian amusement park and spiritual center. The man was soon accused of fraud – he also had to face charges of rape and homosexuality. Other televangelists keep broadcasting their gospel and amassing large amounts of money. Some have gone into politics, like Pat Robertson who founded the conservative Christian Coalition.

# Compréhension de texte

**En tenant compte du contexte, précisez en anglais le sens des expressions soulignées :**

> Bottom-rung workers are also getting a sprinkling of the sacred at the workplace. Companies such as Taco Bell, Pizza Hut, and subsidiaries of Wal-Mart Stores are hiring <u>Army-style chaplains who come in any religious flavour requested</u>. Members of these 24-hour God squads visit employees in hospitals, deal with nervous breakdowns, and respond to suicide threats. They'll even say the vows on a worker's wedding day or deliver the eulogy at her funeral.
>
> Business Week, November 8, 1999 – Religion in the Workplace.

*In the Army, people who need somebody to talk to about their relationship with God have an in-house chaplain; similarly, companies with a large workforce of low- to medium-skilled employees are discovering the benefits of hiring people for the same purpose. As those companies tend to have a high rate of diversity among their workers, they may request the services of many different religions. Interestingly, the word "flavor" usually refers to the varied sorts of ice-cream or soft drink people may order at a restaurant or buy in a supermarket. The word is associated with consumer products and the whole expression "who come in any religious flavor" smacks of the rhetoric of advertisements. It sounds as if religion was a product in demand on the market – and company managers were eager to satisfy the demand. There is undoubtedly a touch of irony here.*

> Monasteries and spiritual centres throughout the United States find that demand is booming. Type the words "spiritual retreat" into an Internet search engine and it will offer you dozens of websites describing centres for Christians, Jews, Buddhists, Native Americans, Hindus, New Agers. If you cannot actually go there, you can at least <u>take a breather from the hustle and bustle</u> by making a virtual retreat in cyberspace.
>
> The Economist, August 19th 2000 – The lure of silence

*As more people are seeking spiritual retreat among Trappist or Buddhist monks, monasteries find it increasingly hard to satisfy the demand. Fortunately they have turned digital and come out with virtual retreats on the Internet for the overworked professionals who can, so to speak, take a breath of fresh air on the web, away from long working hours, the continuous buzzing of phones, road gridlocks, and e-mail checking. But can they, really? The real spiritual retreat works in secluded places, miles away from the hectic life of cities, where one can enjoy the silence and slow pace of life. What if, with the click of a mouse, you try to get away from it all on your office computer?*

> When we see social needs in America, my administration will look first to faith-based programs and community groups, which have proven their power to save and change lives. We will not fund the religious activities of any group, but when people of faith provide social services, we will not discriminate against them. <u>As long as there are secular alternatives, faith-based charities should be able to compete for funding on an equal basis</u> and in a manner that does not cause them to sacrifice their mission.
>
> President George W. Bush on January 29, 2001, when announcing the creation of a White House office for religion-based and community groups that perform social services.

*The decision of the George W. Bush administration to finance religious groups performing social services with federal money may have appeared as a violation of church-state boundaries such as they are defined in the First Amendment. This is why the President was eager to insist that federal funding would be granted only when non-religious agencies are already providing the same sort of social services. As many observers have noted, religious groups are more efficient than public agencies in such social work as saving youngsters from crime or in keeping families together. The new policy was presented as a new experiment putting religious and non-religious social workers on an equal footing – and letting them compete for the best result. Even in dealing with poverty and crime, competition, the engine of a free market economy, will decide who is the best performer.*

# 14     The Right to Bear Arms

*Monique Chéron-Vaudrey*

Gun violence is probably the most \*dumbfounding feature of American life. It is often argued that Americans' readiness to pull out their guns is a deeply-rooted tradition in the country. Indeed the United States was forged through a War of Independence and a Civil War which turned it into a united nation. The conquest of the whole territory was achieved through wars against the Spaniards and the Indians. But similar violent experiences gave rise to many nations throughout the world without \*fostering such passion for firearms.

The 2nd Amendment to the Constitution (see p. 228), written in the early days of the new republic, gave a constitutional ground to those who, much later on, claimed their rights to keep their firearms.

Yet we can hardly believe that one sentence written more than two centuries ago keeps the country from adopting more relevant rules on gun control. We must also bear in mind that the images of the pioneer, of the lonesome cowboy, play a major role in the American mythology; they personify the individual entrepreneur, the man who relies only on himself to fight his way to freedom and happiness, using his own \*gumption – and his gun, too. This is what western movies are all about: when it comes to that, you had better be a fast gun if you want to survive. In the American mind, the gun is the guarantor of one's freedom and one's identity as a self-sufficent person. Moreover, the general distrust of the Federal government in Washington reinforces many people's feelings that if they need protection, they had better rely only on themselves.

## The historical background

Already at the time of the English colonies, every freeman was required to have a gun for his own protection. After independence, the question of how to protect the republic against its enemies was very simply and pragmatically solved. It was unnecessary at the time to bear the cost of a regular army while ordinary citizens could do the job they had already performed in the war against the English. The 2nd Amendment provided for civilian militias to ensure the protection of the community. But, apart from a few \*skirmishes with the Indians, there was no enemy to speak of, and very few militia-men cared to apply for a gun or to learn how to use it properly.

The real change occurred with the Civil War. For the first time huge military forces were involved in an armed conflict. The war broke out just as industrialisation was on its way. Gun manufacturers started taking impressive orders from the Union and Confederacy. When the war was over, all soldiers were allowed to take their guns home. This definitely \*triggered a new attitude to firearms. Guns so far, had been a rare and disregarded commodity, but from then on, millions of households would have one, ready for use.

On the other hand, the war had allowed the firearms industry to develop mass production and put the kind of product people asked for on the market – at a reasonable price. Firearms soon became widespread accessories as crime soared in the South, but also in New York and other cities of the North-East – and in the Wild West. Yet gun violence long remained restricted to traditional crime and not until the past few decades has gun-ownership become a national issue.

### A new mystique

Starting in the 70s, a new mystique, popularized and supported by the National Rifle Association (NRA), has striven to give a glamorous image of the gun and contended that the right to bear arms is an inalienable part of American freedom. That, since the days of independence, the country has had the opportunity to set up a regular army, plus federal and local police forces – making the "well-regulated militia" somewhat redundant – is of no avail to them. More recently, in the 1990s, unofficial militias started *mushrooming throughout the country.

### The NRA

The NRA was founded in the *aftermath of the Civil War as a kind of shooting club for former soldiers. It essentially worked for the promotion of rifle practice, gun safety, and gave training courses for hunters. But in the 1970s, the NRA decided to refurbish its image and transformed itself into a powerful lobby, supported by gun-manufacturers. It started active lobbying in Washington, especially among Republican Congressmen and brought its support to Ronald Reagan. It later boasted its first major blow to gun control legislation in 1986 when pulling to pieces the Gun Control Act of 1968. Since then, the NRA has been *instrumental in defeating all serious attempts in Congress to curb gun violence.

Today, it is estimated that the NRA influences 20 to 30 million voters. It pours money into Republican coffers and exerts heavy political *clout in Congress. It may be responsible for the Republican majority in Congress – or so the Democrats claim.

As the NRA saw its image somewhat shattered by aggressive activism and disturbing gun violence, they elected Charlton Heston as president in 1998, in the hope that the famous actor (who portrayed Moses in *The Ten Commandments*) would appeal to mainstream America. Despite growing protest among citizens on Washington's inability to act against gun violence, the gun lobby, as the NRA and its supporters are often called, manages either to win a majority of votes against gun restrictions or to secure *loopholes in the legislation so that gun lovers can keep buying and using guns.

### A partisan issue

Since Republicans in their majority support the NRA line, Democrats regularly voice their determination to restrict gun use. Several *school shootings which devasted the country under the

Clinton administration provided the Democratic President with an opportunity to call for more anti-gun legislation. In so doing, the Democrats can easily win the support of a growing number of Americans, women in particular, who have become active in the anti-gun fight.

Democrats advocate raising the minimum age for buying a gun to 21, limiting the purchase of guns to one in a month, outlawing possession of semi-automatic weapons by juveniles or adding *mandatory *safety locks on guns. But it must be noted that even the most outspoken politicians who favor gun control never go as far as suggesting banning guns.

## *The industry fights for its market share*

Meanwhile gun manufacturers have actively worked at developing their market share. New weaponry has invaded the market – often products imported from abroad such as explosives and semi-automatic weapons. In the 80s, soaring drug-related crime provided a booming new outlet for the industry. A lot of children in the ghettos fall victims to stray bullets during *shoot-outs between rival gangs.

With technological advances, more sophisticated guns have rolled onto the market. Gun lovers just do not buy one firearm, they start a collection! Yet, once you have bought a whole arsenal, you are not likely to shop for more items every year. So the industry is targeting new potential buyers, in particular women and children. The NRA indeed provides the necessary *shooting ranges and special training for the new customers. But as the industry is facing a sharp decrease in production, repeated government efforts to curb gun violence and an *onslaught of lawsuits filed by several cities, it now admits a few changes are called for.

## *Bucking the trend?*

With recent school shootings, an increasing number of Americans question the lax legislation on gun control, and it is likely that stricter limitations will be implemented in the near future. But it is equally likely that gun ownership will in no way decrease – no politician would risk losing votes on such a controversial issue. Unfortunately, this love affair with guns has horrendous consequences on the people least likely to have control over their own lives. Owning a gun has always represented a symbol of power. With a firearm you can have people respect you, you can obtain what you could not if you were not armed – which is extremely appealing to the weak and *downtrodden, and to maniacs as well. This is just what happened in Littleton in 1999. And this is probably what happens with serial killers – seemingly a typical American product – who are fascinated by gun violence and who, in turn, fascinate large sections of the public when their *killing sprees are reported in the media.

# Vocabulary

| | |
|---:|:---|
| aftermath | conséquences, séquelles |
| clout | influence |
| criminal-background check | vérification des antécédents judiciaires d'un acheteur d'armes à feu |
| downtrodden | opprimé |
| dumbfounding | ahurissant |
| foster (to) | stimuler, favoriser |
| gumption | débrouillardise |
| gun, firearm | arme à feu |
| gunfire | coup de feu, fusillade |
| gun license | permis de port d'arme |
| gun-rights advocate | partisan du maintien des droits |
| gun show | foire aux armes à feu |
| handgun | arme de poing |
| instrumental in (to be) | contribuer à |
| killing spree | accès de folie meurtrière |
| loophole | lacune |
| mandatory | obligatoire |
| mushroom (to) | se multiplier |
| onslaught | assaut |
| pull the trigger (to) | tirer sur la gâchette |
| safety lock | serrure de sécurité |
| school shooting, workplace shooting | fusillade à l'école, sur le lieu de travail |
| shoot at somebody (to) | tirer sur quelqu'un |
| shoot somebody dead (to) | abattre quelqu'un |
| shoot-out | fusillade |
| shooting-range | stand de tir |
| shotgun | fusil |
| skirmish | escarmouche |
| toll of handgun violence | victimes des violences par armes à feu |
| trigger (to) | déclencher |

**Further idiomatic vocabulary**

| | |
|---:|:---|
| be given the bullet (to) | se faire virer |
| be within gunshot (to) | être à portée de tir |
| big guns | « huiles » |
| bite the bullet (to) | accepter une situation désagréable |
| gun slinger | bandit armé |
| hit the bull's eye (to) | frapper dans le mille |
| shoot'em up | film violent |
| smoking gun | preuve flagrante |

# Focus...

About 212 million firearms are in in circulation in the country – about 67 million are handguns.

One household in three has firearms, which means that those who have guns are sometimes armed to the teeth.

Guns are used defensively 2.5 million times a year.

35,000 firearm deaths are recorded every year, through homicide, suicide, or accident.

14 children are killed each day by firearms.

The firearm-related death rate among American children under 15 is 12 times higher than among children in 25 other industrialised countries, according to a 1997 study. The children's homicide rate is five times that in all those nations combined.

A recent decline in murders and violent crimes only returns America to the violent-crime levels of the mid-80s.

"We are addicted to gun violence. We celebrate it, romanticize it, eroticize it. Above all, we market it – through movies, videos, television, radio, books, magazines and newspapers." Addicted to Guns, by Bob Herbert, *The New York Times*, January 1, 2001

◆ **Militias:**

> These groups developed in the 1990s; they arm themselves, they claim, to defend the Constitution. They often describe themselves as patriots, and harbor their distrust and contempt of the US government, guilty in their eyes of surrendering its sovereignty to the UN. They tend to accuse the Federal Government of various conspiracies, all aimed at depriving American citizens of their rights. They usually are heavily armed and hold regular training sessions in anticipation of a fight against government forces to defend their freedom. A lot of paranoia pervades such groups indeed. Many of them are just fringe groups who enjoy parading in combat dress. But some can take action in the most frightening way as was illustrated with the 1995 bombing of the federal building in Oklahoma City. There, Timothy Mc Veigh, one of those militiamen, had planted more than 2,000 kilos of explosives, killing 168 people.
>
> Many are white supremacists at the same time and some will go on killing sprees against blacks, Jews, Asians. It is estimated today that

there are about 15,000 armed militiamen with a following of about 100,000 unarmed sympathisers.

◆ **Children killing children**

1999   In Columbine High School, Littleton, Colorado, two teenagers gunned down twelve fellow students and one teacher before committing suicide.

1998   In Jonesboro, Arkansas, two boys, aged 13 and 11, picked 10 firearms from their families' armory and killed five elementary-school children.

◆ **Gun manufacturers**

The first one was the Springfield Armory (Massachusets); it was established by George Washington to defend the young republic after the War of Independence.

Smith and Wesson is the largest handgun producer. They are eager to show their goodwill in securing better control on the use of guns and recently agreed to go far beyond the law in requiring new restrictions on how retailers sell their guns. They also started developing a "smart" gun that can only be used by its owner – in exchange for which some state municipalities have agreed to drop their charges against the company.

Colt was founded in 1846. Its 44 revolver was a great accessory in the conquest of the West. The company is also developing "smart" guns.

Many manufacturers are just medium-sized companies but the business is still highly profitable despite the various threats of tougher legislation. Indeed each gun control bill spurs gun lovers into buying more of the cherished product before it is banned... Most have become aware that they had better get along with gun control measures. As one CEO put it, "When guns get into the wrong hands, it doesn't help the industry."

How they reach out for new markets:

– cowboy action shooting: participants dress up in rodeo costumes and re-enact scenes from the Wild West;
– guns designed for women; women now account for 25 percent of the gun market. The Outdoors-Woman program, monitored by the US Fish and Wildlife Service offers women in most states training in outdoors skills which may include mule-packing or fly-fishing but are essentially centered on rifle training;
– smart guns, specially designed to keep children from misfiring accidentally, are being developed in an effort to comply with new restrictions on gun use.

# Commentery of a cartoon

*Extrait de l'épreuve écrite du concours IEP Aix-en-Provence, 1999.*

Write a short essay about the situation or event which inspired [...] the cartoon.

*This cartoon was inspired by the killing of twelve high-school students in 1999 in Littleton's (Colorado) Columbine high school. Two teenagers, feeling estranged from their fellow students, had decided to "make a point" with this killing spree before committing suicide. The country woke up in horror at hearing the news. There were public prayers, some limited gun-control measures proposed by the Administration, and soon things went back to normal, that is, guns kept circulating among adults and children alike.*

*The cartoon purposefully conveys an impression of attention and earnestness as befits the activity of teaching. But this is no ordinary classroom. As can be read on the sheet of paper posted on the blackboard, this is Columbine high school and the middle-aged teacher reading the wording of a math test is in fact Uncle Sam as can be inferred from the top hat lying on his desk. In front of him, the broad-shouldered, dark-suited individual who seems to be dozing off while taking the test embodies the US lawmaker.*

Civilisation américaine

*The concerned American citizen asks the direct, commonsense question, "when will the nation wake up to the outrage?" The figures mentioned, alone, ought to call for immediate and drastic action. Yet the congressman sitting before him obviously misses the point – or, rather, just does not want to see it.*

*It illustrates the contradictions that pervade American attitudes when it comes to gun control. As school shootings have become a fact of American life over the past few years, an increasing number of people are now urging lawmakers to take action. After all, it is everybody's own children who are in jeopardy if school shootings cannot be prevented. But kids would not be in a position to bring firearms into schools if those firearms were not so easily available at home in the first place.*

*Let us bear in mind that more than 200 million firearms are in circulation in the United States. Some families are armed to the teeth and the gun is often considered as a household appliance. Among the 3 million members of the NRA, quite a few are keen to give their sons early training in the numerous shooting clubs of the country. So it is no wonder that children should lay their hands on guns and use them against their own classmates.*

*It is indeed extremely shocking that Congress should turn a blind eye to children shooting at other children, but this is only the latest outcome in decades of lax attitudes to gun ownership and use. Many congressmen indeed have close ties with the gun lobby, but even those who don't refrain from proposing legislation that would drastically limit the use of guns. Lawmakers are no heroes, they just want to make sure they will be reelected and consequently avoid angering voters. Many Americans are convinced that the right to bear arms, inscribed in the Constitution, cannot be infringed. The NRA propaganda makes it clear that those who support any form of gun control want to strike a blow to freedom in America. They claim that the best way to a safer America is a better armed America – regardless of the casualties. So it is very unlikely that lawmakers are going to pass unpopular legislation any time soon.*

# MORE ABOUT...
## ...GUN CONTROL

### THE GUN CONTROL LEGISLATION

The Gun Control Act – 1968 – was the first step to limit gun use. After the death of President Kennedy (in 1963) it banned the selling of guns through mail-order catalogues (the gun which had been used to kill the President had been bought this way) and included measures to restrict inexpensive European imports by establishing quality and safety standards.

### THE BRADY LAW

In 1994, the Brady law (after the name of a President Reagan secretary who was shot in an assassination attempt against the president) provided for a mandatory five-day waiting period before you could buy a handgun. The waiting period was later reduced to 3 days – it then expired when the instant *criminal-background checks became available.

### CONCEALED-WEAPONS PERMITS

Since 1985, 31 states have adopted concealed-weapon permits for citizens with no criminal record. You are allowed to carry a gun in your briefcase, your handbag or your car's glove compartment. The idea is that with such permits, criminals would be deterred from assaulting a victim who might carry a concealed handgun. It has reduced the number of deaths but not in any drastic way.

### THE GREAT *GUN SHOW LOOPHOLE

Gun shows do not have to abide by the laws on gun control. Anybody can buy weapons there, no questions asked, without going through the background check, and indeed without submitting to a waiting period. There are approximately 4,000 gun shows each year across the country, which provide a ready supply of firearms to gang members and all sorts of criminals. Three of the guns used by two teenagers to kill 13 people at Columbine High School in 1999 had been bought by one of the boys' 18-year-old girlfriend.

## Suits Against the Gun Industry

Several city mayors have started filing suits against gun shops and gun-manufacturers. They hope to obtain in courts what they cannot have in Congress. The lawsuits accuse the firearms industry of flooding metroplitan areas with guns – they further allege that the weapons do not incorporate readily available safety devices. Accordingly, they seek hundreds of millions of dollars in damages to pay for public costs of gun deaths and injuries. Suits have been filed in Chicago, New Orleans, Cleveland, New York, Atlanta, etc. They may obtain huge sums of money, but this is unlikely to bring more gun-control legislation. Unlike the tobacco industry, gun manufacturers enjoy dedicated support among the public

## Hollywood and Guns

Gun violence is the hallmark of American films. It is so taken for granted that no one notices in the country, and it has in fact become a means of attracting larger audiences abroad. The now famous character Rambo epitomizes the myth of the loner finding himself in a sea of trouble, who manages to set the world right thanks to his courage, determination – and to his private arsenal of firearms.

Oliver Stone's *Natural Born Killers*, released in 1994, ranks among the most significant films dealing with gun violence. It tells of two young psychos going on a killing spree – and of the fascination it arouses among TV reporters and their audiences as well. The film was definitely meant as a satire of American society. But the message did not get across, at least not the way Oliver Stone had meant. The killing spree inspired several teenagers (including the two in Littleton) who took the plot at its face value and decided to do just the same.

## Presidents Who Fell Victims to Gun Violence

Lincoln in 1865
Garfield in 1881
Kennedy in 1963
Theodore Roosevelt and Ronald Reagan survived assassination attempts

# 15 The Death Penalty

*Monique Chéron-Vaudrey*

At a time when the death penalty has been *abolished in most countries as a *barbaric and inefficient *punishment, the United States stands out as an exception. Despite worldwide protest and condemnation by international bodies, it seems that the country has never been so determined to keep it, with record numbers of executions in 1999 and 2000. This trend is fairly recent and in sharp contrast with previous decades when the death penalty had all but disappeared from verdicts.

## *The death penalty in America*

The practice of capital punishment was imported from Europe by the first settlers. In 1608, Captain George Kendall was executed in Virginia for being a spy for Spain. Death *sentences could be pronounced even for minor *offenses such as striking one's father or trading with Indians. The *abolitionist movement started as early as the late 18th century, under the influence of European philosophers such as Montesquieu and Voltaire, of English Quakers and of Cesar Beccaria's essay, *On Crime and Punishment.* In the early 19th century, many states reduced the number of their capital crimes. Michigan was the first state to abolish the death penalty in 1846. Rhode Island and Wisconsin later made the same decision. With the Progressive Era of reforms in the early 20th century, more states either abolished capital punishment or strictly limited it. This period of reform was short-lived. After the United States entered WWI, in the wake of the panic created by the Russian Revolution and social unrest at home, five of the six abolitionist states reinstated it.

Executions reached a peak in the 30s with 167 executions per year on average. Some criminologists argued that the death penalty was a necessary social measure, but the hardships suffered by people during the Great Depression also accounted for the high number of executions.

## *The turning point of the post-WWII period*

The Universal Declaration of Human Rights in 1948 proclaimed a "right to life," but as it was felt it was too early to call for an international abolition of capital punishment, the United Nations only limited the scope of capital justice in order to protect juveniles, pregnant women and old people. In Western Europe many nations stopped using capital punishment and all had altogether abolished it by the early 80s.

## *In the United States too, capital punishment is questioned*

Meanwhile in the United States, the number of executions dropped in the 50s (715 only, against 1,289 in the 40s) and reached an all-time low in the 60s. Many argued, in accordance with the words of the 8th Amendment, that capital punishment was "cruel and unusual"; the Supreme Court invalidated a great number of capital judgments, ruled against arbitrary sentencing by juries, and forced the states to review their death penalty statutes. A ten-year *moratorium on the death penalty came into effect in 1967 – it was lifted in 1976 and executions started again in 1977.

In the 80s, the Supreme Court issued several rulings showing that capital punishment was becoming a major concern. In one case, the Court banned the execution of insane persons, (but in other cases declared *mental retardation should be a *mitigating factor only when sentencing); the Court also recognized racial disparities as a constitutional violation of "equal protection of the law" and declared unconstitutional the execution of offenders aged 15 or under at the time of their crimes. There was no move toward abolition but at least some *safeguards seemed to be taken to guarantee *due process of law.

### A giant step backward

All this was but 15 years ago – and already it looks a *far cry from today's situation. In the late 1990s, some parts of the country obviously put a premium on combating crime with capital judgments. It would be wrong to blame all Americans for the dozens of executions performed each year because in fact most executions are concentrated in a small number of states – among the 37 states which have kept the death penalty, six have had no execution since 1976, and most have had fewer than ten.

So what has gone wrong in the past few years? America indeed needs to do some *soul searching on the question but hardly seems ready to do so. Yet there are a few hard facts that nobody can ignore. First the *crime rate has been decreasing steadily during the 90s, partly thanks to the booming economy. The main argument of the supporters of the death penalty, that it serves as a *deterrent for criminals, just does not *hold water. As a matter of fact, the crime rate tends to be lower in the states where capital punishment is either banned or not used, while it is higher in the states with a lot of executions. Moreover a comparison with European countries where the death penalty was *done away with several decades ago, shows that the rate of violent crime has risen more slowly than crime in general – and the murder rate remains much lower than in the United States. Obviously, capital punishment does not *deter criminals.

But there are more troubling facts. First, a disproportionate rate of *death-row *inmates are poor black males and – is it a coincidence? – the majority of the ten states with the highest number of executions since 1976 are southern states, where segregation used to be most blatant.

Indigent inmates are in the hands of court-appointed defense attorneys whose incompetence or lack of interest has recently been established – many falling asleep during the long court sessions, others admitting to their total lack of experience in dealing with capital judgments. Comparisons are often made with the O.J. Simpson case in 1995, when the black football player turned media star was declared innocent of the murder of his wife and her boyfriend while there was so much *evidence to the contrary – but O.J. Simpson was no ordinary black citizen, he could afford good lawyers.

Too many death-penalty cases are tainted with police misconduct and use of unreliable evidence.

*DNA testing is a technology that did not exist twenty years ago. But today it is a sure and safe way of proving a suspect innocent. 64 wrongly *convicted prisoners had been freed by early 2000 after such testings. But there is a snag. Only two states (Illinois and New York) give inmates the right to be tested. The police and justice often strongly resist it, sometimes do not preserve evidence after appeals, thus making DNA testing impossible.

Due process of law is not respected in other ways: foreign convicts are allowed the right to foreign legal representation. This provision is not respected. Recently two German death-row inmates were executed despite a call for clemency by German Chancellor Gerhard Schroeder. US officials later admitted the two had not been advised of their consular rights and apologized for the mistake. But indeed nothing could stop their execution.

### Mounting debate over the death penalty

The sheer number of executions, cases of wrongful *conviction and police or justice misconduct have opened a public debate over the death penalty. Several death-row inmates were recently proved innocent after law students had volunteered to investigate on their cases. Human rights groups, religious leaders, members of the justice system are increasingly voicing their opposition to the way the death penalty is applied.

In 1997, the *American Bar Association called for a suspension of the death penalty until changes are made to make certain that "death penalty cases are administered fairly and impartially, in accordance with due process and minimize the risk that innocent persons may be executed". They also oppose the execution of mentally retarded persons and those who were under 18 at the time of their crime.

### Resistance and indifference at the top

But politicians are unmoved. Former President Clinton *bragged about his support for the death penalty; the Democratic platform for Democratic candidate Al Gore insisted more on being tough on crime and punishment – including the death penalty – and called for smarter prevention to stop crime. President George W. Bush, as governor of Texas, personally signed dozens of executions, always confident that justice was being done, and never spending, as he once said, more than fifteen minutes on each case. He remained deaf to repeated appeals for clemency for several *causes celebres* in his own state, so it is likely that no major move will come from the White House in the near future.

# VOCABULARY

| | |
|---|---|
| abolish (to) | abolir |
| abolitionist | partisan de la suppression de la peine de mort |
| abrogation of the death penalty | abrogation de la peine de mort |
| American Bar Association | Association des Juristes américains |
| barbaric | barbare |
| brag about (to) | se vanter de |
| convict (to) | déclarer coupable |
| conviction | condamnation |
| crack down on (to) | sévir contre |
| crime rate | taux de criminalité |
| criminal law | code pénal |
| death row | le couloir de la mort |
| deter crime (to) | dissuader, empêcher la criminalité |
| deterrent | moyen de dissuasion |
| DNA test | test d'ADN |
| do away with (to) | supprimer |
| due process of law | prodédure légale régulière |
| evidence | preuves |
| far cry from | très loin de |
| heinous crime | crime odieux |
| hold water (it does not) | cela ne tient pas la route |
| inmate | prisonnier |
| lethal injection | injection mortelle |
| life imprisonment | prison à vie |
| life without parole | condamnation à vie sans possibilité de remise de peine |
| mentally retarded | handicapé mental |
| mitigating factor/circumstance | circonstance atténuante |
| moratorium | moratoire |
| offense | délit |
| pander (to) | flatter bassement |
| parole | liberté conditionnelle |
| petty crime | petite délinquance |
| punishment | punition |
| redeem (to) | racheter |
| retribution | châtiment |
| safeguard (to)/safeguard | sauvegarder ; garantie |
| sentence/to sentence | condamnation ; condamner |
| soul searching | examen de conscience |

# Focus...

◆ **The Death penalty in the world**

  *International calls for abolition*
  On December 25, 1998, Pope John Paul II called for a worldwide moratorium on the death penalty.
  In 1999, the United Nations' Commission for Human Rights meeting in Geneva reached a consensus for a moratorium that might lead to an abolition.
  In 2000, "Moratorium 2000", a petition calling for a cessation of the death penalty was circulated around the world.

◆ **International ban on child executions**

  The International Covenant on Civil and Political Rights, the American Convention on Human Rights, and the United Nations Convention on the Rights of the Child prohibit the execution of someone who committed a crime while a child.

◆ **Strange bedfellows**

  Five countries around the world still execute child criminals and the mentally-ill:
  Iran, Nigeria, Pakistan, Saudi Arabia and the United States.
  China, Iran and the United States are the only countries which frequently use the death penalty.

◆ **The Death penalty in the United States**

  About 13,000 people have been executed since colonial times.
  Only 13 states do not have the death penalty: Alaska, District of Columbia, Hawaii, Iowa, Maine, Massachusetts, Michigan, Minnesota, North Dakota, Rhode Island, Vermont, West Virginia and Wisconsin.

  Fewer people support the death penalty these days, but a 2000 national poll shows that 66% of Americans are in favor of the death penalty (against 79% in 1989) while 28% say they are against (the figure was 16% in 1989).

  In 2000, the New Hampshire legislature voted in favor of abolition (the Democratic Governor vetoed the bill), and the Republican Governor of Illinois imposed a moratorium.

  From 1976, when the Supreme Court lifted a ten-year moratorium, to early 2001, more than 600 people were executed, with Texas alone accounting for one third of executions. Virginia comes next (81 executions), then Florida (51), Missouri (47), Oklahoma (38), Louisiana (26), South Carolina (25), Georgia (23), Alabama (23), Arkansas (23).

About 90% of the people executed were too poor to pay a decent lawyer. They were defended by notoriously incompetent court-appointed lawyers.

Death Row Statistics (as of Jan. 1, 2001):
number of death row inmates: 3,726
46.14% are white, 42.81% are black, 8.8% are Latino.

◆ **Homicide rates**

A survey by *The New York Times* showed that 10 of the states with no capital punishment have homicide rates below the national average. Half the states with the death penalty have homicide rates above the national average – between 48 and 101 percent higher than in states without the death penalty.

◆ **Cruel and Unusual**

Until the early 20th century, hanging was the most commonly used method of execution. The first electric chair was used in 1890. Now *lethal injection is used in most cases as the least painful means of execution. Some states give the choice between lethal injection and the gas chamber. Four states have kept the electric chair.

◆ **Religious groups and the death penalty**

The Christian Coalition, a powerful group representing about 10 million conservative Christians, supports the death penalty. So do Fundamentalist and Pentecostal churches, and the Mormons.

Most Protestant denominations and the Roman Catholic church oppose the death penalty. Pope John Paul II called for an end to the death penalty during a visit in Missouri; he managed to obtain clemency for Darrel Mease whose execution had been scheduled during the pope's visit.

◆ **Dramatic increase in the prison population**

The number of prison inmates has quadrupled over the past twenty years, reaching 2 million at present. Of the 2 million prisoners, more than 500,000 are black males under 40.

# Essay

## Epreuve d'expression du concours CCIP 2000 – anglais LV2

Treize condamnés à mort exécutés depuis 1985 avaient moins de 18 ans au moment de leur crime. Dix-sept ans pour la plupart, sauf le dernier en date, un débile mental nommé Sean Sellers, "piqué" en février 1999, pour un meurtre commis à l'âge de 16 ans. Si la Cour Suprême refuse les exécutions avant cet âge limite, tous les États américains, sauf Hawaï, ont depuis quatre ans modifié leurs lois pour soumettre dès l'âge de 14 ans des mineurs au droit pénal des adultes. Cinq d'entre eux l'autorisent dès 13 ans. Deux à 12 ans, trois à 10 ans. Deux autres, enfin, ne reconnaissent aucune limite d'âge. Le résultat est sidérant : chaque année, 200 000 jeunes délinquants, écartés des tribunaux pour mineurs réputés trop coulants, passent directement devant des cours pénales d'adultes, pour des infractions allant du meurtre au simple cambriolage. Sur les 17 000 mineurs punis de prison ferme, 2 % le sont pour la vie, et 3 500 d'entre eux, soit 21 %, purgent leur peine en compagnie de détenus majeurs. La tendance ne promet pas de s'inverser, au moment où la droite du Congrès tente encore de faire voter la comparution des adolescents devant des tribunaux d'adultes fédéraux, notoirement impitoyables. De quoi inquiéter les autorités pénitentiaires, qui ont fait savoir à mi-voix qu'elles ne pouvaient garantir la sécurité des jeunes détenus dans les quartiers adultes.

En période électorale, les hommes politiques, les shérifs et les juges élus, les maires et les gouverneurs ont moins intérêt à calmer la grande peur américaine qu'à en faire le théâtre de leur campagne. Et les chiffres de la délinquance, brandis avec un retard calculé, semblent leur donner raison. De 1980 à 1994, le taux de criminalité des adolescents avait plus que doublé. Ils étaient les auteurs de 8 % des homicides du pays. L'horreur était réputée être confinée à la planète des ghettos, mais la tuerie de Littleton, en avril dernier, a conforté l'hystérie des parents de la middle class, échaudés depuis 1996 par une dizaine de canardages mortels dans des écoles proprettes d'Alaska, de l'Arkansas rural, du Kentucky ou du paisible Nord-Ouest.

Pourtant, depuis quatre ans, l'apocalypse est contredite par de nouveaux chiffres. La délinquance juvénile est en chute libre (– 40 %), et 3 % des homicides seulement sont aujourd'hui commis par des moins de 18 ans. Mais le nombre de gamins présentés à des juridictions adultes a doublé, et la moyenne des peines maximales qu'on leur inflige est de deux ans supérieure à celle des grands. La phobie du péril jeune aboutit à une autre aberration : les appels à la suppression pure et simple des juridictions pour mineurs, qui fêtent cette année leur centenaire et gèrent, avec peu de moyens, 1,7 million de comparutions. « Les idées de prévention et de réhabilitation sont passées de mode », déplore Schiraldi.

Presque partout, la justice américaine considère un inculpé de 17 ans comme majeur, et exécutable. Cent cinquante mineurs ont été condamnés à mort depuis 1985. Treize ont été exécutés. Soixante-dix attendent encore avec les 3 500 occupants adultes des couloirs de la mort. Les autres ont vu leur sentence commuée en peine à perpétuité. « On pourrait penser qu'ils sont condamnés pour des crimes atroces », confie l'avocat Victor Streib spécialiste de ce sujet. « Mais il ne s'agit souvent, comme pour les adultes, que de braquages qui ont mal tourné. » Quand on les sangle sur les tables d'injection, après des années d'appels et de recours en grâce, ils ont parfois atteint 30 ans, et perdu depuis longtemps leur visage d'enfant.

L'Amérique terrorisée par ses enfants, Philippe Coste – *L'Express*, 18/11/1999

**Répondre en anglais à la question ci-dessous (200 mots environ) :**

**What picture does this text give of American attitudes to juvenile delinquency?**

*The text shockingly illustrates how American politicians and elected officials (sheriffs and judges are elected) \*pander to the public's call for retribution and act tough on under-age criminals. Juvenile delinquency has been sharply decreasing over the past few years and only 3 percent of homicides are committed by young people under 18. According to the text, it is the horror caused among middle-class parents by the recent school shootings which has spurred a major \*crackdown on juvenile delinquency. Commonsense people might argue that if those juveniles had not been able to get their hands on their parents' arsenal in the first place, there might have been no killing at all. But this is hardly the best way to convince the constituents of voting you back into office on election day.*

*To be sure, not all Americans approve of tough justice on teenagers – the text is silent on this – but it illustrates the attitude of judges, especially in conservative constituencies, who consider that a child who commits an adult's crime should be punished like an adult. For all those who favor severe punishment, including the death penalty, there is no such thing as "mitigating circumstances." Numerous cases of unfair capital judgments show that they are inflicted on mentally-ill people, on young criminals who were children at the time of the crime, and that neither the court nor the juries are disturbed at the idea of sentencing those who most need protection.*

# 16 Scandals

*Sarah Loom*

## An American tradition?

Scandals are a striking and highly-visible feature of contemporary American politics but, despite the media *feeding-frenzy over Bill Clinton's marital infidelities, they are not a new phenomenon on the political scene. What's more, there is no obvious correlation between the gravity of *alleged *misdeeds and the degree of controversy which they generate. Why did Nixon *resign and Reagan and Clinton stay in office? Be it Watergate, Irangate, or all the other little "-gates" which have received *blanket media coverage, it is not easy to differentiate fact from *hype, to specify the level of guilt of those involved or even to determine what crimes (if any) were committed. Nonetheless, the liberal American political system (with its merciless media pursuit of perceived *improprieties, intense political competition and cult of the individual) appears eminently scandal-prone. Whether there are more scandals nowadays than in the past is open to debate – what is certain is that sensitivities to *misconduct have evolved, and that a profound scepticism of public figures has taken root in American society. We shall focus on two aspects: first of all, specifically political scandals involving US Presidents and secondly, presidential *peccadilloes – the froth on the cappuccino of political affairs.

## Political scandals

Awful puns aside, the watershed in American scandals was without doubt Watergate. The only scandal to cause the *resignation of a President, Watergate is the popular term used to refer to an intricate web of political wrongdoings between 1972 and 1974. It was in the Watergate Hotel complex that the Democratic National Committee offices were *burgled on June 17, 1972. The *burglars (G. Gordon Liddy and E. Howard) were rapidly arrested and convicted, but not before revealing compromising information. Links with the CIA came to light, White House aides resigned, and gradually suspicions that Nixon himself had been involved became too strong to ignore. When Nixon released transcripts of Oval Office conversations relating to Watergate which contained suspicious blanks, the whole case *upped a gear and moved to the Supreme Court. The House Judiciary Committee recommended that the President be *impeached on three counts – abuse of presidential powers, obstruction of justice and attempting to impede the *impeachment process. Nixon released further tapes, but by then his involvement in the *cover-up had become impossible to deny. On August 9, 1974, under threat of impeachment, Richard Milhous Nixon became the first ever US chief executive to resign.

While the Irangate scandal is less central in the American collective consciousness than Watergate, it arguably did more to lay bare the inner workings of the White House and the foreign policy machine. Several senior Reagan officials resigned and the President's reputation was undeniably harmed. The whole affair began when a Lebanese weekly, *Al-Shiraa*, revealed that clandestine propositions had been made by the US concerning secret arms sales to Iran. When the public learnt that profits from these sales were diverted in order to provide *covert finance for the Contra rebels in Nicaragua, the scandal erupted. Invoking national security grounds, the Reagan administration succeeded in covering up a number of embarrassing facts and the affair eventually died down.

The music of scandal has a reassuringly familiar beat: accusations are followed by denial and enquiry, exposure always comes hot on the heels of cover-up. However, if Watergate and Irangate gave us the picture of an allegedly shocked Democratic majority in Congress, *the* political scandal of the nineties saw the opposite scenario: a Democratic president facing the *wrath of an outraged Republican majority on Capitol Hill. Whitewater refers to a series of scandals involving Bill and Hillary Clinton's *real-estate investments in Arkansas. Many events took place fifteen years before Clinton came to power, others even before he became Governor of Arkansas in 1979 and the White House *spin-doctor, Mark Fabiani, maintained that the whole affair was a "*politically inspired fishing expedition*". However, it is interesting to note that Clinton refused to hand over certain documents, invoking "executive privilege" – just as "*Tricky Dicky" had done before him...

During the last days of his presidency, Clinton granted a controversial pardon to billionaire fugitive and tax fraudster Marc Rich. Just before the pardon, Rich's ex-wife had donated some $450,000 to Clinton's presidential library fund... Other dubious payments also came to light, including $400,000 paid to Hillary's little brother for his lobbying on behalf of clemency petitions. The scandal, inevitably, was dubbed "Pardongate".

### White House Women

Hillary Clinton may well be the only First Lady ever summoned before a grand jury (Whitewater), but she is upholding a certain tradition. Abraham Lincoln's wife, Mary, ran up dress bills which exceeded her husband's salary, did not attend the assassinated president's funeral in 1865 and subsequently refused to leave the White House for five weeks. In the 1920s, Florence Harding was *slated for her role in scandals involving oil and liquor licences and after Warren Harding's sudden death in 1923 rumours abounded that she had poisoned the President! The *whiff of scandal surrounding Harding's presidency doesn't end there: Harding was known to have had an affair with a woman 30 years his junior, and Washington gossip reported that they were in the habit of making love in a White House broom cupboard. Other presidents (Washington, Wilson, Roosevelt, Eisenhower...) are said to have had extra-conjugal relationships while in office – Jefferson is widely believed to have fathered several illegitimate children with his black slave.

All of these infidelities pale into comparison with those of JFK, whose sex-drive was legendary and whose conquests famously included the film stars Angie Dickinson and Marilyn Monroe. More compromising from a political point of view, however, were his *romps with Judith Campbell (also the mistress of a Mafia *bigwig) and Ellen Rometsch (rumoured to be an East German spy). In the late nineties, Bill Clinton's "inappropriate relationship" with a White House *intern, Monica Lewinsky, and his notorious economy with the truth ("*I did not have sexual relations with that woman!*") very nearly led to a constitutional crisis. Many Americans deemed that Clinton was guilty of *misrepresentation and *perjury and, as such, had committed an impeachable offence. Others felt that his conduct, albeit reprehensible, sordid or unpresidential, was not grounds for impeachment or resignation.

### Where do we go from here?

The Lewinsky affair at least proves one thing clearly – what counts as scandal varies from country to country, and over time. It was not Clinton's behaviour *per se* which was deemed scandalous, but the public's knowledge of it, and the opprobrium which he brought to the *hallowed office of President. The Shorter Oxford Dictionary explains that a scandal creates "a perplexity of conscience occasioned by the conduct of one who is looked up to as an example". As such, when a President lies, takes drugs, is unfaithful or whatever, it is less the actual conduct that leads to scandal than the perceived disgrace to the office and insult to public expectations. Or as Molière put it so appositely, "*To *sin in secret is not to sin at all.*"

Similar behaviour in another cultural context (e.g. Mitterand's illegitimate daughter) has not led to major scandal. It may be that Americans are more troubled than the French by the private sexual conduct of politicians, but here the risk lies in succumbing to cultural stereotyping. We should perhaps ponder the role of the mass media, the use in America of scandal allegations as a political weapon, and above all the tendency to centre election campaigns around individuals rather than policy debates. But are political scandals merely a ridiculous, superficial phenomenon? At a time when significant policy differences between Republicans and Democrats are increasingly hard to discern, scandals at least help voters to differentiate between candidates and parties. Moreover, the outcome of the Clinton – Lewinsky debacle proves that the American public can tell a Watergate from a Monicagate…

## VOCABULARY

| | |
|---|---|
| allege (to)/alleged | alléguer, prétendre ; allégué |
| bigwig | grosse légume |
| "buck"/make a buck (to) (fam. US) | dollar, l'argent ; se faire un petit à-côté |
| burgle (to)/burglar/burglary | cambrioler ; cambrioleur ; cambriolage |
| coverage/"blanket" coverage | couverture médiatique d'un événement ; traiter à fond un événement |
| cover-up | tentatives faites pour étouffer un scandale |
| covert | caché, indirect |
| evidence | preuves |
| feeding-frenzy | acharnement, déchaînement médiatique |
| "FOB" (Friend of Bill) | membre du cercle privilégié de Clinton |
| hallowed | saint, sacré |
| harassment/harass (to) | harcèlement ; harceler |
| hush up an affair (to) | étouffer, faire taire une affaire |
| hype/hype (to) | battage médiatique ; faire un énorme battage autour de quelque chose |
| impeachment/impeach (to) | destitution; destituer |
| impropriety | inconvenance |
| intern (US) | stagiaire |
| misconduct | inconduite, adultère |
| misdeed | méfait |
| misrepresentation | déformation |
| peccadillo | indiscrétion (sexuelle), vétille |
| perjury | parjure |
| real-estate (US) | biens immobiliers ou fonciers |
| resignation/resign (to) | démission ; démissionner |
| romps | ébats |
| sin/sin (to) | péché ; pécher |
| slate (to)/slam (to) someone | éreinter, démolir quelqu'un |
| sleaze | corruption, adultère etc. |
| sleazeball (fam.) | ordure |
| sleazy | louche, sordide |
| spin-doctor | spécialiste en communication (chargé de l'image d'un homme ou d'un parti politique) |
| spin (to) | présenter un événement sous un angle flatteur (pour un homme ou un parti politique) |
| tricky | rusé (cf "Tricky Dicky", surnom de Richard Nixon) |
| up a gear (to) (fam.) | accélérer |
| the whiff of scandal | soupçon d'un scandale |
| withhold evidence (to) | cacher ou taire des preuves |
| wrath | colère |

# Focus...

The American public has little confidence in the office of President: between 1973 and 1993 the proportion of Americans with "hardly any confidence" in the executive rose from 18% to 32%. During the same period, those who professed a "great deal of confidence" fell from 29% to 12%.

◆ **Polls, presidents and popularity**

*"We give the President more work than a man can do, more responsibility than a man should take, more pressure than a man can bear. We abuse him often and rarely praise him. We wear him out, use him up, eat him up."* John Steinbeck, 1966

Nowhere is this contradictory vision of the presidency more apparent than in the swings and roundabouts of Presidential approval ratings. Clinton slipped from 60% down to 43% in the first three months of his first term in office, during the so-called "honeymoon period" – the marked tendency of voters to wish a new President well. Perceived "errors" can lead to even more spectacular slumps: Nixon's rating dropped forty points during Watergate, while Ford's subsequent pardon of Nixon cost him thirty points in a matter of days. Reagan's involvement in the Iran-Contra affair caused a twenty point drop in 1986, and George Bush's rating slumped after the invasion of Panama. The latter holds the record for the highest-ever Presidential rating – 91% approval in the aftermath of the Gulf War.

◆ **Media coverage**

*"A country dying for and of entertainment can't stand for dullness, doesn't want incomprehensible realities – it wants entertainment. That is why almost all media coverage of government centers on the President, his wife, his family and his entourage. These provide a manageably small cast for a national sitcom, or soap opera, or docudrama, making it easy for media people to persuade themselves they are covering the news while mostly just entertaining us."* Russell Baker

Every post-Nixon President has faced a media feeding frenzy in which an adversarial and investigative press corps has hunted scandals. While it is acknowledged that pre-1970s Presidents enjoyed a discreet, even respectful relationship with the media, we have recently witnessed a more judgmental approach, as well as the emergence of hugely popular talk-show hosts whose staple diet consists of attacks on the White House. The actual size of the Washington press corps is also on the up – there are now over 2,000 accredited White House journalists. Coupled with the heightened frequency of media and commercial polls since the late sixties, these changes mean that a near-continuous presidential referendum exists. Clinton himself complained in 1994 *"I don't suppose there's any public figure that's ever been subject to any more violent personal attacks than I have, at least in modern history, anybody who's been President"*, adding *"Sometimes I wonder what planet I'm on"*.

# Commenting on a cartoon

"YOU FOLKS HAVE BEEN SO GOOD TO ME, .... I COULD JUST KISS YOU...."

*A perfect illustration of the "President – Polls – People" triangle, this cartoon by Rick McKee is a brilliant reworking of Grant Wood's painting,* American Gothic. *Wood's Regionalist picture of dour Protestant farmers is perhaps the one painting by an American artist which every American knows. In years to come, the Clinton – Lewinsky affair may well be the only political scandal post-Watergate generations of Americans will remember. Not unsurprisingly, this instantly recognisable painting is a favourite with satirical cartoonists and it is the picture which must have inspired the greatest number of pastiches (except perhaps the* Mona Lisa*). The couple in front of their Gothic farmhouse have come to symbolise archetypal American citizens and they have been reinvented as "preppies, yuppies, hippies, weathermen, pot growers, Ku Kluxers, jocks, operagoers, the Johnsons, the Reagans, the Carters, the Fords, the Nixons, the Clintons..." to name but a few of the countless variations listed in Robert Hughes's book,* American Visions.

*Here McKee reproduces the watchful couple in faithful detail, right down to the brooch and flowered pinafore of the female figure, and the farmer's overalls and striped shirt. However, in place of the Gothic farmhouse backdrop, the artist has chosen to introduce a third*

Civilisation américaine

*character, namely Bill Clinton. McKee skilfully uses all the traits which are the cartoonist's code for the former president (bulbous nose, jutting chin and so on) and as such, "Bubba" is instantly recognisable for the readers. The rotund, almost obese figure of Clinton contrasts sharply with the gaunt, emaciated faces of the farmers and the female figure on the left looks distinctly ill at ease as Clinton suavely slips his arm around her shoulders.*

*This reticence doesn't seem to discourage the libidinous-looking Clinton, however. He announces that he is so indebted to the "folks" in the cartoon that he could kiss them! The direction of his glance shows the reader exactly which character he intends to embrace and the male character on the right of the cartoon looks distinctly worried by just how energetically Clinton might express his gratitude. His eyes (which in Wood's original stare unblinkingly forwards) are shown swivelling around to his right, in order to gaze in fear and horror at what may be about to take place. Wood referred to the female character in his painting at various times as both the man's wife and his spinster daughter – whatever the case, we can imagine that if Clinton lives up to his ruttish reputation, the farmer will make immediate use of his trusty pitchfork. This tool, with which Satan is traditionally depicted as tossing the damned onto the fires of hell, evokes notions of sin and transgression. During the Lewinsky scandal, commentators made much of both of these notions, interestingly enough, so McKee's choice of subject matter/inspiration is particularly fitting on yet another level.*

*Last but not least, the slip of paper in Clinton's podgy hand explains the reason behind his gratitude. Opinion polls play a preponderant role in American politics and, rather surprisingly, when Clinton's "inappropriate relationship" with Monica Lewinsky came to light the President's popularity ratings did not suffer unduly. Whether this meant that Americans implicitly condoned the President's conduct, or whether it was a reaction to Kenneth Starr's "no-holds-barred" prosecution or Clinton's repeated public apologies, remains unclear. What is undeniable, however, is the artist's message here: Clinton owes an enormous debt to ordinary, American folk.*

"I used the famous Grant Wood painting of ordinary, American folk to represent the ordinary, American folk who basically saved Clinton's bacon with their support of his professional conduct, while simultaneously being repulsed by his personal conduct." *Extract from an e-mail sent by Rick McKee to Sarah Loom.*

# 17     The Welfare State

*Sarah Loom*

State *welfare in the USA dates back to Roosevelt's 60-year pledge during the New Deal. The dust-bowl farmers, miners' widows, and ragged children who loomed large as victims of poverty now seem to have been replaced by the public spectre of state-sponsored *single mothers and professional *dole queue members. In a healthy economy where the majority of voters will never have to call on state *welfare payments, many American *taxpayers deem that their taxes are merely subsidising a welfare way of life and perpetuating the cycle of *hand-out dependency. Middle-class taxpayers would appear to be applying the infamous policy of zero tolerance to those less fortunate than themselves, whom they accuse of being "*freeloaders". This "work or *starve" attitude to finding *gainful employment reflects the generally unsympathetic view many Americans have of those fellow-citizens who live thanks to public assistance. It has to be said that the lobbying power of the poor is as weak as their electoral voice. The face of hardship in the days of the Great Depression was largely white to boot, while a majority of welfare recipients in the nineties were black or Hispanic.

If the profile of the typical welfare recipient has changed, then so has the terminology – "clients" now visit "transitional assistance" agencies in order to sign "personal responsibility agreements" aimed at getting them back to work. The Personal Responsibility and Work Opportunity *Act, as one key welfare reform was called, replaced the AFDC (*Aid to Families with Dependent Children*) with the TANF (*Temporary Assistance to Needy Families*) programme, which as its name suggests is intended as a temporary measure.

## Bill's *bills

The welfare reforms voted during Bill Clinton's two terms as President were far and away the most radical in recent decades. Although he had previously twice vetoed less far-reaching proposals passed by the Republican Congress, in May 1996, Clinton finally endorsed a radical overhaul of America's welfare system, thus honouring his 1992 election pledge "*to end welfare as we know it*". These reforms were lauded – or slammed, according to political proclivities – as the most dramatic change in US social policy in half a century. Proposals included *punitive measures such as cutting off *benefits for those who refused to take jobs, even reducing payments to parents of kids who played truant.

Coming as it did during a pre-election run-up period, Clinton's welfare scheme was seen by many critics as an about-turn for the President, even as a calculated attempt to appropriate "right-wing" policies and therefore steal thunder from Republican opponents. Clinton was accused of having moved away from his early-90s, liberal "New Democrat" stance towards the political centre and this turnaround even earned him the *moniker "Republican Bill". Similar accusations of electioneering were levelled at Clinton during the 2000 Gore – Bush presidential race, when he was accused of trying to buff up the old-fashioned, "tax'n'spend" image of the Democrats by introducing billion-dollar welfare and *childcare plans.

On a different level, Clinton's welfare reforms were seen as an embarrassing climb-down for the former First Lady, Hillary Rodham Clinton, an avowed defender of children's rights. During the 1992 Presidential campaign, for instance, much was made of Mrs Clinton's dedication to children's issues. She even penned a best-seller on the subject: *"It Takes a Village"*. Activist groups such as The Children's Defence Fund publicly condemned Clinton's reform proposals as "disturbing" and demanded to know why the First Lady was lying so low while her husband cut welfare provision.

### The "nitty-gritty" of reforms

As a result of welfare reform legislation, federal responsibility was transferred to state and city government and the "Temporary Assistance to Needy Families" programme was introduced. Block grants for needy families under the TANF programme mean that each state must now require welfare recipients to "participate in work activities". The *bottom line is that any job-seeker who fails to comply with sweeping work-related TANF requirements now risks benefit curbs. Numerous states also impose sanctions if families fail to comply with additional stipulations relating to the immunisation of children, regular school attendance and so forth. When sanctions are imposed, some or all family members lose TANF cash benefits and these cuts may be partial or complete, temporary or permanent, depending on the policies chosen by each state. Such ostensibly aggressive sanctions were destined to eliminate families who, although capable of complying with work requirements, simply refused to do so. They were intended as a strong message to "freeloaders" and "the professional unemployed" and indeed many states (such as Wisconsin) have since adopted sanction policies that are actually **more** *stringent and far-reaching than Federal law requires.

### The new poor

Although results published by the non-partisan *GAO in 1998 (two years after the implementation of welfare reform) appear to go some way in proving the efficiency of the Clinton legislation, many analysts have noted the emergence of a new "*underclass" of particularly needy Americans. They point to disturbing rises in several *poverty and inequality indices, in spite of a *dip in the general overall poverty rate and the lowest unemployment rate in 30 years.

Several categories of American appear to be at particular risk of slipping through the welfare net. For example, in 1998 55% of children in single-mother families lived in poverty (60% for black kids and 67% for Hispanic children). Under the new legislation, single mothers are required to work for their benefits. Unmarried teenage moms get nothing at all unless they live at home and go to school – such "good conduct" earns them vouchers for food and diapers. Mothers who decline to name the father of their child and give information concerning his whereabouts face benefit cuts of up to 25%, in an attempt to force fathers to keep up with their *child support payments. In addition to these measures, a single mother whose youngest child is older than five must prove that she is unable to find a babysitter in order to qualify for welfare.

Other target categories – so-called "legal aliens", for instance – also risk losing the right to cash payments and food stamps, as do those convicted of drug-related offences. Pregnant women and adults following drug rehabilitation programmes are exempt. Under the reforms, legal immigrants must now work and pay taxes for a decade before becoming eligible for assistance. In addition to this targeting of certain "high-cost" categories, a two-year time limit has been imposed on all job-seekers and any able-bodied American's entitlement to benefit is now capped at 5 years (in an individual's entire working life).

Significantly, a 1999 survey of 26 large cities by the US Conference of Mayors found that the need for emergency food aid over the past decade had increased by 18%, while the demand for emergency shelter had risen by 12%. The charity Second Harvest has noted serious shortfalls since the mid-nineties in emergency food programmes due to massively increased demand in several cities. Although it is questionable whether this worrying evolution can be directly attributed to welfare reform, it seems to be indicative of the emergence of an economically vulnerable sub-section in contemporary American society. However, partisans of welfare reform quote GAO data which appear to show that on the whole Americans are finding work more quickly: in Maryland, 17% of welfare recipients found work in 1997 compared to only 4% in 1995, while in California the percentage climbed from 9% to 19% over the same period.

Whether these successful job-seekers were encouraged by the two-year benefit cap or were finding work more easily as a result of economic growth is impossible to say. Reliable statistics are hard to come by in this area, although one possibility is that fewer people without jobs are now going into further education than in the past, pushed instead to find employment. If this is indeed the case, then the 21st century may witness the emergence of both an economic *and* an intellectual subclass in America – are the potential savings from welfare reform worth such a risk?

# Vocabulary

| | |
|---:|:---|
| act | loi |
| benefits | allocations |
| bill | projet de loi |
| bottom line | l'essentiel |
| by-product | conséquence (indirecte) |
| childcare | assistance à l'enfance |
| child support | allocations familiales, pension alimentaire |
| CHIP | **the Children's Health Insurance Programme** |
| dip (in figures) | baisse |
| dole queue | nombre de chômeurs |
| emergency care | soins d'urgence |
| free prescription | ordonnance gratuite |
| freeloader/freeload (to) | parasite ; vivre en parasite |
| gainful/"in gainful employment" | dans un emploi rémunéré |
| GAO | General Accounting Office |
| hand-outs (fam.) | aide, aumône |
| hardship | privation |
| healthcare | services médicaux |
| health center | centre médico-social |
| health insurance gap/income gap | différence de couverture médicale, de revenus |
| HMO | **Health Maintenance Organization** |
| jobless figures | taux de chômage |
| low income families | familles à revenues faibles |

(those with incomes below 200% of the Federal Poverty Line i.e. $26,240 per annum for a family of two adults and one child)

| | |
|---:|:---|
| Medicaid | assistance médicale pour les personnes de moins de 65 ans vivant en dessous du seuil de pauvreté |
| Medicare | régime d'assurance maladie pour les personnes âgées de plus de 65 ans |
| Medigap | assurance complémentaire privée |
| moni(c)ker | surnom |
| pledge | engagement, promesse |
| poverty/poverty line | pauvreté, la misère ; seuil de pauvreté |
| punitive measures | sanctions, mesures dissuasives |
| single mother | mère célibataire |
| starve (to) | mourir de faim |
| stringent (measures) | (mesures) draconiennes |
| taxpayer | contribuable |
| underclass | classe sociale très défavorisée |
| welfare | aide sociale, assistance publique |
| welfare payments/welfare check | prestations sociales ; chèque d'allocations |
| welfarite (péj.) | assisté |

# Focus...

During the period 1996 – 1998, **10 million US households** did not have access to enough food to meet their basic needs.

In 1997, **26 million Americans** sought emergency food aid from the charity "Second Harvest".

One in six American cities has **chronic unemployment rates** despite an overall dip in *jobless figures.

In spite of a 4% overall unemployment rate, in January 2000 92% of American cities claimed there were **not enough low-skilled jobs** to meet the requirements of welfare reform laws.

**Savings of up to $55 billion** are expected to result from welfare reform.

**Americans on welfare**: 1993 = 14.1 million; 1996 = 12.2 million; 1999 = 7.3 million.

◆ **Debunking the dependency myth**

A recent study of 13,000 households proves that majority of welfare recipients are first generation users, a conclusion which somewhat undermines the "professional freeloader" theory referred to above:
- 25% of beneficiaries said their parents rarely used welfare;
- 10% grew up in households that frequently used welfare;
- only 5% were chronic users who also grew up in "welfare households".

The author of the report, Mark Rank, maintains: *"The bottom line is that rather than being a learned lifestyle, welfare dependency is simply a by-product of poverty"*.

◆ **Reform casualties**

GAO figures show that in 1998, around 5% of families receiving TANF benefits lost part of their allowances as a result of sanctions, while 16,000 families per month completely lost assistance under full-family penalties. If we look more closely at those who have suffered, it is clear that sanctioned families generally have the lowest educational levels (half typically not having finished high school) as well as more limited work experience and a higher incidence of domestic violence, disabilities, physical and mental health problems and so on. Childcare is also a continuing problem, as almost half of all welfare families need childcare. Under the old law, families were entitled to assistance, as were those "transitioning off" welfare. The Child Care and Development Fund no longer provides such guarantees – only 10% of potentially eligible *low-income families are thought to benefit from the childcare assistance they need.

◆ **And now for the good news...**

According to findings from the 1999 National Survey of America's Families, low-income families are broadly-speaking better-off today than in 1997. National poverty rates declined for both adults (13% down to 11%) and children (21% down to 18%). California, Florida, Mississippi, Washington and Wisconsin saw a considerable shift of families from low to high-income brackets, while other states (such as Alabama and Colorado) witnessed a rise in the number of insured adults and children. In short, fewer Americans are now on welfare than at any time since 1967.

# Essay

**What is the state of welfare in the US today?**

*Under federal law, all US states now demand that that welfare recipients participate in work activities and are obliged to impose financial sanctions on families who, without good reason, refuse to do so. As outlined above, these benefit cuts may be permanent or temporary, total or partial, according to the individual policy adopted by each State. However, a significant number of States actually impose penalties which go beyond federal requirements:*

*36 impose "full-family" sanctions, thus cutting off welfare benefits for the entire family (18 of these after the **first** instance of non-compliance),*

*39 states continue sanctions for a set period of time, regardless of whether the recipient has come into line with TANF requirements during that time period.*

*These stringent sanctions are aimed at penalising "freeloaders" and "*welfarites" but recent research from The Center on Budget and Policy Priorities would seem to indicate that sanctioned families are not by and large those who refuse to comply, but those who are faced with substantial barriers in finding work. Such families are characterised by a high incidence of health problems, as well as below-average education levels. These difficulties are frequently compounded by a lack of adequate transport or acceptable childcare facilities. In addition, there is evidence that penalised families neither know what the TANF requirements are, nor understand the consequences if they fail to abide by the rules.*

*The National Jobs for All Coalition is campaigning for a number of changes to welfare law, and has proposed a programme of "welfare repair" which it claims will counterbalance excessive TANF requirements. Recommendations include:*

1. *Ascertaining whether suitable jobs are available before imposing work-related requirements*
2. *Ensuring that welfare reform does not create a dual labour force (same wages and conditions as for "regular" jobs)*
3. *Enforcing a minimum wage*
4. *Guaranteeing affordable high-quality childcare to all parents who need it*
5. *Increasing government and state funding for education and training*

## Comparison of two differing sanction procedures

### 1) South Carolina

One of the highest sanction rates in the entire US can be found in South Carolina. The South Carolina Appleseed Legal Justice Center provides the example of a single mother with ongoing mental and physical health problems, whose child has a severe heart disability. The mother in question faced TANF sanctions in 1999 when she missed an appointment with her caseworker because she was at the hospital with her child who was undergoing cardiac surgery. The mother appealed for the sanction to be lifted via South Carolina's conciliation process. The state declined to acknowledge the mother's difficulties and lifted the sanction on condition that the mother promised not to miss any other appointments.

A month later, the mother was sanctioned again, this time because she was late for a job training programme when the bus she needed to take was an hour late. The caseworker stated that the woman did not have good cause for missing the training session and, as a result, the woman's entire family had their benefits cut. As we go to press, the woman in question is currently trying to obtain a fair hearing with the help of her attorney...

In 1998, South Carolina reported an average of 628 new families per month lost their access to welfare as a result of sanctions. More worrying than this, however, is the number of families who do not return to assistance after sanctions: around 9,500 per month.

### 2) Mesa County, Colorado

Welfare programmes in other states, such as Colorado, are the responsibility of individual counties and this flexibility has enabled counties to set up a whole range of procedures in order to avoid such inappropriate or unfair sanctions. Mesa County, for instance, has a number of services which help families comply with TANF requirements in the first place, as well as a pre-sanction review process. During this process, social workers look at why an individual has not complied, what barriers and needs he or she faces in finding work, and finally propose solutions which address their particular difficulties. Social workers can find specialised childcare for disabled kids, or help families with transport problems buy a car. They can even help families find what is known as a "good cause exemption" and therefore avoid non-compliance sanctions! Understandably, the sanction rates in Mesa County are exceptionally low and almost 70% of families who are referred for problems of non-compliance finally avoid punitive measures.

# 18 The New Economy

*Sarah Loom*

## Just what is this so-called "new economy"?

The late nineties saw many analysts referring to a new paradigm in economics and the term "the new economy" has been coined in response to the fact that the USA and many other industrialised countries have been enjoying a sustained period of economic growth and low unemployment, without signs of an attendant *hike in inflation. Generally speaking, this economic evolution has been achieved because *information technology and global competition have allowed companies to offer more for less – thus enhancing productivity without fuelling inflation. The "new economy" is no longer based on those old-fashioned *commodities oil, coal, copper and so on but, as one expert put it, "our energy comes more and more from electrons that flow through computer chips made of sand". Technology, which depends much less on oil or coal than manufacturing does, now drives economic growth.

However, while such talk of a new economy is associated with the *boom years of a healthy economy, it has to be said that productivity – even in America – has actually been growing very slowly. Besides, a term like "the new economy" is something that crops up every time economic figures look very good. In the UK in the late 80s, for instance, there was a much *hyped "economic miracle" which the early nineties recession wiped out. Again, in 1994, the then Chancellor of the Exchequer, Kenneth Clarke, made much of what he termed the Goldilocks economy – "not too hot and not too cold !"

Difficulties in giving a cogent definition of the new economy aside, it does have to be said that new technology and the Internet in particular have changed the rules of economics. Technology and the web are going to have an increasingly central role to play in everything we do at home and at work, and increasing numbers of ordinary Americans (and Europeans) have a huge proportion of their wealth tied up in *stocks and *shares. The take-off of real-time, low-cost Internet share *dealing for "the man in the street" has brought the formerly rarefied world of *trading a step closer to becoming an everyday concern, and in 2000 almost half of American households owned stocks, either directly or through mutual funds and pension plans (compared with just 4% in 1952).

## NASDAQ in freefall

When the stocks of the *tech-heavy NASDAQ index took a dive (or rather a series of increasingly spectacular *nosedives) in 2000, many small *investors got their fingers burnt. Instead of tripping over one another to buy hi-tech stocks, investors sold out as quickly as they could, while other money just went back to the *blue-chip values and old economy stalwarts of the Dow Jones. What lies behind the volatility of the new economy?

It would appear that the overvaluation of Internet companies is at the root of this retrenchment in blue chip stocks. Dot.coms and other Internet *start-ups represented a new sector of *investment in the late nineties, and institutions (and individuals) tended to buy indiscriminately. Demand exceeded supply, particularly for hi-tech stocks, thus pushing up prices. In the nineties we witnessed a tidal wave of enthusiasm for anything with a dot.com after its name. Many of the newer companies in the booming new economy TMT sectors (telecom, media, technology) had never made a profit, but their shares went on rising as investors bought them, both on expectations of future growth and in the mistaken belief that the market would continue to rise. Markets witnessed the inevitable trend (symptomatic of a strong flotation market) to take fledgling Internet companies to *IPO earlier, which gives investors a much higher level of risk.

As such, unlike traditional blue-chip companies, hi-tech share prices reflect perceptions of what profits might be, rather than what they have been in the past. Such perceptions are exceedingly volatile, for a CNN news bulletin, a rumour, or an odd bit of information can have a phenomenal effect on share prices – it's known as the "CNBC effect". All share prices are determined by the interaction of buyers and sellers, but notions of worth are clearly more volatile when it comes to dot.com stocks and Internet ventures. The seminal economist Maynard Keynes once said that determining share prices was like judging a beauty contest where the judges have to decide not just who the most beautiful contestant is but who everyone else thinks the winner will be. This analogy fits the new economy perfectly, but with the added complication that judges only have baby photos to go by!

### The dot.com dream

According to a survey by US net monitoring company, Webmergers.com, the rate at which dot.coms became dot.gones exceeded one a day in the last quarter of 2000. Around 400 Internet firms are currently listed on US stock markets, with around 75% of them destined to disappear within five years. However, it would appear that certain types of Internet *venture are more vulnerable than others. The buzzwords in this sector are "B2B" and "B2C": on the one hand, we have B2B or "business to business" market places (where companies trade goods and services amongst each other), and on the other B2C or "business to consumer" web *retailers, selling goods or services to consumers on-line.

Over three-quarters of the companies closing down in 2000 were in the B2C sector and online retail ventures are quite clearly most at risk. Cyberspace spending is set to become part of our economic landscape, but online retailers find themselves in a dilemma: customers who demand both low prices and fast but costly delivery, and investors who get impatient and want to see profits.

What's more, government watchdogs in the US are standing by to impose heavy fines on companies who fail to live up to their cyber-promises. However, B2Bs still promise hefty growth rates in 2001 and beyond, although it remains an extremely volatile sector overall.

### A future for futures?

The 2000 NASDAQ *slide begs two questions: first of all, is this decline symptomatic of a general economic down period (that's *Fed-speak for a recession), and secondly has the tech stock meltdown effectively killed off the nascent new economy which we outlined above? What is clear is that there are very real fears that the US economy is heading into a recession. This hard landing after the euphoria of the boom years may be compounded even further by the move away from traditional savings schemes toward stock market *wheeling and dealing. Americans save virtually nothing, but for years lack of savings didn't seem to pose a problem as people invested money in the stock market, which was rising at 20% per year. When the stock market goes up, Americans feel wealthy and this translates into increased consumer spending. In a country where consumer spending makes up nearly two thirds of the nation's economic activity, those figures suddenly sound quite scary. Now the worry is that as consumers see their investments fall, they may well stop the very spending that fuelled a decade of growth. The consequences of the 2000 hi-tech *slump were perhaps felt hardest by the army of small investors who had bought hi-tech shares. All of a sudden, Internet stocks didn't seem quite so sexy.

What has not been affected by the NASDAQ slump, however, is the dramatic impact of *IT and web-based business strategies on the wider economic picture. Thanks to new technologies, we are witnessing major restructuring or "unbundling" in countless markets and industries (such as the media, high street banking, credit cards, telecommunications and so forth) which in itself constitutes a new way of doing business, a fresh business model, another form of "new economy".

In short, the old new economy is dead. Long live the **new** new economy.

# VOCABULARY

| | |
|---|---|
| assets and liabilities | actif et passif |
| boom/booming economy | marché en plein essor ; très forte hausse |
| blue-chip shares | placements de premier ordre, valeurs de père de famille |
| "bear market" (= falling market) | marché à la baisse, marché baissier |
| "bull market" (= rising market) | marché à la hausse, marché haussier |
| commodity | produit de base, matière première |
| dealing/"wheeling and dealing" | (trouver des combines pour) acheter et vendre des actions |
| downturn | baisse |
| "Fed" | Federal Reserve Bank of the United States |
| "Fed-speak" | langage euphémique utilisé par cette institution |
| hike | hausse |
| hype/much hyped | battage médiatique ; fortement médiatisé |
| investor/invest (to)/investment | actionnaire; placer de l'argent ; placement, investissement |
| IPO (Initial Public Offering) | première cotation en bourse |
| IT (Information Technology) | informatique |
| layoff/lay off (to) | licenciement ; licencier |
| merger | fusion |
| nosedive | chute spectaculaire, plongeon |
| pink slip/ "pink-slip" (to) someone (fam. US) | licenciement ; licencier |
| plummet (to) | dégringoler |
| pundit | expert (souvent ironique) |
| retailer | détaillant |
| securities | valeurs, titres |
| stocks (US)/shares (GB)/shareholder | actions ; actionnaire |
| slide/slump/slump (to) | baisse ; baisser |
| sluggish | stagnant |
| start-up | jeune entreprise internet (« jeune pousse ») |
| stockbroker | agent de change |
| stock market | la bourse |
| stock options | droit préférentiel de souscription pour les employés d'une entreprise |
| takeover bid | une offre publique d'achat, une OPA |
| tech stocks | actions de la nouvelle technologie |
| tech-heavy (adj.) | à une forte prépondérance d'actions nouvelle technologie |
| trade (to)/trading/"trading day" | vendre des actions ; vente d'actions en bourse |
| unload shares (to) | se débarrasser, se défaire de ses actions |
| value/an overvalued stock | valeur ; action cotée à un prix excessif |
| venture | tentative commerciale, entreprise |

# Focus...

◆ **Tech stocks *plummet**

If we look at the combined value of NASDAQ firms, the losses in 2000 were indeed quite spectacular:

Value on March 10: **$6,711 billion**

Value on December 20: **$3,399 billion** – a decline of over **3.3 billion dollars**.

The market **doubled** in value between August 1999 and March 2000 only to **halve** again by the end of November.

Much hyped dot.com casualties include Clickmango.com, the online health products retailer, which was forced to wind down and Boo, the highly-publicised B2C fashion retailer. Big web names also seem to be having trouble staying afloat in the choppy waters of the new economy. Even PC giant Microsoft's shares slipped to around $50 in December 2000, wiping around $20 billion off its stock market value.

◆ **An era of *pink-slipping**

A recent cover of the influential new economy magazine *The Industry Standard* says it all: *"Pink slips in paradise: the era of dot.com *layoffs has begun."* Scores of workers, many lured in the boom years to internet jobs by the promise of *stock-option packages, were *laid off when the stock market *slumped and investment capital dried up. As well as job losses in the hi-tech sector, Old Economy stalwarts were also hard hit, with nearly half a million redundancies announced in the month of November 2000 alone.

◆ **Is this a recession?**

According to the latest available statistics, the US economy expanded at an annual rate of 2.2% in the third quarter of 2000. While this represents a sharp drop from the 5.2% annualised rate given for the first half of the year, it is still reassuringly far from meeting the criteria which define a dreaded recession (two successive quarters of negative growth). Even stock market losses pale into comparison next to the darkest days of 1929 (when there was a 12.8% slide on October 28, followed by an 11.7% fall the following day) or the October 1987 crash when the market lost 22.6% in a single trading day.

◆ **And now for the good news...**

Even though the plunge in new economy hi-tech stocks has been spectacular, market *pundits are talking more in terms of a correction than an actual crash. The NASDAQ did indeed fall by over 45% between March and December 2000, but it still remained up 25% over the previous 12 months. As such, we are not (yet) facing what is known as a "*bear market". Similarly, despite highly-mediatised layoffs in both old and new economy sectors, the American job market actually remained relatively strong, with unemployment rates hovering around the 4% mark. Compared with previous recession rates of 7.5% (in 1992) and 9.7% (1982), jobless figures at the turn of the 21st century are at their lowest since 1969.

# Commentery of a cartoon

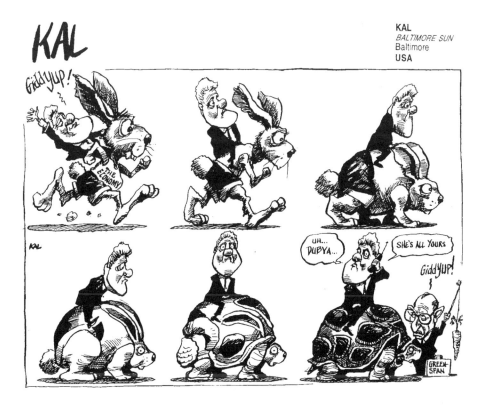

By way of introduction, I'd say that this cartoon epitomises both a political and an economic turning point in recent US history. Drawn by the prolific and much-loved American cartoonist Kevin Kallaugher and published in January 2001 (shortly after the highly-publicised bout of legal wrangling which finally declared George W. Bush the 43rd President of the United States), what at first appears to be a mere light-hearted reworking of the hare and the tortoise fable, is in fact a biting satire of the state of the American economy.

If we break down the six drawings which make up this cartoon, the first thing we note is the sense of movement: the top left-hand drawing represents a hare sprinting confidently along. Dust is flying up around his feet, his ears are pricked up in expectation of certain victory and his jockey, head thrown back, arm flung perilously in the air, is urging him on to glory with a forceful "Giddy up!" The running shorts and singlet emphasise speed and athleticism, as well as allowing the artist to inscribe the words "the economy". The reader instantly understands the symbolism of the hare, and this allows him to associate the over-confident jockey with the man holding the reins of the American economy – ex-President, Bill Clinton. The caricature of Clinton includes all the familiar visual traits which are US artists' shorthand for the ex-president: a bulbous nose, jutting chin, a round face and so on. Clinton is also represented by Kal with his eyes firmly shut – a detail which is surely meant to evoke the President's irresponsible, reckless attitude to America's thrusting "new economy".

However, the president is soon brought down to earth with a bang and the transformation of his mount is as rapid as it is spectacular. In the next four elements of the cartoon, the hare morphs into a tortoise: his ears begin to droop and are gradually absorbed into a hard, bulky shell; his strong, muscular legs become ever more cumbersome and dumpy, while his back is seen to curve, bringing his proud head inexorably groundward. The surprise of the poor, dumbfounded hare is matched only by the disappointment of its poor, dumbfounded jockey. Clinton's eyes open and his confident smile turns into a sulking, angry grimace. In the fifth drawing, the artist shows Clinton facing forwards, as if he were searching for a solution to his country's economic slowdown, perhaps asking the readers for an explanation.

In the final frame, we can see that "Bubba" has found a solution – stuck atop a lumbering tortoise economy, he whips out his mobile phone and calls George W. Bush, graciously handing over the exhausted economy with an unconvincing "She's all yours!" The tortoise itself looks highly sceptical at this prospect, and the use of "DUBYA" serves to highlight this even further. Indeed, American satirists have coined the nickname "Dubya" (as in George Dubya Bush) with its overtones of "dumb" or "dumber" as an oblique reference to Bush's supposed lack of brainpower or intellectual finesse! Even the tortoise doesn't look as if it trusts Bush to kickstart the American economy out of a threatened recession. In fact the only glimmer of hope lies with the little gnome-like figure in the bottom right-hand corner of the cartoon. A glance at the inscription on the typical businessman's briefcase informs the reader that this unconvincing knight in shining armour is none other than Alan Greenspan, head of the Fed and a favourite of American political satirists. In other cartoons he is the unflappable cowboy on the back of a *bull (market, that is), or shown desperately trying to find preposterous gadgets to slow growth, like some sort of mad professor. In another Kal cartoon, Greenspan plays the laconic neighbourhood barber, whose whizzing electric shaver tries in vain to trim the exuberant head of hair belonging to a character symbolising the US economy.

Here the only solution a subdued Greenspan has found to America's economic *downturn is a proverbial carrot-on-a-stick, coupled with a feeble "Giddy up" addressed to a sceptical tortoise. The moral of the story is clear – the flagging economy as Clinton hands over the Presidency of the States to his successor is in pretty poor form.

# 19     Globalisation

*Guy Richard*

For better or worse, globalisation is here to stay. The Fall of the Wall was an apt symbol of the demise of the Old Order and it opened a breach through which financial markets and new technologies started rushing. Ever since, time and space have taken on a new significance. Likewise, a new militancy has emerged and it took to the streets of Seattle, Prague and Nice. Such an upsurge of civil society showing a distrust of all things political is a phenomenon politicians will have to reckon with. Concerned citizens seem to be pitted against money-grabbing multinationals and unaccountable international bodies like the WTO. Is this a portent or merely a sideshow?

Ever since the sixties, the world has become an increasingly fast-paced, complex "village" in which it is getting easier for people to travel and connect through high-tech means of communication. Therefore, is the world becoming a global community, or merely a huge market where goods and services can be exchanged with a click of a mouse? Are citizens now enjoying a golden age of shared wealth, prosperity and boundless opportunities? Not quite so. More and more critics now argue this is a *free-for-all in which the gap between the haves and the have-nots is far from narrowing. International bodies like the World Bank, the IMF or, more recently, the WTO are under the fire of a variety of groups. Seattle, Prague, Nice, Genoa and Gotheburgh are now associated with riots and violence. Why such an outcry? Is globalisation to be feared or praised? Can it be claimed such demonstrations are telltale manifestations of a current malaise with the world in which we are living?

## Anything new under the sun?

As a matter of fact, free trade is not something new. It was the basic doctrine championed by liberal British economists like Adam Smith and David Ricardo. In France, Montesquieu also extolled the virtues of free trade and even equated it with gentility.

There is no denying free trade boosts economic growth, creates jobs and fosters a higher standard of living. Equally unquestionable is the fact that economic prosperity has been achieved in the past fifty years by western economies, though the price may have been high in terms of pollution, exploitation and the waste of natural resources.

Globalisation might also be a boon for developing countries whose products can find new markets and which can benefit from transfers of technologies and investments, as witness Asia's "Tigers". A whole raft of measures is meant to *alleviate world poverty and promote growth through a lowering of trade barriers, more affordable imports and a freer flow of capital investments. These are noble intentions indeed, but it may be nothing but *wishful thinking, given that the gap between the "knows" and the "don't knows", in educational and technological terms seems to be all but unbridgeable. Thus, globalisation seems to be having mixed results (at least for the time being) and is crystallising all sorts of protests.

## Much ado about nothing?

Although it is now made up of 135 countries, the WTO is viewed essentially as a rich men's club dominated by the vested interests of developed countries. Such perceptions tend to cloud the issue, as the WTO is vilified as a bogeyman, responsible for all the evils the world is now being confronted with. Unions are up in arms against dumping and favour protectionist measures. They advocate a linkage between imports and labour standards or even imports and human rights, as was the case during the US-led talks between the WTO and China, while developing countries argue their low production costs (in which child labour undeniably plays a part) are their assets. For them, (over)regulating their labour standards would cut their economic edge. Besides, they claim such an issue should be debated in another international body, namely, the ILO (International Labour Organisation).

Environmentalists allege such a headlong pursuit of productivity and unrestrained industrialisation can only *hasten deforestation, overfishing, despoliation, climate changes and overall exploitation. However true this may be, it is somewhat hypocritical to deny developing countries the very opportunities generations of westerners have benefited from over the last fifty years. Therefore, fears raised in Seattle and Prague may be somewhat exaggerated, though there are worrying trends, all the more so as globalisation is often perceived as Americanisation.

## Down with American economic (and cultural) imperialism?

José Bové's *wrecking of a McDonald's outlet, megamergers, the worldwide dominance of CNN in the media or of Hollywood in the entertainment industry, epitomise a US-influenced global village. Politicians seem to be losing to the markets and the rise of the megacorporation may *toll the death knell of the sovereign nation-state. It is only natural that the man in the street should lose his bearings and wonder where an everchanging world is heading for.

In order to fight this overbearing dominance of the markets, Tony Blair's "Third Way" may have suggested a new approach after the Seattle fiasco. Britain's Prime Minister remarked:

"*Our conclusion could not be that open markets and free trade are wrong, but that we have to make a sincere effort to convince the world of their benefits.*"

New Labour has always been wary of "free market fundamentalism" and a dawning notion of "corporate social responsibility" (as opposed to shareholder return) should be injected into the new World Order. This may have happened at Davos 2000, the get-together of corporate leaders, economists and analysts. More recently, global warming, poverty and disease were on the Davos 2001 agenda. Do such concerns mirror a corporate change of mind… or heart? Still, such awareness cannot bear its fruit overnight and unrelenting pressure may have to be exerted by civil society (through boycott campaigns, for example).

The "Erika" *oilspill is ample proof such action will inevitably have to be taken. Besides, culture is no ordinary consumer good and the Hollywood *juggernaut in itself justifies France's demands for a "cultural exemption".

The problems raised in Seattle, Prague and Nice are undoubtedly burning topics and the unions' demand for a "social chapter" in the European construction can be viewed as a necessary safeguard to defend workers' interests. Actually, you cannot call for a border-free continent for capital and goods and deny workers the same type of framework. Negotiators in global trade talks have to see the writing on the wall.

Yet, were it not for the WTO, the situation might play into the hands of the "*bullies" (i.e. multinationals) at the expense of the underdogs, who would still be worse off. There are inevitably fouls during a soccer match and the referee is there to take action. Shooting the referee would mean far more fouls, definitely not fewer. However imperfect the referee (and the WTO) may be, they should be given a chance – and time – and the situation might play itself out, provided there are watchdog groups ready to *blow the whistle. This may be what the antiglobalisation crowds are good for.

# VOCABULARY

| | |
|---|---|
| abide by standards (to) | respecter des critères |
| alleviate (to)/ease (to) poverty | soulager la pauvreté |
| banana war | guerre de la banane (États-Unis contre Europe) |
| beef ban | l'interdiction de la viande de bœuf |
| belt-tightening policy | politique d'austérité |
| blow the whistle (to)/whistle-blower | dévoiler, révéler qqch. |
| bridge the gap (to) | réduire l'écart |
| bully/bully sb. into doing sth. (to) | brute ; obtenir qch. de qqn par intimidation |
| child labour | travail des enfants |
| cost-cutting measures | mesures d'austérité |
| cross-border cooperation | coopération transfrontalière |
| free-for-all | pagaille, mêlée générale |
| gadfly | « casse-pieds », « empêcheur de tourner en rond » |
| garb (in the) | sous couvert de |
| growth hormone | hormone de croissance |
| hamper (to) commerce | entraver le commerce |
| hasten (to) growth | accélérer la croissance |
| hostile take-over bid | OPA hostile |
| information highway | autoroute de l'information |
| juggernaut | mastodonte, rouleau compresseur (fig.) |
| know-how/expertise | savoir-faire |
| market share | part de marché |
| mergers and consolidations | fusions d'entreprises |
| NAFTA | ALENA (accord douanier entre les États-Unis, le Canada et le Mexique, 1990) |
| oilspill | marée noire |
| pension funds | fonds de pension |
| referee | arbitre |
| relocate (to)/relocation | délocaliser ; la délocalisation |
| retaliate (to)/ take retaliatory measures (to) | prendre des mesures de rétortion |
| see the writing on the wall (to) | savoir à quoi s'attendre |
| stiff/cut-throat competition | concurrence acharnée |
| stock market meltdown | effondrement des marchés boursiers |
| take a stake in (to) | prendre une participation dans |
| toll the death knell of sth. (to) | sonner le glas de qqch. |
| trade deficit | déficit commercial |
| wishful thinking | vœux pieux |
| wreck a building (to) | saccager un bâtiment |

# Focus...

◆ **It is a bumpy road to globalisation: a few landmarks**

| | |
|---|---|
| 1944 | The Bretton-Woods Conference: the monetary system was to be based on the gold/US dollar convertibility. The World Bank and the International Monetary Fund (IMF) were founded. |
| 1947 | The founding of GATT (General Agreement on Tariffs and Trade). |
| 1971 | President Nixon announces an end to the gold/dollar convertibility. |
| 1973 | The introduction of a "floating" currency system. |
| 1995 | GATT becomes the World Trade Organisation (WTO). |
| 1995 | Financial crisis in Mexico, which is bailed out by the US and the IMF. |
| 1997 | Financial meltdown in South-East Asia (Thailand, then Indonesia and South Korea) which prompted an IMF intervention. |
| 1998 | A financial meltdown in Russia, with IMF intervention. |
| Nov.1999 | The WTO summit in Seattle was disrupted by anti-globalisation crowds. |
| Feb.2000 | The Davos World Economic Forum (WEF): more disturbances. |
| Sept.2000 | The Prague summit: scuffles with the police. |
| Jan. 2001 | An anti-WEF alternative summit in Porto Alegre (Brazil), during the Davos Forum. |

◆ **The World Trade Organisation: arbiter or bogeyman?**
- Membership: 135 countries (with some 30 countries applying for membership).
- Its action: first limited to goods, and subsequently extended to include intellectual property rights and trade in services.
- Its mission: to enforce trade agreements and ensure an easier flow of goods and services.
- Its jurisdiction: the stakes are high in five different fields: agriculture, labour, environment, services, dumping.
- Its ultimate aim: to be committed to setting a global trade agenda, a long-term task.

◆ **The gadflies***

**Ralph Nader**: 66, a lawyer who first came to prominence in 1965 with his book "*Unsafe at any Speed*", an attack on car-manufacturers the result of which was to make safety belts mandatory. He turned from a consumer activist to a radical and denounced both G. W. Bush and Al Gore as "part of the same corporate party" during the 2000 US presidential election. He garnered 2% of the votes, taking on globalisation and multinationals and depicting the WTO as an unaccountable body which ignores labour and environmental standards. His aim is to set up a permanent progressive party.

**José Bové**: 46 (born in France, but raised in the US from age 1 to 7), a farmer radical who rose to fame in July 1999 for wrecking a McDonald's outlet in Millau. He used his incarceration as a soap-box for the causes he champions (the fight against "junk food", genetically-modified food, the WTO's power) and defends each country's right to preserve its own way of life and food, with protective tariff barriers if necessary.

**James Tobin**: a Nobel Prize for Economics winner, the champion of taxation on all cross-border capital transfers to deter stock speculation and short-term capital. A very popular proposal (especially among anti-globalisation groups like "ATTAC"), it has never been enforced and some critics argue it is more utopian than enforceable as it would mean (all but) impossible international cooperation, transparency and putting an end to "fiscal havens".

**A motley crowd of trade unionists, environmentalists, NGOs, right-wingers, anarchist fringers** who wreaked havoc in the streets of Seattle, Prague, and more recently, in Nice (Dec. 2000), Quebec City (April 2001), Gotheburgh (June 2001) and Genoa (July 2001).

Yet, reducing the activists' message to such violent street scenes would be an oversimplification.

# Essay 1

Comment on the following quotation, taken from *Newsweek* (27/12/1999 p.78):

"Paradox: some of the most outspoken critics of modern capitalism are themselves American." Michael Elliot

*Globalisation has been in the headlines for a few years and its effects are making themselves felt in many different fields. It seems there is no stopping it, all the more so as it is often associated with Americanisation. Reactions to world summits (Seattle, Prague, Nice) have often been violent and the WTO is under criticism for being an instrument of US domination. Now, it turns out "some of its most outspoken critics are themselves American". Is this really paradoxical? What are these protesters actually taking to the streets for?*

*It is true many American advocacy groups are vocal and want to have their say on at least three topics: labour rights, the environment and global capitalism. Trade unionists in declining industries (like steelworks) argue emerging countries practice dumping and that the rules are unfair. Production costs are also lowered by child labour and alleging these are unfair practices is understandable. Developing countries counter that such an argument smacks of protectionism (in the \*garb of morality) only meant to prevent them from exporting their own goods.*

*Pollution has been a growing concern for over a decade and guidelines set by the Rio summit in 1992 have not been met, including by the US. The Bush Administration has made it clear the US will not ratify the Kyoto Protocol about the emission of greenhouse gases and such an attitude may also look somewhat hypocritical as it means denying the Third World the opportunities western countries have profited from for over 200 years. For Americans, a factory south of the US-Mexican border means pollution whereas for Mexicans, it means jobs. Such conflicting views prompted former Mexican President E. Zedillo to accuse "ecowarriors" of "trying to protect the developing countries from development". Besides, economic growth in such a country would also alleviate the burden on the US in terms of illegal immigration.*

*However utopian and generous such US pressure groups may be, theirs may also be self-serving motivations. Another paradox lies in*

*the fact that globalisation makes antiglobalisation possible, given that protesters make ample use of new technologies (the Internet, faxes, mobile phones) and amenities (cheap fares on flights) to organise their own demonstrations. There is an upside to such gatherings though: the emergence of a new civil society, an awareness that might pressure business executives to make new technologies available to as many people as possible, through distance learning, the discovery of an AIDS vaccine, or a fairer, wider distribution of the dividends of economic growth. As globalisation cannot be rolled back, why not try to make the most of it? This can be achieved only through a combination of persuasion and pressure. It is time politicians took precedence over corporate leaders. This is a daunting long-haul task in which civil society will have to exert pressure, wherever people may live. This is a sphere in which, once again, Americans may set the trend and pave the way.*

# 20 Hollywood and the *entertainment industry

*Monique Chéron-Vaudrey*

Americans have made Hollywood their dream factory – and the rest of the world has followed suit.

Much of 20th century culture will be remembered worldwide through the films made in Hollywood, thanks to the talent of numerous filmmakers, and to the *business acumen of the film *moguls. Very early on, Hollywood's studios developed into a successful and powerful entertainment industry exporting its production abroad. Whenever it met major difficulties, the industry was flexible and inventive enough to find new ways to keep going. For the past fifty years, the European cinema has been trying to resist the *juggernaut of American films – with little success. It has even grown into a *bone of contention and initiated several protective drives among governments, such as the French "exception culturelle."

## The early beginnings

At the dawn of the 20th century, film-making started on the East Coast, in New York and New Jersey but soon moved to California. Southern California was a place of choice because of its sunny weather, its wide variety of landscapes, its cheap electricity and its large labor force.

The men who founded the American cinema were Eastern European Jews who had experienced *destitution and were naturally attracted by the movie industry because it was new, open to all, and did not require big investments. They showed their own talent at judging the public taste and analyzing the American *psyche, as only European-borns could do. Moreover their Jewish origin had *bestowed on them a sense of humor the like of which has been found nowhere else (it runs from the Marx Brothers to today's Woody Allen movies). They invented fast rhythm, *screwball scenarios, added a touch of European gloss and romanticism – all things which immediately enthralled Americans.

They were not just inventive – they knew how to develop a profitable business. In a matter of years, the giant studios were set up: Universal came first in 1912, followed by Metro-Goldwyn-Mayer, Twentieth Century-Fox, Warner Brothers. Success brought money and the first Hollywood stars could boast of *mind-boggling salaries. The star system was born and large audiences were set dreaming with tales of luxury and fantasy about the *denizens of *Tinseltown.

After WWI, in Europe, American films soon were in great demand. Already during the war, Washington had realized how powerful movies could be for propaganda purposes and had helped the industry penetrate foreign markets. The movie industry invaded the old continent with its products, set up its own network of subsidiaries

Civilisation américaine

and *thwarted all efforts by European filmmakers to build a competitive industry. Major European actors and *directors even chose to settle in Hollywood where the real thing was. The triumph of Nazism over part of Europe only led the process some steps further. Meanwhile, Congress granted tax breaks to ease the flow of capital into the studios. Hollywood already had the lion's share while European cinema was only coming to life.

## Hollywood and American values

In Puritan America the cinema was soon regarded as suspicious. A number of scandals affecting Hollywood stars in the early 20s prompted the studio moguls to take action and show they were tough on moral values. They asked Will H. Hays to lay down a code for scenarios as well as rules for the artists. Film directors were required to avoid long kisses, clergy in comic roles, attractive treatment of adultery, nudity and sympathy for crime. Not surprisingly, the values of patriotism, family-life, fidelity, respect for religion, truth-telling, hard work and optimism were highlighted.

Another onslaught on "immorality" was launched in 1933 by the Catholic-inspired Legion of Decency which saw moving pictures as "a grave menace to youth, to home life, to country and to religion." A year later, a cardinal asked for a total boycott of movies. The industry's revenues soon plummeted, both through the boycott and the hardships of the Depression. No wonder that studios subsequently submitted to new restrictions: the Production Code Administration set up in 1934 enforced strict rules for film content – they covered the same fields which had previously been defined by Hays but this time the Code was government-enforced. This censorship lasted for a period of 30 years.

When The US entered WWII, Hollywood worked hand in hand with Washington, pushing the idea that it was a "people's war," as the New Deal administration had put it. Many of the screenwriters who most readily went along with the new line happened to be Communists or their sympathizers. A decade later, in the McCarthy period, they were *blacklisted by the studios.

## The dream factory has forged a lasting culture

Most Hollywood productions quickly *fall into oblivion – if they are *released at all. But looking back on 100 years of cinema production, we are impressed by the variety and quality of American films. Hollywood invented the *slapstick comedy, the western, the musical, the "film noir," the horror film, and – like it or not – special effects. Among the classics, we can quote *Citizen Kane*, *Casablanca*, *Gone With the Wind*, *Annie Hall*, and, depending on one's tastes, *The Godfather*, *Star Wars*, *E.T.*, are sure winners as well.

Indeed American films reach for a worldwide audience but reflect American culture and ethics: they often emphasize the epic of the lonesome hero or the Rambo-like character – alone against all the baddies of the planet – and a lot of films use violence as a powerful magnet (sometimes as the main theme of a scenario). This is no doubt *unnerving for foreign audiences but unlikely to influence other cultures as it is sometimes said. Serious critics even argue that Hollywood reaches for the lowest common denominator of the audience, producing simple stories with a minimum of spoken words. There is some truth in this as recently the industry has been targeting younger audiences and has concentrated on a new type of film – which by no means reflects the rich variety of Hollywood productions.

### The *blockbuster syndrome

The new trend is to invest a lot of money in films likely to attract large audiences, to spend millions on the marketing and create a lot of *hype around the blockbuster. Such movies are made to feed theme parks, merchandising and licensing needs – movies that the audience will see two or three times. They target teenagers to 30-year-olds. They are expensive big-studio movies with equally expensive superstars. This recent move is an effort to boost profits as *box office returns have been steadily decreasing since the end of WWII and the advent of television.

### The film industry today

Blockbusters and *popcorn movies have spurred an *outcry about the *dumbing down of the country and the poor image of American culture given in such productions. In their love-hate relationship with Hollywood, many European *moviegoers insist that such movies are a threat to the Seventh Art. Well, the question is – is it art? Of course not. The cinema is an entertainment and the blockbuster a consumer product designed to meet the demands of large audiences. Today's Hollywood is not just about blockbusters anyway. *Producers like Coppola, Scorcese, Tarantino, the Coen brothers and Woody Allen keep the legend alive. And Spielberg or Lucas are talented people, not just *peddlers of low culture entertainment. But as *market forces prevail in today's entertainment industry, not just Hollywood, but also television and home videos are deeply affected by laws where culture and the public's interests are dismissed as insignificant (see p. 395-396).

### The Seventh art at risk?

The Seventh Art, as the French love to call the cinema, will no doubt survive – but the way quality things survive when they are not an easily marketable commodity. The future certainly looks gloomy for independent films in an industry where the box office reigns supreme. Yet Hollywood studios keep releasing high quality films that travel all over the world, just as European cinema survives with films that deserve praise while attracting large audiences – even in America. Lamenting over the low culture expressed in Hollywood productions will not change the industry's stance. As long as there is a market for it, it will keep catering for the public's wishes. The only question maybe is for Europe's film industry to work out sustainable competition with Hollywood, but so far, protectionism and state subsidies have been the most commonly used weapons to resist the pressure.

# VOCABULARY

| | |
|---:|:---|
| bark up the wrong tree (to) | se tromper d'adresse |
| bestow on (to) | conférer à |
| blacklist (to) | mettre sur liste noire |
| blockbuster | superproduction |
| bone of contention | pomme de discorde |
| box office return | recette au box-office |
| business acumen | sens des affaires |
| denizen | habitant |
| destitution | extrême pauvreté |
| director | metteur en scène |
| dumbing down | abêtissement |
| entertainment | divertissement |
| fall into oblivion (to) | tomber dans l'oubli |
| feature film | film long métrage |
| film buff | mordu de cinéma |
| glued to the tube | scotché à la télé |
| hype | battage publicitaire |
| juggernaut | mastodonte |
| market forces | loi du marché |
| mind-boggling | qui dépasse l'imagination |
| mogul | nabab du cinéma |
| moviegoer | amateur de cinéma |
| network TV | les grands réseaux nationaux de television (NBC, CBS, ABC) |
| onslaught | assaut |
| outcry | tollé |
| peddler | colporteur, marchand |
| popcorn movie | film grand public (de piètre qualité) |
| producer | producteur |
| psyche | psychisme |
| release a film (to) | faire paraître un film |
| screenwriter | scénariste |
| screwball | cinglé, tordu |
| series | feuilleton |
| silver screen | métaphore pour l'écran, la toile |
| slapstick comedy | grosse farce |
| state of the art | le dernier cri |
| thwart (to) | contrecarrer |
| Tinseltown | surnom de Hollywood, « la ville des paillettes » |
| tycoon | magnat |
| unnerving | déconcertant |

# Focus...

## ◆ A few landmarks

1902     The first purpose-built theater opens in Los Angeles.

1903     The first successful fictional narrative film, *The Great Train Robbery* (12 minutes) is released.

1911     The first studio opens in Hollywood.

1915     Universal City, the first Hollywood studio is built.
            *Birth of a Nation*, by D.W. Griffith, is the first great film produced in Hollywood.

1927     *The Jazz Singer* is the first talking movie.

1928     A new snack is introduced in a Chicago Theater, buttered popcorn.
            First Academy Awards.

1930     *The Big Trail* with John Wayne introduces wide-screen action.

1934     Opening of the first drive-in in Los Angeles.

1939     Invention of the multiplex.

1952     Introduction of the 3-D movie.

1974     First "Sensurround" film.

1975     Sony's Betamax, the first videocassette player, rolls onto the market.

1999     George Lucas' *Star Wars* Episode One is released in digital form.

## ◆ Some opinions on Hollywood and television

"We're a country of wishes and expectations, frozen into some idyll where all things are possible. The movies came as the perfect medium to sustain and expand this American condition. We are the country of movie stars because the stars, like ourselves represent a kind of extended infantilism, beauties waiting for the big chance."

Jerome Charyn

"We don't have the Medicis. Before a film is anything else and it may by accident turn out to be art – but before it's anything else, it's a product. It's paid for by businessmen who expect to get their money back, and if they don't, they won't keep putting up the money. American movies are the most popular movies everywhere, and it is true that the quality is far from uniformly terrific."

Sydney Pollack, interview published in the *International Herald Tribune*, November 16, 1999

"Movies are powerful – they steal up on you in the darkness of the cinema to inform or confirm social attitudes. They can help to create a healthy, informed, concerned, and inquisitive society or, alternatively, a negative, apathetic, ignorant one."

*Movies and Money*, by David Puttnam (Knopf – 1998)

◆ **Among many, two Hollywood figures**

### Steven Spielberg

Hollywood's most successful director and producer is in many regards a symbol of both Hollywood and American success stories. Born in 1946, he made his first film when he was eleven, using his father's home-movie camera; he barely graduated from high school, was rejected from UCLA's film school and only got a C in his television production course at California State University. He shot his first *feature film *Firelight* in 1964 (later remade as *Close Encounters of the Third Kind*). His first blockbuster and worldwide success *Jaws* was released in 1975. Then came other successes (*Raiders of the Lost Ark, E.T. the ExtraTerrestrial, Jurassic Park, Schindler's List, Saving Private Ryan*).

Spielberg excels at selecting the stories that will make good films, simple stories in the tradition of the folk tale, where man's goodness will eventually triumph over the forces of evil. He is a highly creative and imaginative figure, a master of special effects and battlefield scenes, and he is also an expert manager – a rare quality among Hollywood moguls. He launched his own company, Dreamworks, with two partners in 1994.

With the vast amounts of money he has amassed, Spielberg has recently turned to philanthropy. He has given money for Jewish culture and education and set up a foundation for ailing children in hospital wards.

### Spike Lee

At the other end of the Hollywood spectrum Spike Lee (born in 1957) stands as the black filmmaker who has had the greatest cultural and artistic impact. A man of many talents (as director, producer, author, actor and entrepreneur) he challenges stereotypes about race, class and gender identity and has probably opened new roads for black American voices to be heard. He became famous in 1989 with his third film, *Do the Right Thing*, a meditation on racial tensions. The making of *Malcolm X* in 1992 brought him international fame. Spike Lee has written several books, made music videos, commercials for the small screen and produced a documentary on the bombing of a Birmingham (Alabama) church which killed four black little girls in 1963. He has his own production and record company, called Forty Acres and a Mule.

# Essay

**Concours Ecricome 88 – LV1**

The cinema is an art form, an industry, a business and a source of entertainment. Which one(s) of those four aspects is/are in crisis? Justify your opinion with examples. 200 words or more.

*A lot of people complain about the crisis hitting cinema. Yet it seems to be alive and well! The point is that cinema is an entertainmant but sometimes it is also an art form; in addition, it is an industry – and a profitable business too. There may be some opposite forces from art to business which are the cause of this crisis.*

*The cinema was born as an entertainment and has remained so to this day. Indeed as films are meant to give an image of ourselves, the cinema soon developed into something more, telling us moving stories about men and women – it developed into an art form. Some classic films such as* La règle du jeu *by Jean Renoir are now on the curriculum in French lycées, just like novels by Balzac or Victor Hugo.*

*But it is a special kind of art form: it has to attract large audiences, because cinema is also an industry. Shooting a film requires a lot of technology, engineering, qualified workers and expensive movie stars. The money spent for a low-budget film is usually far beyond the money invested to run a medium-sized company.*

*Because the investment is so huge, it has to make a profit. No wonder cinema has now become a business as well as an art form. As such, films have to be consumer products – there is harsh competition to make use of \*state-of-the-art technology (special effects in particular), and to have the most popular movie-stars. Every film is launched with an advertizing campaign similar to that of a new car or a new cosmetic. Films have to meet the expectations of the mainstream. This is why cinema is not primarily an art form. Art cannot adapt to consumer demand!*

*The difficulty is to make both a box-office hit and a work of art.* Titanic *was a blockbuster and showed great craftsmanship but it could hardly claim to be a work of art – just good entertainment. But if we take the example of Luc Besson's* The Fifth Element, *there is no denying that it was not just a blockbuster, there was some artistic inspiration in it as well.*

*So, while the film industry is fast expanding, we can say that cinema is certainly one of the most popular forms of entertainment* *today, but definitely, the artistic dimension in film productions is limited to only a few exceptional movies. Those in Europe who argue that cinema is an art and nothing else are probably \*barking up the wrong tree. You can't prevent the film industry from seeking profit and making consumer products. The difficulty is to let talent find its way among dozens of popcorn movies. But talent is rare anyway. And such celebrities as Coppola, Scorcese, Fellini, etc. are proof that the film business does not always thwart talent.*

*To conclude, it is hard to say that the cinema is in crisis when we consider its place in our world, both from the economic point of view and the artistic one. Simply, the requirements of an industry are often in contradiction with the aspirations of the artist who wants to have his own way, regardless of the production cost and of the box office.*

# MORE ABOUT...
## ...TELEVISION

### THE ADVENT OF TELEVISION

Hollywood studios suffered a major blow after WWII when the success of television emptied movie theaters. But the industry soon took action and started producing TV programs, films and *series.

Meanwhile national TV *networks competed for large audiences and advertizing revenues. Programs catered to all tastes and all age groups – children being a prime target. Quality suffered in the process and TV commercials gradually took up an ever increasing share of viewing time.

Television was just the technology that many American people craved for: it fulfilled their desire for entertainment, for all forms of cheerfulness and for something appealing to the senses rather than to the mind. Moreover this entertainment was available in the comfort and privacy of the home. TV networks provided viewers with as much entertainment as possible.

By the early 60s, television had superseded newspapers as an information source. News became entertainment, too. Information was less a priority than sensation. Some major events reported live like President Kennedy's assassination and the historical Moon landing (or, more recently, the Gulf War) contributed to transforming news into something else, not far from the TV show.

### TODAY'S TELEVISION

Today, TV channels just give the public what they ask for. They make heavy use of celebrities as this is what attracts the largest audiences. Anybody will do – the ordinary citizen who hits the headlines for some reason will reach celebrity status, too. Criminals are a brand of celebrity in particularly great demand. So TV channels will fight over the interview of a serial killer. Another big hit is the reality show: it is based on the idea that the real world can be as fascinating as fiction; it has a voyeuristic lure with real-life characters exposing their personalities. But watching people's daily life is dull and boring, so game show elements are added, with participants accepting to "live" awkward situations. The prize for debasing oneself is indeed fame and there is no lack of candidates.

### TV VIEWERS AT RISK

The current concern is about sex and violence on television. It is not just sex films broadcast any time of day on cable-TV that worry parents (the Supreme Court recently upheld the right of TV channels to do so in the name of the First Amendment's right to free speech), it is also the constant sex talk in sitcoms or the violent or sexually explicit content of many films. Violence has appalling effects on children. On television, perpetrators of violent acts go unpunished three times out of four. Murder is seen as a normal way to solve a conflict and violence an acceptable means of expressing how one feels about a situation.

Now the reason why there is so much sex and violence is that people are watching. For some people, TV is like an addictive drug (America is the country of the couch potato who spends hours *glued to the tube eating pizzas and ice-creams) and TV programmers are the drug pushers. As the TV industry is driven by the market forces only, it is dominated by greedy and ruthless people who believe that the physical or psychological effects of TV on some parts of the population – in particular children or lesser-educated people, is none of their business. In this deregulated age, there is indeed no government intervention apart from the planned V-chip, a device to block transmission of violent programs, and TV ratings defining categories of audiences for TV programs (children, adults, all audiences, etc.).

## CONSUMER PROTEST

Surveys show that television has a major influence in developing value systems and shaping behavior. Medical experts say there are associations of heavy TV-viewing with obesity and negative psychological characteristics. The less experienced, the less educated, the more isolated are the main victims of today's television. For those TV viewers, life shown on television becomes more real than their own lives. Children are the most exposed as TV has often become a kind of electronic baby-sitter. When they reach adult age, many will have spent more time in front of the TV screen than at school or talking with their family and friends. Concerned parents have built associations giving advice on how to teach children to live away from the tube. Since 1994 an interest group has launched the "TV-Turn Off Week," scheduled in April.

## A POWERFUL MEDIA AND ENTERTAINMENT INDUSTRY

Hollywood studios and televion are no longer two separate worlds. In order to compete for the audience of the 6 billion inhabitants of the planet, the former studios have merged with other conglomerates to form just half-a-dozen global information and entertainment companies: News Corp. Time Warner, Walt Disney, Viacom, Sony, Vivendi-Universal. With their financial and industrial power, they are fighting on every level: films, broadcasting, cable and satellite, theme parks. The new competition is now on the Internet, and soon digital television.

Hollywood is still the powerhouse that feeds TV channels, develops the market of video cassettes and DVDs, provides new ideas for the merchandizing that follows every blockbuster.

Just a handful of conglomerates are now monitoring the films we see, the programs we watch, the entertainment our children enjoy, even the information we can have access to. The question is, what room will be left for free speech and creativity?

# 21 The Vietnam War and the American Psyche

*Guy Richard*

After its defeat at Dien Bien Phu, France had to recognize the independence of Indochina. Vietnam, Laos and Cambodia became independent with the signing of the Geneva Agreements, which called for elections which were to be held two years later. But the situation rapidly spun out of control: popular discontent prevailed in South Vietnam because of President Diem's corrupt, authoritarian regime which favoured *cronyism and the countryside was an ideal breeding ground for a guerrilla force which started organising a rebellion with the help of North Vietnam and its communist allies.

## The "American War"

In response to the domino theory, two Democratic Presidents (J.F. Kennedy and L.B. Johnson), first sent military "advisers" (16,000 by 1963) and the US found itself more and more *bogged down in the Vietnamese quagmire to check the progression of the Vietcong (also called "VC" or the "National Liberation Front": NLF). American involvement was to reach a peak of 536,000 troops in 1968.

The US military resorted to different strategies: economic aid to the country, pacification programmes, covert political intervention (to oust President Diem who was eventually overthrown and killed in Nov.1963) and heavy bombing campaigns in North Vietnam.

But it was of no avail, as insurgents could rely on a constant flow of new troops and equipment coming along the Ho Chi Minh trail. Besides, the enemy was very *elusive in a type of war US soldiers were not used to fighting. In addition, apart from a few elite troops, the capacity and willingness to fight of the ARVN (Army of the Republic of Vietnam) was always controversial.

## Deeper into the quagmire

On the home front, Americans increasingly questioned their Administration's decision to fight a "dirty little war", all the more so as it claimed more and more US lives. Non-violent marches and teach-ins were organised on many campuses across the US.

In Vietnam, the world's most powerful army, backed by the most sophisticated weaponry (fighter-bombers, helicopters, aircraft carriers, napalm and defoliants) did not seem to be able to quash the uprising of a ragtag bunch of guerrillas.

## The point of no return

1968 was to be a turning-point, from both a military and a psychological point of view. The Vietcong, who were said to have been contained, took advantage of the Tet holiday to mount a full-scale offensive which showed how efficient and coordinated the insurgents could be and Americans were shell-shocked. The *death toll kept rising and each new funeral in the remotest part of the US proved the futility of the war effort.

Vietnam actually caused Johnson's downfall. He had pledged he would not run for President in 1968 and the Republican candidate, Richard Nixon, announced he had "a secret plan" to end the war. When he was elected in Nov. 1968, there were 536,000 US troops in Vietnam.

### Nixon's "secret plan"

According to Nixon, the key to victory in Vietnam was a deeper involvement of the Vietnamese themselves in their own conflict, that is why he advocated a "vietnamization policy" whose direct consequence was a gradual *withdrawal of US troops.

When Nixon was reelected in Nov.1968, US troops in Vietnam had dropped to 24,200.

Peace talks, which had been *under way in Paris since 1968, reached an agreement and a ceasefire was proclaimed in 1973. The Nobel Peace Prize award to Henry Kissinger and his North Vietnamese counterpart, Le Duc Tho (who refused it), may have been premature since North Vietnamese troops were to come sweeping down to Saigon two years later. Congress refused President Ford's request for emergency aid to the South Vietnamese.

### The final days and after...

The picture of the last Americans leaving from the roof of the US embassy by helicopter was to remain engraved in the American psyche. Moreover, 135,000 South Vietnamese were eventually admitted into the US after the fall of Saigon (cf. chapter on "A Nation of Immigrants", p. 275). An idealistic commitment had turned into a nightmare and the Americans realised they had been cheated into a "bright shining lie". The US had suffered a military setback, the first ever, and American foreign policy would keep a low profile in the next decade. (cf. chapter on "The US as Global Policeman", p. 415).

Paradoxically, it was the Gulf War (1991) which brought into sharp focus the Vietnam Veterans' (Vietvets') plight. GIs who had taken part in "Operation Desert Storm" were given a hero's welcome in *ticker tape parades. Americans were eager to express their gratitude since Saddam Hussein's annexation of Kuwait had been checked thanks to American might. Such a welcome had always been denied Vietvets who were often scorned, put to shame and dubbed "baby killers" when they came back home. Many had to be hospitalised because they suffered from Post Traumatic Syndrome (PTS) and found it hard to adjust to civilian life, inasmuch as their sacrifice was never acknowledged or *belatedly so, since they were given a parade in the streets of New York in ... March 1985, twelve years after the last GI had left Vietnam.

Movies had dealt with the war but, because of the ambivalence of the conflict, Hollywood had never regarded it as a money-getter (unlike World War II and its many movies set both in Europe and in the Pacific) and, apart from *The*

*Green Berets*, starring John Wayne in 1968, no Vietnam movie could draw any clear line between the "goodies" and the "baddies" and they all highlighted the fighting man's confusion, fears and dilemma.

The dedication of the Vietnam Veterans Memorial (cf. chapter on "Sites of Memory", p. 405) marked the emotional climax of a *cathartic process, when a nation could at long last come to terms with its past. This *long-overdue recognition was a concrete symbol of reconciliation, but it had been a purely private initiative and President Reagan did not attend the *dedication ceremony.

### The unfinished war

Vietnam has kept cropping up in the American psyche, as exemplified by the plight of the Vietnamese "boat people" in the 1980s, whom the American Administration was more and more reluctant to admit, as it considered theirs was an economic motivation.

John McCain's 2000 campaign was partly based on his *POW experience. Although his qualities of personal integrity are unquestionable, would he have been so popular during the Republican primaries if he had not been a war hero too? He spent five and a half years in North Vietnamese jails after his plane had been *shot down over Hanoi.

### An open wound: the *Missing-in-Action (MIAs)

About 2,400 US soldiers are still reported missing in Vietnam and some claim they may still be held captive in Vietnam, China or Far East Russia. This is a hope many families still cling to. Investigations have been carried out (with the help of Vietnamese authorities) for twenty years and have produced very little evidence, apart from a few remains which were repatriated. Some Hollywood movies, starring Sylvester Stallone or Chuck Norris, capitalized on such an emotional theme. Thus, some veteran groups still keep the flame alive and the memory of Vietnam will not die.

### Echoes of the war

The embargo on Vietnam, one of the world's poorest countries with a $400 annual per capita income, was not lifted until 1994. Diplomatic relations were resumed in 1995.

One of President Clinton's last political acts was his visit to Vietnam in mid-November 2000. A Democratic President may have written the final chapter of an emotion-filled saga started by another Democratic President almost forty years ago. Even though no apologies were made for US involvement, President Clinton acknowledged the "staggering sacrifice" of the Vietnamese.

He also handed over 350,000 documents on MIAs, hoping the gesture would fuel a new search for remains of *downed pilots. "The past may still haunt, but it does not have to divide", he declared. He added: "once we met as adversaries, to-day we work as partners". As a matter of fact, Nike is Vietnam's biggest private employer…

# Vocabulary

| | |
|---|---|
| anti-war movement | mouvement d'opposition à la guerre |
| back a regime (to) | soutenir un régime |
| be called up (to be)/drafted/the draft | être incorporé ; la conscription |
| belated/ adv.belatedly | tardif, qui arrive en retard ; tardivement |
| body bag | sac servant à transporter les morts |
| body count | bilan des pertes |
| bogged down (to get) | s'enliser |
| bomb to rubble (to) | réduire à l'état de ruines |
| catharsis/cathartic process | catharsis ; processus de catharsis |
| cronyism | « copinage » |
| death toll | pertes en vies humaines |
| dedicate a monument (to) | inaugurer un monument |
| dodge (to)/evade the draft (to)/ | être insoumis ; l'insoumission |
| draft dodger/evader | insoumis |
| elusive enemy | ennemi qui se dérobe |
| escalate a war (to) | pratiquer l'escalade (lors d'un conflit) |
| escalation | escalade |
| fight a losing battle (to) | mener un combat perdu d'avance |
| flee (fled/fled) a country (to)/n. flight | fuir un pays ; la fuite |
| grunt | fantassin |
| given one's due (to be) | recevoir son dû |
| heal (to)/healing process | guérir ; le processus de guérison |
| impose (to)/lift an embargo (to) | imposer ; lever un embargo |
| long overdue (to be)/long-overdue recognition | que l'on n'a que trop attendu |
| MIA (Missing-In-Action) | disparu (au combat) |
| POW (Prisoner Of War) | prisonnier de guerre |
| powers that be (the) | autorités (en place) |
| pull out (to)/withdraw troops (to) | retirer des troupes |
| puppet regime | régime fantoche |
| reported missing (to be)/unaccounted for | être porté disparu |
| resume relations (to)/resumption | rétablir des relations ; le rétablissement |
| shoot down (to)/down a plane (to) | abattre ; « descendre » un avion |
| storm (to)/take over (to) | prendre d'assaut ; s'emparer du pouvoir |
| swamp | marais, marécage |
| sweep/sweep across a country (to) | offensive ; s'emparer d'un pays |
| ticker tape parade | retour triomphal (sous une pluie de serpentins) |
| trauma/adj. traumatic/ vb. traumatize (to) | traumatisme ; traumatisant ; traumatiser |
| under way (to be) (for talks, a process) | être en cours (négociations, processus) |
| withdrawal/pullout/pullback | retrait |

# Focus...

## ◆ The Domino Theory

"If someone sets up a row of dominoes and knocks over the first one, it is certain that the last one will go over very quickly. It would be the beginning of a disintegration that would have the most profound consequences."

President Eisenhower, 1954

Such an argument was to be taken up by President Johnson in 1965 to justify an American intervention in Vietnam:

"We are there because we have a promise to keep... We are also there to strengthen world order... We are also there because there are great stakes in the balance...To withdraw from one battlefield means only to prepare for the next."

## ◆ A turning-point: the Tet Offensive (January 1968)

On the eve of Tet, the Vietnamese New Year, the Vietcong launched an all-out, coordinated attack on Vietnam's major cities and VC commandos went as far as the American Embassy compound. Although it was a defeat for the Vietcong, the onslaught had a traumatic impact on American public opinion. It took South Vietnamese and US troops weeks to repel the communist forces and there was fierce fighting, especially in Hue (cf. Stanley Kubrick's *Full Metal Jacket*). It showed the insurgents, helped by North Vietnamese regulars, were far from being subdued, in spite of the American Command's optimistic picture.

## ◆ Vietnam as a divisive issue

- A slogan, written on a GI's helmet: "the Unwilling led by the Unqualified fighting the Unnecessary for the Ungrateful".
- General Le May, on bombing North Vietnam: "We'll bomb them back to the Stone Age".
- A more qualified assessment, by Neil Sheehan, an American journalist, in October 1966:

"Americans, because they are Americans, arrive in Vietnam full of enthusiasm and with the best of intentions. After a prolonged period of residence, they leave with their enthusiasm a victim of the cynicism that pervades Vietnamese life and their good intentions lost somewhere in a paddy field."

### ◆ The human toll

|                   | The US  | South Vietnam                     |
|-------------------|---------|-----------------------------------|
| Dead              | 58,000  | 254,000                           |
| Missing in action | 2,400   | unavailable                       |
| Wounded           | 303,700 | 783,000                           |
| Civilian casualties | --    | 430,000 dead and 1,000,000 wounded |

1,027,100 North Vietnamese and Vietcong dead, no data available for their number of wounded.

### ◆ Escalation

Number of US troops in Vietnam:

1961:   3,200        1969:   475,200
1965:   184,300      1970:   334,600
1967:   485,600      1971:   156,800
1968:   535,100      1972:   24,200

Tons of bombs dropped on Vietnam, Laos and Cambodia.
Under Johnson's presidency:   2.9 million tons.
Under Nixon's presidency:     4.2 million tons.

### ◆ A few more data

Some 2.9 million Americans went to Vietnam for a one-year tour. Out of the roughly 303,000 wounded, 100,000 came back with severe physical disabilities (cf. *Born on the Fourth of July* – Oliver Stone, 1990).

50,000 may have been affected by the cancer-causing herbicide "Agent Orange". Many still suffer from PTS (Post Traumatic Syndrome).

### ◆ The war that will not die

In 1985, a 20-volume history distributed by TIME/LIFE and entitled *The Vietnam Experience* was originally printed to sell about 120,000. It was soon out of print and was to sell four times as many.

# Essay

## The Aftermath Of The War

In its May 1985 issue, *National Geographic* published an article about the Vietnam War entitled "To Heal a Nation". The author described the emotional appeal of the Wall:

"Reflecting faces, the polished granite draws beholders into a special union with loved ones. From the day of dedication, visitors have reached out to touch the names they know or made a rubbing of a friend's name to take back home as a memory".

Has the wound actually healed, or is it here to stay? Give examples.

*The Vietnam war came to an end some 25 years ago but the healing process is far from over.*

*Among the crowds waiting to draw nearer the chevron-shaped wall are Vietvets who scrutinize a specific granite panel. They seem to be staring at the wall, in search of some friend's name, someone they may have fought with, or a friend of theirs who was reported missing. Their right hand is often leaning on the wall so that they have both physical and visual contact with the wall. Furthermore, their reflection can be seen on the granite wall itself and many of them are dressed in their battle fatigues and have a bush hat on, the sort of clothes they would have worn back in Vietnam. The whole scene conveys an impression of grief, remembrance and emotion and is the very symbol of how the past can still influence the present.*

*More than 58,000 US soldiers died in Vietnam and about 2,400 were unaccounted for. No-one has heard from them ever since. They must have died, but many families still cling to the faint hope some may still be alive in some remote POW camp. Spontaneously, many relatives and friends leave behind personal offerings and memorabilia which are collected for storage by the National Park rangers in charge of the site. Others come to reminisce or get information from the "American Foundation for Accountability of POW- MIA" stall, whose flag is displayed for all to see. It is a simple banner indeed, made up of the profile of a man with his head bowed. He really looks despondent as no-one seems to care for him anymore. A watch-tower with a guard and some barbed wire can be seen in the background. This foundation is still lobbying politicians to pressure*

*Vietnamese authorities. But isn't it a lost cause? Why would the Vietnamese keep prisoners for so long? Wouldn't they have used them as bargaining chips in talks over the resumption of diplomatic relations, the lifting of the embargo, or simply to boost their image on the international scene?*

*Many MIA families still do not want to accept their relatives' fate, others regularly come to the wall to pay tribute to their dead. Both attitudes show that, in spite of some definite improvement in the relations between the US and Vietnam in the past ten years, and of the belated recognition Vietvets were eventually given, the wound of Vietnam is here to stay and may only heal for those who went there once their generation gets older. But the soldier's average age in Vietnam was 19... Younger generations may find it easier to forget, Vietvets will not.*

# 22 Sites of Memory

*Guy Richard*

Does history repeat itself? Does studying one's country's important dates and places lead to a better understanding of today's events? These are questions every responsible citizen can reflect on, wherever he may live. The answer is quite obvious for Europeans since they live in countries with a centuries-old history. Cathedrals, castles, war memorials, D-Day beaches in Normandy, dot a history-rich continent. Europe is steeped in history, some may even argue it is sometimes overburdened with it, but these landmarks are sites of memory visited by thousands of tourists every year.

Unlike the Old World, the US has never been invaded or occupied and seems to be free of the burden of History. Yet, Americans do have places which *remind them of their past, which they visit in order to take stock of their roots or reassess their country's history. Each place is unique and performs a specific function. One of them, Wounded Knee, *reminds them of the injustices visited upon Native-Americans, while the Statue of Liberty and Ellis Island *encapsulate a dream to which millions of immigrants have responded for decades. Another one pays tribute to the dead and veterans of a conflict whose echo still reverberates in the US today: the Vietnam War. But, beyond such diversity, the American way of coming to terms with the past may have some specific characteristics worth studying in its historical context.

### Wounded Knee

Location: a tiny hamlet (pop. 40) on Pine Ridge Reservation, South Dakota.

Importance: the site of one of history's most infamous massacres that put an end to "Indian Wars" and resistance. Roughly 300 Indians, mostly old men, women and children were shot dead.

Time: December 1890, at the time when the Frontier was coming to an end for different reasons.

Pioneers had pushed westwards for more than two centuries and had settled on the Frontier, the imaginary line that separated settled territories from virgin lands on which many Indian tribes roamed. There was a minor push eastwards starting from California too. The Gold Rush in 1848 and the completion of the first transcontinental railroad in 1869 had also contributed to driving Native-Americans west.

They were in a critical situation by 1890 since they were landless and had nowhere to go but reservations, a humiliating predicament for proud people used to being free.

- the Sioux chief, Sitting Bull, had been arrested and killed two weeks earlier;
- there were fewer and fewer buffaloes, which were the key to their economy. Buffaloes were *slaughtered indiscriminately by white hunters (cf. Bill Cody, nicknamed "Buffalo Bill") whereas Native-Americans would kill them one by one to preserve Mother Earth's legacy;
- they were starving, all the more so as weather conditions are very hard in winter in South Dakota.

What happened: There was a revival of the Ghost Dance, which Indians alleged would make them invincible. Such a phenomenon caused the Whites to worry for they regarded it as a call to arms and a harbinger of things to come: open rebellion. They then decided to disarm the Indians, which was a humiliating situation. It meant the Indians could not be trusted. There was a misunderstanding during the search for weapons in the camp and the Whites thought they were being shot at. All hell broke loose and when the smoke cleared, about 300 Indians were lying dead, mown down by the cavalry's machine-guns. The wounded were carted to a church nearby. As it was a few days after Christmas, some garlands were still hanging overhead reading: "Peace on earth, good will to men". History can sometimes be hard on the losers...

This massacre was to mark the end of Indian resistance and Native-Americans would not become US citizens until 1924. They could not make themselves heard and could only stage symbolic demonstrations.

In 1969, they occupied Alcatraz Island (in San Francisco Bay), issued the "Alcatraz Manifesto" in which they denounced their exploitation, past and present.

In 1973, a group of roughly 200 Indians of different tribes occupied Wounded Knee as a reminder of the 1890 massacre. They issued a statement in which they declared "the Red Giant is on one knee, but he is ready to stand up". They were eventually overwhelmed by US marshals.

There is no memorial at Wounded Knee, nothing but a plain sign reminding visitors of this sorry episode. The US does not seem to have come to terms with this grim chapter of its settlement and Native-Americans do not have the political clout to lobby for a formal recognition of past grievances.

### The Statue of Liberty

Location: In New York harbour, one mile from Ellis Island.

Nicknames: "Lady Liberty", "Mother of Exiles".

1865: A group of French patriots decided to give a monument to the American people as a token of friendship on the occasion of the coming centennial of the Independence of the US. Bartholdi, the famous French sculptor, volunteered with a project. For him, there were political undertones as well since the allegory of Liberty would also contrast with Louis Napoleon Bonaparte's authoritarian regime.

It was to be erected with private funds and would be fraught with symbols:
- she has just broken the shackles of slavery, still lying at her feet;
- she rises up, flourishing a lighted torch in her right hand to "enlighten" the world;
- she takes a step forward;
- she is wearing a crown with seven spikes;
- she holds a book in her left hand. A date (July IV, MDCCLXXVI), ie. the Declaration of Independence, is inscribed on its front page.

1886: The statue was dedicated by President Cleveland. A few months earlier, money had been raised by Joseph Pulitzer, the famous journalist, to have a pedestal built. Public contributions poured in.

1903: Emma Lazarus's famous sonnet, first published in 1883, was placed on a plaque inside the pedestal as a tribute to her. It eventually came to be associated (in the mainstream of American consciousness) with immigration, a somewhat ironical twist of History at a time when authorities were trying to close the "Golden Door".

*"Give me your tired, your poor,*

*Your huddled masses yearning to breathe free,*

*The wretched refuse of your teeming shores,*

*Send these, the homeless, the tempest-tossed to me,*

*I lift my lamp beside the Golden Door."*

In the early 1980s: a quarter-billion dollars was needed for the restoration of Lady Liberty.

A $70 million amount was raised by the Statue-of-Liberty/Ellis Island Foundation, a charitable corporation chaired by Lee Iacocca, the then CEO (Chief Executive Officer) of Chrysler.

1986: Lady Liberty, in full regalia, was dedicated by President R.Reagan.

### Ellis Island

Location: In New York harbour, one and a half miles off the lower tip of Manhattan.

Nicknames: America's Gate, Island of Tears (be it in English, French, German or Italian).

1815-1860: 6 million immigrants arrived in the US and the Administration decided to build a processing centre on the Battery (i.e. the southern tip of Manhattan): Castle Garden.

1855: Castle Garden was opened and 70% of immigrants were screened there.

In the 1880s: A xenophobic movement against immigration developed and the US Congress responded with a few restrictive measures, including…

1882: The Chinese Exclusion Act, which was to be passed again in 1892 and 1902.

1892: Castle Garden was closed and replaced by Ellis Island. The first structure was destroyed by fire in 1897 and a brick beaux arts building was erected.

1900: Inauguration of the new structure which was designed to process half a million arrivals a year.

1903: New restrictive measures were taken against anarchists, prostitutes and epileptics who were barred from entering the US.

1907: The peak year for immigration with 1.2 million entrants.

1921&1924: Two sets of Immigration Acts (commonly referred to as "the quota laws") were passed in Congress to curb immigration. They especially targeted Latin immigrants from the Mediterranean Basin.

1954: Ellis Island was closed and buildings fell to decay, vandals and pigeons.

Sept. 1990: After a 7-year, $160 million restoration program, under the auspices of the Statue-of-Liberty/Ellis-Island Foundation and with the co-operation of the National Park Service in charge of the site, the refurbished Main Building was opened to the public, complete with a "Wall of Honour" to pay tribute to the thousands of families who helped to build America (cf. document, p.416).

The architects wanted to bring the immigrants' pain and heartbreaking experience back to life, to have "a monument to the masses". The great Registry Room, where so many fates were sealed, was restored painstakingly to its original bareness where "a babble of incomprehensible tongues rose to the ceiling". The crowd and noise must have been dizzying, officials would just "bring the cattle in and ship them out, it was impersonal".

It is meant to be a gripping place dedicated to all those who tried their luck in the New World and for whom the stakes were high. Restorers would like visitors "to muse on what the place was like", where immigrants were ushered into America whose gate often took the shape of a small metal wicket: immigrants' dreams bumped against reality and bureaucracy. The medical and legal tests filled them with awe, the "staircase of separation" was where families sometimes had to part.

Ellis, once a gate to America, now opens onto the past, an island is being redeemed.

### *The Vietnam Veterans Memorial*

Between 1959 and 1975, the US got more and more deeply involved in South East Asia and eventually had to pull out of the Vietnamese quagmire. The "Vietnam syndrome" was a traumatic experience which the US was to live with for more than three decades since it also reverberated across the 1980s and shaped a whole generation. To some extent, it can be alleged the

Vietnam experience is still in its healing process and some of the scars of this conflict which divided the nation can still be felt nowadays (cf. chapter on "the Vietnam War and the American Psyche", p.397)

Indeed, it was the first armed conflict American forces did not win.

1980: Three Vietnam Veterans ("Vietvets") came up with the idea of a memorial which would serve different purposes. It was meant:

- to speed up the cathartic process;
- to enable veterans to pay each other the tribute denied to them elsewhere;
- to feel and display grief and gratitude to those who sacrificed their lives;
- to relieve some of the guilt of survival.

From the outset, the idea set off a controversy. Some critics did not see why a memorial should be dedicated to losers. But the three veterans went ahead and created the Vietnam Veterans Memorial Fund. They would not ask for government money, but for land. Besides, they wanted the plot of land they would be allotted to be highly symbolic.

April 1980: After much lobbying, the bill was voted unanimously in the Senate. Two acres were to be given to the Fund, which eventually managed to raise $9 million from the American people.

July 1981: President Carter signed the bill into law. The memorial would be built on Washington's Mall, "America's myth-yard", a place emblematic of the watershed events in American History. It was to be set near the Lincoln Memorial, another potent landmark.

A competition was launched for the design of the memorial and it was won by Maya Lin, a 20-year old Asian-American, born in the USA who had never seen war. It was only a coincidence (or an ironical turn of history?), since the entries were anonymous. She had designed a monument which, unlike war memorials which generally rise out of the ground, would cut into the earth, a chevron-shaped wall, almost 250 feet long, which would look like a wound. Some critics denounced it as "a black *gash of shame", claiming it was unheroic, below ground and death-oriented. Its black granite panels on which the names of the 58,000 Americans, killed in action or unaccounted for, would be etched, would reflect visitors, thus establishing a link between the dead and the living, it would "look back to death and forward to life".

It was placed in a symbolic embrace of the past so that one end reaches out to Washington's Monument and the other to the Lincoln Memorial. The first names appear in the centre of the monument, on the east end of the wall, below "1959", the year of the first American casualties in Vietnam, and descend along each panel to the narrow end of the wall. They begin again at the narrow end of the west wall, descending again until they reach the centre of the monument and end with the date "1975" on the panel adjacent to the one bearing "1959", thus closing the *traumatic cycle.

As could be expected, it was deemed too bare a monument and the necessary construction permit was first denied. A solution was found in the form of a heroic-sized group of bronze statues which was to be placed in front of the memorial. The "three fightingmen" (one black, one Hispanic and one white) seem to be searching for their own names or those of some friends on the wall.

The Vietnam Veterans Memorial was dedicated on Nov. 13, 1982 (i.e. on Veterans Day) and the 58,000 names were read aloud in Washington's National Cathedral during a vigil. It was an emotional event which lasted 56 hours.

Since its dedication, the Vietnam Veterans Memorial has been a meeting place for veterans or families who lost a son, a brother, a father or a boyfriend. Their names, listed in chronological order of death, year after year, the reflectiveness of the granite panels and the combination of grief, compassion and pathos make the place one fraught with heart-felt emotion. In spite of the heated debate it caused, it is gradually achieving an act of national reconciliation.

Do these five landmarks, dedicated to various groups of people who have shaped America since the turn of the century, share any common features?

First, the American Administration does not seem to have played any significant role in the decision to have them erected. Private foundations (in the case of the Statue of Liberty and Ellis Island) took the initiative and worked jointly with the federal department in charge of the site. A determined group of citizens can also talk a few politicians into action and lobby the US government into giving flesh to an abstract idea, even a controversial one. The campaign, spearheaded by a few Vietnam veterans, climaxed with the completion of their memorial, a project the Federal Government stepped in only to give a plot of land on the Mall.

No monument marks the site of the Indians' last stand at Wounded Knee. There is nothing but a plain sign bearing the story of the episode and the word "battle" is often spray-painted by an anonymous hand and replaced by "massacre", a more fitting word. Indeed, Native-Americans find it hard to voice their grievances for several reasons. There is no Indian lobby, no Indian Senator or Congressman in Washington DC and such a lack of political representation is detrimental to the advancement of their cause.

If such monuments somehow contribute to the healing process of history's wounds, the plight of Native-Americans has often been swept under the carpet and there is still plenty of guilt and denial around. As long as the Whites have not come to terms with that grim chapter of their settlement, no healing is likely to begin.

There is also an emotional dimension to all these landmarks: not only do visitors want to see, but they also want to touch and empathise. This is a yearning on which designers play, especially with Ellis Island's Wall of Honour and at the Vietnam Veterans Memorial with the names of the fallen GIs etched in granite panels. It is as if such an approach made history, generally an abstract notion, more concrete and understandable. A person's name is something unique and the ultimate link between past and present. Having thousands of families' names inscribed at Ellis Island or gritblasted on the Veterans Memorial is a means to materialise the generations of people who built America or sacrificed their lives when called up. Visitors to the Vietnam Veterans Memorial reach out to touch a name they know, they can make a rubbing of it which they take back home. The power of a familiar name turns the memorial into a place to mourn and to reflect. Many even leave behind personal offerings such as wreaths, war medals, photographs of the loved ones, or even toys. Such an emotional element can also be found in British or Commonwealth memorials of the Great War, in Flanders fields for instance.

These American sites are places where people are remembered, honoured, mourned, where History can be revisited graphically. They *encapsulate the American experience, both in its glory and its less reputable aspects. Through the emotion they convey, they are emblematic of the ambivalence of many human endeavours. They are eventually the milestones a nation needs to come to terms with its past and to look ahead.

# Vocabulary

| | |
|---|---|
| aftermath (of the war) | suites (de la guerre) |
| assess (to), reassess (to) | évaluer, réévaluer |
| bone of contention | pomme de discorde |
| controversial, contentious | controversé |
| display (to) | exposer |
| disputable, questionable, debatable | contestable, discutable |
| dispute, question a fact (to) | contester un fait |
| encapsulate (to) | résumer, symboliser |
| epitomise sth (to) | incarner, être le parfait exemple de qch. |
| fight a losing battle (to) | livrer un combat perdu d'avance |
| fulfil an ambition (to) | réaliser une ambition |
| gash | coupure, entaille |
| heal (to)/healing process | guérir ; un processus de guérison |
| icon (adj. iconic) | symbole |
| in the wake of | au lendemain, à la suite de |
| item, artifact, artefact | objet (exposé) |
| landmark | monument célèbre |
| milestone | événement marquant |
| lobby/lobby sb. (to) | groupe de pression ; faire pression sur qqn |
| make a dream come true (to) | réaliser un rêve |
| overwhelmed with grief (to be) | être au comble de la douleur |
| POW = Prisoner of war | prisonnier de guerre |
| raise funds (to) | collecter des fonds |
| remind sb. of sth. (to) | rappeler qch. à qqn |
| scar | cicatrice |
| shed, cast light on sth (to) | faire la lumière sur qch. |
| slaughter, massacre/slaughter (to), massacre (to) | massacre ; massacrer |
| soul-searching | examen de conscience |
| sponger | parasite |
| stage (to)/mount (to) an exhibition/exhibit (to) | organiser une exposition |
| stem, curb immigration (to) | limiter, freiner l'immigration |
| stir, ignite, set off, spark a controversy (to) | déclencher une polémique |
| thorny, delicate, sensitive, touchy issue | question épineuse, délicate, sensible |
| trauma/traumatic/traumatise (to) | traumatisme ; traumatisant ; traumatiser |
| wound/wound (to) | blessure ; blesser |

# Essay

**Comment on the document and show how relevant to the American Experience such an approach is.**

> Back in the early 1990s, visitors to the newly-refurbished Ellis Island Museum were given a leaflet about the "Wall of Honor" which read:
>
> **IF YOU DON'T KEEP THEIR NAMES ALIVE, WHO WILL?**
>
> An invitation to place the name of a member of your family who immigrated to America in the only national museum created to honor them.
>
> Whether your ancestor first set foot on American soil at Ellis Island or entered through another gateway, here is a unique opportunity to show your gratitude. And to present your family with a gift that will be meaningful now and for generations to come.
>
> When you make a $100 tax-deductible contribution to restore Ellis Island, the name you designate will be permanently placed on the newly-created American Immigrant Wall of Honor.
>
> By acting now you ensure that the Ellis Island Immigration Museum will be a place to honor your own heritage, as well as a monument to the great American traditions of freedom, hope and opportunity.
>
> Keep the Dream Alive.
>
> Write to: Ellis Island Foundation
>
> P.O. Box ELLIS, New York, Y.10163.

*This document is a leaflet handed to visitors at Ellis Island. It must have been a remembrance of things past to many American tourists whose ancestors one day had decided to leave their forefathers' lands for a destination they did not know anything about, an adventure filled with incalculable uncertainty of overpowering proportions.*

*Indeed, this is a sort of appeal to readers made through these immigrants, across generations. The document focuses on the notion of memories which have to be handed from one generation to the next, as a kind of historical legacy. This is a device which must be very effective with Americans, as many of them have ancestors who emigrated to the US, so they should all feel concerned and respond to this appeal. They are requested to send a one hundred dollar cheque to have the name of their family placed on the "wall of honour". Why such a wall?*

*Contrary to what some critics of immigration currently allege, immigrants did contribute to the making, wealth and diversity of the U.S, although they may sometimes have been regarded as burdens or* *spongers who strained social services. These people had to overcome a lot of difficulties in order to come to the U.S; it must have taken them courage to leave everything behind. That is why the US can show them "gratitude" and "honour" them.

In a way, they responded to the American tradition of "freedom, hope and opportunity", which may be a reference to the promise of "life, liberty and the pursuit of happiness" enshrined in the Declaration of Independence. Therefore their names and endeavours must not fall into oblivion.

The final word – Dream – is an important eye-catching device too. Indeed, readers are expected to "keep the [American] Dream alive" and "every name etched on the wall will be a reminder of past sacrifices and hopes". But the Dream should not become a myth and "will be meaningful now and for the generations to come", which means would-be immigrants who now want their dream of a new life in the US to come true should not be denied the opportunity the people referred to in the leaflet were given.

Families' names thus become a bridge between past and present and demonstrate that honouring one's country's heritage also contributes to building the future.

# 23     The US as Global Policeman

*Guy Richard*

## From the early 17th century to the turn of the 19th century: Keep off the grass!

Americans were so busy settling their vast continent that foreign affairs were not originally something they were actually concerned with.

The Monroe Doctrine (quotation 1) was first and foremost a warning issued to major European powers to avoid any further territorial encroachment upon the American continent. Such a *de facto* gentlemen's agreement was to be observed until the turn of the century, as the US was busy settling its ever-expanding territory, either through purchases, annexations or treaties.

At the time of the annexation of Texas in 1845, J. O'Sullivan invoked America's "Manifest Destiny" (quotation 2), in which Providence played a role. Accordingly, westward expansion was closely associated with a religious design.

When the Frontier eventually came to an end, in 1890 (quotation 3), such a watershed sent a shockwave across the US as its inhabitants felt there was no more outlet for the discontented. Such frustration was to find a new expression, both in politics and in the economy, in the emergence of American imperialism, whose first manifestation was war in Cuba in 1898. The US was definitely looking outward and this policy was to be carried out, with ups and downs though, in the next fifty years. It also confirmed the US considered Latin America as its backyard, and would not put up with any foreign interference in what it referred to as "the Western Hemisphere".

This was the heyday of Theodore Roosevelt's "big stick" and "gunboat diplomacy" (quotation 4): American forces could land in any Central or Latin American country unchallenged.

## The United States as a reluctant warrior

However, the world scene was not something American Administrations were keenly interested in and the Great War had been raging for three years before W. Wilson decided to send troops to Europe. His idealism (quotation 5) was opposed by the Senate that failed to ratify the Treaty of Versailles, short of a two-thirds majority. The League of Nations, Wilson's *brainchild, remained an idea American public opinion was reluctant to embrace and Wilson's successors conducted an isolationist policy.

Not until the "sneak attack" on Pearl Harbor did F.D. Roosevelt commit US troops and the use of the atom bomb marked the beginning of a new era. The "Iron Curtain" had just fallen and F.D. Roosevelt's last political achievement had been to coax Stalin into agreeing on the principle of the United Nations.

Civilisation américaine

American public opinion once again wanted the "boys" to come home and it took European governments much persuasion to have US troops stationed on their soil and to be protected under the US nuclear "umbrella" at a time when both blocs *glared at each other during the Berlin blockade (1948/1949) or fought in Korea (1950).

## The Cold War and the Vietnam War

The US provided the backbone of NATO, created in 1949 to fight communist expansionism. It then appeared the stakes were too high to have a head-on confrontation between East and West and war was waged by *proxy on faraway battlegrounds.

The world was on the brink of war during the missile crisis in Cuba (1962) and the imposition of a blockade by the US is still having dire consequences forty years after the stand-off.

America's gradual involvement in Vietnam was a traumatic experience whose healing process is still under way (cf. Chapters on "Sites of Memory", p. 405 & "The Vietnam war and the American Psyche", p. 397), but such a "dirty little war" taught the US a lesson: no troops should be engaged without a consensus, an approach which is still firmly held nowadays. From then on, American military interventions abroad were to be limited, both in scale and in duration, with some strings attached to their media coverage, whose impact American Administrations had often deemed negative during the Vietnam War.

Still, US troops were dispatched to Grenada (1983) to topple a Marxist regime, to Haiti (1984 & 1994) to restore democracy and to Somalia (Operation "Restore Hope", under a UN mandate in 1995), but the latter ended in an inglorious retreat after the death of 18 US Marines.

Such caution did not prevent some *covert actions though, like the CIA-led coup in Chile (Sept. 1973) to overthrow the democratically-elected government of S. Allende and favour A. Pinochet's junta, to preserve the economic interests of US multinationals. US might also made itself felt in Latin America (through overt or covert operations) in El Salvador or Nicaragua in the '80s and '90s.

1989 was a watershed as it made the US the world's only superpower. Even if this did not mean "an end to History", Americans tended to revert to an isolationist policy: US bases were closed in the Philippines, fewer GIs were stationed in Europe at a time when military budgets were being slashed.

## Since the early 1990s: the US as a (major) fighting partner

It took the invasion of Kuwait by Saddam Hussein for the US to head a coalition, under a UN mandate, to liberate the tiny state from Iraqi troops. The US was definitely the backbone of the Alliance, providing it with the sophisticated hardware any modern warfare requires. It was a conflict American public opinion readily embraced for three reasons. It was morally a black-and-white, clear-cut conflict, Saddam Hussein being depicted as the villain. Besides, oil supplies were also at stake... It was a short confrontation: Allied forces were poised to attack, and once the order was given, it was a matter of days before victory. Above all, it was a (practically) casualty-free conflict: fewer than 300 for the US and about 80 for the Allies, whereas Iraqi casualties may have run into the hundreds of thousands...

The concept of a "clean war" had by then taken root in American public opinion. Such a safe approach accounted for the Senate's (and the Pentagon's) reluctance to commit ground troops in Bosnia after the Dayton Agreements (Nov. 1995): how many troops? For how long? With what mandate? The same would apply to Kosovo in 1999.

But such a wary attitude does not mean American Administrations have remained passive, far from it. For example, President Clinton's diplomatic activities have been decisive in (partly) settling the Irish conflict and the US was instrumental in the signing of the Good Friday Agreement in April 1998. The Middle East was also an American concern (the Camp David summits and the Wye Plantation Agreement), so was Bosnia (the Dayton Agreements in 1995).

US military might was once again all-important during the Kosovo crisis, "smart bombs" and "surgical strikes" allegedly made a ground intervention unnecessary.

Foreign affairs have always played a negligible role in US presidential elections. During the 2000 campaign, G.W. Bush was often made fun of by the media for his *fuzzy knowledge of places and names of heads of state and diplomatic moves do not generally make the headlines in the dailies of mainstream America.

There have been two exceptions though: the hostage crisis in Iran was a pressing issue during the 1980 campaign. The hostages were to be released 30 minutes after R. Reagan had been sworn in, on January 21, 1981... In 1992, President Bush's campaign ads were based on the Fall of the Wall, the disintegration of the USSR and the newly-found détente. But Bush Sr lost...

The US is currently a giant which is urging its European partners to shoulder a bigger share of the burden of their defence through NATO, its enlargement and a higher financial contribution. But is it not a giant with clay feet, as demonstrated by the recent bomb attack on the USS "Cole" in Aden in Nov. 2000?

The "Powell Doctrine" holds that America should not commit forces to combat unless the mission is clear, vital US interests are at stake, the American public agrees, the exits are well marked and victory is assured. What impact will this have on such issues as the National Missile Defence (NMD), the embargo on Iraq, the relations with North Korea and other rogue states, the commitment of US troops in the Balkans?

Accordingly, will the US be tempted to leave Europe and other countries out in the cold? Is it not time the European Union took its fate in its own hands, as partly exemplified by the blueprint of a common European defence structure and defence policy?

# VOCABULARY

| | |
|---|---|
| advocate a rapprochement policy (to) | prôner une politique de rapprochement |
| airlift | pont aérien |
| bear the brunt of an offensive (to) | supporter l'essentiel d'une offensive |
| brainchild | trouvaille, création |
| bring sb. to heel (to) | ramener qqn à la raison |
| call for air support (to) | demander un soutien aérien |
| carry out/conduct/implement a policy (to) | appliquer ; conduire ; mettre en œuvre une politique |
| commit troops (to)/commitment | engager des troupes ; un engagement. |
| covert operation | opération clandestine |
| détente policy | politique de détente |
| disintegrate/implode (to) | (se) désintégrer ; imploser |
| enlarge (to)/the enlargement | élargir ; l'élargissement |
| face-off | face-à-face, épreuve de force |
| fuzzy knowledge | connaissances vagues, floues |
| gather intelligence (to) | recueillir des renseignements |
| glare at sb. (to) | fusiller qqn du regard |
| guer(r)illa warfare | guérilla |
| hatch a plot (to) | fomenter un complot |
| hold a summit (to) (meeting) | organiser un sommet |
| impose/lift an embargo (to) | imposer ; lever un embargo |
| intelligence agency | service de renseignements |
| make/wage war (to) | faire la guerre |
| military hardware | matériel militaire lourd |
| overwhelm sb (to)/ an overwhelming victory | écraser qqn ; une victoire écrasante |
| poles apart (to be) | être diamétralement opposés |
| prevail (on sb.) (to) | l'emporter sur qqn |
| proxy (to fight by) | se battre par personne interposée |
| spy on sb (to) /a spy/spying/espionage | espionner qqn ; espion ; espionnage |
| stage a coup (to)/a takeover/ to take over | organiser un coup d'état ; prendre le pouvoir |
| stalemate/be stalemated (to) | impasse ; être dans l'impasse |
| "surgical strike" | « frappe chirurgicale » |
| swing of the pendulum | oscillation du pendule |
| tear down a wall (to) | abattre un mur |

# FOCUS...

**1.** "We should consider any attempt on their part [*European powers*] to extend their system to any part of this hemisphere as dangerous to our peace and safety. With the existing colonies or dependencies of any European power we have not interfered and shall not interfere."

The Monroe Doctrine (1823)

**2.** In 1845, J.O' Sullivan denounced the European powers' "avowed object of thwarting our policy and hampering our power, limiting our greatness and checking the fulfilment of our Manifest Destiny to overspread the continent allotted by Providence for the free development of our yearly multiplying millions."

**3.** In 1920, F.J. Turner, an American historian, claimed in his famous *Significance of the Frontier in American History*: "He would be a rash prophet who would assert that the expansive character of American life has now entirely ceased... the Frontier has gone, and with its going has closed the first period of American History."

**4.** President Theodore Roosevelt urged that "the nation speak softly and carry a big stick."
In 1904-1905, the Roosevelt Corollary (to the Monroe Doctrine) warned Latin American countries that "chronic wrong-doing, or an impotence which results in a general loosening of the ties of civilized society...may force the United States, however reluctantly... to the exercise of an international police power."

**5.** "Article 10 [*of the League of Nations Covenant*] provides that every member of the League covenants to respect and preserve the territorial integrity and existing political independence of every other member of the League as against external aggression." W. Wilson (1919)

**6.** "In the future days, which we seek to make secure, we look forward to a world founded upon four essential human freedoms [*freedom of speech, freedom of worship, freedom from want, freedom from fear*] in such a thorough fashion that no nation will be in a position to commit any act of aggression against any neighbour, anywhere in the world." F.D. Roosevelt (1941)

**7.** "We shall pay any price, bear any burden, to assure the success of liberty". J.F. Kennedy (1961)

"Ich bin ein Berliner." J.F.K. (1963, in front of the Wall)

**8.** "America cannot, and will not, conceive all the plans, design all the programs, execute all the decisions and undertake all the defense of the free nations of the world." R. Nixon (1972)

**9.** "This will be another American century." George Bush Sr (1988)

"America is the last, best hope of mankind."

**10.** "America cannot walk away from its interests or responsibilities." B. Clinton (1995)

**11.** "We look to the US as the world leader in technology, fashion, music and movies." A 23-year old Vietnamese, during President Clinton's visit to Vietnam, in Nov. 2000 (Newsweek 27/10/2000).

# Essay

In his book *Diplomacy*, published in 1994, Henry Kissinger described American foreign policy as "a constant push and pull between idealism and national interests".

**How relevant is such an assessment, especially at the dawn of the new millennium?**

*Henry Kissinger, Nixon's State Secretary and the architect of the rapprochement policy with China in the early 1970s, claimed the preservation of national interests should be pursued though a "balance of powers", thus playing China against the Soviet Union. However efficient such a policy may have been in the "cool war", can it still be implemented at a time when the US remains the sole superpower after the Fall of the Wall?*

*There is no denying American foreign policy has often shifted between isolationism and interventionism since the 1890s. American commitment in the Great War was soon followed by an isolationist policy and the US had to be talked into stationing troops in Europe in 1945. The Vietnam War was a traumatic experience Americans found hard to recover from. Wilson's "beneficent policeman" eventually landed in an Asian quagmire and, apart from a few interventions in the Western Hemisphere, America's "backyard", US Administrations have been reluctant to get involved overseas since the early 1980s.*

*The Gulf War and later, the wars in Bosnia and Kosovo were waged by the US under the aegis of "umbrella organisations", the UN and NATO, and the US now seems unwilling to play a major role at the very time its world leadership goes unchallenged. Why?*

*The concept of a high-tech, zero-casualty conflict is now something which appeals to American public opinion whose concerns for foreign affairs have always been minor ones. Accordingly, the US would like NATO member states and the new entrants to take the lion's share in NATO's funding and later, to assume joint leadership in the alliance's new challenges: the fight against world terrorism, drugs, nuclear proliferation and ethnic strife.*

*"What good is peace in the Mideast without peace in the Middle West?", a* Newsweek *journalist wrote in September 1993, thus mirroring the urgency of domestic problems and the lack of interest for foreign affairs in mainstream America. Besides, world leadership*

*can no more be expressed in purely military terms in a context of US hegemony. A worrying trend is that the "global village" itself could become America's 21st century backyard and US dominance can make itself felt in more ways than one. Globalisation and the pull exercised by the American way of life worldwide (as epitomised by Microsoft, Nike, Disney and McDonald's) could prove mightier than "Stealth bombers" and other sophisticated \*military hardware.*

# Index

abolitionist, 347
abortion, 186, 224, 225, 236, 241
American Civil Liberties Union, (ACLU), 248
Act of Supremacy, 169
Act of Union, 20, 97
Adams, Gerry, 106
affirmative action, 223, 293-302, 305, 313, 321
AFL-CIO, 237
Africa, 284, 304
Afro-Caribbeans, 177, 184
amendments to the Constitution, 220, 221
Amish, 304
Asians, 177-179, 181, 183, 184, 213, 243, 304
Atlanta, 258, 292
Attlee, Clement, 43, 51, 57, 58, 76

B2B, 372
B2C, 372, 375
Bagehot, Walter, 8
ballot initiative, 223
balseros, 254
Bangladeshi, 11, 178, 179
Baptists, 173
Beatles, The, 135, 136
Bevan, Aneurin, 94, 96
Beveridge Report, 79
Beveridge, William H., 79, 80, 91
Bible Belt, 287, 331, 333
Big Apple, 261
Big Brother, 155
big government, 262
big stick policy, 415, 419
Bill of Rights, 214, 220, 241, 330
Black Muslims, 284

black people, 243, 283-294, 300, 304, 317
Blair, Tony, 9, 15-17, 23, 31, 32, 35, 44, 45, 47, 50, 51, 53, 57, 58, 65, 67, 69, 74, 76-79, 80, 81, 89, 102, 107, 115, 120, 125, 175, 176, 178, 187, 274
blockbuster, 389
blue-chip values, 372
boarding-schools, 117, 124
born-again Christians, 334
British Empire, 33, 37, 112, 161
Brixton riots, 179, 182
Burke, Edmund, 18, 20, 52
Burlington House, 144
Bush, George, W., 213, 248, 331, 336, 349, 378

Cabinet, 45, 71
California, 250, 305, 387
Callaghan, James, 51
Calvinist, 330
Cambridge, 79, 113, 114, 117, 119, 123
Carnegie, Andrew, 253
Carroll, Lewis, 133, 135
Catholics, 103, 106, 107, 111, 170, 173, 175, 333
censorship in Hollywood, 388
*Chariots of Fire*, 129
charity, 146, 329
Chatsworth, 137, 144
checks and balances, 219, 220
Chicago, 258
Christians, 132, 169, 170, 183
Christian Coalition, 334, 352
Church of England, 24, 169-176
Churchill, Winston, 39, 43, 59, 74

civil rights, 236, 289, 291-293, 311
Civil Rights Acts, 215, 297
Civil War, 214, 337
Clarke, Kenneth, 45, 53
class structure, 27, 28, 96, 114, 122, 123, 152, 153
clean war, 417
Clinton, Bill, 78, 106, 107, 224, 237, 298, 308, 349, 355, 356, 362, 377, 378
CNBC effect, 372
Coca-Cola, 301
Cold War, 241, 247, 416
Commission for Racial Equality, 178
Commonwealth, 13, 33, 35, 37-40, 43, 101, 106, 125, 177, 183, 184
Commonwealth Games, 34, 123
compassionate conservatism, 213, 331
Congress, 206, 209, 229, 233, 235
Conservatives, Conservative Party, (see also Tories), 9, 15, 44, 45, 51, 52, 53, 55, 57, 59, 60, 67, 78, 80, 98, 152, 181, 187, 195
constitution (US), 209, 211, 214, 219-228, 239
consumer society, 259
containment policy, 215
Coronation Oath, 24, 170
couch potato, 396
creationism, 334
Crisp, Quentin, 133
Cromwell, Oliver, 23, 101
Cuba, Cubans, 253, 254, 415, 416

Davos, 380
Dayton Agreements, 417
death row, 348
Declaration of Independence, 214, 220, 227
Democratic Left, 110
Democrats, 211, 212, 233, 338, 339, 349
devolution, 97
Devonshires, 137, 144
discrimination, 248, 284, 295, 297, 311
Disraeli, Benjamin, 53
diversity, 297, 310, 311, 313, 321, 325, 329
DNA testing, 349
dominions, 33
domino theory, 397
dot.com, 372, 375
Du Bois, W.E.B., 290
Dublin, 122

Ebonics, 315
eccentricity, 131-136
*Educating Rita*, 121
Equal Employment Opportunity Commission (EEOC), 301, 302
electoral college, 210
Eliot, T.S., 133
Elizabeth I, 20, 105, 112
Ellis Island, 407
Emin, Tracey, 133
employment, 79, 83, 85, 86, 190
enlightenment, 145
*entente cordiale*, 274
entrepreneur, entrepreneurship, 267-274
equal rights, 185
Establishment, 27, 29, 30, 113, 161, 169
ethnic minorities, 275-280, 293, 294, 312
ethnicity, 303, 305, 330
Eton, 25, 117, 123

euro, 45
European Free Trade Agreement, 44
European Union (EU), 40, 43, 44, 47, 49, 50, 99, 101
EU enlargement, 45
Europhiles, 49
Eurosceptics, 49
evil empire, 243
Executive Order, 215, 220, 279

Fabian Society, 21, 51, 57, 58
Falklands war, 60, 61, 63
Food and Drugs Administration (FDA), 207
Federal Reserve Bank (Fed), 374, 378
Federalists, anti-Federalists, 212
Fianna Fail, 109
Fine Gael, 110
First World War, see World War I
first-past-the-post system, 15, 16, 55, 97
Fleet Street, 154
football, 124, 125, 128, 184
Ford, Henry, 258
Founding Fathers, 210, 214, 219, 239
Four Freedoms, 243
Fourth Estate, 159, 244
fox-hunting, 123, 151, 152
Frears, Stephen, 163, 166, 184
Free Cinema Movement, 167
free enterprise, 267
free speech, 230, 231, 236, 241, 245, 248, 313, 396
freedom, 239-248, 258, 300, 317, 337
freeloaders, 363, 364, 369
Frontier, 214, 249, 257, 261, 405, 415, 419

Gaitskell, Hugh, 58

Garvey, Marcus, 284, 304
gate crashing, 251
gated communities, 304
Gates, Bill, 234
Gay Pride, 197
General Motors, 298
Gilbert, Lewis, 121
globalisation, 159, 265, 269, 271, 379
Gold Rush, 249
Goons, The, 133
Great Old Party (GOP), 212
Great Depression, 215, 347
Great Society, 212
Green Belt, 138
Green Party, 56
Gulf War, 216, 398
gun control, 231, 233, 337
gunboat diplomacy, 415

Hamilton, Alexander, 212
Harrow, 117, 123
Harvard, 327
health care plan (US), 237
Heaney, Seamus, 107
Heath, Edward, 60, 80
hereditary peers, 32
Heseltine, Michael, 45
Hindus, 9, 169-171, 183, 333
Hirst, Damien, 133
Hispanics, 213, 304, 307
Hollywood, 162, 163, 247, 263, 309, 346, 387-396
Home Rule, 105
homelessness, 61, 137, 139
Homestead Act, 257, 261
hooliganism, 9, 124
House of Commons, 13-17, 23, 31, 32, 56, 77, 105, 123, 179, 185
House of Lords, 13, 23, 31, 32, 68, 69, 149, 169, 176, 179, 190
House of Representatives, 208, 220

immigrants (US), 204, 205, 214, 239, 240, 257, 289, 303, 317,
impeachment, 223, 355, 357
Indians, 178, 220, 303, 304
information superhighway, 155
information technology, 371
Initial Public Offering (IPO), 374
Irangate, 355
Irish Greens, 110
Irish Labour Party, 110
Irish Republican Army, 9, 63, 105, 106, 111
Ishiguro, Kazuo, 144
Islam (see also Muslims), 333
Ivy League, 323

James II, 109
Jefferson, Thomas, 212, 283
Jehovah's witnesses, 333
Jenkins, Roy, 16, 56, 181
Jewish, Jews, 9, 103, 129, 169, 177, 183, 184, 333
John Paul II, 351
Johnson, Lyndon B., 215, 297, 397
Johnson, Magic, 288
Joyce, James, 107, 133

Kal (cartoonist), 343, 377
Kennedy, Charles, 45, 215, 328
Kennedy, John F., 255, 397, 420
Keynes, John Maynard, 79, 372
King, Martin Luther, 288, 292, 299
Kosovo, 417
Ku Klux Klan, 245, 283, 287
Kuwait, 416

Labour, Labour Party (see also New Labour), 9, 15, 21, 44, 50-55, 59, 65, 67, 68, 77, 87, 98, 152, 160, 167
Las Vegas, 258
Latinos, 304
Lear, Edward, 133, 135
Lee, Spike, 392
Legion of Decency, 388
Lennon, John, 111, 135
Lewinsky, Monica, 357, 361
Liberal Democrats, 14, 53, 98
life peerage, 31
Lincoln, Abraham, 212, 214, 283
Livingstone, Ken, 17
Loach, Ken, 166, 167
lobbies, lobbying, 45, 197, 229-238, 248, 305, 338, 344
London Mayor, 69
Lord Mayor of London, 17
Los Angeles, 258

Macmillan, Arthur, 44
Major, John, 60, 61
manifest destiny, 261, 415, 419
Marielitos, 254
Mayflower, 287
McCarthy Joseph, McCarthyism, 215, 247, 331, 388
McCormick, 258
melting pot, 299, 303, 307
Member of Parliament (MP), 13, 14, 16, 59, 71, 72, 77
mergers, 264, 265
Methodism, 173
Mexico, 214
Microsoft, 302
Milligan, Spike, 133, 135
miners' strike, 60, 63
missile crisis, 416
*Mississippi Burning*, 292
Massachusetts Institute of Technology (MIT), 320
Monicagate, 245, 331, 357

Monroe doctrine, 214, 415, 419
Monroe, Marilyn, 357
Monster Raving Loony Party, 136
Monty Python, 133
Mormons, 304
Mounbatten, Lord, 106
MSPs, 98
multiculturalism, 285, 294, 303, 305, 309
Murdoch Rupert, 60, 154, 157, 158
Muslims, 9, 103, 169-171, 183, 333
*My Beautiful Launderette*, 163, 167, 184

National Association for the Advancement of Colored People (NAACP), 284, 288
Nader, Ralph, 211, 233
NAFTA, 237
NASA, 207
NASDAQ, 371, 373, 375, 376
National Executive Committee (NEC), 52
National Health Service (NHS), 9, 21, 61, 68, 69, 74, 76, 87-96, 177
National Missile Defence, 417
National Rifle Association (NRA), 338
National Trust, 9, 137, 146, 149
NATO, 416, 417
New Deal, 80, 81, 262, 363
New Economy, 371-375
New Frontier, 212, 250
New Labour, 32, 44, 45, 51, 57, 58, 63, 69, 79, 80, 84, 88, 89, 94, 97, 152, 187
New York, 258, 261
Nixon, Richard, 215, 224, 355, 359

Index

425

Old Bailey, 160
Olympic Games, 123, 125, 130
Open Universities, 114, 118, 121, 122
Oxbridge, 29, 30, 114, 117, 119, 120
Oxford, 59, 77, 113, 114, 117, 119, 123, 129

Paine, Thomas, 52
Pakistani, 11, 178, 179
Pardongate, 356
Parks, Rosa, 291
Parliament, 24, 31, 64, 99, 104, 161, 175, 176, 189
Parnell, Charles Stewart, 105
Patient's Charter, 92
Payne, John H., 143
Pearl Harbor, 215
Pentagon Papers, 244
Pilgrim Fathers, 214, 239, 281, 303
pioneers, 257
Plaid Cymru, 98, 99, 101, 102
Pledge of Allegiance, 333
political correctness, 311-318, 331
poll tax, 61, 63, 64
polytechnics, 114, 115
poverty, 259, 285, 295, 363
poverty line, 206
Powell, Colin, 309
Powell Doctrine, 417
Powell, Enoch, 179, 181
Presbyterianism, 173
Prime Minister, 13, 16, 21, 23, 24, 32, 34, 58-60, 69, 74, 175, 176, 187
pro-choice, 213
pro-life, 213, 241
Prohibition, 215, 221
Protestants, Protestantism, 319, 329, 331, 333, 352
public schools, 19, 30, 117, 120, 123

Puritans, Puritanism, 313, 327, 329, 330, 388

Question Time, 14
quotas, 215, 297, 298, 408

Reagan, Ronald, 213, 216, 399
recession, 371, 373, 378
Republicans, 211, 212, 233, 338
Robinson, Mary, 109
Rockwell, Norman, 243
Rodriguez, Elian, 254
Roosevelt, Franklin D., 212, 225, 240, 243, 328, 415
Rosenberg, Julius & Ethel, 247

Saint Patrick, 109
salad bowl, 307
Salem, 331
Salisbury, Lord, 143
Scholastic Aptitude Test (SAT), 319, 323, 325
Scarman Report, 179, 182
Schuman Plan, 43
Scottish Nationalist Party, 101
Scottish Parliament, 68, 97, 98, 101, 103, 104
Seattle, 250, 379, 383
Securities and Exchange Commission (SEC), 207
Second World War, see World War II
segregation, 215, 224, 240, 244, 284, 297, 299, 300, 348
self-made man, 249, 253
self-regulation, 160
self-reliance, 268
Senate, 206, 220
Shadow Cabinet, 14, 52
share dealing/trading, 371
Sherman Act, 214
Sikhs, 9, 169, 170, 183
Silicon Valley, 250

Simpson, O.J., 348
Sinn Fein, 99, 105, 106, 109, 110
skyscraper, 258
slaves, slavery, 220, 223, 283, 287, 289, 299, 303
SMEs, 274
social Darwinism, 251
South, southern states, 250, 284, 291, 297
Soviet Union, 247, 417
Speakers' Corner, 132
Spielberg, Steven, 392
spoils system, 211
St Andrews, 114
St Paul's 117
Standard Oil, 263
Star Wars, 216
start-ups, 372
stately homes, 18, 137, 144
Statue of liberty, 406
Statue of Westminster, 37
stock market, 373
stocks and shares, 371
Strauss, Levi, 253
struggle for life, 249
subsidiarity, 97
Sunbelt, 250
Supreme Court, 208, 220, 221, 225, 241, 245, 284, 295, 298, 348
Synge, John Millington, 107

TANF, 363
televangelism, 334
television, 389, 391, 395, 396
Tet Offensive, 401
Texas, 214, 351
Thatcher, Margaret, 8, 12, 59, 60, 61, 64, 65, 78, 80, 154, 162, 167, 168, 175, 187, 192, 195
Third Way, 380
thirteen colonies, 208, 303, 330
TMT, 372

tobacco industry, 225, 231, 235, 238
Tories (see also Conservatives), 52, 53, 55, 163
Tortilla Curtain, 251
trade unions, 58, 64, 83, 84, 154
Trimble, David, 107
Trinity College, 122

Ulster, 111
underclass, 364`
undocumented aliens, 277
unemployment, 59, 79, 80, 81, 83
Union Jack, 63, 112, 177
United Nations, 347
Universal Declaration of Human Rights, 244, 290, 347
urban sprawl, 259

victimization, 294, 297, 305

Vietnam Veterans Memorial, 408

Wall of Honour, 408
Walpole, Sir Robert, 143
Washington, Booker T., 284
Washington, George, 212
WASPs, 240, 268, 275, 307
Watergate, 215, 244, 245, 355-357
welfare, Welfare State (GB), 9, 51, 59, 65, 68, 79, 80, 87
welfare, Welfare State (US), 212, 213, 331, 363-370
Welsh Assembly, 97, 98, 99, 101
West, 258, 261, 342
Westminster, 19, 31, 55, 68, 97-99, 101, 105, 117, 133
Westminster Parliament, 102
Whigs, 52, 55
white people, 213, 283, 284, 289, 293, 294, 300, 303, 305, 317
white supremacy, 288, 341

Whitehall, 99
Whitewater, 356
Wilde, Oscar, 132, 193, 198
Wilson, Harold, 32, 44, 51, 80, 114
Wimbledon, 125
Winchester, 117
winner-take-all, 210
Woods, Tiger, 326
World Trade Organization (WTO), 250, 379-381, 383
World War I (WWI), 39, 146, 185, 215, 241, 243, 262, 284, 308, 347, 387
World War II (WWII), 33, 39, 95, 96, 137, 144, 146, 153, 158, 162, 170, 177, 194, 215, 240, 243, 247, 259, 347, 388
Wounded Knee, 405

Yeats, W. B., 107

zero tolerance, 363

Achevé d'imprimer en octobre 2002
sur les presses de Normandie Roto Impression s.a.s.
61250 Lonrai
N° d'impression : 02-2476
Dépôt légal : novembre 2002

*Imprimé en France*